Object-Oriented Software Engineering

Practical software development using UML and Java

Second edition

Object-Oriented Software Engineering

Practical Software Development using UML and Java

Second edition

Timothy C. Lethbridge
Robert Laganière

The McGraw·Hill Companies

London • Burr Ridge, IL • New York • St. Louis • San Francisco •Auckland
Bogotá • Caracas • Lisbon • Madrid • Mexico • Milan • Montreal • New Delhi
Panama • Paris• San Juan • São Paulo • Singapore •Tokyo • Toronto

Object-Oriented Software Engineering
Timothy C Lethbridge
Robert Laganière
ISBN 0-07-70109082

 Education

Published by McGraw-Hill Education
Shoppenhangers Road
Maidenhead
Berkshire SL62QL
Telephone: 44 (0) 1628 502 500
Fax: 44 (0) 1628 770 224
Website: http://www.mcgraw-hill.co.uk

British Library Cataloguing in Publication Data
A catalogue record for this book is available from the British Library

Library of Congress Cataloguing in Publication Data
The Library of Congress data for this book has been applied for from the Library of
Congress

Publishing Director: Catriona King
Development Editor: Karen Mosman
Marketing Manager: Alice Duijser
Senior Production Manager: Max Elvey

Text Design by Mike Cotterell
Cover design by Ego Creative
Typeset at Neuadd Bwll, Llanwrtyd Wells
Printed and bound in the UK by Bell & Bain Ltd, Glasgow

Contents

Foreword

If a builder build a house for someone, and does not construct
it properly, and the house which he built falls in and kills its
owner, then that builder shall be put to death
Article 229 of the Code of Hammurabi (1780 BC).

This earliest recorded attempt to regulate the engineering profession reminds us, in the bluntest way possible, that the paramount purpose of engineering and engineering design is to serve the user. One would assume that the engineer's responsibility to users is so self evident that it goes without saying. Various professional engineering societies have inculcated this into the core of the rules that regulate the conduct of their members.

However, in the relatively young discipline of software engineering, this has not yet fully permeated the professional culture. Part of it is due to the essential nature of the software: like no other engineering medium, software provides the shortest path from concept to reality. With no metal to bend, heavy weights to lift, or large teams of people to mobilize, creativity is practically unhampered. In the heady and seductive process of embodying ideas through software, users are often forgotten or relegated to secondary status. In some cases, they are even seen as a distraction whose idiosyncrasies merely get in the way of 'elegant and clean' design. Software developers are notorious for their impatience with anything that separates them from programming – the medium has become the message. Symptomatically, the terms 'hacking' and 'hacker' have no equivalent in any other engineering discipline.

It is interesting to note the dramatic impact that the concept of 'use case' has had on the software community. This idea, introduced by Ivar Jacobson and his colleagues a little over a decade ago, was lauded as revolutionary. Its essence lies in the formal introduction of the concept of a user (an 'actor') into the software design process. (The layperson can hardly be blamed for wondering 'what took them so long?' Hammurabi knew this almost 4000 years ago.)

Clearly, there is an imbalance of motivations here that needs to be set right: the creative urge needs to be made subservient to the need to support the user. This is something that has to be instilled from the first steps in a software engineering education, and the book by Tim Lethbridge and Robert Laganière is an important contribution to this.

The authors build the book around nine 'themes', auspiciously starting with 'understanding the customer and user'. (Many software practitioners do not even differentiate between customers and users.) The themes are not dry theorems but distillations of practical and proven domain knowledge drawn from a wealth of experience in industrial software development. The book abounds with pragmatic detail that is rarely found in textbooks. In fact, it is the kind of textbook that, as a young engineering student, I wished I had, because it describes the proverbial 'real world'.

The book does not shirk theory, quite to the contrary. However, the theory comes alive because it is set in its full and proper context, comprising not only the technical but the social and cultural aspects that often play an important role in molding the theory. The reader not only learns why a particular technological approach is good, but also its drawbacks and, perhaps equally importantly, its history. (Some things – like the QWERTY keyboard – can only be understood properly if one is familiar with their history.) They carefully point out the controversial issues in modern software engineering without taking sides, meticulously listing the arguments for each viewpoint.

The 'engineering' side of software engineering is extremely well represented here and not just because the authors emphasize a user-centric approach. Themes such as 'incorporating quantitative thinking', 'evaluation of alternatives in requirements and design', 'risk management', or 'communicating effectively' are all proven and effective techniques evolved from centuries of engineering experience and which, unfortunately, are still not adequately applied in software engineering. Yes, software is different from other forms of engineering in many, many ways, but not so different that it cannot benefit from these lessons learned. For example, the lack of quantitative thinking, including elementary risk analysis, is probably one of the most common causes of software project failures. And, no matter which statistics you read, more software projects fail than succeed. (Thankfully, the engineers who design buildings and airplanes have a much better record than their software counterparts.)

Model-driven development is another important thread throughout the book. This relatively new approach to software development, which promises to be the first true technological generational advance since the invention of the compiler, is covered in detail, from the basic principles of object orientation to the latest modeling languages and their use. The way of the future lies here.

So, from the nuts and bolts of objects to the high vistas of software architecture, from writing code to testing, from software development processes to project management – it's all gathered here. The breadth and depth of the material covered is striking and impressive, yet it has been brought together quite seamlessly, all the pieces in their rightful places, in balance. Although primarily conceived as a textbook, it will undoubtedly serve its readers as a reference for years to come.

If a builder build a program for someone, and does not construct it properly...

Bran Selic
August, 2004
Ottawa, Canada

Preface

Our focus in this book is software engineering knowledge and skills that readers can put into immediate practical use. The book is designed to be used in second-year post-secondary software engineering courses, although it has been used in introductory software engineering courses at all levels. It will also be valuable to programming practitioners who want to develop a better understanding of modern software engineering.

We have taught software engineering courses for fourteen years, and have attempted to tune the book so that it is both useful and enjoyable to students. Feedback from former students has been gratifying – some have reported that they regularly use it as a reference in their jobs. Our industrial experience performing software development, consulting and professional training has also allowed us to focus on material that is important to the employers of these students.

Using the book in a software engineering degree program

Software engineering is becoming an established discipline, separate from computer science and computer engineering. As a witness to this, in 2004 The IEEE Computer Society and the ACM approved *Software Engineering 2004* (SE2004), a document outlining what should be taught in any undergraduate software engineering program. Timothy Lethbridge played a leading role in that project, and this book is specifically designed as a textbook for SE2004 course SE201. See the web site http://sites.computer.org/ccse.

At the University of Ottawa, we teach the material in this book over a 12-week period during the first semester of the second year. By that time, students have completed two semesters of computer science – including object-oriented programming in Java. They take a course in data structures and algorithms in parallel with this course, and subsequently take advanced software engineering courses that expand their knowledge of the material we introduce here.

Students who have studied the material in this course should be particularly employable in summer jobs, co-op and sandwich work terms, and other forms of industrial placement. Employers are looking for students who understand what constitutes a good requirement, can apply fundamental design principles, can use UML properly, can translate requirements and designs into good quality programs, and can effectively test those programs. This book gives a practical grounding in all of these skills.

The book is structured so that in a 12-week course or unit, it can be taught using three hours a week of classroom instruction, plus regular supervised and unsupervised laboratory time. Each year we assign a selection of the exercises, many of which students work on in groups. This second edition of the book updates many exercises and introduces many new ones.

Suggested background

Prior to studying this book, readers should understand the basic notions of object-oriented programming, although Chapter 2 gives a brief review of these concepts. We have selected Java as the language used for programming examples since it is a complete, simple and popular object-oriented language. Motivated readers who know other object-oriented languages should be able to pick up the necessary Java from the material provided in Chapter 2 and the book's web site, and as they work through the exercises.

Material on the web site

We have prepared a web site with many resources to support readers and teachers. The address is http://www.lloseng.com.

Here you will find sets of presentation slides, source code, answers to exercises, links to all the web-based references, a knowledge base summarizing many of the concepts presented, videotapes of lectures, and various other learning aids.

There is also a publisher's website at http://www.mhhe.com/lethbridge, where you will find lecturer's password-protected resources.

Themes taught throughout the book

Woven throughout the book are nine themes that we believe are basic to contemporary software engineering. Each of these themes is revisited in many chapters, and is taught in the context of concrete examples and exercises.

1. **Understanding the customer and the user**. We emphasize domain analysis as well as gathering and validating requirements. We place these in the context of use case analysis and usability. Readers are asked to think in terms of what the customer's problem really is, what is realistic, etc. The purpose of software engineering is described at the beginning of the book as solving customers' problems, rather than developing software for its own sake.

2. **Basing development on solid principles and reusable technology**. We emphasize the necessity for software engineers to understand design principles and have a thorough grasp of suitable technology before embarking on a project. To ensure this is the case for the design work in this book, we first review object-oriented principles. Later we discuss frameworks, a series of design principles, and many design and architectural patterns.

3. **Visual modeling using UML**. We present key elements of UML, particularly class, interaction and state diagrams. We do not cover all of UML and we do not restrict our discussion to UML alone since it does not cover all of software engineering. We emphasize that UML diagrams do not solve problems by themselves, but are one of the many tools that software engineers should use as a regular part of their work. For the second edition, we have updated the book so that it is compliant with UML 2.0.

4. **Evaluation of alternatives in requirements and design**. Throughout the book we present alternatives with their advantages and disadvantages. We encourage readers to record the rationale for each choice.

5. **Object orientation**. We cover all aspects of object-oriented development, including analysis, design, and programming. Ensuring that the reader sees how to take projects all the way to implementation means that he or she gets more than just an abstract view of the development process, and appreciates the reasons for many design principles.

6. **Quantitative and logical thinking**. We cover the essentials of software metrics in several different chapters so that students can learn to think quantitatively. We also promote the judicious application of logic as embodied in OCL and assertions.

7. **Iterative and agile development**. We strongly emphasize that readers should follow an iterative approach to development. As project work, readers are asked to perform requirements analysis, design and implementation very near the beginning of the book, and then again several times throughout the book. To accomplish this we introduce a complete project in Chapter 3. Initially, readers are asked to make only a small change to this project in order to begin to understand it. In Chapter 4, readers are then asked to write and review requirements for new features to add to the system – again they design and implement the features. Later, readers learn more details of topics such as design and quality assurance, and are asked to apply what they learn to successively more advanced changes to their project. Concepts from the agile movement are also emphasized: developing in very small increments, test-first development, etc.

8. **Communicating effectively using documentation**. We encourage readers to practice writing informative but concise documentation; we provide templates and examples of each type of document.

9. **Risk management in all software engineering activities**. Throughout the book, we discuss many aspects of risk management, including evaluating potential costs and risks on a regular basis, balancing risks with benefits, avoiding doing work that is not worthwhile, and evolving plans as we learn more information. We point out that the knowledge learned from the other themes above can be applied to reduce risk.

Changes in the second edition

In the second edition, we have made a wide variety of small changes to keep up with changes in the field. The following are some of the more significant changes:

■ Covers UML 2.0.

■ Moves all discussion of use cases to Chapter 4.

■ Introduces model-driven development.

■ Discusses web-based software architectures and middleware.

■ Integrates discussion of agile approaches, and techniques made popular by those approaches including refactoring and test-driven development.

■ Covers more of the essentials of measurement and metrics.

■ Incorporates many new and changed exercises. All exercises have been given a new numbering scheme to prevent confusion with those in the first edition.

Structure of the book

Size The book is small enough so that instructors can realistically require students to read it all during a 12-week course. We present a suggested schedule below.

Depth Rather than covering all aspects of software engineering, we present in reasonable depth a cohesive collection of material that will give readers a foundation in topics central to the field. We focus on material that is immediately applicable in industrial software projects.

Examples and exercises Readers can practice applying the concepts, since we provide an extensive set of examples and exercises. One set of project exercises is based on a fully implemented small system, which we provide. This means that, rather than always programming from scratch, readers are able to spend their time thinking about higher-level analysis and design issues, yet they can still practice implementation of their ideas. Readers also come to appreciate reuse, since the implemented system is based on a framework that is applicable to a wide variety of client–server systems. The exercises vary widely in difficulty; some are easy and simply encourage the reader to think about what they have read; others are intended to motivate advanced readers. Many exercises have fully explained answers available in the student's answer manual; other answers are available in a manual only available to instructors.

Sequencing The sequence of material in the book is designed to allow students to rapidly start work on real problems requiring analysis, design and implementation. As readers perform several iterations of project work, we introduce topics they will need in each iteration. The early part of the book, for example, introduces the knowledge about object orientation and architecture that they will need to understand the project work. Then we move on to requirements and object-oriented analysis, focusing initially on use cases and static modeling. Later, we introduce dynamic modeling.

Use of this book in a 12-week course

The following is a suggested schedule for using this book in a second-year university course. For the main body of the book, Chapters 3 to 10, the allocated time corresponds roughly to the length of each chapter.

The authors use this book in a 12-week course, where each week has three hours of lecture as well as three hours of lab and tutorial time. Students are expected to read all the chapters, although the lectures focus most heavily on the core material in Chapters 3 through 10, and particularly Chapters 3, 5, 8 and 9.

We also anticipate that students work on a selection of exercises with deliverables about four times during the course. We also expect them to deliver three iterations of the project. We have provided suggested project activities at the end of many chapters.

Week 1 Chapters 1 and 2: Introduction and review (1 week).

Weeks 2–3 Chapter 3: Reuse and the client–server framework (1.5 weeks).
Project work: learning to use the client–server framework by making a minor change to a system implemented using it.

Weeks 3–4 Chapter 4: Domain analysis, use cases and requirements (1.5 weeks).
Project work: adding features following requirements analysis.

Weeks 4–5 Chapter 5: OO analysis and modeling (1.5 weeks).
Project work: adding features that require considerable modeling.

Week 6 Chapter 6: Design patterns (1 week).

Week 7 Chapter 7: Use cases and user interfaces (0.5 weeks).
Project work: adding a GUI.

Weeks 8–9 Chapter 8: Dynamic modeling (1.5 weeks).

Weeks 9–10 Chapter 9: Design principles and architecture (1.5 weeks).
Project work: detailed design of some features.

Week 11 Chapter 10: Testing (1 week).
Project work: preparing a test plan.

Week 12 Chapters 11 and 12: Introduction to project management and review (1 week).

Other orderings are possible. In particular, the order in which Chapters 6 through 11 can be covered is flexible. Also, parts of many chapters could be skipped in order to give greater emphasis to other material.

Acknowledgements

We would like to thank the following people who helped us improve this book:

- Those who have contributed insights or helped edit the book. There are too many to mention them all, but we would especially like to thank Rohit Bahl, Bob Probert, K. Teresa Khidir, François Bélanger and Klaas van den Berg who made particularly large contributions.

- Judy Kavanagh, who worked on the knowledge base of the accompanying web site and helped refine the glossary.

- The University of Ottawa students in SEG2100 and SEG2500 with whom we used this book and its beta versions for several years. Many of the approaches to explaining things in the book arose from trying to answer tricky student questions. Students have also pointed out many improvements, which we have incorporated.

We would also like to thank our families who have had to put up with ridiculous work schedules when deadline crunches approached.

The publishers would also like to thank the following reviewers who provided helpful feedback on the first edition of this textbook: Muthu Ramachandran, Leeds Metropolitan University, UK; Klaas van den Berg, Twente University, The Netherlands; Renaat Verbruggen, Dublin City University, Republic of Ireland; Paul Krause, University of Surrey, UK; Filip Vanderstappen, Erasmus University, The Netherlands; Gero Wedemann, Fachhochschule Stralsund, Germany; Radmila Juric, University of Westminster, UK; Willem-Jan van den Heuvel, University of Tilburg, The Netherlands.

We would also like to thank the reviewers who read and commented on the manuscript of the new edition: Boris Cogan, London Metropolitan University, UK; Nicolas Gold, UMIST, UK; Cecilia Mascolo, University College London, UK; Bruce R. maxim, University of Michigan-Dearborn, USA; Nikolay Y. Nikolaev, Goldsmiths College, University of London, UK; Steve O'Connell, University of Southampton, UK; Hakan Petersson, Chalmers University of Technology, Sweden; Rebecca H. Rutherford, Southern Polytechnic State University, USA; Karel van den Berg, Twente University, The Netherlands.

All the review comments were extremely helpful in developing the new edition of this textbook.

Guided tour

Learning Objectives
Each chapter opens with a set of learning objectives, summarising what readers should learn from each chapter.

Boxes
The book includes example boxes that are designed to illustrate how you can apply the main techniques learned. They may also offer extra explanations of important ideas explored in the text.

Figures and Tables
Each chapter provides a number of figures and tables to help you to visualise the software engineering models and concepts, and to illustrate and summarise important ideas.

Exercises

Each chapter in the book features a range of questions and exercises that test your understanding of the techniques you have read about, and apply software engineering methodology to real-world situations. Solutions are available on the supporting website.

Definitions

Key terms are explained by clear and straightforward definitions so that you can check you have understood. They are boxed in the text for easy reference and revision.

Chapter summary and 'for more information' section

This section briefly reviews and reinforces the main topics you will have covered in each chapter to ensure you have acquired a solid understanding of the key topics. A section entitled 'for more information' directs you to useful websites, journal articles, books and a variety of other resources to aid further study.

Appendices of notation

These appendices at the end of the book provide essential references for your studies, including summaries of the UML notation, documentation types, system descriptions, and a comprehensive glossary.

Technology to enhance learning and teaching

This book is supported by a publisher's web site: http://mhhe.com/lethbridge.

The McGraw-Hill Online Learning Center contains a range of resources for lecturers to support their teaching of Object-Oriented Software Engineering.

Available for lecturers:

■ Chapter-by-chapter PowerPoint slides to support delivery of topics in lectures

■ A full set of solutions to the exercises within the text, plus code.

Visit the web site to find out how to contact your local representative for a password.

The authors have also developed a comprehensive web site to support the book at: http://lloseng.com. Take advantage of the study tools offered to reinforce the material you have read in the text, and to develop your knowledge of software engineering further.

Resources for students include:

■ Answers to selected textbook exercises, enabling students to test their progress

■ Source code and documentation

■ Useful Web links and further reading

■ A searchable glossary of key terms

For lecturers: Primis Content Center

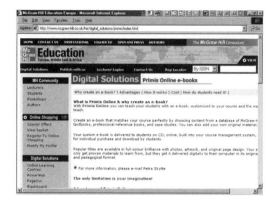

If you need to supplement your course with additional cases or content, create a personalised e-Book for your students. Visit http://www.primiscontentcenter.com or email primis_euro@mcgraw-hill.com for more information.

Study skills

We publish guides to help you study, research, pass exams and write essays, all the way through your university studies.

http://www.openup.co.uk/ss/

Computing skills

If you would like to brush up on your computing skills, we have a range of titles covering MS Office applications such as Word, Excel, PowerPoint, Access and more: http://www.mcgraw-hill.co.uk/app.

Software and software engineering 1

The software engineer's job is to solve problems economically by developing high-quality software. In this first chapter we will present important issues that all software engineers should understand to do their jobs well.

In this chapter you will learn about the following

- How does software differ from other products? How does software change over time? What do we mean when we talk about high-quality software? What types of software are there and what are their main differences?

- How are software projects organized? How successful are typical projects?

- How can we define software engineering? Why will following a disciplined approach to software engineering help us produce successful software systems?

- What activities occur in every software project?

- What should we keep in mind as we perform any software engineering activity?

1.1 The nature of software

Similarly to mechanical engineers who design mechanical systems and electrical engineers who design electrical systems, software engineers design software systems. However, software differs in important ways from the types of artifacts produced by other types of engineers:

- Software is largely intangible. Unlike most other engineering artifacts, you cannot feel the shape of a piece of software, and its design can be hard to

Offshoring: an exaggerated fear?

The software engineering labor market has been increasingly affected by the recent trend towards offshoring: this occurs when organizations in developed countries outsource software development to countries that have much lower labor costs yet have highly educated populations and are politically stable. India and some Eastern European countries have particularly benefited from this. Many economists believe offshoring represents a healthy redistribution of wealth that will result, in the longer run, in increased wages and consumer demand in the recipient countries. Citizens of these countries are also becoming big consumers of software, increasing the total market.

However, fear that offshoring will contribute to a lack of jobs is one factor that has caused a sharp drop in university computing enrolments in many developed countries. This fear is exaggerated for three reasons.

First, students studying computing still have a much higher chance of finding a job in their field than students studying most other subjects. Second, as we will learn in this book, close and constant interaction with end-users is essential to the development of quality software; it will always therefore remain important to have a significant part of the development team close to the user. And thirdly, as software development becomes distributed, there will be an increasing need for the disciplined approaches to modeling, requirements, architecture and quality assurance as taught in this book.

visualize. It is therefore difficult for people to assess its quality or to appreciate the amount of work involved in its development. This is one of the reasons why people consistently underestimate the amount of time it takes to develop a software system.

■ The mass-production of duplicate pieces of software is trivial. Most other types of engineers are very concerned about the cost of each item in terms of parts and labor to manufacture it. In other words, for tangible objects, the processes following completion of design tend to be the expensive ones. Software, on the other hand, can be duplicated at very little cost by downloading over a network or creating a CD. Almost all the cost of software is therefore in its development, not its manufacturing.

■ The software industry is labor intensive. It has become possible to automate many aspects of manufacturing and construction using machinery; therefore, other branches of engineering have been able to produce increasing amounts of product with less labor. However, it would require truly 'intelligent' machines to fully automate software design or programming. Attempts to make steps in this direction have so far met with little success.

■ It is all too easy for an inadequately trained software developer to create a piece of software that is difficult to understand and modify. A novice programmer can create a complex system that performs some useful function but is highly disorganized in terms of its design. In other areas of engineering, you can create a poor design too, but the flaws will normally be easier to detect since they will not be buried deep within thousands of pages of source code. For example, if a civil engineer designed an unsafe bridge, it would normally be easy for inspectors to notice the flaws since they know exactly what to look for in each drawing and calculation. A poorly designed software system will usually at least partly work, but many other types of engineering artifact will not work at all if they are badly designed.

■ Software is physically easy to modify; however, because of its complexity it is very difficult to make changes that are correct. People tend to make changes without fully understanding the software. As a side effect of their modifications, new bugs appear.

■ Software does not *wear out with use* like other engineering artifacts, but instead its *design deteriorates* as it is changed repeatedly. As mentioned in the previous point, changes tend to introduce new defects; consequently the changed software tends to be worse in terms of design than the original. Over time, the designs of successive versions of software may show significant deterioration to the point where a complete redesign is needed.

Taken together, the above characteristics mean that much existing software is of relatively poor quality and is steadily becoming worse. At the same time, there is strong demand for new and changed software, which customers expect to be of high quality and to be produced rapidly. Therefore, software developers have often not been able to live up to the expectations of their managers and customers – many software projects are either never delivered, or are delivered late and over budget. Furthermore, many software systems that are delivered are never put to use because they have so many problems; others require major modification before they can be used.

  This whole situation has been called the *software crisis*, despite the fact that the crisis has been going on for several decades. The term 'crisis' was chosen with the hope that the problems which arose as the software industry expanded would be resolved by implementing improved software engineering methods. Although this sentiment still holds true, we now realize that the difficulties of the software industry are, to some extent, a natural consequence of the complex nature of software, coupled with the laws of economics and the vagaries of human psychology.

  It is an objective of this book to teach you how to engineer software so that it meets expectations and doesn't contribute to the crisis. To do that, you will have to learn techniques that allow you to minimize or hide the complexity, and take account of economic and psychological realities.

Types of software and their differences

There are many different types of software. One of the most important distinctions is between *custom* software, *generic* software and *embedded* software.

  Custom software is developed to meet the specific needs of a particular customer and tends to be of little use to others (although in some cases developing custom software might reveal a problem shared by several similar organizations). Much custom software is developed in-house within the same organization that uses it; in other cases, the development is contracted out to consulting companies. Custom software is typically used by only a few people and its success depends on meeting their needs.

Examples of custom software include web sites, air-traffic control systems and software for managing the specialized finances of large organizations.

Generic software, on the other hand, is designed to be sold on the open market, to perform functions that many people need, and to run on general-purpose computers. Requirements are determined largely by market research. There is a tendency in the business world to attempt to use generic software instead of custom software because it can be far cheaper and more reliable. The main difficulty is that it might not fully meet the organization's specific needs. Generic software is often called *Commercial Off-The-Shelf* software (COTS), and it is sometimes also called *shrink-wrapped* software since it is commonly sold in packages wrapped in plastic. Generic software producers hope that they will sell many copies, but their success is at the mercy of market forces.

Examples of generic software include word processors, spreadsheets, compilers, web browsers, operating systems, computer games and accounting packages for small businesses.

Embedded software runs specific hardware devices which are typically sold on the open market. Such devices include washing machines, DVD players, microwave ovens and automobiles. Unlike generic software, users cannot usually replace embedded software or upgrade it without also replacing the hardware. The open-market nature of the hardware devices means that developing embedded software has similarities to developing generic software; however, we place it in a different category due to the distinct processes used to develop it.

Since embedded systems are finding their way into a vast number of consumer and commercial products, they now account for the bulk of software copies in existence. Generic systems, on the other hand, account for most of the software running today on general-purpose computers. Although custom software has fewer copies than either of the other types, it accounts for many more distinct systems and hence is what most developers work on.

It is possible to take generic software and customize it. The risk in doing this, however, is that when a new release of the generic software is issued, the customization work may have to be re-done.

Table 1.1   Differences among custom, generic and embedded software

	Custom	*Generic*	*Embedded*
Number of copies in use	Low	Medium	High
Total processing power devoted to running this type of software	Low	High	Medium
Worldwide annual development effort	High	Medium	Medium

You can also take custom software and try to make it generic; however, this can be a complex process if the software was not designed in a flexible way.

Table 1.1 summarizes some of the important characteristics of custom, generic and embedded software.

Another important way to categorize software in general is whether it is *real-time* or *data processing* software. The most distinctive feature of real-time software is that it has to react immediately (i.e. in real time) to stimuli from the environment (e.g. the pushing of buttons by the user, or a signal from a sensor). Much design effort goes into ensuring that this responsiveness is always guaranteed. Much real-time software is used to operate special-purpose hardware; in fact almost all embedded systems operate in real time. Many aspects of the custom systems that run industrial plants and telephone networks are also real-time.

Generic applications, such as spreadsheets and computer games, have some real-time characteristics, since they must be responsive to their users' inputs. However, these tend to be *soft* real-time characteristics: when timing constraints are not met, such systems merely become sluggish to use. In contrast, most embedded systems have *hard* real-time constraints, and will fail completely if these are not met. Safety is thus a key concern in the design of such systems.

Data processing software is used to run businesses. It performs functions such as recording sales, managing accounts, printing bills etc. The biggest design issues are how to organize the data and provide useful information to the users so they can perform their work effectively. Accuracy and security of the data are important concerns, as is the privacy of the information gathered about people. A key characteristic of traditional data processing tasks is that rather than processing data the moment it is available, it is instead gathered together in batches to be processed at a later time.

Some software has both real-time and data processing aspects. For example, a telephone system has to manage phone calls in real time, but billing for those calls is a data processing activity.

Software varies in terms of its age. Much custom software written in the 1960s and 1970s is still in use today. That software differs from newly developed software in terms of programming languages, data storage technologies, user interface technology and design techniques. Many of the web-based user interfaces we use today, e.g. for banking, are just new *front ends* on much older custom data processing software.

Usage of the word 'software' – a common mistake made by non-native speakers of English.

Many non-native speakers of English erroneously say sentences such as the following: 'I will create *a software* to update the database'. The error is that you cannot talk about 'a software'. When the word 'software' is used as a noun, it is a mass noun, like 'water' and 'sand', and cannot be preceded by the indefinite article 'a'. Therefore you have to say, 'I will create *some software* to update the database', or 'I will create *a piece of software* to update the database'. You can also use the word software as an adjective, as in 'I will create *a software system* to update the database'. In this latter case the indefinite article is referring to 'system', not 'software'.

Exercise

E1 Classify the following software according to whether it is likely to be *custom*, *generic* or *embedded (or some combination)*; and whether it is *data processing* or *real-time*.

(a) A system to control the reaction rate in a nuclear reactor.

(b) A program that runs inside badges worn by nuclear plant workers that monitors radiation exposure.

(c) A program used by administrative assistants at the nuclear plant to write letters.

(d) A system that logs all activities of the reactor and its employees so that investigators can later uncover the cause of any accident.

(e) A program used to generate annual summaries of the radiation exposure experienced by workers.

(f) An educational web site containing a Flash animation describing how the nuclear plant works.

1.2 What is software engineering?

Not all software development should be called software engineering, in the same way as not all construction is civil engineering. A do-it-yourselfer can build a wooden footbridge spanning a 60-cm-wide stream in his or her garden, but it requires a civil engineer to build a bridge across a wider span that public vehicles will traverse. Similarly, a self-trained shareware author may write a small program to track a personal stock portfolio, but it requires a software engineer to develop a complete trading and accounting system for a large brokerage company.

Definition: *software engineering* is the process of solving customers' problems by the systematic development and evolution of large, high-quality software systems within cost, time and other constraints.

Each of the words in this definition has been chosen carefully. Let us therefore split up the definition and examine each component.

Solving customers' problems

Solving customers' problems should be the *goal* of every software engineering project. Before finalizing any software engineering decision, you should therefore ask yourself whether the proposed alternative will help achieve this goal. In particular, it is important to recognize activities that are not consistent with this goal, such as adding unnecessary features. Software engineers have the responsibility to recognize situations when it would be most cost effective *not* to develop software at all, to develop *simpler* software or to purchase *existing* software.

The problems being solved by software engineers are usually related to human activities. Software engineers must therefore learn to communicate and negotiate effectively with people, to understand how people do their work, and to understand what impact any proposed software may have on its users' productivity.

Systematic development and evolution

Software development becomes an engineering process when the developers apply well-understood techniques in an organized and disciplined way. Software engineering is a young field, and its technology and techniques are still undergoing rapid development. Nevertheless, there are many well-accepted practices that have been formally standardized by bodies such as the IEEE, ISO (International Organization for Standardization) and various national standards bodies.

Sometimes a software engineering team sets out to develop completely new software. However, most development work involves modifying software that has been already written – this is because software is normally continually changed over a period of years until it becomes obsolete. Ensuring that this constant change, called *maintenance* or *evolution*, is done in a systematic way is an integral part of software engineering. We will discuss this in more detail in Section 1.6 below.

Large, high-quality software systems

A small system can often be successfully developed by a programmer working alone. However, large systems with many functions and components become too complex unless engineering discipline is applied. A system of many thousands of lines of code cannot be completely understood by one person, and certainly would take one person far too long to develop, therefore teamwork is essential to software engineering. One of the hardest challenges is dividing up the work and ensuring that the teams communicate effectively and produce subsystems that properly connect with each other to produce a large but functioning system.

The techniques discussed in this book are therefore *essential* for large systems, although many of them are also *useful* for small systems.

The end product that is produced must be of sufficient quality. Some software engineering techniques are aimed at increasing the quality of the design, whereas others are used to verify that sufficient quality is present before the software is released. Quality is discussed in more detail in Section 1.5 and Chapter 10.

Cost, time and other constraints

One of the essential characteristics of engineering is that you have to consider economic constraints as you try to solve each problem. The main economic constraints are: 1) resources are finite, 2) it is not worth doing something unless the benefit gained from it outweighs its cost, and 3) if somebody else can perform some particular task more cheaply or faster than us, they will probably succeed instead of us. Software engineers, like other engineers, therefore must ensure their systems can be produced within a limited budget and by a certain due date. Achieving this requires careful planning and sticking to the plan in a disciplined way. Furthermore, creating a realistic plan in the first place requires a great deal of knowledge about what is required to produce a system, and how long each activity should take.

Unfortunately, failure to stick to cost and time budgets has been widespread in software engineering projects. The reasons for this are many, but include the inherent complexity of software, the relative immaturity of software engineering and its technologies, lack of knowledge and experience on the part of software engineers, the inherent human tendency towards over-confidence, and pressure to offer excessively low prices and short development times in order to obtain contracts or make sales.

Other definitions of software engineering

We have presented our definition of software engineering. Here are two other definitions:

- IEEE: (1) The application of a systematic, disciplined, quantifiable approach to the development, operation, maintenance of software; that is, the application of engineering to software. (2) The study of approaches as in (1).
- The Canadian Standards Association: The systematic activities involved in the design, implementation and testing of software to optimize its production and support.

1.3 Software engineering as a branch of the engineering profession

People have talked about software engineering since 1968 when the term was coined at a NATO conference. However, only since the mid-1990s has there been a shift towards recognizing software engineering as a distinct branch of the engineering profession. Some parts of the world, notably Europe and Australia, were somewhat ahead of others in this regard.

In most countries, in order to legally perform consulting or self-employed work where you call yourself an 'engineer', you must be licensed. Similarly, a company that sells engineering services may be required to employ licensed engineers who take formal responsibility for projects, ensuring they are conducted following accepted engineering practices.

Prior to the 1940s, very few jurisdictions required engineers to be licensed. However, various disasters caused by the failure of designs eventually convinced almost all governments to establish licensing requirements. Licensing agencies have the responsibility to ensure that anyone who calls himself or herself an engineer has sufficient engineering education and experience. To exercise this responsibility, the agencies accredit educational institutions they believe are providing a proper engineering education, and

Ethics in Software Engineering

It is very important as a software engineer-in-training that you develop a sense of professional ethics. Many people perform software development work without fully realizing some of the ethical issues that can arise. The following are highlights of the IEEE/ACM code of ethics. For details about the IEEE and the ACM, see the 'For More Information' section at the end of the chapter.

Software engineers shall:

■ Act consistently with the public interest.

■ Act in the best interests of their client or employer, as long as this is consistent with the public interest.

■ Develop and maintain their product to the highest standards possible.

■ Maintain integrity and independence when making professional judgments.

■ Promote an ethical approach in management.

■ Advance the integrity and reputation of the profession, as long as doing so is consistent with the public interest.

■ Be fair and supportive to colleagues.

■ Participate in lifelong learning.

scrutinize the background of those who are applying to be engineers, often requiring them to write exams.

We can characterize the work of engineers as follows: engineers *design* artifacts following well-accepted practices, which normally involve the application of science, mathematics and economics. Since engineering has become a licensed profession, adherence to *codes of ethics* and taking *personal responsibility* for work have also become essential characteristics. Some people only include in engineering those design activities that have a potential to impact public safety and well-being; however, since most people who are trained as engineers do not in fact work on such critical projects, most people define engineering in the broader sense.

Historically, engineering has evolved several specialties, most notably civil, mechanical, electrical and chemical engineering. *Computer engineering* evolved in the 1980s to focus on the design of computer systems that involve both hardware and software components. However, most of the practitioners performing what we have defined above to be software engineering have not historically been formally educated as engineers.

Many of the earliest programmers were mathematicians or physicists; then in the 1970s the discipline of *computer science* developed, and educated many of the current generation of software developers. The computer science community recognized the need for a disciplined approach to the creation of large software systems, and developed the software engineering discipline.

In the mid-1990s the first jurisdictions started to recognize software engineering as a distinct branch of engineering. For example, in the United Kingdom those who study software engineering in computer science departments at universities have been able to achieve the status of Chartered Engineer, after a standard period of work experience and passing certain exams. In North America, the State of Texas and the Province of Ontario were among the first jurisdictions to license software engineers (in 1998 and 1999 respectively).

In parallel with the process of licensing software engineers, universities have been establishing academic programs in universities that focus on software engineering, and are clearly distinct from either computer science or computer engineering. Since considerable numbers of these graduates are now entering the workforce, software engineering has become firmly established as a branch of engineering.

1.4 Stakeholders in software engineering

Many people are involved in a software engineering project and expect to benefit from its success. We will classify these *stakeholders* into four major categories, or roles, each having different motivations, and seeing the software engineering process somewhat differently.

- **Users**. These are the people who will use the software. Their goals usually include doing enjoyable or interesting work, and gaining recognition for the work they have done. Often they will welcome new or improved software, although some might fear it could jeopardize their jobs. Users appreciate software that is easy to learn and use, makes their life easier, helps them achieve more, or allows them to have fun.

- **Customers** (also known as *clients*). These are the people who make the decisions about ordering and paying for the software. They may or may not be users – the users may work for them. Their goal is either to increase profits or simply to run their business more effectively. Customers appreciate software that helps their organization save or make money, typically by improving the productivity of the users and the organization as a whole. If you are developing custom software, then you know who your customers are; if you are developing generic software, then you often only have *potential* customers in mind.

- **Software developers**. These are the people who develop and maintain the software, many of whom may be called software engineers. Within the development team there are often specialized roles, including requirements specialists, database specialists, technical writers, configuration management specialists, etc. Development team members normally desire rewarding careers, although some are more motivated by the challenge of solving difficult problems or by being a well-respected 'guru' in a certain area of expertise. Many developers are motivated by the recognition they receive by doing high-quality work.

- **Development managers**. These are the people who run the organization that is developing the software; they often have an educational background in business administration. Their goal is to please the customer or sell the most software, while spending the least money. It is important that they have considerable knowledge about how to manage software projects, but they may not be as intimately familiar with small details of the project as are some of the software developers. For this reason, it is important that software developers keep their managers informed of any problems.

In some cases, two, three or even all four of these stakeholder roles may be held by the same person. In the simplest case, if you were privately developing software for your own use, then you would have all four roles.

Exercise

E2 How do you think each of the four types of stakeholders described above would react in each of the following situations?

(a) You study a proposal for a new system that will completely automate the work of one individual in the customer's company. You discover that the cost of developing the system would be far more than the cost of continuing to do the work manually, so you recommend against proceeding with the project.

(b) You implement a system according to the precise specifications of a customer. However, when the software is put into use, the users find it does not solve their problem.

1.5 Software quality

Almost everybody says they want software to be of 'high quality'. But what does the word 'quality' really mean? There is no single answer to this question since, like beauty, quality is largely in the eye of the beholder.

Figure 1.1 shows what quality means to each of the stakeholders. They each consider the software to be of good quality if the outcome of its development and maintenance helps them meet their personal objectives.

Attributes of software quality

The following are five of the most important attributes of software quality. Software engineers try to balance the relative importance of these attributes so as to design systems with the best overall quality, as limited by the money and time available.

■ **Usability**. The higher the usability of software, the easier it is for users to work with it. There are several aspects of usability, including learnability for novices, efficiency of use for experts, and handling of errors. We will discuss more about usability in Chapter 7.

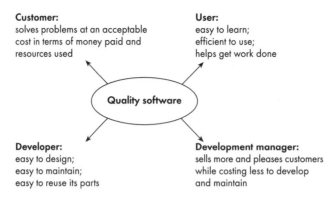

Figure 1.1   What software quality means to different stakeholders

- **Efficiency**. The more efficient software is, the less it uses of CPU-time, memory, disk space, network bandwidth and other resources. This is important to customers in order to reduce their costs of running the software, although with today's powerful computers, CPU-time, memory and disk usage are less of a concern than in years gone by.

- **Reliability**. Software is more reliable if it has fewer failures. Since software engineers do not deliberately plan for their software to fail, reliability depends on the number and type of mistakes they make. Designers can improve reliability by ensuring the software is easy to implement and change, by testing it thoroughly, and also by ensuring that if failures occur, the system can handle them or can recover easily.

- **Maintainability**. This is the ease with which you can change the software. The more difficult it is to make a change, the lower the maintainability. Software engineers can design highly maintainable software by anticipating future changes and adding flexibility. Software that is more maintainable can result in reduced costs for both developers and customers.

- **Reusability**. A software component is reusable if it can be used in several different systems with little or no modification. High reusability can reduce the long-term costs faced by the development team. We will discuss reusable technology in Chapter 3.

All of these attributes of quality are important. However, the relative importance of each will vary from stakeholder to stakeholder and from system to system. For example, reliability and efficiency are usually both of concern to customers and users; however, in a safety-critical system for controlling a nuclear power plant, reliability would be far more important than efficiency – assuming that faster hardware could be bought if efficiency became a problem. On the other hand, efficiency might be highly important in a program for biologists that calculates how proteins fold – such a program might take days to run, but if it fails no disaster will occur. The program can simply be corrected and re-run.

Often, software engineers improve one quality at the expense of another. In other words, they have to consider various *trade-offs*. The following are some examples of this:

■ Improving efficiency may make a design less easy to understand. This can reduce maintainability, which leads to defects that reduce reliability.

■ Achieving high reliability often entails repeatedly checking for errors and adding redundant computations; achieving high efficiency, in contrast, may require removing such checks and redundancy.

■ Improving usability may require adding extra code to provide feedback to the users, which might in turn reduce overall efficiency and maintainability.

One of the characteristics that distinguishes good engineering practice is setting *objectives* for quality when starting a project, and then designing the system to meet these objectives. The objectives are set in such a way that if they are met, all the stakeholders will be happy. Also, since there is no need to exceed the objectives, they help engineers to avoid spending more effort than is necessary.

To compete in the market successfully, it is sometimes necessary to *optimize* certain aspects of designs. This means achieving the best possible levels of certain qualities, while not exceeding a certain budget and at the same time meeting objectives for the other qualities.

Exercise

E3 For each of the following systems, which attributes of quality do you think would be the most important and the least important?

(a) A web-based banking system, enabling the user to do all aspects of banking on-line.

(b) An air traffic control system.

(c) A program that will enable users to view digital images or movies stored in all known formats.

(d) A system to manage the work schedule of nurses that respects all the constraints and regulations in force at a particular hospital.

(e) An application that allows you to purchase any item seen while watching TV.

Internal quality criteria

Above, we have largely been talking about *external quality attributes* that can be observed by the stakeholders and have a direct impact on them. There are also many *internal quality criteria* that characterize aspects of the design of software and have an effect on the external quality attributes. The following are a couple of examples:

■ The amount of commenting of the code. This can be measured as the fraction of total lines in the source code that are comments. This impacts maintainability, and indirectly it impacts reliability.

■ The complexity of the code measured in terms of the nesting depth, the number of branches and the use of certain complex programming constructs. This directly impacts maintainability and reliability.

In Sections 2.10 and 9.2, when we talk about design, we will discuss additional internal quality criteria that affect the externally visible qualities.

Quality for the short term vs. quality for the long term

It is human nature to worry more about short-term needs and ignore the longer-term consequences of decisions. This can have severe consequences. Examples of short-term quality concerns are: Does the software meet the customer's immediate needs? Is it sufficiently efficient for the volume of data we have today?

These questions are important, and must be answered. However, if you take an exclusively short-term focus you are likely to ignore maintainability, and also to ignore the longer-term needs of the customers. This is a mistake made by numerous software engineers over the years, resulting in much higher costs later on. Unfortunately, at the height of excitement about new projects with impending deadlines and markets to capture, even seasoned developers fall into the same trap.

1.6   Software engineering projects

Software engineering work is normally organized into projects. For a small software system, there may only be a single team of three or four developers working on the project. For a larger system, the work is usually subdivided into many smaller projects.

We can divide software projects into three major categories: 1) those that involve modifying an existing system; 2) those that involve starting to develop a system from scratch, and 3) those that involve building most of a new system from existing components, while developing new software only for missing details.

Evolutionary projects

Most software projects are of the first type – modifying an existing system. The term *maintenance* is often used to describe this process; however, for many people the word maintenance implies keeping something running by simply fixing problems, but without adding significant new features. The reality of software change is somewhat different: there tends to be constant pressure from users and customers not only to fix problems but also to make many other kinds of changes. After several years of such changes, software systems are often significantly larger and barely resemble their original state. We will thus use the term *evolution* to more accurately describe what happens to software over its life-span.

Evolutionary or maintenance projects can be of several different types:

- *Corrective* projects involve fixing defects.

- *Adaptive* projects involve changing the system in response to changes in the environment in which the software runs. For example, it might be necessary to make changes so that the system will continue to work with a new version of the operating system or database, or with a new set of tax laws.

- *Enhancement* projects involve adding new features for the users.

- *Re-engineering* or *perfective* projects involve changing the system internally so that it is more maintainable, without making significant changes that the user will notice.

In reality, most evolutionary projects involve more than one of the above.

In many cases, a software engineering team must undertake evolution of a system when the original developers are no longer available, or when their memory of the design is starting to fade. Such a system is called a *legacy* system.

A team can take great pride in evolving a high-quality product such that it continues to meet the needs of customers. However, it is important to ensure that the product does not become a 'victim of its own success'. This occurs when customers constantly want new features added, so the software becomes so large and bloated that it becomes difficult to maintain at a high level of quality.

Greenfield projects

Projects to develop an entirely new software system from scratch are significantly less common than evolutionary projects. Developers often enjoy such brand new, or *greenfield*, projects because they have a wider freedom to be creative about the design.

In a greenfield project you are not constrained by the design decisions and errors made by predecessors. However, it takes a lot of work to build a complex system from scratch.

Projects that involve building on a framework or a set of existing components

The third type of software project can be considered neither evolutionary nor new development. This type of project, which is becoming increasingly common, starts with a *framework*, or involves plugging together several *components* that are already developed and provide significant functionality.

A framework is a software system especially designed to be reused in different projects, or in the various products of a *product line*. A framework contains important functionality, but must be adapted to handle the requirements of particular customers or products.

For example, imagine an application framework for ticketing. Such a system would have basic capabilities for reserving and printing tickets for events or travel. These functions would be well designed and tested by the original developers of the framework. However, many details would need to be added to handle the particular needs of each new organization that adopts the framework. Selling tickets for a theater can be quite different from selling tickets for a sporting event, a tropical holiday package or even a cinema.

As an example of the use of components, imagine you had an accounting package and a package for tracking meetings, appointments etc. You might hook these together to create a product for a lawyer's office. The meetings and appointments would automatically result in charges for time being recorded in the accounting package. The code that you write to connect the two component packages is called *glue*.

The use of frameworks or components allows you to benefit from reusing software that has been shown to be reliable. Yet, at the same time, it gives you much of the freedom to innovate that you would have if you were performing greenfield development.

In Chapter 3 we will discuss frameworks in detail. We will also present a framework that you will use in exercises and projects throughout this book.

1.7 Activities common to software projects

The following subsections briefly describe many of the activities commonly found in software engineering projects. We will discuss most of these in more detail later in the book.

Requirements and specification

In order to solve the customer's problems, you must first understand the problems, the customer's business environment, and the available technology which can be used to solve the problems. Once you have done this, you can meet with the customers and users to decide on a course of action that will solve the problems. If you decide that developing or modifying software is the best course of action, then you can decide in detail what facilities the software should provide.

This overall process may include the following activities.

- **Domain analysis:** understanding the background needed so as to be able to understand the problem and make intelligent decisions.

- **Defining the problem:** narrowing down the scope of the system by determining the precise problem that needs solving.

- **Requirements gathering:** obtaining all the ideas people have about what the software should do.

- **Requirements analysis:** organizing the information that has been gathered, and making decisions about what in fact the software should do. The term 'requirements analysis' is often used more broadly to include some of the other steps in this list.

- **Requirements specification:** writing a *precise* set of instructions that define what the software should do. These instructions should describe how the software behaves from the perspective of the user, but should not describe any details of the implementation.

One of the most important principles of requirements is to separate the 'what' from the 'how'. The 'what' refers to the requirements – what is needed to solve the problem. The 'how' refers to how the solution will be designed and implemented.

Although initial requirements should be established early in a project, the customers' needs tend to change. Requirements analysis therefore should be continued throughout the life of a software system. We will discuss requirements in detail in Chapter 4.

Design

Design is the process of deciding how the requirements should be implemented using the available technology. Important activities during design include:

- Deciding what requirements should be implemented in hardware and what in software. This is called *systems engineering* and is normally only necessary for embedded and other real-time systems. Even for these systems, there is a trend towards implementing more and more facilities in software so that the hardware can be simpler and more generic.

- Deciding how the software is to be divided into subsystems and how the subsystems are to interact. This process is often called *software architecture*; there are several well-known ways of structuring software which are called *architectural patterns* or *styles*. In Chapter 3 we will introduce the client–server architecture, and in Chapter 9 we will look at other architectural patterns.

- Deciding how to construct the details of each subsystem. Such details include the data structures, classes, algorithms and procedures. This process is often called *detailed design*.

- Deciding in detail how the user is to interact with the system, and the *look and feel* of the system. This is called *user interface design*, and will be discussed in Chapter 7.

- Deciding how the data will be stored on disk in databases or files. We do not discuss this topic in this book – it is addressed in many specialized books.

Agile versus conventional development

There is a community of software engineers who practice what is called *agile* development. Agile methods emphasize the ability to quickly modify software and have been found to work well for small to medium-sized systems. The most well-known such method is called eXtreme Programming (XP). We will contrast agile methods with more conventional methods at several places in this book.

One way in which agile and conventional methods differ is in how they treat requirements and design. Agile practitioners gather requirements in very small increments, and design and implement each increment before gathering the next small requirements increment. They fully acknowledge that this may require the design to be changed to accommodate the new requirements, and use techniques called *refactoring* to make the necessary design changes. Conventional practitioners, on the other hand, prefer to develop a design that will be robust in the face of changing requirements. We will revisit all these ideas at various points in the book.

Quite often, for large systems, software engineers work on architectural design in conjunction with high-level requirements. This allows them to divide a system effectively into subsystems. Detailed requirements can then be developed for each subsystem. For smaller systems and lower-level subsystems though, it is conventional to develop the requirements before starting the design since otherwise the design may have to be re-done if requirements change.

Modeling

Modeling is the process of creating a representation of the domain or the software. Various modeling approaches can be used during both requirements analysis and design. These include:

- **Use case modeling**. This involves representing the sequences of actions performed by the users of the software. We will discuss this in Chapter 4.

- **Structural modeling**. This involves representing such things as the classes and objects present in the domain or in the software. This is the topic of Chapters 5 and 6.

- **Dynamic and behavioral modeling**. This involves representing such things as the states that the system can be in, the activities it can perform, and how its components interact. This is the topic of Chapter 8.

Modeling can be performed visually, using diagrams, or else using *semi-formal* or *formal languages* that express the information systematically or mathematically. In this book, we will primarily use semi-formal notations and diagrams – in particular a visual language called *UML*.

Programming

Programming is an integral part of software engineering. It involves the translation of higher-level designs into particular programming languages. It

Pair programming
One of the recommended approaches in the agile method 'eXtreme Programming' is called *pair programming*. In this technique, two programmers always work together in front of a single computer. The idea is that their constant interaction should stimulate good ideas and prevent errors. Whether this approach should be widely adopted is still being studied and debated.

should be thought of as the final stage of design because it involves making decisions about the appropriate use of programming language constructs, variable declarations etc. Most people who call themselves programmers also perform many higher-level design activities. People who limit their work to programming (i.e. who do no higher-level design or analysis) are often today called 'coders'.

One of the objectives of software engineering researchers has been to automate programming. There has been some success in this regard – some tools now generate much of the code for you from models typically represented in UML. However, there will always be a need for some programming done by humans.

We assume that readers of this book have some object-oriented programming background. We will use Java for the example code in this book, and you will be asked to translate designs into programs so you can get a feel for the effects of various design decisions. If you know an object-oriented language other than Java (e.g. C++, C# or Smalltalk) it should not be difficult to learn enough Java to use the book effectively.

Quality assurance

Quality assurance (QA) encompasses all the processes needed to ensure that the quality objectives discussed in Section 1.5 are met. Quality assurance occurs throughout a project, and includes many activities, including the following:

■ **Reviews and inspections**. These are formal meetings organized to discuss requirements, designs or code to see if they are satisfactory.

■ **Testing**. This is the process of systematically executing the software to see if it behaves as expected.

Quality assurance is also often divided into validation, which is the process of determining whether the requirements will solve the customer's problem, and verification, which is the process of making sure the requirements have been adhered to.

In various chapters, we present checklists that you can use to conduct reviews. Testing and some other aspects of quality assurance are presented in detail in Chapter 10.

Deployment

Deployment involves distributing and installing the software and any other components of the system such as databases, special hardware etc. It also involves managing the transition from any previous system.

Deploying a new release of a large system with many users can pose great difficulties – the amount of work is often under-estimated. To keep this book short, we have decided not to discuss deployment.

Managing software configurations

Configuration management involves identifying all the components that compose a software system, including files containing requirements, designs and source code. It also involves keeping track of these as they change, and ensuring that changes are performed in an organized way. All software engineers must participate in the configuration management of the parts of the system for which they are responsible.

Managing the process

Managing software projects is considered an integral part of software engineering. All software engineers assist their managers to some extent, and most will, at some point in their careers, become managers themselves.

Management issues are discussed briefly in Chapter 11. In addition to leading the other activities described above, the manager has to undertake the following tasks:

■ **Estimating the cost of the system**. This involves studying the requirements and determining how much effort they will take to design and implement.

■ **Planning**. This is the process of allocating work to particular developers, and setting a schedule with deadlines.

Both cost estimates and plans need to be examined and revised on a regular basis, since initial estimates will only be rough.

1.8 The themes emphasized in this book

The nine general themes discussed below are emphasized through many of the chapters in this book. They represent general principles or unifying approaches that can be used in any software project.

Theme 1: understanding the customer and user

Interaction with customers and users should occur in virtually all of the software engineering activities discussed in the previous section. These two groups of stakeholders are most heavily involved in requirements analysis, user interface design and deployment, but also may play a role in design, quality assurance and project management.

If software engineers can learn how users and customers think and behave, then it will be easier to produce software that meets their needs. Ensuring that they feel involved in the software engineering process will result in fewer mistakes being made and greater acceptance of the finished product.

Theme 2: basing development on solid principles and reusable technology

A fundamental tenet of engineering is that once techniques or technology become well established, their use should become routine. Civil engineers, for example, have a well-established set of principles, which they use to decide what kind of bridge to build. They also have standard bridge designs that they adapt for most routine bridge projects.

Even though software engineering is still a maturing discipline, many principles have become well established. We discuss these principles throughout the book.

As for technology, we base our designs on Java, a language with wide acceptance. Furthermore, in Chapter 3 we present a *framework* – a collection of classes that forms the basic structure upon which many different applications can be built. We demonstrate how this framework can be used to rapidly build several different applications.

Applying well-understood principles and reusing designs means that we are building on the experience and work of others, rather than 'reinventing the wheel'. The creative task of the engineer is to put knowledge to use in innovative ways to solve problems. This contrasts with the role of the scientist, which is to seek out new knowledge.

Theme 3: object orientation

Object-oriented (*OO*) techniques are based on the use of classes that act as abstractions of data, and that contain a set of procedures which act on that data. It is now widely recognized that object orientation is an effective design approach to manage the complexity inherent in most large systems.

In this book we discuss three major areas of software engineering in an object-oriented context: analysis, design and programming. In Chapter 2, we review basic OO principles and OO programming; then, in the rest of the book, we approach analysis and design from a primarily OO perspective. We will ask you to implement your designs in the OO language Java, so that you can see the consequences of your design decisions.

Theme 4: visual modeling using UML

The Unified Modeling Language (UML) is a set of notations for representing software requirements and design. It is now widely accepted as the standard approach to representing many aspects of software.

We will teach you in some detail how to use several different aspects of UML, including class diagrams (Chapter 5), state diagrams and interaction diagrams (both in Chapter 8).

Theme 5: evaluation of alternatives in requirements and design

There is rarely a single straightforward answer to any problem in software engineering. Whether you are developing requirements or performing design, there are often several alternatives that must be assessed systematically to decide which is best.

In both requirements analysis and design we will encourage you to list alternatives, and discuss their advantages and disadvantages before making a decision. We will also encourage you to document your reasoning, frequently called *rationale*, so that others can understand your decisions.

Theme 6: incorporating quantitative and logical thinking

It is becoming increasingly necessary to incorporate mathematical thinking into software development. We will present basic ways to measure aspects of software systems and software engineering processes. The objective of doing this measurement is to help make predictions of development time and quality in order to better control these factors. This topic, commonly known as *software metrics*, is covered in the chapters on object-orientation (Chapter 2), requirements (Chapter 4), design (Chapter 9), testing (Chapter 10) and project management (Chapter 11).

We will also show several ways to make use of *logic* in order to develop software: in Chapter 5 we will introduce *OCL*, a language for formally describing properties of designs; and in Chapter 9 we will show how logic can be used in a technique called defensive programming.

Theme 7: iterative and agile development

Traditionally, software engineering has been performed following what is called the *waterfall* model. In this approach you first develop requirements; once these are complete you move on to design, and then to programming, testing and deployment. An outdated view held that you should completely finish each of these steps before moving on to the next; then, when you complete deployment, you are finished. In contrast, the currently accepted view is that software engineering is, and should be, a highly *iterative* process. So-called *agile* techniques are the most highly iterative of all (see the sidebar 'Agile versus conventional development' earlier in this chapter).

It is typical to develop the first iteration of a system as a *prototype*, with only rough requirements and little functionality. Doing this serves to help establish the requirements for the next iteration. Several iterations of prototypes may be needed before the stakeholders are finally satisfied with the requirements, at which time you can proceed with a more rigorous process involving more complete specification and design.

Even after delivering software to customers, you typically continue to build a series of new releases, each one involving most of the activities discussed in Section 1.6. Iterative development results in delivering smaller units of work (prototypes or releases) quite frequently. This means that the first release can be in the customers' hands earlier than if you had tried to develop a fully fledged system. It also means that if the system turns out to be a disaster, less work has been wasted.

We will practice the iterative approach in this book, starting in Chapter 3, by asking you to make a series of small changes to a project. You will do the requirements, design and implementation of each change, with changes becoming more sophisticated as you learn more of the material in the book.

We discuss processes the waterfall, iterative and other approaches in more detail in Chapter 11.

Theme 8: communicating effectively using documentation

Software engineers communicate with each other orally both in meetings and at each other's desks; however, it would never be possible to run a large project if all information had to be conveyed in this manner.

Agile documentation

Agile developers prefer to write very little documentation. Some would prefer that anything that needs documenting be put in code comments and nowhere else.

Writing clear documentation is therefore an essential skill. Documentation should be written at all stages of development and includes requirements, designs, user manuals, instructions for testers and project plans. One of the keys to writing good documentation is to understand the audience. You must provide the information the readers will need, and organize it in such a way that the readers can find it easily. For example, the audience for design documentation includes other software engineers with whom you are currently working, as well as those who will need to make changes later. Both groups need to understand what you did and why you did it.

Unfortunately, unless it is managed appropriately, writing documentation can waste resources and can be a source of rigidity in software development. The waste of resources can occur if documentation is never read – this will be the case if it is excessively voluminous, poorly written or not made readily available. Excessive documentation means that the readers cannot find what they want easily, and 'can't find the forest for the trees'. It is therefore as bad as if you had not created enough documentation to start with.

Forcing software developers to write documents prematurely just to meet specific deadlines can mean that the overall objective becomes writing documents, instead of solving problems. Furthermore, such documents can entrench poorly made decisions that are hard to change.

In this book, we will encourage you to write documentation but we will emphasize that it should be as short and succinct as possible, and it should serve the purpose of documenting your decisions and communicating them to others. Furthermore, documentation should be written in the context of risk management, discussed below, which means that it is always subject to change.

We will give you outlines of each type of document as well as several example documents. You will have the opportunity to practice writing the documents and also reviewing them in groups.

When writing documentation you should also be aware that there are often standards that you should adhere to. It is important that documentation used within a company have a standard format so that people can more easily use it.

Theme 9: risk management in all software engineering activities

Whereas documentation allows future readers to keep an eye on the past, we must also constantly keep an eye on the future. *Risk analysis* is a key software engineering activity in which we constantly assess any new information to determine whether it will cause problems for the project. If you believe there is a significant risk that a certain type of problem will arise, then you can take steps to reduce the risk.

Software is an investment that should provide benefits; and risks are natural in any investment. The objective must be to reduce risks to acceptable levels, while still achieving the benefits. Taking action to reduce risks is like adjusting your investment portfolio. Sometimes you put more effort into certain tasks to ensure the project is completed successfully; at other times you must cut parts of the system to avoid losses.

The last numbered section of every chapter will discuss the difficulties and risks to be considered in the material covered by that chapter. In the next section we begin this process by reviewing the most important risks in software engineering.

1.9   Difficulties and risks in software engineering as a whole

The following is a selection of general factors, or challenges, that can have a major impact on the success of a software engineering project. Software engineers should regularly analyze whether any of these poses a risk, and take the suggested corrective action if necessary.

Some of these points serve as a review of what we said earlier in this chapter. We will discuss many of them in more detail in subsequent chapters.

After each challenge listed below, we list some suggestions for resolution. These suggestions can be used both to reduce risk and solve problems. However, since each situation is different, the suggestions will not always work – experience and good judgment must be your ultimate guide. As you read through the rest of the book, you will learn more details about how to go about resolving the difficulties.

■ **Complexity and large numbers of details**. Software systems tend to become complex because: a) it is easy to add new features, b) software developers typically add features without fully understanding a system, and c) the system may not have been originally designed to accommodate the features.
Resolution. Design the system for flexibility right from the start. Divide the system into smaller subsystems, so that each one is naturally simpler. Resist the urge to add new features, and consider removing those that are not needed. Use tools designed to help you more fully understand the structure of a software system. Budget sufficient time to learn about the software before making changes. When faced with an over-complex system, redesign parts of it as necessary.

■ **Uncertainty about technology**. You can never be sure whether the technology on which a system depends will work as expected. Hardware tends to be reliable, but special-purpose hardware or future versions of the hardware may differ from what you expect. Software libraries and other software systems with which a system interacts can be expected to have bugs and incompatibilities.
Resolution. Avoid technology sold by just a single vendor and which has relatively few other customers. Widely used technology is more likely to be supported and to have had its defects removed. Avoid obscure features of any technology. Balance the benefits of your use of third-party technology with the risks of problems. Create prototypes to try out the technology you will be using.

■ **Uncertainty about requirements**. Until a system is delivered and in use, you can never be quite sure whether it meets the customer's needs.
Resolution. Understand the application domain so you can communicate effectively with clients and users. Follow a good requirements gathering and analysis process. Prototype to get an early view of potential problems. Continually interact with users and clients to keep up to date on their needs. Design with change in mind.

■ **Uncertainty about software engineering skills**. Software engineering is heavily labor-intensive; however, skills of team members can vary dramatically and probably are the biggest single factor affecting success of a project.
Resolution. Make sure software engineers have sufficient general education, plus training in the technology to be used. Make sure they have sufficient experience by 'practicing' on prototypes or systems that are of lesser importance. Put in place a mentoring system so that the software engineers can effectively learn from others.

■ **Constant change**. Both technology and requirements can be expected to change regularly.
Resolution. Design for flexibility to accommodate potential changes. Stay aware of things that may change. Adjust the requirements or design as soon as important changes are discovered. Avoid changing too much too frequently, however.

■ **Deterioration of software design**. Software deteriorates due to successive changes that introduce bugs.
Resolution. Build flexibility and other aspects of maintainability into the software from the start so that changes are easier to make. Ensure software engineers have sufficient training. Ensure changes are not rushed. Perform quality assurance activities on each change.

■ **'Political' risks**. Not everybody will be happy with the requirements. Not everybody may want the system. Competition or organizational changes might render the system less important or might result in project cancelation. Various stakeholders may not understand certain software-engineering practices and may want you to do things with which you disagree.

Resolution. Participate in promoting and marketing the project. Enhance your negotiating and other 'people' skills. Regularly evaluate how the system will impact all the stakeholders, and work closely with them to foster increased understanding of issues.

1.10 Summary

We have emphasized in this chapter that software engineering is an emerging engineering specialty in which you focus on solving a customer's problem by developing high-quality software.

Since software is relatively intangible, our ability to work with it is different from other engineering products. It is possible for a beginner to rapidly program a significantly sized system, make changes to source code in a matter of minutes, and distribute thousands of copies at little cost. Unfortunately, developing systems in a rapid and ad hoc way like this leads to excessive complexity and increasing numbers of problems.

To perform good software engineering, it is necessary to incorporate discipline into software development. Some ways of doing this include carefully understanding users and their requirements, taking time to perform design, and carefully evaluating the quality of the software. You also must keep systems small at first to reduce the risk of failure, focus on delivering systems within a fixed amount of time, and constantly reassess what you are doing so that you can take action when problems arise.

Throughout the rest of this book we will present many different software engineering techniques so that you can learn how to achieve the goal of solving customers' problems more effectively.

1.11 For more information

At the end of each chapter we will discuss sources of information that you can consult to learn more about the material in that chapter. In this chapter, we list general software engineering resources; in later chapters we list resources covering specific issues.

The resources include web sites, books and periodicals. We have only listed web sites that we believe to contain reasonably reliable information or useful sets of links, which have stood the test of time, and are likely to be maintained. This book's web site (www.lloseng.com) contains a page with all the links shown in the book, updated as necessary.

Software engineering magazines published by major organizations

- *IEEE Software*, http://www.computer.org/software/
  The IEEE Computer Society is one of the two most important international organizations that focus on software engineering. They produce many software

engineering publications, but *IEEE Software* is probably the one most readable by practitioners.

■ *IEEE Computer*, http://www.computer.org/computer/
Also published by the IEEE Computer Society, this magazine covers a broader spectrum of computing topics, including software engineering. All members of the society receive this.

■ *Communications of the ACM*, http://www.acm.org
The Association for Computing Machinery (ACM) is the other main international organization involved in the development of software engineering. *CACM* is not exclusively about software engineering, but has many articles on this topic. It is included with membership in the ACM.

Other selected software engineering Internet sites

■ The Software Engineering Body of Knowledge (SWEBOK), www.swebok.org
The goal of this project, initiated by the ACM and the IEEE, is to gather together all the most important and widely accepted knowledge in software engineering. The SWEBOK initiative is under continuous development, and is an excellent resource to find detailed background material about the field.

■ The ACM/IEEE software engineering code of ethics, http://www.acm.org/serving/se/code.htm

■ The Community for Software Engineers, www.software-engineer.org

■ The Wikipedia entry for software engineering: http://en.wikipedia.org/wiki/Software_engineering

■ The Software Engineering Institute (SEI) at Carnegie Mellon University, www.sei.cmu.edu
One of the foremost research institutes on software engineering.

General software engineering books

■ Roger Pressman, *Software Engineering: a Practitioner's Approach*, 6th edition, McGraw Hill, 2004. This is one of the classic books covering all areas of software engineering in considerable depth. http://www.rspa.com/about/sepa.html

■ Stephen R. Schach, *Object-Oriented and Classical Software Engineering*, 6th edition, McGraw Hill, 2004. http://www.mhhe.com/catalogs/0072865512.mhtml

■ Ian Sommerville, *Software Engineering*, 7th Edition, Addison-Wesley, 2004, http://www.software-engin.com/

■ Bernd Bruegge and Allen Dutoit, *Object-Oriented Software Engineering: Using UML, Patterns and Java*, 2nd edition, Prentice Hall, 2004

■ Shari Lawrence Pfleeger, *Software Engineering: Theory and Practice*, 2nd edition, Prentice Hall, 2001.

The profession of engineering

■ Greatest achievements of engineering: http://www.greatachievements.org

■ Professional Engineering Institutions (UK): http://www.pei.org.uk

■ Canadian Council of Professional Engineers: http://www.ccpe.ca

■ National Society of Professional Engineers (US): http://www.nspe.org

Review of object orientation

2

As we mentioned in the last chapter, software engineers must have a good understanding of the computing technology with which they work. In this chapter, we review an important area of that technology: object-oriented programming.

It is our expectation that most readers will have learned the basics of object-oriented programming in Java before reading this book.

If you do not know Java, but know another object-oriented language, such as C++, C#, Delphi or Smalltalk, then the exercises at the end of this chapter will help you make the transition to Java. We recommend you also make use of Java learning resources, some of which we list at the end of the chapter.

Our goal with the use of Java in this book is to give you practical illustrations of software engineering concepts.

In this chapter you will learn about the following

- The basic principles of object orientation.

- Classes and objects.

- Instance variables, attributes and associations.

- Methods, operations and polymorphism.

- Organizing classes into inheritance hierarchies.

- Evaluating alternative implementations of simple designs in Java.

2.1 What is object orientation?

Object-oriented systems make use of *abstraction* in order to help make software less complex. An abstraction is something that relieves you from having to deal with details. Object-oriented systems combine procedural abstraction with data abstraction. To help you better understand what this means, we will first take a look at these two types of abstraction.

Procedural abstraction and the procedural paradigm

From the earliest days of programming, software has been organized around the notion of *procedures* (also in some contexts called *functions* or *routines*). These provide *procedural abstraction*. When using a certain procedure, a programmer does not need to worry about all the details of how it performs its computations; he or she only needs to know how to call it and what it computes. The programmer's view of the system is thus made simpler.

In the so-called procedural paradigm, the entire system is organized into a set of procedures. One 'main' procedure calls several other procedures, which in turn call others.

The *procedural paradigm* works very well when the main purpose of programs is to perform calculations with relatively simple data. However, as computers and applications have become more complex, so has the data. Systems written using the procedural paradigm are complex if each procedure works with many types of data, or if each type of data has many different procedures that access and modify it.

Data abstraction

Data abstractions can help reduce some of a system's complexity. *Records* and *structures* were the first data abstractions to be introduced. The idea is to group together the pieces of data that describe some entity, so that programmers can manipulate that data as a unit.

However, even when using data abstraction, programmers still have to write complex code in many different places. Consider, for example, a banking system that is written using the procedural paradigm, but using records representing bank accounts. The software has to manage accounts of different types, such as checking, savings and mortgage accounts (a checking account would be called a cheque account or current account in some countries). Each type of account will have different rules for the computation of fees, interest, etc. Such a system would have procedures like the following pseudocode in many different places:

```
if account is of type checking then
  do something
else if account is of type savings then
  do something else
else
  do yet another thing
endif
```

Imagine also that clients can hold several accounts of different types, and some accounts can be held jointly; also the different account holders might have different rights. Rules to deal with issues like these would be scattered throughout the code, making change very difficult.

The object-oriented paradigm: organizing procedural abstractions in the context of data abstractions

Starting in the late 1960s, programmers began to see the advantage of organizing programs around data abstractions. They realized that they could make systems much simpler by putting all the procedures that access or modify a particular class of objects in one place, rather than having the procedures spread out all over the system. This idea is the root of the *object-oriented* (OO) paradigm which, by the 1990s, had become accepted as the best way to organize most systems.

> **Definition:** The *object-oriented paradigm* is an approach to the solution of problems in which all computations are performed in the context of objects. The objects are instances of programming constructs, normally called classes, which are data abstractions and which contain procedural abstractions that operate on the objects.

In the object-oriented paradigm, a running program can be seen as a collection of objects collaborating to perform a given task.

Figure 2.1 summarizes the essential difference between the object-oriented and procedural paradigms. In the procedural paradigm (shown on the left), the code is organized into procedures that each manipulate different types of data. In the object-oriented paradigm (shown on the right), the code is organized into classes that each contain procedures for manipulating instances of that class alone. Later on, we will explain how the classes themselves can be organized into hierarchies that provide even more abstraction.

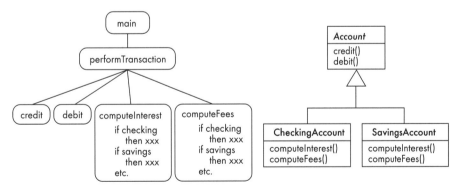

Figure 2.1   Organizing a system according to the procedural paradigm (left) or the object-oriented paradigm (right). The UML notation used in the right-hand diagram will be discussed in more detail later

2.2   Classes and objects

Classes and objects are the aspects of object orientation that people normally think about first. In this section, we will define in more detail what we mean by these two terms.

Objects

An object is a chunk of structured data in a running software system. It can represent anything with which you can associate *properties* and *behavior*. Properties characterize the object, describing its current *state*. Behavior is the way an object acts and reacts, possibly changing its state.

Figure 2.2 shows some of the objects and their properties that might be important to a particular banking system. The notation used in Figure 2.2 to represent objects is UML. We will show you some very simple UML notation in this chapter; we will explain it in more detail in Chapter 5 and subsequent chapters.

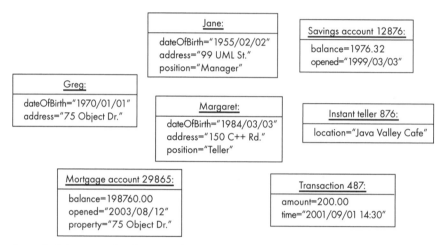

Figure 2.2   Several objects in a banking application

The following are some other examples of objects:

- In a payroll program, there would be objects representing each individual employee.

- In a university registration program, there would be objects representing each student, each course and each faculty member.

- In a factory automation system, there might be objects representing each assembly line, each robot, each item being manufactured, and each type of product.

In the above examples, all the objects represent things that are important to the users of the program. You use a process often called *object-oriented analysis* to decide which objects will be important to the users, and to work out the structure, relationships and behavior of these objects.

When performing object-oriented analysis, you do not initially need to understand how objects are physically represented using a particular programming language, nor whether they are stored in random-access memory or on disk. It is best to leave consideration of such issues until you have completed object-oriented analysis, and moved on to *object-oriented design* (OOD). We will discuss object-oriented analysis and design in detail starting in Chapter 5.

Classes and their instances

Classes are the units of data abstraction in an object-oriented program. More specifically, a class is a software module that represents and defines a set of similar objects, its *instances*. All the objects with the same properties and behavior are instances of one class.

For example, Figure 2.3 shows how the bank employees Jane and Margaret from Figure 2.2 can be represented as instances of a single class Employee. Class Employee declares that all its instances have a name, a dateOfBirth, an address and a position.

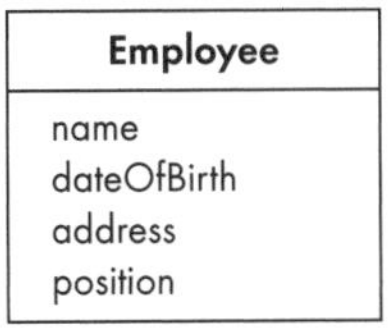

Employee
name
dateOfBirth
address
position

Figure 2.3   A class, representing similar objects from Figure 2.2

As a software module, a class contains all of the code that relates to its objects, including:

- Code describing how the objects of the class are structured – i.e. the data stored in each object that implement the properties.

- The procedures, called *methods*, that implement the behavior of the objects.

In other words, in addition to defining properties such as name and address, as shown in Figure 2.3, an Employee class would also provide methods for creating a new employee, and changing an employee's name, address and position. We will talk more about the contents of a class in Sections 2.3 and 2.4.

Sometimes it is hard for beginners to decide what should be a class and what should be an instance. The following two rules can help:

- In general, something should be a class if it could have instances.

- In general, something should be an instance if it is clearly a single member of the set defined by a class.

For example, in an application for managing hospitals, one of the classes might be Doctor, and another might be Hospital. You might think that Hospital should be an instance if there is only one of them in the system; however, the fact that in theory there could be multiple hospitals tells us that Hospital should be a class.

Example 2.1   *In the following, we indicate whether each item should be a class or an instance. If it should be a class, we describe its instances. If it should be an instance, we describe its class.*

Film: class; instances include 'Star Wars' and 'Casablanca'.
Reel of film: class; instances are physical reels.
Film reel with serial number SW19876: instance of `ReelOfFilm`.
Showing of 'Star Wars' in the Phoenix Cinema at 7 pm: instance of class `ShowingOfFilm`.

Exercise

E4   Which of the following items do you think should be a class, and which should be an instance? For any item that should be an instance, name a suitable class for it. If you think an item could be either a class or an instance, depending on circumstances, explain why.

(a) General Motors
(b) Automobile company
(c) Boeing 777
(d) Computer science student
(e) Mary Smith
(f) Game
(g) Board game
(h) Chess
(i) University course SEG 2100
(j) Airplane
(k) The game of chess between Tom and Jane which started at 2:30 pm yesterday.
(l) The car with serial number JM 198765T4

Naming classes

One of the first challenges in any object-oriented project is to name the classes. Notice that the class names mentioned in the last subsection such as `Employee`, `Hospital` and `Doctor` are *nouns*, have their first letter *capitalized* and are written in the *singular*. These are important conventions that should be followed in all object-oriented programs in languages like Java and C++. Being consistent about capitalization ensures that readers of the program can tell what is a class and what is not. Using the singular ensures that readers can tell that an instance of the class is a single item, not a list or collection. If you want to give a class a name consisting of more than one word, then omit the spaces and capitalize the first letter of each word, for example: `PartTimeEmployee`.

It is also important to choose names for classes that are neither too general nor too specific. Many words in the English language have more than one meaning, or are used with a broad meaning. For example, the word 'bus' could mean the physical vehicle, or a particular run along a particular route, as in, 'I will catch the 10:30 bus (but I don't care which vehicle is used)'. You might choose to call

Usage of the words 'Instance', 'Object' and 'Class'

A common question is: what is the difference between an instance and an object? The answer is that they refer to the same thing; the difference is one of grammar and usage in the English language. 'Instance' is a role term, meaning that it is used to talk about the role an object plays, in this case as an instance of a class.

It might be easiest to see this by analogy. There are many similar pairs of words in normal English usage; 'Daughter', a role term, 'Girl', a non-role term; or 'Father', a role term, 'Man', a non-role term. If, for example, you saw some girls walking down the street and said, 'I see several daughters', people would know what you meant, but it would sound funny. You would normally instead say, 'I see several girls.' On the other hand it would be quite reasonable to say, 'Jane has several daughters.'

Thus it is possible to say, 'instances are stored in memory', although it sounds better to say, 'objects are stored in memory'. You also can say, 'class `Passenger` has 10 objects', but it would sound better if you said, 'class `Passenger` has 10 instances'.

You will sometimes read documents where the word 'object' is used when the author really ought to have said 'class'. For example, you might hear somebody incorrectly say, 'I just finished designing the `Passenger` object.' Although you would know what they mean in this context, in other contexts using these terms loosely can be confusing. For example, if somebody says, 'the `Employee` object is stored in the database', you might wonder if they mean all the objects of the class, or just one particular object.

the class that represents physical vehicles `BusVehicle` and the class that represents runs along a route `BusRouteRun`. Sometimes it is possible to be too specific in naming a class: for example, when filling out a form, you may be asked to specify the 'city' as part of an address. But not everybody lives in a city! Therefore, rather than creating a class called `City` to store, for example, a person's place of birth, you should perhaps use the more general class name `Municipality`.

Another principle is to name classes after the things their instances represent in the real world. Unless you are dealing with low-level system design, you should avoid using words in class names that reflect the internals of a computer system such as 'Record', 'Table', 'Data', 'Structure', or 'Information'. For example, a class named `Employee` would be acceptable, but one named `EmployeeData` would not.

Exercises

E5 Some of the following are not good names for classes in the scheduling system of a passenger rail company. For each name, indicate whether it is a bad class name, and if so, explain why and suggest a better name or names:

(a) `Train`

(b) `Stop`

(c) `SleepingCarData`

(d) arrive

(e) Routes

(f) driver

(g) SpecialTrainInfo

E6 Identify all the classes you can think of that might be part of the following systems, and choose good names for them.

(a) A restaurant reservation system.

(b) A video rental store.

(c) A weather forecasting system.

(d) A video editing tool.

2.3 Instance variables

A variable is a place where you can put data. Each class declares a list of variables corresponding to data that will be present in each instance; such variables are called *instance variables*.

Attributes and associations

There are two groups of instance variables, those used to implement attributes, and those used to implement associations.

An *attribute* is a simple piece of data used to represent the properties of an object. For example, each instance of class Employee might have the following attributes:

- name
- dateOfBirth
- socialSecurityNumber
- telephoneNumber
- address

An *association* represents the relationship between instances of one class and instances of another. For example, class Employee in a business application might have the following relationships:

- supervisor (association to class Manager)
- tasksToDo (association to class Task)

We will talk about selecting and representing attributes and associations in much more detail in Chapter 5.

Variables versus objects

One common source of confusion when discussing object-oriented programs is the difference between *variables* and *objects*. These are quite distinct concepts.

At any given instant, a variable can refer to a particular object or to no object at all. Variables that refer to objects are therefore often called *references*. During the execution of a program, a given variable may refer to different objects. Furthermore, an object can be referred to by several different variables at the same time.

The *type* of a variable determines what classes of objects it may contain. We will explain the rules regarding this in later sections.

Variables can be local variables in methods; these are created when a method runs and are destroyed when a method returns. However, objects temporarily referenced by such variables may last much longer than the lifetime of the method as long as some other variable also references the object.

Exercises

E7 Identify the *attributes* that might be present in the following classes. Try to be reasonably exhaustive.

(a) `Series` (in a scheduling system for an independent television station)

(b) `Passenger` (in an airline system)

(c) `Event` (in a personal schedule system; a meeting might be a kind of event)

(d) `Clasroom` (in a university course scheduling system)

(e) `PhoneCall` (in the system of a mobile telephone company)

(f) `AssemblyLine` (in a factory automation system)

E8 Identify some *associations* that might involve the classes listed in the previous exercise. For each association, indicate the other class that would be involved.

Instance variables versus class variables

If you declare that a class has an instance variable called `var`, then you are saying that *each instance* of the class will have its own slot named `var`. Therefore, for example, each `Employee` has a `supervisor`. The actual data put into these variables will vary from object to object: employees will have different instances of `Manager` as their supervisors.

Sometimes, however, you want to create a variable whose value is shared by all instances of a class. Such a variable is known as a *class variable* or *static variable*. If one instance sets the value of a class variable, then all the other instances see the same changed value.

Class variables are often overused by beginners in cases when they should use instance variables. Class variables are, however, useful for storing the following types of information:

- Default or 'constant' values that are widely used by methods in a class.

- Lookup tables and similar structures used by algorithms inside a particular class.

Terminology for instance variables and class variables
You may read the term 'data member'; this is C++ terminology that means an instance variable. A 'static data member' is a class variable. The term 'field' is also often used to collectively refer to both instance and class variables.

2.4 Methods, operations and polymorphism

The word '*method*' is used in object-oriented programs where the words '*procedure*', '*function*' or '*routine*' might be used in other programs. Methods are procedural abstractions used to implement the behavior of a class.

An *operation* is a higher-level procedural abstraction. It is used to discuss and specify a type of behavior, independently of any code that implements that behavior. Several different classes can have methods with the same name that implement the abstract operation in ways suitable to each class. The word 'method' is used because in English it means 'way of performing an operation'.

We call an operation *polymorphic*, if the running program decides, every time an operation is called, which of several identically named methods to invoke. The program makes its decision based on the class of the object in a particular variable. Polymorphism is one of the fundamental features of the object-oriented paradigm.

Definition: *polymorphism* is a property of object-oriented software by which an abstract operation may be performed in different ways, typically in different classes.

C++ terminology for methods
For readers coming from the world of C++, the term 'function member' or 'member function' is normally used in that language instead of 'method'. Also, the term 'virtual' is used to indicate methods that are implementations of a single polymorphic operation. Hence, polymorphic methods are sometimes called 'virtual functions'.

As an illustration of polymorphism, imagine a banking application that has an abstract operation `calculateInterest`. In some types of account, interest is computed as a percentage of the *average* daily balance during a month. In other types of account, interest is computed as a percentage of the *minimum* daily balance during a month. In a mortgage account, to which you can only deposit (make a payment) but from which you cannot withdraw except initially, interest may be computed as a percentage of the balance at the *end* of the month.

In the banking system, the three classes `CheckingAccount`, `SavingsAccount` and `MortgageAccount` would each have their own method for the polymorphic operation `calculateInterest`. When a program is calculating the interest on a series of accounts, it will invoke the version of `calculateInterest` specific to the class of each account.

Exercise

E9 For each of the following sets of classes, find an appropriate superclass and the polymorphic operations that should be included in this superclass. Explain the way these operations would behave in each subclass and identify some operations that might be present in only one of the subclasses.

(a) `Square`, `Circle`, `Rectangle`

(b) `Truck`, `Ambulance`, `Bus`

(c) `Techician`, `AdministrativeAssistant`, `Manager`

2.5 Organizing classes into inheritance hierarchies

If several classes have attributes, associations or operations in common, it is best to avoid duplication by creating a separate *superclass* that contains these common aspects. Conversely, if you have a complex class, it may be good to divide its functionality among several specialized *subclasses*.

For example, imagine you are creating a banking application in which there are several kinds of accounts. Some things are common to all accounts, such as having a balance and an owner, as well as being able to deposit money in the account, open it and close it. Other things differentiate the accounts – for example, a mortgage account has a negative balance as well as a property (e.g. a house) as collateral; a savings account might have certain privileges associated with it such as higher interest for keeping a high balance in it. In this example we would say that class `Account` should be the superclass of subclasses `SavingsAccount`, `CheckingAccount` and `MortgageAccount`.

The relationship between a subclass and an immediate superclass is called a *generalization*. The subclass is called a *specialization*. A hierarchy with one or more generalizations is called an *inheritance hierarchy*, a generalization hierarchy or an *isa hierarchy*. The reason for the latter name will become clear shortly.

C++ terminology for superclass and subclass
In C++, a superclass is called a 'base class', while a subclass is called a 'derived class'.

You can draw inheritance hierarchies graphically as shown in Figure 2.4. The little triangle symbolizes one or more generalizations sharing the same superclass, and points to the superclass. It is clearest when such diagrams are drawn with the superclass at the top and the subclasses below, although other arrangements are also allowed.

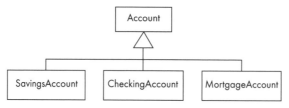

Figure 2.4   **Basic inheritance hierarchy of bank accounts**

It is also possible to show inheritance hierarchies textually using indentation, like this:

```
Account
    SavingsAccount
    CheckingAccount
        MortgageAccount
```

> **Definition:** *inheritance* is the *implicit* possession by a subclass of features defined in a superclass. Features include variables and methods.

You control inheritance by creating an inheritance hierarchy. Once you define which classes are superclasses and which classes are their subclasses, inheritance *automatically* occurs.

For example, all the features of Account are also present in `SavingsAccount`, `CheckingAccount` and `MortgageAccount`. Figure 2.5 expands on Figure 2.4, showing a variety of attributes and operations possessed by `Account` that would also be inherited by the three subclasses. Attributes are shown in the middle of the class box; operations are shown at the bottom. The inherited features are not explicitly shown in the subclasses to make the diagram clearer; however, any new features exclusive to each subclass are shown.

Organizing classes into inheritance hierarchies is a key skill in object-oriented design and programming. It is easy to make mistakes and create invalid generalizations. One of the most important rules to adhere to is the *isa* rule. The isa rule says that class A can only be a valid subclass of class B if it makes sense, in English, to say, 'an A *is a* B'. For example it makes sense to say 'a `SavingsAccount` is an `Account`' ; it does not make sense to say the inverse, 'an `Account` is a `SavingsAccount`'. You should test all superclass–subclass pairs (generalizations) against the isa rule. It is for this reason that inheritance hierarchies are often called isa hierarchies.

When you detect a violation of the isa rule, it is a clear indication that you have made an invalid generalization. However, not all cases where the isa rule holds are good generalizations. Other important points you should check are:

■ If you have given the subclass or superclass ambiguous names (such as 'Bus' as described earlier), you will often create bad generalizations.

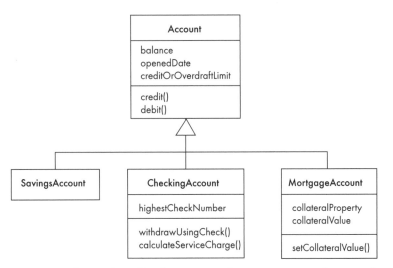

Figure 2.5 Inheritance hierarchy of bank accounts showing some attributes and operations

■ A subclass must retain its distinctiveness throughout its life. For example if you decided to create a subclass `OverdrawnAccount`, the isa rule appears to hold: 'An overdrawn account is an account'. However, an overdrawn account will not remain a distinct type of account once enough money is deposited into it. Therefore this is not a good generalization; in fact, the class `OverdrawnAccount` should not be a separate class.

■ *All* the inherited features must make sense in each subclass. In Figure 2.5 you must ensure that each of the three subclasses can have a `balance`, an `openedDate` and a `creditOrOverdraftLimit`. You must also make sure that it makes sense to perform the operations `credit` and `debit` in each subclass, and that all methods of these operations will behave consistently. You may think that debit would not apply to `MortgageAccount`; however, remember that when the account is first created, a large debit is made. We will discuss this issue more in the next section.

It is a common mistake for designers to overlook these three checks. If the checks are overlooked, the resulting code then needs many special conditions to deal with unwanted inheritance, and it becomes hard to understand.

Key conclusions we can draw from the above are: generalizations and their resulting inheritance help to avoid duplication and improve reuse; but poorly designed generalizations can actually cause more problems than they solve.

The Liskov Substitution Principle

The *Liskov Substitution Principle* says this: if you have a variable whose type is a superclass (e.g. `Account`), then the program should work properly if you place an instance of that superclass or any of its subclasses in the variable. The program using the variable should not be able to tell which class is being used, and should not care.

Example 2.2   *Organize the following set of classes into hierarchies:* Circle, Point, Rectangle, Matrix, Ellipse, Line, Plane.

Figure 2.6 shows one possible solution – there can often be more than one acceptable answer to this kind of question.

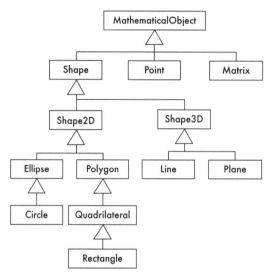

Figure 2.6   A possible inheritance hierarchy of mathematical objects

The following are some possible changes to Figure 2.6 that can be debated:

■ You could consider a Point to be a degenerate Shape. But how many dimensions does it have? A point could have any number of dimensions. Perhaps what is needed is to have separate classes Point2D and Point3D.

■ A Line, similarly, can be 2-dimensional or 3-dimensional.

■ The fact that Circle is shown as a subclass of Ellipse is interesting. Mathematically, a circle has all the properties of an ellipse. An ellipse has two foci; in a circle these two foci are constrained to be *equal* to each other – at the center. In an object-oriented system, subclasses must have all the properties of their superclass; in the case of the ellipse, a valid operation is to change one of the foci. This implies we should be able to change one focus of a Circle, which is a bit odd. We could permit this as long as doing so automatically changes the other focus so that the circle remains a circle with one center. However, this solution is not entirely satisfactory since every instance of Circle must still have two attributes to store the foci. An alternative sub-hierarchy, showing a different way of arranging the attributes of circles and ellipses, is shown in Figure 2.7. Yet another option is to get rid of the Circle class entirely and just use the Ellipse class; you might then add a Boolean attribute constrainAsCircle to Ellipse if you wanted certain ellipses to always remain circles.

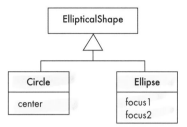

Figure 2.7   An alternative approach to defining ellipses and circles that avoids difficulties that would occur if `Circle` were a subclass of `Ellipse`

Exercises

E10   Which of the following would not form good superclass–subclass pairs (generalizations), and why? Hint: look for violations of the isa rule, poor naming, and other problems.

(a) `Money – CanadianDollars`

(b) `Bank – Account`

(c) `OrganizationUnit – Division`

(d) `SavingsAccount – CheckingAccount`

(e) `Account – Account12876`

(f) `People – Customer`

(g) `Student – GraduateStudent`

(h) `Continent – Country`

(i) `Municipality – Neighborhood`

E11   What problems could arise by making `Quadrilateral` and `Rectangle` subclasses of `Polygon`? What alternatives are possible? What are the advantages and disadvantages of each alternative?

E12   Organize each of the following sets of items into inheritance hierarchies of classes. Hints:

■ For each set of items, you will have several distinct hierarchies.

■ You will need to add additional classes to act as superclasses. You will also need to change some names, and you will discover that two items may correspond to a single class.

■ Think of important attributes present in your classes. Make sure that attributes in a superclass will be present in each of its subclasses.

■ Remember to use the isa rule.

a) Vehicle   Car   Sports car
    Airplane   Amphibious vehicle   Engine
    Jet engine   Electric motor   Wheel
    Transmission   Truck   Bicycle

b) Edition of book   Copy of book   Volume
    Issue of newspaper   Magazine   Work of literature
    Newspaper   Issue of magazine   Publication
    Chapter   Author   Publisher
    Copy of issue of
    magazine

c) Schedule   Bus   Trip
    Chartered bus   Bus route   Express bus
    Luxury bus   Tour bus   Route
    Unscheduled trip

d) Student   Course   Professor
    Graduate student   Course section   Program of studies
    Teaching assistant   Administrative assistant   Technician
    Classroom   Time slot   Meeting room
    Building   Gymnasium   Registration system
    Laboratory   Tutorial   Exam

e) Currency   Exchange rate   Bank
    Financial instrument   Credit card   Debit card
    Check   Credit Union   Bank machine
    Visa   MasterCard   Loan
    Bank account   Bank branch   Canadian dollars
    US dollars

f) Hotel room   Meeting room   Ballroom
    Suite   Hilton (the hotel chain)   Ottawa Hilton
    Meeting organizer   Catered function   Booking
    Guest   Reservation   Meeting
    Conference   Conference room   Item on bill

g) Insurance policy   Claim   Deductible
    Insurance client   Insured property   Automobile policy
    Home policy   Life insurance   Beneficiary
    Policy renewal

h) Telephone   Phone line   Digital line
Phone call   Conference call   Call waiting
Extension   Feature   Call on hold
Caller   Call forwarding   Forwarded call
Telephone number   Voice mail message   Voice mail
Voice mail box

2.6   The effect of inheritance hierarchies on polymorphism and variable declarations

Much of the power of the object-oriented paradigm comes from polymorphism and inheritance working together. In this section we will investigate this *synergy*.

Figure 2.8 shows an expanded version of the hierarchy of two-dimensional shapes from Figure 2.6, also incorporating the `EllipticalShape` class from Figure 2.7, as well as a modified `Polygon` hierarchy. We will use Figure 2.8 to illustrate several important points; you should study it and try to understand it before proceeding.

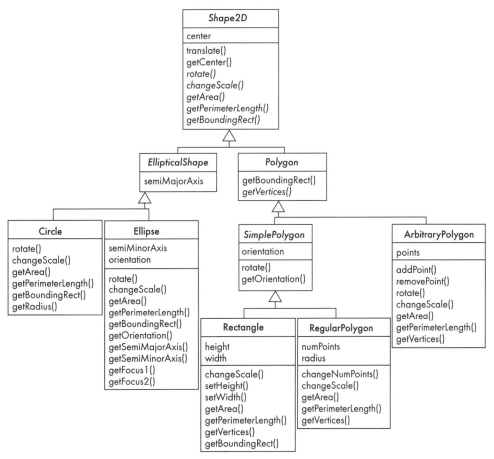

Figure 2.8   A hierarchy of shapes showing polymorphism and overriding

Figure 2.8 is a four-level hierarchy with four generalizations. The classes at the very bottom of the hierarchy are called *leaf classes*.

The following explains certain details of some of the classes:

■ An `Ellipse` is defined using the lengths of two axes: the longer one is called the *major* axis, and the shorter one the *minor* axis. The *semi-major* axis is half the major axis; in a circle, the semi-major axis and the semi-minor axis are equal to the radius.

■ A `RegularPolygon` is any shape whose vertices can be all placed on the circumference of a circle and whose side lengths are equal; for example, an equilateral triangle, square or regular pentagon.

■ An `ArbitraryPolygon` is any polygon that is neither a rectangle nor regular. It is defined by a set of points.

Class `Shape2D` lists seven operations. Since this is the ultimate superclass of the hierarchy, these seven operations are all inherited by each of the other eight classes. This means that each operation must *make sense* and *behave consistently* in all the classes. In this example, the various subclasses will use different methods for most operations. We will discuss this further, below.

Three of the operations in `Shape2D` modify the shape. The effect of these operations is illustrated in Figure 2.9.

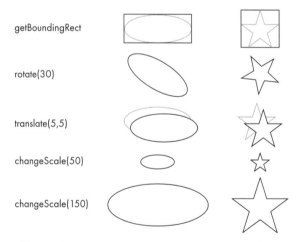

getBoundingRect

rotate(30)

translate(5,5)

changeScale(50)

changeScale(150)

Figure 2.9   Effects of certain operations on an `Ellipse` and an `ArbitraryPolygon`

■ `rotate`: takes one argument, the number of degrees to rotate the shape. The shape is modified as a result of the rotation.

■ `translate`: takes two arguments, an x-amount and a y-amount and moves the shape in the x- and y-directions.

■ `changeScale`: takes one argument, a percentage, and makes the shape bigger or smaller, keeping its center the same.

The getCenter operation simply returns the value of the center instance variable. The getArea and getPerimeterLength operations compute a value and return it. The getBoundingRect operation returns a non-rotated Rectangle that would be just big enough to fit around the shape – this is also illustrated in Figure 2.9.

Abstract classes and abstract methods

There are separate methods in four different classes to compute the operation rotate. Each method takes advantage of properties unique to its class:

- Circle: rotating a circle does not change it! Therefore the rotate method in class Circle would do absolutely nothing. The method would exist but would immediately return.

- SimplePolygon and Ellipse: these classes have an attribute called orientation, which the rotate method simply has to modify.

- ArbitraryPolygon: rotating one of these would be a little more complex. See a textbook on computer graphics to learn precisely how to do it.

However, it is not possible to write a method to rotate instances of the superclasses of these four classes. This is because there is not enough information available in those classes to do the rotation. This leads us to two important conclusions:

1. The rotate operation found in Shape2D is an example of an *abstract operation*. If a class has an abstract operation, it means that no method for that operation exists in the class, although the operation makes logical sense for it and for all the classes below it in the hierarchy. Abstract operations are shown in italics in Figure 2.8. Leaf subclasses have to have or inherit implementations of each operation – in other words, you can have abstract operations anywhere except leaf classes.

2. The four classes, Shape2D, EllipticalShape, Polygon and SimplePolygon, must be *abstract classes*. An abstract class is one that cannot have any instances. Any class, except a leaf class, can be declared abstract; however, a class that has one or more abstract methods *must* be declared abstract. The main purpose of an abstract class is to hold features that will be inherited by its subclasses. If a class is not abstract, then it is said to be *concrete*, and instances of it can be created. Leaf classes must be concrete, although it is also possible to have concrete classes higher in the inheritance hierarchy.

You should also note the following other interesting facts about abstract classes and methods in the shape hierarchy of Figure 2.8:

- In addition to rotate, all but two of the other operations in class Shape2D are abstract. As required, these have concrete implementations by the time the leaf classes are reached. However, the concrete implementations do not actually have to be defined *in* the leaf classes – they can be defined higher in the hierarchy. For example, rotate is defined in the abstract class SimplePolygon.

■ Class `SimplePolygon` is abstract, even though it has two concrete methods. This is because it neither has nor inherits concrete implementations of operations `changeScale`, `getArea` and `getPerimeterLength`.

■ There is an abstract operation `getBoundingRect` in class `Shape2D` of Figure 2.8. It has a concrete implementation in `Polygon`, since it is possible to design a general algorithm for computing the bounding rectangle if you can compute the vertices of a shape – and class `Polygon` does have such a method, called `getVertices`.

■ Class `Polygon` declares the operation `getVertices`, yet the operation does not exist in its superclass `Shape2D`. This is because it only makes sense to talk about vertices of polygons; no vertices exist in smooth-curved shapes such as ellipses.

■ Operation `getVertices` is abstract in `Polygon`, even though the concrete method `getBoundingRect` calls it. Such calling of an abstract operation by a concrete method is quite legal and in fact is considered good design practice.

■ Operation `getVertices` has concrete implementations in the three leaf classes below `Polygon`, but not in the immediate subclass `SimplePolygon`, because there is not enough information to compute the vertices in that class.

■ The attribute `semiMajorAxis` is present in `EllipticalShape`; however, it is not accessed by any method in that class. This is because `Circle` accesses it using the method name `getRadius` – it would be odd to be able to talk about the semi-major axis of a circle even though mathematically it is equivalent to the radius.

Overriding

In addition to the implementation of `getBoundingRect` in `Polygon`, there is also another concrete implementation in class `Rectangle` (which is a *subclass* of `Polygon`). This second concrete implementation is said to *override* the version of `getBoundingRect` that otherwise would be inherited from `Polygon`. The `getBoundingRect` method in `Rectangle` computes the same result as the method in `Polygon`, but the overriding version in `Rectangle` can be more efficient: in those cases where the `Rectangle` is not rotated, its bounding rectangle is the `Rectangle` itself.

In general, there are three valid reasons for overriding methods: *restriction*, *extension* and *optimization*:

■ **Overriding for restriction** occurs when the overriding method prevents a violation of certain constraints that are present in the subclass, but were not present in the superclass.

For example, imagine there was a `changeScale(x,y)` method in `Shape2D` that allowed a shape to be distorted by having its width and height modified by different percentages. It would be reasonable to use this method to modify any `ArbitraryPolygon`, `Ellipse` or un-rotated `Rectangle`. However, scaling a `Circle` in this way would mean that it would no longer be a `Circle` – it would be an `Ellipse`.

C++ terminology for abstract operations

You may hear the term 'pure virtual function'. This is C++ terminology for 'abstract operation'.

You might therefore consider creating an overriding version of changeScale(x,y) in Circle which throws an exception if x and y are not equal to each other. Similarly, non-uniform scaling of a RegularPolygon should be forbidden.

As another example of overriding for restriction, imagine adding a concrete version of debit in MortgageAccount in Figure 2.5 that restricts your ability to withdraw money from the account: MortgageAccount might allow you to only withdraw a fixed amount when the account is first opened. Any other attempt to withdraw money would throw an *exception*.

Overriding for restriction can have some undesirable effects. It is important to ensure that all polymorphic methods implementing an abstract operation behave consistently. For example, if the implementations of debit in some classes may throw an exception, while other implementations of debit do not declare that they too may throw the exception, then consistency is being violated. The programmer can solve this problem by declaring that the exception *may be thrown* by any of the polymorphic implementations of debit, even though he or she knows that certain of the methods will not in practice do so. Users of the operation must therefore always *prepare* for the exception (in Java, by using a try–catch construct).

- **Overriding for extension** occurs when the overriding method does basically the same thing as the version in the superclass, but adds some extra capability needed in the subclass. For example, in Figure 2.5, there might be a version of debit in SavingsAccount that would charge an additional fee if your bank balance was less than $1500.

- **Overriding for optimization** occurs when the overriding method in the subclass has exactly the same effect as the overridden method, except that it is more *efficient*. Above, we described a case of this in which getBoundingRect can often be computed more efficiently in the Rectangle class than in the general case.

Exercises

E13 This question requires knowledge of very basic geometry. Describe in one paragraph how the different polymorphic implementations of the following operations from Figure 2.8 would work in classes Rectangle, RegularPolygon, Circle and their superclasses. You do not need to write any code; instead just describe what attributes would be used and/or modified, and the formula to be used (if any).

(a) translate

(b) changeScale

(c) getArea

(d) getCenter

E14 Explain how you would incorporate the operations flipHorizontally and flipVertically into the hierarchy of Figure 2.8. Describe which classes (if any) should declare these to be abstract operations, and which classes should have methods for them.

E15 Explain how you would incorporate the following classes into the hierarchy of Figure 2.8. Describe the attributes and operations that would be present in these classes.

(a) IsoscelesTriangle

(b) Square

(c) Star

E16 Describe what the methods addPoint and removePoint in class ArbitraryPolygon would have to do. Hint: think about what attributes would be affected, and how. You do not need to write any code.

E17 Imagine you want to create an operation called getEnclosingCircle in the hierarchy of Figure 2.8. This operation would compute the smallest circle that can completely enclose any shape. Describe the methods that you think would be needed to implement this operation.

Variables and dynamic binding

Imagine you are programming in an object-oriented language and declare a variable called aShape that has type Shape2D. What this means is that as the program runs, the variable can contain objects of any concrete class in the hierarchy of Shape2D.

If you then attempt to invoke the operation getBoundingRect on the variable aShape, the program will make the decision about what method to run 'on the fly'. The decision-making process is called *dynamic binding* (or sometimes *late binding* or *virtual binding*).

You can imagine that the following procedure is used to perform dynamic binding:

1. The program looks in the class of the object actually stored in the variable. If there is a concrete method for the operation in that class, then it runs the method.

2. Otherwise, it checks in the immediate superclass to see if there is a method there; if so, it runs the method.

3. The program repeats step 2, looking in successively higher superclasses until it finds a concrete method and runs it.

4. If no method is found, then there is an error.

Therefore, for example, if you had an instance of RegularPolygon in the aShape variable, and invoked the operation getBoundingRect, the program would look first in RegularPolygon, then SimplePolygon and finally Polygon before it finds a method to run.

If aShape had contained an instance of Rectangle, however, then the program would find a getBoundingRect method in that class immediately.

It would be inefficient if programs ran the above dynamic binding algorithm for every procedure call, therefore an optimized approach using a lookup table is used instead. However, programmers do not normally need to be aware of the optimized mechanism.

Dynamic binding is what gives polymorphism its power. It relieves programmers from the burden of having to write conditional statements to explicitly choose which code to run; with dynamic binding, that work is done automatically by the programming language.

Dynamic binding is only needed when the compiler determines that there is more than one possible method that could be executed by a particular call. Therefore, for example, if you declared a variable to have type Rectangle, and you could be sure that Rectangle would have no subclasses, then only a Rectangle could be put in that variable. In such a case, the compiler can statically determine precisely which method to call.

Exercise

E18 In which of the following situations would dynamic binding be needed? Assume that the compiler knows that no new classes or methods can be added to the hierarchy.

You have a variable of type:	You invoke the operation:
a) Rectangle	getPerimeterLength
b) SimplePolygon	getCenter
c) Polygon	getBoundingRect
d) EllipticalShape	getScale
e) RegularPolygon	translate

Interfaces

An interface in Java is very much like an abstract class, except that it can have neither instance variables nor concrete methods – it is basically a named list of abstract operations. We instead create several *implementing classes* (rather than subclasses) of an interface that must implement the abstract operations. A class can implement multiple interfaces, but can have only one superclass.

You will see many interfaces built into Java: for example `Comparable` is an interface that defines operations that allow objects to be compared, and `Runnable` is an interface that allows an object to execute as a thread.

A key feature that gives interfaces their power is that you can declare a variable with an interface as its type. This means that an instance of *any* class that implements the interface can be put in the variable. With the variable, you can then call any of the operations defined in the interface – dynamic binding operates in the same way as with generalization.

We will see in Chapters 5, 6 and 9 that interfaces are very useful for creating good-quality designs.

2.7   Concepts that define object orientation

We have looked at several important aspects of object orientation. It is now time to summarize what we have presented and, at the same time, point out the essential features that distinguish an object-oriented language or system from one that is not object oriented. To be called object oriented, a language needs to have the following features:

■ **Identity**. The language must allow a programmer to refer to an object without having to refer to the instance variables contained in the object. Every object has a unique identity; therefore objects that contain instance variables with the same values must be recognized as different objects.

■ **Classes**. The programmer must be able to organize the code into classes, each of which describes the structure and function of a set of objects.

■ **Inheritance**. There has to be a mechanism to organize these classes into inheritance hierarchies, where features inherit from superclasses to subclasses.

■ **Polymorphism**. There has to be a mechanism by which several methods, in related classes, can have the same name and implement the same abstract operation. There must consequently be a dynamic binding mechanism that allows the choice of which method to run to be made during execution of the program.

Sometimes, languages or systems are sold that purport to be object oriented; however, without these key capabilities the term object oriented should not be applied. The term 'object based' is sometimes used instead of 'object oriented' for technologies which have features like objects or classes but which are perhaps missing inheritance, polymorphism or both.

The following four concepts are enhanced by the presence of the points listed above, and are also integral to object-oriented languages and systems. They allow us to engineer software effectively. We will revisit some of these issues later in the book.

■ **Abstraction**. As discussed at the beginning of the chapter, creating an abstraction means creating a simplified representation of something that you can work with in place of the original thing. Abstractions help you deal with complexity because you can reason about the simpler abstractions instead of the full details of something. There are many abstractions in an object-oriented program:

❏ An **object** is an abstraction of something of interest to the program, normally something in the real world such as a bank account.

❏ A **class** is an abstraction of a set of objects; at the same time it also acts as an abstract container for the methods that operate on those objects. The abstraction is improved if fewer methods are public.

❏ A **superclass** is an abstraction of a set of subclasses: you can declare a variable to be of a certain class, and not care that instances of its subclasses may be put in the variable. An **interface** is a similar but even better abstraction since it has fewer details defined (only abstract operations).

❏ A **method** is a procedural abstraction that hides its implementation: you can call the method without having to know the implementation.

❏ An **operation** is an abstraction of a set of methods. Better abstraction is achieved by giving an operation fewer parameters.

❏ **Attributes** and **associations** are abstractions of the underlying instance variables used to implement them.

■ **Modularity**. An object-oriented system can be constructed *entirely* from a set of classes, where each class takes care of a particular subset of the functionality (functionality related to a given type of data), rather than having the functionality spread out over many parts of the system.

■ **Encapsulation**. A class acts as a container to hold its features (variables and methods) and defines an interface that allows only some of them to be seen from outside.

■ Abstraction, modularity and encapsulation each help provide **information hiding**. This arises when software developers using some feature of a programming language or system do not need to know all the details; they only need to know sufficient details to use the feature. The result is that the developers have less confusing detail to understand and will therefore make fewer mistakes. Hence they can work effectively with larger systems.

Exercise

E19 Search the Internet for programming languages, databases or other tools on the market that call themselves object oriented. See if you can determine whether the claim of being object oriented is valid.

History of object orientation – programming languages

The first object-oriented programming language was *Simula-67*. This language allows programmers to simulate the way objects behave in the real world. For example, a simulation application might model cars approaching an intersection controlled by traffic lights. The objects in this simulation would include cars, lights and traffic lanes. When running a Simula program, each object is represented by a 'chunk' of data. All the procedures that operate on that object are found together in a class, so that the programmer can easily change the behavior of a car or a traffic light without having to search through the entire program.

Although Simula-67 was intended as a special-purpose simulation language, software developers gradually recognized that a wide variety of programs would be easier to develop and understand if organized this way. Although Simula is still used today, mostly in Scandinavia, it never gained widespread popularity.

In the early 1980s a new object-oriented language called *Smalltalk* gained popularity. Smalltalk was developed at Xerox PARC (Palo Alto Research Center). This research lab is also credited with giving rise to many other inventions, which we take for granted today: graphical user interfaces, the mouse, the laser printer, etc.

Smalltalk has many features that were innovative at the time. It has a simple syntax that is quite unlike that of other popular languages. It has a large library of reusable code – and programmers have access to all the source code for the library. Smalltalk popularized bytecode, platform independence and garbage collection, as now found in Java.

Smalltalk is still used today and has a loyal following, but it was rapidly overtaken in the late 1980s by a new language called *C++*. The developer of C++, Bjarne Stroustrup, recognized the advantage of object orientation but also recognized that there were tremendous numbers of programmers of the C language who wanted to take advantage of their C expertise and C's execution speed. He thus added object-oriented extensions to C and the new language became rapidly dominant.

However, over 15 years of experience has shown that C++ has certain drawbacks. Its syntax is quite complex and it is too easy to create code that has bugs. Large C++ programs have thus been found to be hard to maintain – they deteriorate rapidly as many programmers make changes.

In 1991, a group of engineers at Sun Microsystems started a project to design a programming language that could be used in consumer 'smart devices'. Knowing the strengths and weaknesses of C++, Smalltalk, and a third language called *Objective-C*, they invented a language initially called Oak. This borrowed the C syntax from C++, and many of its other essential features from Smalltalk. Some of the more troublesome features of C++, such as multiple inheritance and the ability to create pointers to arbitrary parts of memory, were eliminated.

Unfortunately, the team faced difficulties trying to sell Oak. It was only when the Internet gained popularity, with the advent of the World Wide Web in 1994, that Sun saw an opportunity to exploit the technology. The new language, renamed Java, was formally presented in 1995 at the SunWorld '95 conference.

More recently, Microsoft has entered the fray with its language *C#* (C-Sharp). C# has very many similarities with Java, but some subtle and interesting differences. C# is one of several languages that can run on Microsoft's *Common Language Runtime*, and is part of its *.Net* framework. Anyone who knows Java should be able to learn C# quite easily.

We will continue this history of object orientation in Chapter 5, where we will look at methods and notations for describing object-oriented systems.

2.8 A program for manipulating postal codes

On the book's web site (www.lloseng.com) you will find a Java program designed to illustrate the most important features of Java, including inheritance, polymorphism, string manipulation, access control. The program also illustrates an important software engineering concept: separation of the user interface from the functional part of a system.

The example is divided into three elements, as illustrated in Figure 2.10. The first element is a hierarchy representing postal codes of different countries. The second element is a new exception class. The third element is the PostalTest class that allows the user to enter postal codes and test the facilities of the PostalCode hierarchy.

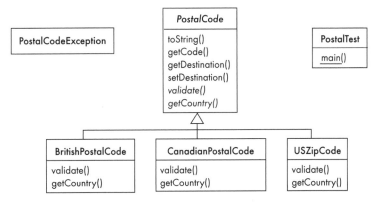

Figure 2.10   Classes for manipulating postal codes, showing public methods

The PostalCode hierarchy

The following are some design decisions you should study in PostalCode and its subclasses:

■ PostalCode is declared as abstract, meaning that no instances can be created. Two of its operations, **validate** and **getCountry**, are abstract, meaning that they must be given concrete implementations in subclasses.

■ The operation **validate** is protected, and is called by the constructor. Its concrete implementations in each subclass will throw a PostalCodeException (described below) if the format of the code is invalid.

■ All the instance variables are declared **private**. All other classes, including subclasses, can only access them using methods. This helps to improve encapsulation.

■ There is a **toString** method, as should be provided in most Java classes.

There are three examples of subclasses of PostalCode. Each of these implements the two abstract operations. For example, the **validate** method of one subclass,

`CanadianPostalCode`, ensures that the format is XNX NXN, where N is a number and X is a letter; the first letter is also taken from a restricted set. The other implementations of `validate` ensure that US postal codes have an all-numeric format, while British postal codes adhere to their more complex alphanumeric format.

The `PostalCodeException` class

`PostalCodeException` illustrates the concept of the user-defined exception class. Instances of this class are thrown when an error is found while validating a postal code. A class that manipulates postal codes could choose to handle such exceptions in any way it wishes.

The user interface class `PostalTest`

The user interface class, `PostalTest`, has only a static `main` method and one private static helper method called `getInput`. The code prompts the user for input and then attempts to create an instance of one of the subclasses of `PostalCode`. If a `PostalCodeException` is thrown, it tries to create an instance of other subclasses until none remain. Then it prints out information about the result. Clearly this is not a sophisticated user interface, nevertheless it is sufficient to test the facilities of the `PostalCode` hierarchy.

It would be possible to put all the code from `PostalTest` into `PostalCode` – the `main` method in `PostalCode` would then simply be used to test the class. This is, in fact, a design alternative that some people would choose. We prefer to advocate the complete separation of the classes that do the user interface work from the functional classes.

`PostalTest` is a rather degenerate class in the object-oriented sense, since it will never have any instances. If any instances were created, then they could do nothing since there are no constructors, instance variables or instance methods. The `main` method and its helper methods are class methods (also called static methods), reminiscent of the procedural paradigm. For the purposes of having a simple test class, we believe this is acceptable; however, you should be careful not to force class methods to do work that would be better done in instance methods.

Exercises

E20 Run the postal code program. Then carefully read through the code for all six classes. Use the Java documentation to look up any methods or classes you do not understand.

E21 The way the program is written, letters in Canadian postal codes are only accepted if they are upper case. On the other hand, letters in British postal codes are accepted whether they are upper case or not. This is inconsistent.

Modify the program so that user input of upper or lower case is accepted, and the input is converted to upper case immediately.

E22 Describe how you would design the following modifications to the postal code program. Think carefully about whether there should be one method, or several different polymorphic methods. In the latter case, think about whether there should be an abstract method in the superclass and concrete methods in the subclasses, or else a concrete method in the superclass and one or more overriding methods in the subclasses.

(a) There should be an operation `length` that returns the number of characters in a postal code.

(b) There should be a file that contains postal codes, one per line. There should then be an operation called `isOnRecord` that returns `true` if a postal code is in this file. Do not worry for now about the efficiency of this operation in the case of very large files, although you should be aware that this would be a concern in a production-quality system. Hint: investigate class `FileInputStream`.

(c) For each country, there should be a file that contains, on each line, a postal code prefix followed by the name of a destination of such postal codes. For example, class `BritishPostalCode` might use the file `BritishPostalDestinations.txt`, and on one of its lines it might contain 'SW Southwest-London'. The parts of the program that set the destination should read these files.

E23 Implement the designs you prepared in the above exercise.

E24 Add a new subclass representing postal codes for the fictitious country of Ootumlia, whose format is always one or two letters, followed by a space, followed by two numbers. You will have to modify the `PostalTest` class to accommodate your new subclass, although you must not modify the `PostalCode` class.

2.9 Classes for representing geometric points

In this section we illustrate the use of the mathematical class library in Java. We also illustrate how a seemingly simple problem can be solved in several rather different ways. You will have the chance to analyze the advantages and disadvantages of various alternatives.

The classes described in this section represent points on a 2-dimensional plane. From mathematics, we know that to represent a point on a plane, you can use x and y coordinates, which are called *Cartesian coordinates*. Alternatively, you can use *polar coordinates*, represented by a radius (often called rho) and an angle (often called theta). In the code we have provided, you can interchangeably work with a given point as Cartesian coordinates or polar coordinates.

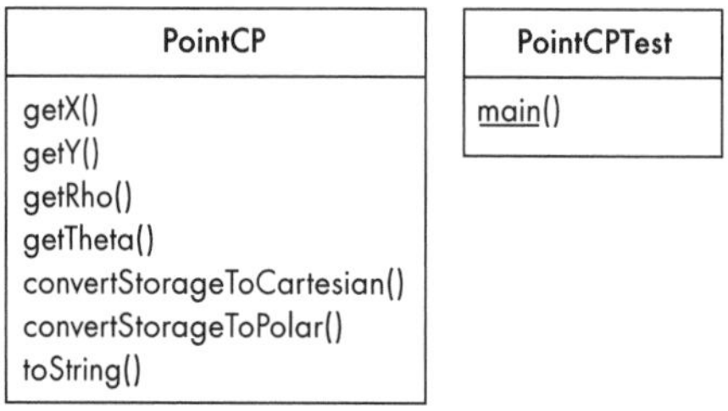

Figure 2.11 Classes for representing points using both Cartesian and polar coordinates. Only the operations are shown

Java already has classes for representing geometric points. Take a few moments to look at classes Point2D and Point in the Java documentation.

We will call the point class presented here PointCP; its main distinguishing feature from the built-in Java classes is that it can handle both Cartesian and polar coordinates. We also provide a class called PointCPTest which, like PostalTest, simply provides a user interface for testing. The public methods of both classes are shown in Figure 2.11. The code for these classes can also be found at the book's web site (www.lloseng.com).

Class PointCP contains two private instance variables that can either store x and y, or else rho and theta. No matter which storage format is used, all four possible parameters can be computed. Users of the class can also call methods convertStorageToPolar or convertStorageToCartesian in order to explicitly convert the internal storage of an instance to the alternative format.

The above design of PointCP is certainly not the only possible design. Table 2.1 shows several alternative designs; the above design is Design 1.

Exercises

E25 Answer the following questions with respect to the above designs of the PointCP class.

(a) Discuss why it might be useful to allow users of class PointCP (Design 1) to explicitly change the internal storage format, using convertStorageToCartesian or convertStorageToPolar.

(b) What might be a potential hidden weakness of these methods? Hint: what could happen if one is called, then the other, and this process is repeated numerous times?

(c) Write a short program to test whether the weakness you discussed in part b is, in fact, real.

E26 Create a table describing the various advantages (pros) and disadvantages (cons) of each of the five design alternatives. Some of the factors to consider are: simplicity of code, efficiency when creating instances, efficiency when

Table 2.1   Alternative designs for the PointCP class

	How Cartesian coordinates are computed	*How polar coordinates are computed*
Design 1: Store one type of coordinates using a single pair of instance variables, with a flag indicating which type is stored	Simply returned if Cartesian is the storage format, otherwise computed	Simply returned if polar is the storage format, otherwise computed
Design 2: Store polar coordinates only	Computed on demand, but not stored	Simply returned
Design 3: Store Cartesian coordinates only	Simply returned	Computed on demand, but not stored
Design 4: Store both types of coordinates, using four instance variables	Simply returned	Simply returned
Design 5: Abstract superclass with designs 2 and 3 as subclasses	Depends on the concrete class used	Depends on the concrete class used

doing computations that require both coordinate systems, and amount of memory used.

E27   Implement and test Design 5. You will also have to make some small changes to PointCPTest. Hints: a) Do you still need the variable typeCoord? b) Do still you need the third argument in the constructor?

E28   Run a performance analysis in which you compare the performance of Design 5, as you implemented it in the previous exercise, with Design 1. Determine the magnitude of the differences in efficiency, and verify the hypotheses you developed in E26.

E29   To run a performance analysis, you will have to create a new test class that randomly generates large numbers of instances of PointCP, and performs operations on them, such as retrieving polar and Cartesian coordinates. You should then run this test class with the two versions of PointCP – Design 1 and Design 5.

E30   Summarize your results in a table: the columns of the table would be the two designs; the rows of the table would be the operations. The values reported in the table would be the average computation speed. Make sure you explain your results.

E31 Study the `PointCPTest` class. It has a complex pair of loops for obtaining input from the user.

(a) Discuss whether you think the design is clear, and if not, why not.

(b) Design, but do not yet implement, an alternative to `PointCPTest` that does not have the nested loops. What are the drawbacks of this alternative design?

(c) Implement and test your alternative design.

E32 In Design 5 of Table 2.1, we suggested creating an abstract superclass. Another alternative (we can call it Design 6) would instead involve turning `PointCP` into an interface. Different classes corresponding to designs 1 to 4 would implement this interface.

(a) Design and implement this approach (with two different implementing classes).

(b) What advantages and disadvantages does this approach have?

2.10 Measuring the quality and complexity of a program

It is very important for engineers to be able to measure properties of the materials and devices they work with. A civil engineer, for example, needs to know the load capacity of a beam so that he or she can decide on its required thickness or support. In software engineering, we work with pure information as represented in programs, designs and other documents. Our goals of measurement include: better prediction of the time and effort required for development, and, as was discussed in Section 1.5, improved control of aspects of quality such as reliability, usability and maintainability.

A *metric* is a well-defined method and formula for computing some value of interest to a software engineer. Below are some of the metrics relevant to the basic principles of object-oriented programming and design we have discussed in this chapter. Each metric is useful as a rough *indicator* of some quality such as maintainability, or of work involved in development. However, each metric also has disadvantages, which we will address.

Lines of code: You will often notice people describe the amount of work they have accomplished in terms of the number of lines of code they have written. This is a very easy metric to compute and is easy to understand. In large systems, the term *KLOC* is used, which means *thousands* of lines of code. A program with more lines of code will typically take more time to develop and maintain than a program with fewer lines of code. Unfortunately, this is not always the case: a smaller program may be more technically complex than a larger program and therefore require more development time; also, either program may be better designed and therefore have fewer defects; finally, a programmer can add duplicate or unneeded lines to make the system appear bigger than it should be.

For these reasons it is considered unfair to judge a programmer's abilities based solely on the number of lines of code she or he has developed; it is also not reasonable to predict future maintenance based exclusively on this metric.

Uncommented lines of code: Sometimes instead of counting all the lines in a source code file, only the lines containing actual source code statements are included; blank lines and those with just comments are left out. This can result in a less biased metric: a programmer could otherwise add extra unneeded comments or blank lines to make the amount of code appear greater. However, the other problems with lines of code mentioned above still remain.

Percentage of lines with comments: It is considered a sign of more maintainable code if it has lots of informative comments – in some systems up to 50% is desirable for this metric. However, the comments have to be *informative*. Also, well-structured code with better choices for variable and method names can be self-documenting and therefore require fewer comments.

Number of classes: This is often a good indicator of the overall size of a design. Its main weakness is that the number of classes can be affected significantly by the quality of the design. Some programmers, particularly when they are used to procedural programming, will create too few classes that are too complex; on the other hand, some programmers will create redundant and useless classes.

Number of methods per class: If a class has a very large number of methods it is often a sign that it is too complex.

Number of public methods per class: Similar to the above, this should be very small. Too many public methods suggests that methods that ought to be private are being made public; alternatively, classes may simply be too complex.

Goals, Questions, Metrics (GQM)

When working with software engineering metrics, the recommended practice is to first think of your high-level *goals*: e.g. 'To improve maintainability'. Then you should think about the *questions* you can ask of the system or the process that will help achieve these goals: e.g. 'How much information is provided to the maintainer?' or 'How complex is the system?' Finally you choose or develop *metrics* that will answer your questions: e.g. 'Percent lines with comments' can help answer the 'how much information?' question.

Merely computing numbers for metrics without goals and questions is not considered an efficient way to work.

Number of public instance variables per class: Ideally this should be zero – it is good practice to make them all as private as possible.

Number of parameters per method: A low number is better here – most methods should take zero or one parameter.

Number of lines of code per method: It is considered better to have more, but smaller methods. In

Chapter 6 we will see a design pattern that directly leads to this.

Depth of the inheritance hierarchy: Very complex inheritance hierarchies can be quite difficult to maintain. At the same time, having no inheritance at all limits opportunities for reuse.

Number of overridden methods per class: A number too high here suggests problems in the design. A subclass is supposed to be a specialization of its superclass, not something completely different.

Exercises

E33 Compute values of each of the metrics described above for the following. Where appropriate, compute values for the entire system, each package, each individual class, and each method.

(a) The PostalCode system.

(b) The various designs of the PointCP system.

(c) Some other system you have developed.

E34 Analyze your data from the previous exercise. Rank the metrics in the order in which you think they might:

(a) Act as indicators of the amount of work that would have been required to develop the code.

(b) Act as indicators of the maintainability of the system.

2.11 Difficulties and risks in programming language choice and OO programming

The following are some of the factors arising from the material in this chapter that can pose a risk to software engineering projects:

■ **Language evolution and deprecated features**. Every programming language evolves, such that code written for earlier versions will not run or gives warning messages threatening that it will not run in the future. This has been true for Java – a list of deprecated classes and methods is available as part of the standard Java documentation.
Resolution. Pay careful attention to the documentation describing which features of Java are deprecated.

■ **Efficiency can be a concern in some object-oriented systems**. Most implementations of Java run using a virtual machine. This means that Java code tends not to be as efficient as code written in a language such as C++. Java's exception handling and safety checking also can consume considerable

CPU time. But even object-oriented C++ code can be less efficient than purely procedural code if it uses dynamic binding extensively and allocates objects excessively. Some projects have failed because, when complete, the system did not provide adequate performance.

Resolution. Prototype the system early, especially those parts that involve complex algorithms, in order to determine whether performance will be satisfactory. Learn about the different programming strategies that make a Java program run faster. Consider languages other than Java for number-crunching applications. Profile the running system to discover places where inefficiencies lie, then selectively rewrite code to eliminate the worst inefficiencies.

2.12 Summary

In this chapter, we have reviewed the main principles of object orientation. Object-oriented systems use classes and objects to provide software engineers with a useful combination of data and procedural abstraction.

Some of the key features of object-oriented systems are that they provide inheritance hierarchies and polymorphism. It is important to learn to use these facilities correctly, since abusing them can result in designs that are difficult to maintain. For example, you should check carefully to ensure that all generalizations follow the 'isa' rule, and you should make sure that all features present in a superclass also make sense in each subclass.

2.13 For more information

The following are just a few of the many books and web sites that present information about basic object orientation and Java. Since Java is evolving, and since new books and web sites about it appear almost weekly, check your favorite bookstore and search the web for other material.

Books to help you learn Java and OO principles

- C. Thomas Wu, *An Introduction to Object Oriented Programming with Java*, 3rd edition, McGraw Hill, 2004. http://www.drcaffeine.com

- Walter Savitch, *Java: An Introduction to Computer Science and Programming*, 3rd edition, Prentice Hall, 2003

- Ken Arnold, James Gosling and David Holmes, *The Java Programming Language*, 3rd edition, Addison-Wesley, 2000. The book by the originators of Java; for those who already know something about programming. http://java.sun.com/docs/books/javaprog/

- Bruce Eckel, *Thinking in Java*, 3rd edition, Prentice Hall, 2002. Online version: http://www.mindview.net/Books/TIJ/

■ C. S. Horstmann, *Core Java*, Volumes I and II, 6th edition, Prentice Hall, 2002, http://www.horstmann.com/corejava.html

Book on programming in general

■ J. Bentley, *Programming Pearls*, 2nd edition, Addison-Wesley, 2000, http://www.cs.bell-labs.com/cm/cs/pearls/

Book on metrics

■ N. Fenton, and S. Pfleeger, *Software Metrics: A Rigorous and Practical Approach*, 2nd edition, Course Technology, 1998

Web sites about Java

■ Sun's official web site: http://java.sun.com contains a wealth of information, including official documentation, tutorials and downloads. You will be particularly interested in *The Java Tutorial:* http://java.sun.com/docs/books/tutorial and the Javadoc pages: http://java.sun.com/javadoc

■ The Java Lobby: http://www.javalobby.org is an excellent site containing Java news and products

■ JavaWorld, an online magazine about Java: http://www.javaworld.com

Tools to help you develop Java code

We recommend that you use an integrated tool to help you develop Java code. The following are some popular alternatives:

■ Borland JBuilder: Borland Corporation: http://www.borland.com

■ CodeWarrior: http://www.metrowerks.com

■ The Eclipse open source development environment: http://www.eclipse.org

Project exercises

The following are additional advanced exercises to help you tune up your Java and programming skills.

E35 Write a package that implements some of the hierarchy of two-dimensional shapes, discussed earlier in this chapter, including the abstract classes and the concrete classes `Circle` and `Rectangle`. Your main program should construct some random shapes of the concrete classes, do some transformations on these shapes, and then print out as much information as possible about the resulting shape, including perimeter, area, and bounding rectangle. Use the `PointCP` class presented earlier where possible. Hints:

■ For a circle, the area is πr^2 and the perimeter (i.e. the circumference) is $2\pi r$.

- To compute the bounding rectangle of an object you have to compute its maximum and minimum points in the x- and y-directions.

- As a challenging bonus, you can try to implement `ArbitraryPolygon`. Use one of the collection classes to store the points. To compute the area, you can divide it into triangles and sum the area of the triangles. The area of a triangle is 0.5 × base × height. To compute the bounding rectangle you will have to search through the points to find the maximum and minimum x- and y-coordinates.

- As another bonus you can try to implement the class `Ellipse`. The area is π × a × b where a is the semi-minor axis and b is the semi-major axis. The approximate perimeter is $\pi(3(a+b) - \sqrt{(a+3b)(3a+b)})$. Computing the bounding rectangle of an ellipse is a challenging problem if the ellipse is rotated.

E36 Compare the performance of `ArrayList`, `Vector` and ordinary arrays. You should do a series of experiments where you do each of the following tests with the three types of collection, timing the execution of each run. You should run each case several times on the same computer to obtain stable average timings.

(a) Construct very large collections by putting random integers into each collection one at a time. The random integers should range in value from zero to nine. You should make each collection large enough so that the run takes at least 10 seconds to add the integers in the case of an `ArrayList`. You will have to do some initial experiments to find out what is a good size. You would use the same size of collection for `ArrayList`, `Vector` and the array. The `ArrayList` and `Vector` can be created by successively adding items and allowing them to grow, while the array has to be created at its full size and then populated with its contents. You could also try to experiment with the case where you *do* create the `ArrayList` and `Vector` initially with their full size.

(b) Construct very large collections as in (i). Then use iterators to sum the elements. Subtract the construction time to get a measure of how much time the iteration takes. Use a `for` loop for the array, and an `Iterator` for the `Vector` and `ArrayList`.

(c) Again, construct collections as in (i). Then iterate through the collections removing all the even numbers. Subtract the construction time to get a measure of how much time deletion takes. You can only easily do this for `Vector` and `ArrayList`.

(d) Once again, construct collections. Then iterate though them adding an extra element after every number 9 encountered. Subtract the original construction time to get an idea of how long adding elements randomly into collections takes. You can only easily do this for `Vector` and `ArrayList`.

Write up the results of your experiments as a formal laboratory report. Present your data in suitable tables, and draw conclusions from an analysis of the data. From your conclusions, develop recommendations to designers.

Basing software development on reusable technology 3

In the last chapter, we refreshed your knowledge of the object-oriented paradigm, an important software development technology that can be used to construct complex software systems. It would be nice, however, if instead of developing an entire system from scratch, you could simply adapt an existing system to meet your needs. In other words, *reuse* is one of the keys to successful software development. We will start our exploration of the software development process by looking at a technology called *frameworks* that promotes reuse.

In this chapter we will also introduce the client–server architecture, one of the most widely used ways of structuring software systems. We will then introduce a framework specifically designed for this book that allows software developers to rapidly build many different client–server systems.

In this chapter you will learn about the following

- Frameworks, reusable software subsystems that implement important facilities which many applications can use.

- The client–server architecture, an important way of designing programs in which the software is divided into two main parts: a client program which runs on each user's computer, and a server program with which each user's client communicates in order to obtain services.

- A client–server framework written in Java. We will use this as the basis for many of the exercises presented in the book.

3.1   Reuse: building on the work and experience of others

Where feasible, software engineers should avoid re-developing software that others have already developed; in other words, they should try to *reuse* others' work.

In order to facilitate reuse, software engineers should also make their designs *reusable*. This means designing and documenting software so that it is understandable and flexible enough be used in a variety of different systems.

The following are some of the types of reuse practiced by software engineers, in increasing order according to the potential amount of work that can be saved by the reuse:

- **Reuse of expertise**. Software engineers who have many years of experience working on projects can often save considerable time when it comes to developing new systems because they do not need to re-think many issues: their past experience tells them what needs to be done. If such people write articles describing their experiences, this can help others to do better engineering work.

- **Reuse of standard designs and algorithms**. There are thousands of algorithms and other aspects of designs described in various books, standards documents and articles. These represent a tremendous wealth for the software designer, since all he or she needs to do is to implement them if they are appropriate to the current task.

- **Reuse of libraries of classes or procedures, or of powerful commands built into languages and operating systems**. Libraries and commands represent implemented algorithms, data structures and other facilities. Software developers always do this kind of reuse to some extent since all programming languages come with some basic libraries. The more powerful the facilities that come with a programming language, the more powerful and 'high level' the language is. Applications like spreadsheets, word processors and database programs have built-in languages with commands for such things as sorting, searching and displaying dialogs. Using these languages, which are often called *fourth-generation languages*, is an important form of reuse.

- **Reuse of frameworks**. Frameworks are libraries containing the structure of entire applications or subsystems. To complete the application or subsystem, you merely need to fill in certain missing details. A framework can be written in any programming language and can vary considerably in sophistication and detail. We will discuss them in more detail in Section 3.3.

- **Reuse of complete applications**. You can take complete applications and add a small amount of extra software that makes the applications behave in special ways the client wants. For example, you might take a standard email application and add a feature that would always update its 'address book' with data from the company's employee and client databases. This type of reuse is often called reuse of commercial off-the-shelf or *COTS* software, and the extra code written is often called *glue* code. It is common to write the glue code using *scripting* languages which run using an interpreter.

> **Newton on reuse**
> Reuse is not a new concept. It was Isaac Newton who said, 'If I have seen further it is by standing on the shoulders of giants.'

The elements reused in the latter three types of reuse are often collectively called *components*.

Unfortunately, reuse is not as extensive in software engineering projects as might be desirable. Some of the reasons for this are outlined in the next section. In this book, we want to encourage you always to think in terms of reuse when you develop software. Therefore, as a major part of this chapter, we will present a reusable framework that will form the basis for many examples and exercises.

Exercises

E37 Search the Internet in order to build a list of sources of information about the following things which can be reused during software development. Rate each source on a scale from low to high, where low means the source is very uninformative (perhaps just offering to sell a product), and high means it provides a wealth of practical information.

(a) Wisdom and experience about software design (e.g. tips, guidelines etc.).

(b) Written descriptions of standard algorithms.

(c) Class libraries.

(d) Code repositories.

(e) Fourth-generation languages.

(f) Macro packages you can add to spreadsheet or word processor programs.

(g) Frameworks.

(h) Scripting languages used to glue together COTS programs.

E38 Pick a couple of the best sources of information from the last exercise and discuss how they can help you achieve the reuse objective.

3.2 Incorporating reusability and reuse into software engineering

In order for reuse to occur, software developers must not only reuse existing good-quality components, but must also contribute to reusable components that others can use.

Encouraging reuse: breaking the vicious cycle

Reuse and design for reusability, especially of frameworks, need to be made part of the *culture* of software development organizations. In the many organizations that do *not* practice reuse, software engineers tend to start design from scratch for each new application either because there are no reusable components available to reuse, or because they do not feel confident about reusing whatever is available.

Developers are often willing to reuse packages of code delivered with a programming language, but are reluctant to develop new ones, and are especially reluctant to develop entirely new frameworks.

There are several reasons for this reluctance:

■ Developing anything reusable is seen as not directly benefiting the current customer – after all, the current customer only needs *one* application, so why take the extra time needed to develop something that will benefit *other* applications? This argument often seems particularly convincing when developers are under extreme deadlines.

■ If a developer has painstakingly developed a high-quality reusable component, but management only rewards the efforts of people who create the more visible 'final product', then that developer will be reluctant to spend time on reusable components in the future.

■ Efforts at creating reusable software are often done in a hurry and without enough attention to quality. People thus lose confidence in the resulting components, and in the concepts of reuse and reusability.

Therefore many organizations suffer from a vicious circle: developers do not develop high-quality reusable components, therefore there is nothing good enough to reuse. Since there is nothing good enough to reuse, software developers take so much time to develop applications that they lack time to invest in reusable frameworks or libraries.

This cycle can only be broken if software engineers and their managers recognize the following points:

■ The vicious cycle exists, and costs money.

■ In order to save money in the longer term, some investment in reusable code is normally justified.

■ Developers should be explicitly rewarded for developing reusable components.

■ Attention to quality of reusable components is essential so that potential reusers have confidence in them.

■ Developing reusable components will normally simplify the resulting design, independently of whether reuse actually occurs.

■ Developing and reusing reusable components improves reliability, and can foster a sense of confidence in the resulting system.

The latter three points are worth further discussion.

The quality of a software product is only as good as its lowest-quality reusable component. It is no wonder then that many developers refuse to reuse components in which they lack confidence. To combat this, development of reusable components should be treated just like development of complete applications. You need to do proper domain and requirements analysis for the component; to design and document it properly; and to ensure its quality through testing and inspection. We will discuss these activities later in the book. In addition, it is important that software engineers be always available to properly maintain a reusable component. If all of the above are performed, then the component should be of high quality and hence it is more likely to be reused.

The process of developing reusable components, as part of a larger software project, can have significant benefits, even if the components are never reused outside the project. Looking at a problem at a more general level tends to make it easier to understand: details relevant to only certain specific cases are discarded, which leads to better abstractions and a simpler structure of the resulting design. Also, the very process of developing reusable components separately from their target system reduces the interconnections among parts of the system, a quality we will call low coupling, and discuss in detail in Chapter 9. This low coupling makes the resulting application easier to understand, modify and test.

In addition to simplifying design, reusable software tends to be more reliable. The more places the reusable components are used, the more testing they get. Also, they will be used in different contexts, thus their weak points are more likely to be exposed. When developing a new system, you can substantially increase confidence in it by composing it mostly of components that have already been thoroughly validated.

Making it possible to find reusable components

Even if reusable components are available, software engineers must be able to find them easily. An essential activity therefore is to carefully *catalog* and document all the reusable components.

This catalog must be easy to search and must be kept up to date. In particular, it is important to drop or *deprecate* older components that have been found to be unreliable or have been superseded by better components. Deprecating a component means declaring that it should not be used in subsequent designs, but remains available to support existing designs that incorporate it.

3.3 Frameworks: reusable subsystems

Developing and using frameworks is an excellent way to promote reuse and reusability.

> **Definition:** a *framework* is reusable software that implements a generic solution to a generalized problem. It provides common facilities applicable to different application programs.

The key principle behind frameworks is as follows: applications that do different but related things tend to have similar designs – in particular, the patterns of interaction among the components tend to be very similar. This can be true even if the applications are in quite different domains. To develop a framework, you identify the common design elements and develop software that implements these design elements in a reusable way.

The key thing that distinguishes a framework from other kinds of software subsystem is that a framework is intrinsically *incomplete*. This means that there are certain classes or methods that are *used* by the framework, but which are missing.

The missing parts are often called *slots*. The application developer fills in these slots in an application-specific way to adapt the framework to his or her needs. The more slots that the application developer must fill, the more complex the framework is to use. At the same time, a framework with many slots tends to be more flexible and therefore you are more likely to be able to reuse it to create a wide range of applications across different domains.

Frameworks also usually have *hooks*: these are like slots, except that they are places where developers can add *optional* functionality of different kinds. We will see examples of hooks and slots in the framework we present later in this chapter.

Developers using frameworks not only fill slots and hooks, but they also use the services that the framework provides, i.e. methods that perform useful functions. The set of services, taken together, is often called the *Application Program Interface*, or *API*.

A framework enables the reuse of both design and code. The user of a framework not only reuses the overall design envisioned by the framework's designer, but also a body of code that implements that design.

The following are some examples of frameworks:

■ **A framework for payroll management**. Most businesses have software that includes a payroll module. The rules and features needed in a payroll system will differ considerably, depending on the type of business, the local jurisdiction and other software the company uses. However, basic elements such as making regular payments, and computing taxes and other deductions, will always exist. Although it is possible to purchase complete payroll applications, many businesses are of sufficient complexity that such applications do not implement all the needed features and rules. Instead of developing a custom payroll package from scratch, several businesses could adapt a common framework to their individual needs.

■ **A framework for a frequent buyer 'club'.** In order to encourage loyalty, many companies have a system that awards points to customers based on the amount they purchase. The details of such systems will differ from company to company, but they all have a lot in common. A company implementing a new frequent buyer club would do well to base it on a framework in order to avoid the cost of developing a system from scratch. An airline frequent-flier plan could be built using the same framework since it is merely a special kind of frequent buyer club.

■ **A framework for course registration.** Each institution has its own academic rules, hence it is difficult to create a commercial application that can be bought off the shelf to automate student information systems. However, when software engineers are developing or replacing student information systems, they could benefit from basing their designs on a common framework.

■ **A framework for e-commerce web sites.** Most e-commerce web sites are built on the same general model. There is a list of products to pick from; when an item is selected it is added to a shopping cart; the site then prompts for personal information and arranges for secure payment. Individual web sites will want to have special features to differentiate themselves in the market. However, developers could save a lot of work if they had a framework that implemented the above general model.

Frameworks and product lines

A *product line* (or *product family*) is a set of products built on a common base of technology. The various products in the product line have different features to satisfy different market requirements. Many consumer products are sold in product lines. For example, a company producing microwave ovens will likely produce a very basic model that they can sell cheaply, and successively more expensive models with increasingly sophisticated features.

The software industry is following the product-line model more and more. Underlying a software product line is a framework containing the software technology common to all the products in the line. Each product is then produced by varying the modules used to fill the hooks and slots; new product variations can be produced quickly and easily.

For example, the software controlling a line of microwave ovens will be based on a common framework. Each model in the line will then have different combinations of software and hardware features. Doing this is far more economical than designing each model separately.

Product lines are also found in many generic software products: you can often purchase stripped-down 'demo' or 'lite' versions of software, as well as 'pro' versions with extra features. Sets of software versions each tailored to specific languages or countries also represent product lines.

Horizontal and vertical frameworks

A framework can be *horizontal* or *vertical* (Figure 3.1). A horizontal framework provides general application facilities that a large number of applications can use. For example, if many applications need to have a 'preferences' dialog that allows users to specify many kinds of options, then a horizontal framework could be designed that would provide general 'preferences dialog facilities' for many different types of applications.

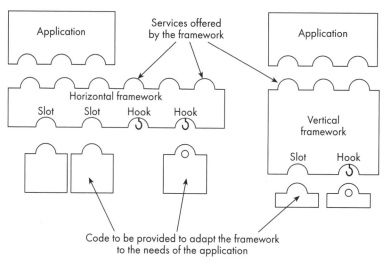

Figure 3.1   Horizontal and vertical frameworks showing services (at the top) and fillers of hooks and slots (at the bottom). One of the hooks is not filled

A vertical framework, often also called an *application framework*, provides facilities that will allow easy development of a more specific class of application programs. The microwave oven, frequent-buyer and course registration frameworks are vertical in nature, while the e-commerce framework might be a hybrid – a vertical framework composed of several horizontal frameworks that perform the sub-functions (such as general secure payment facilities).

A vertical framework will have a more complete implementation, and may have fewer slots and hooks. An interface in Java can be considered an extreme example of a horizontal framework: there is no implementation, and all the specified methods represent slots that must be filled.

An application will typically use only a subset of the framework's services. For example, a framework for a rental store could do such things as manage membership, handle deposits, process rentals and returns, and compute penalties for late returns. A developer using this framework to build an application for a video rental store would likely ignore the facilities for handling deposits, but would take advantage of the membership facilities. When building a car-rental system, the opposite would be true.

In Section 3.6, we will be studying a framework for the development of client–server applications. This is a horizontal framework, since it is usable by a very large number of applications that require a client–server architecture, but does not itself provide any functions for the end-user.

Object-oriented frameworks

In the object-oriented paradigm, a framework is composed of a library of classes. The set of services – the API – offered by the framework is defined by the set of all *public methods* of the public classes.

Some of the classes in an object-oriented framework should be abstract. To use the framework in the context of a new application, the developer creates concrete classes that extend these abstract classes. The abstract methods in the abstract classes are the slots that are filled when concrete methods are created in the concrete subclasses.

Example 3.1   *Imagine you are designing a framework that different libraries (of books, not code) would be able to adapt to meet their needs. What kind of facilities would you want to provide if you were designing such a framework? In what ways do libraries differ such that they would need to use a framework rather than a complete application?*

Answer: common facilities a library framework might provide include:

■ A user interface providing standard kinds of searches (e.g. by author, title and subject) and the ability to browse through lists of books and periodicals, or authors.

■ Basic classes representing books, clients, loans etc., along with common operations that can be done with those classes.

Differentiating features of library systems might include:

■ The cataloging scheme (e.g. Dewey Decimal or Library of Congress).

■ The kind of information kept about each client and book (e.g. clients may have different privileges, such as to be able to borrow only certain types of books).

■ Rules for types and lengths of loans, putting items on hold, payment of fines etc.

■ The particular types of items that can be borrowed from the library. All libraries have books, but libraries may contain such specialized items as videos, maps or rare books that need special treatment.

■ Specific data unique to this library such as a specific style of barcodes placed on books, multilingual support, etc.

■ Specific hardware the library possesses, such as particular types of barcode scanners and checkout machines.

■ The security mechanisms, such as who has authority to do what kind of operations. Login passwords in a university library might, for example, be integrated with login passwords for other university systems.

■ Integration of the system with other systems such as online library resources, existing databases of books and periodicals, accounting systems (e.g. for fines).

Exercises

E39 Imagine you are designing a framework for the following classes of applications. Describe what services you might put in the framework. Answer this question using a simple list of things the system should be capable of doing.

(a) A *reservation* framework. This could be expanded into an application to reserve anything that needs reserving, e.g. dental appointments, meetings, tickets at the theater, etc.

(b) A *scheduling* framework. This could be expanded for scheduling meetings, trains, classes etc.

(c) A *language-processing* framework. This could be expanded to process a programming language, a database query language or a command language.

(d) An *editing* framework. This could be expanded to allow editing of text, spreadsheets, and elements of different kinds of diagrams. Think about common features of editing tools provide.

E40 For each of the three frameworks in the last exercise, what differentiating features would software developers need to provide to build specific applications? What hooks and slots should therefore be available?

E41 List as many types of applications as you can think of that might benefit from the development of the frameworks in Exercise E39, so as to reduce the work required to develop similar applications from scratch.

E42 Imagine an airline company asks you to develop the software for its frequent-flier program. You choose to attack the development of this system by first developing a framework. You consider two approaches:

(a) Developing and then adapting a *vertical* framework that provides the facilities needed by several types of frequent-flier programs.

(b) Developing and then adapting a more *horizontal* framework that encompasses any frequent-buyer program such as a hotel priority club, a book club or a video rental store membership club.

For each of these two approaches, sketch the resulting framework in terms of: (i) the services it would have to offer, (ii) the slots that should be present, and (iii) the hooks that would be useful.

E43 Prepare arguments for both sides of the following debate question: 'Resolved: when asked to develop a new frequent-flier system, developing a new frequent-flier framework would be a waste of time.'

3.4 The client–server architecture

Software architecture is the branch of software engineering that deals with how to organize and connect a set of software modules so that they can work together with each other. There are many well-known architectures – one of the most widely used is the client–server architecture. We will use this as the basis for much of the design work in this book; we will look at other architectures in Chapter 9.

We present the client–server architecture here since we want to introduce a client–server framework upon which we will build some example applications. You will find, in the coming sections, all the details you need to learn in order to understand how our client–server framework works. Once you understand this material, you will be able to reuse the framework to build a wide variety of applications.

A *distributed system* is a system in which computations are performed by separate programs, normally running on separate pieces of hardware, that co-operate to perform the task of the system as a whole. A *server* is a program that provides some service for other programs that connect to it using a communication channel. A *client* is a program that accesses a server. A client may access many servers to perform different functions, and a server may be accessed by many clients simultaneously. A *client–server system* is a distributed system involving at least one server and one client. A *peer-to-peer system* is a client–server system in which programs can act as both client and server for each other.

Figure 3.2 illustrates a server program communicating with two client programs. The vertical lines represent the three programs involved. After connecting, Client 1 sends a message, receives a reply and disconnects. Client 2 connects while Client 1 is still connected; it simply sends a message and then disconnects. This diagram is an example of a UML *sequence diagram*; we will study such diagrams in more detail in Chapter 8.

In general, the components of a client–server system interact as follows:

■ The server starts running.

■ The server waits for clients to connect. This waiting process is called *listening*.

■ Clients start running and perform various operations, some of which require connecting to the server to request a service.

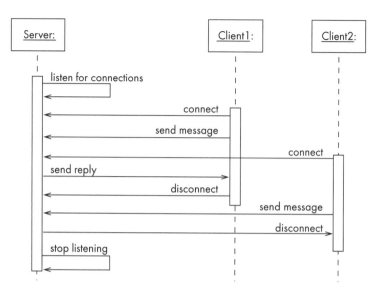

Figure 3.2   A server program communicating with two client programs

■ When a client attempts to connect, the server *accepts* the connection if it is willing.

■ The server waits for messages to arrive from connected clients.

■ When a message from a client arrives, the server takes some action in response, then resumes waiting.

■ Clients and servers continue functioning in this manner until one of them decides to shut down.

Normally, the action taken by the server includes sending a message back to the client. Most servers have to be able to handle connections from many clients and respond to messages from all the connected clients. How this is accomplished will be described below.

It is possible for the same program to be both a client and a server at the same time. For example, a database server might connect to another server in order to obtain additional data. It is also possible for the client and server to be located on the same computer, and run as separate processes. However, it is quite typical for them to be located on separate computers, perhaps in different geographical locations.

Table 3.1 lists some important kinds of systems that use the client–server architecture.

Comparing the client–server architecture to alternatives

You could also have some mechanism other than client–server communication for exchanging information. For example, one program could write a file, and another program could read the file, or else both programs could read and write

Table 3.1   Example client–server systems

System	Clients	Server
The World Wide Web	Browsers that display web pages and post forms, e.g. Netscape Navigator or Microsoft Internet Explorer	Web servers that manage sets of web pages (as well as CGI programs and servlets), and send information to browsers when sent a URL
Email	Programs that read and send email. For example, Microsoft Outlook, Eudora	A post-office program that receives email from remote sites and holds it until an email-reading client is activated. The program also forwards outgoing mail from the client to other sites
Network file system	Programs on any computer that access files that happen to be on other computers	A program whose main purpose is to allow clients on other computers to access files. Unix NFS and Novell NetWare are examples
Transaction processing system	Programs that send specific requests to perform some kind of transaction, such as debiting a bank account or booking an airline ticket	A program that centralizes all the functions of some business and processes transactions when they arrive
Remote display system	Programs that want to display information on the screen. Many Unix programs are capable of displaying graphical output on any computer running an X-Windows server	A program that manages the screen and allows applications, perhaps running on other computers, to display their output. A Unix X-Windows server is an important example
Communication system	A program that allows users to send a message or maintain a conversation with users on another computer	A program that routes messages. It can have features such as 'forwarding' that people are familiar with from the telephone network
Database system	Any application program that wants to query a database	A database management system that responds to requests to query or update the database

the same database. This could work for some kinds of communication, but would normally result in more complex and slower programs.

A single program that does everything can also be an alternative to a client–server system. However, the client–server architecture can have the following advantages:

- The computational work can be distributed among different machines. Designers can choose to centralize some computations on the server and distribute others to the clients. If everything is done on the server, then a powerful computer may be needed. On the other hand, if the clients take care of some computations then the server's workload will be lighter.

- The clients can access the server's functionality from a distance.

- The client and server can be designed separately, therefore they can both be simpler than a program that does everything. The development work can be done by independent groups, each only concerned with one part of the system (plus how the client and server communicate). Since the groups may be able to work on the client and server in parallel, they may be able to complete the whole system sooner.

- All the data can be kept centrally at the server, thus making it easier to assure its reliability. For example, it can be easier to ensure that regular backups are made of a single server's data, rather than trying to separately back up data saved by many separate programs.

- Conversely, distributing data among many different geographically distributed clients or servers can mean that if a disaster occurs in one place, the loss of data is minimized.

- The information can be accessed simultaneously by many users. It is possible to accomplish this using a single large program, but that approach tends to be more complex.

- Competing clients can be written to communicate with the same server, and vice versa; for example, different web browsers can communicate with the same web server. This can encourage innovation.

Exercises

E44 For each of the following systems, discuss under what circumstances it would be worth making it into a client–server system, as opposed to just creating a single program that does everything. In the case of a client–server system, indicate what work could be done by the server, and what by the client. In answering this question, make your best judgment, using whatever knowledge you already have about software applications.

(a) A word processor.

(b) A system for doctors to look up patient records when visiting a patient.

(c) A home alarm system that monitors various sensors such as motion detectors, smoke detectors and window-opening sensors.

E45 If you were designing a server for the following classes of applications, list the kinds of main activities that you might expect the server to do:

(a) A server for an airline reservation system.

(b) A server that contains the master list of toll-free telephone numbers that different telephone companies will need to access.

(c) A server that forms the center of a building alarm system; clients are individual controllers for devices around the building.

(d) Your favorite site for buying books on the Internet.

(e) A web-based course registration system.

Capabilities that must be provided when designing a server

A server has the following main activities to perform:

1. The server must **initialize** itself so that it is able to provide the required service. For example, a server that handles airline reservations might load data describing the available flights.

2. It must **start listening** for clients attempting to connect. Until it starts listening, any client that attempts to connect will not succeed.

3. It must handle the following types of *events* originating from clients, which can occur at any time:

   ❏ It **accepts connections** from clients. This process will normally involve some form of validation to ensure that the client is allowed to connect. While a client is connected, the server keeps a record of the connection.

   ❏ It **reacts to messages** from connected clients. This is the most important thing the server does. In an airline server a message could be a request to book a passenger, or a query to find out who is booked. In response to a message from a client, a server can do many types of things, including performing computations and obtaining information. Normally the server will send some information back to the requesting client; it might also send a message to another client or broadcast messages to many clients at once.

   ❏ It **handles the disconnection** of clients. A client can request disconnection by sending a message to the server or by simply disconnecting itself; it might 'disappear' if it crashes, or if its network connection goes down; finally, the server might *force* a client to disconnect if the client is not 'behaving' well.

4. The server may be required to **stop listening**. This means that it will no longer

accept new client connections, but it will continue to serve the currently connected clients. This may happen when the number of connected clients becomes too high; in such a situation the server rejects new clients so that it does not run out of resources such as memory. When it has enough resources again, it can start listening again. The server may also choose to stop listening prior to shutting down, allowing the connected clients time to terminate their work.

5. It must cleanly **terminate**, i.e. shut down, when necessary. Shutting down cleanly means doing such things as notifying each client before terminating its connection.

The above main activities of a server are illustrated in Figure 3.3, which is an example of a UML state diagram. We will examine such diagrams in detail in Chapter 8; for now, we believe that the diagram is sufficiently self-explanatory.

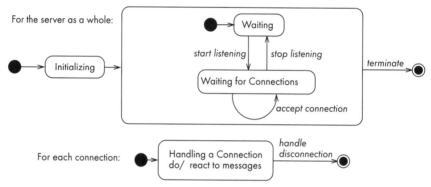

Figure 3.3   The main activities performed by a typical server

Later on in this chapter, we will see that in order to perform its work effectively, a server needs to use several concurrent threads.

Capabilities that must be provided when designing a client

A client has the following main activities to perform:

1. Like the server, a client must **initialize** itself so that it is able to communicate with the server. For example, it needs to know the network address of the server.

2. It performs some work, which includes:

❑ Making a decision to **initiate a connection** to a server. If connecting to the server fails, or the server rejects the connection, the client may try again or may give up.

❑ **Sending messages** to the server to request services.

3. It must handle the following types of events originating from the server, which can occur at any time:

❏ It **reacts to messages** coming from the server. Often, messages received from the server alternate with messages sent to the server – in other words, the messages from the server are replies to the client's requests. Sometimes, however, an unanticipated message might arrive from the server; for example, to announce that some new data is available or that the server is shutting down.

❏ It **handles the disconnection** of the server. This might occur because the server crashed or the network failed. It might also occur because either the client or server requested disconnection. The important issue is that the client knows it is no longer connected and makes decisions accordingly; one possible action is to attempt to reconnect.

4. It must cleanly **terminate**. This includes disconnecting from a server if it is still connected.

The above main activities of a client are illustrated in Figure 3.4, which shows one possible sequence of activities. Note that the 'regular' work of the client may need to proceed concurrently with the process of responding to events originating from the server. This is indicated in Figure 3.4 by the horizontal bars that show execution dividing into two distinct paths. We will consider concurrency in more depth in the next subsection.

Figure 3.4 is an example of a UML activity diagram; we will discuss these further in Chapter 8.

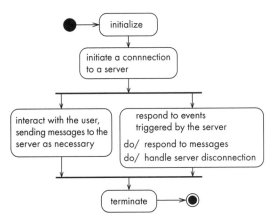

Figure 3.4   The main activities performed by a typical client

Concurrency in client–server systems

Client–server systems are inherently concurrent because the server runs at the same time as the clients, normally (but not necessarily) on different computers.

However, there is an added level of concurrency in both the client and server sides. As mentioned above, the client will normally be doing the following things concurrently:

■ Waiting for interactions with the end-user, and responding when interactions occur.

■ Waiting for messages coming from the server, and responding when messages arrive.

These generally have to be implemented using multiple threads of control that can be concurrently executed. Without this mechanism, when the client is waiting for one kind of input, it will not be able to respond to the other kind of input. An exception to this can occur in clients that do not need to interact with the user in any way.

Similarly, the server should normally have concurrent threads which do the following:

■ Waiting for interactions with the user who is in charge of the server, and responding as necessary. As with the client, some servers can dispense with user interaction, but most will need a thread to handle basic controlling commands.

■ Waiting for clients to try to connect and establishing connections as needed.

■ For *each* connected client, waiting for messages coming from that client, and responding when messages arrive.

Servers thus normally operate with at least two concurrent threads, and in general n+2 threads where n is the number of connected clients. Figure 3.5 illustrates the various threads executing in a typical client–server system. In this diagram only one client (client A) is shown communicating with the server; however, a thread for a second dormant client (client B) is also shown.

Thin- versus fat-client systems

The work of a client–server system can be distributed in several different ways. In a *thin-client* system, the client is made as small as possible and most of the work is done in the server. In the opposite approach, called a *fat-client* system, as much work as possible is delegated to the clients. The two approaches are illustrated in Figure 3.6.

An important advantage of a thin-client system is that it is easy to download the client program over the network and to launch it. In Java, *applets* are usually thin clients because it is desirable for them to download rapidly. An advantage of fat-client systems is that since more computations are distributed to the clients, better use is made of available computational resources; the server can therefore be smaller or can be made to handle more clients.

One of the main considerations in choosing between a fat-client and a thin-client system is how intensively the system will use the network to communicate

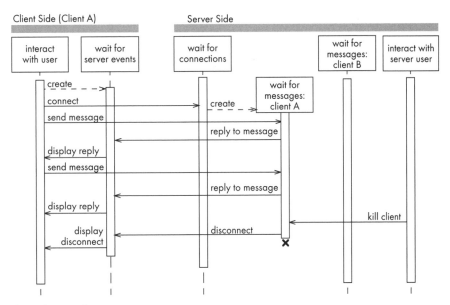

Figure 3.5   Threads in a client–server system

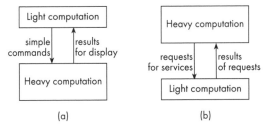

Figure 3.6   A thin-client system (a) and a fat-client system (b). The clients are at the top and the servers are at the bottom

– making the wrong choice can sometimes result in an overloaded network. Depending on the nature of the system, either a fat-client or a thin-client system may take the fewest network resources. In some cases, a thin-client system will need to communicate the least because it generally sends only simple user requests to the server. On the other hand, a thin client might need to communicate with the server much more frequently than a fat client and to download voluminous results of the server's calculations.

Exercise

E46   In each of the following systems, list: (i) the work normally performed on the server side; (ii) the work normally performed on the client side; (iii) the types of information transmitted in both directions over the network; (iv) whether the system is thin-client, fat-client or intermediate; (v) what could be done to increase or decrease the proportion of work done on the client side; (vi) what effects such changes would have on the network.

(a) to (e) The systems from Exercise E45.

(f) The world wide web in general (with browsers and web servers).

(g) The email system that you use.

Messages in a client–server system: communications protocols

The types of messages the client is allowed to send to the server form a *language*. The server has to be programmed to understand that language. Similarly, another language consists of the types of messages the server is allowed to send to the client.

When a client and a server are communicating, they are in effect having a conversation using these two languages. As with a human conversation, there have to be rules to ensure, for example, that the communicating parties take turns to speak. The rules also describe the sequences of messages that the client and server must exchange, in order to reach agreement on something or to accomplish some other task.

The two languages and the rules of the conversation, taken together, are called the *protocol*. The design of protocols can be very complex; in simple systems, such as those discussed in this book, the protocol is merely a list of service requests and their responses.

Example 3.2   *Sketch a protocol for a simple program for manipulating files on a remote computer.*

The following illustrates the kinds of messages sent between clients and the server.

Messages to server	*Possible replies to client*
getFile *name*	fileContent, accessDenied, noSuchFileOrDir, failed
saveFile *name content*	successful, accessDenied, failed
rename *oldname newname*	successful, accessDenied, noSuchFileOrDir, failed
delete *name*	successful, accessDenied, noSuchFileOrDir, failed
listDir	fileList, accessDenied, failed
changeDir *name*	successful, accessDenied, noSuchFileOrDir, failed
createDir *name*	successful, accessDenied, failed

The above protocol does not deal with such things as security and logging in; nor does it suggest how the information would be presented to the user in a friendly way.

Exercise

E47 Propose a simple protocol for the systems described in question E45.

Tasks of the software engineer when developing a client–server system

When designing a client–server system, the software engineer should make use of a framework that provides much of the underlying mechanism. We will describe such a framework later; however, the designer still has four key things to design:

1. The primary work to be performed by both client and server; i.e. the computations to be performed, data to be stored, etc.

2. How the work will be distributed – thin client, fat client, or intermediate.

3. The details of the set of messages that will be sent from the client to the server and vice versa in order to accomplish the main activities, i.e. the communications protocol.

4. What has to happen in the client and server when they start up, handle connections, send and receive messages, and terminate.

3.5   Technology needed to build client–server systems

In order to build a client–server system you need a computer network as well as software facilities for sending and receiving messages. There are several standards for data communication, and most modern programming languages include suitable data communication packages. This section discusses basic Internet and Java technology you can use to construct client–server systems.

Some important network concepts

In order to be able to understand how a client and a server communicate with each other, you must understand a few basic concepts about computer networks. Many books have been written about networks, but the few details discussed here will be enough to enable you to understand client–server design.

Since most computers today are connected to the Internet, we will assume that clients and servers will communicate with each other using the Internet's main communications mechanism, *TCP/IP*.

'IP' stands for 'Internet Protocol'. The main function of IP is to route messages from one computer to another. Long messages are normally split up into small pieces which are sent separately and then reassembled at the destination computer. Since the Internet is a large heterogeneous network of many computers and other devices, this routing process is quite complex. Luckily, Internet users rarely need to worry about the complexity.

How to find out the IP address and host name of a computer

Using a web browser, you can normally find out the IP address of your computer (and a lot of other information about your network connection) at privacy.net/analyze/.

In Windows XP you can find the IP address by first opening the 'Network Connections' control panel. Then click on the icon for a connection and look in the 'Details' tab. You can also issue the command 'ipconfig /all' to obtain very detailed information including your host name.

On Mac OS X, you can find out the IP address by looking at the 'TCP/IP' tab of the 'Network Preferences' panel.

On most varieties of Unix, including Mac OS X, or Linux, you can find out your host name by issuing the commands `hostname` or `uname -n`. You can normally look up the IP address corresponding to a host name using `ypcat hosts | grep <hostname>`. In addition, you can look up the host name corresponding to an IP address using the same command sequence.

On many computers (including both Windows and Mac) you can issue the command `netstat -a -p TCP` to determine which ports are in use.

'TCP' stands for 'Transmission Control Protocol'. TCP handles connections between two computers. A connection lasts for a period of time, during which the computers can exchange many IP messages. In addition to simply exchanging data, the computers use TCP to establish the connections, and to assure each other that the messages they have sent each other have been satisfactorily received. There is another mechanism called UDP that can be used instead of TCP; however, we will not discuss UDP here.

Each computer using IP is called a *host* and has a unique address. In IP Version 4, you may see this address written as four numbers (each from 0 to 255), separated by dots, such as 128.37.100.100; in IP version 6, to which many networks are moving, the address appears as eight hexadecimal numbers separated by colons. More commonly, however, you will see an IP address as a more human-understandable dot-separated series of words such as 'www.mcgraw-hill.com'. The numeric and word forms can be used interchangeably. The numeric form is normally called the *IP address*, while the word form is normally called the *host name*. If you strip off the first component of the host name (everything up to and including the first dot) then the remaining part typically represents a sub-network on which the host is running; this is often called a *domain*. In the above example, 'mcgraw-hill.com' is a domain. The '.com' is a *top-level domain*.

Several servers can run on the same host. Each server is identified by a *port* number, which is an integer from 0 to 65535. In order to initiate communication with a server, a client must know both the host name and the port number. By convention, port numbers from 0 to 1023 are reserved for use by specific types of servers; for example, web servers normally use port 80. Knowing this convention, a web browser that is only given a host name (in a URL) can connect to a web server by assuming that the server is at port 80. We therefore should not use port 80 for any other kind of server since confusion will result. In this book, we will by default run servers on port 5555 if it is not already occupied by some other server. In general, when you create a new server, you must pick a port number and publish both the host name and port number so that clients know where to connect. Taken together, the host name and port number are often just called the *address* of the server. By convention, if a client wants to talk to a server on the same computer, it can use the special host name *localhost* (IP address 127.0.0.1).

Establishing a connection in Java

Java includes a package specially designed to permit the creation of a TCP/IP connection between two applications: it is called `java.net`. The class `Socket` is the central element of this package; instances of this class encapsulate information concerning each connection. Both the client and the server must have an instance of `Socket` in order to exchange information.

Before a connection can be established, the server must start listening to one of the ports. To do this, it uses the resources of the class `ServerSocket`. This is typically done as follows:

```
ServerSocket serverSocket = new ServerSocket(port);
```

where `port` is the integer representing the port number on which the server should be listening.

In order for a client to connect to a server, it uses a statement like the following, passing the host name (or numeric IP address) and port number of the server:

```
Socket clientSocket = new Socket(host, port);
```

For the connection to be accepted, the server must have a thread constantly listening for connections using a statement like the following, embedded in a loop:

```
Socket clientSocket = serverSocket.accept();
```

The above statement will wait indefinitely in the `accept` method until a client tries to connect, then it will try to create an instance of `Socket` to handle the new connection. If this is successful, both client and server now have instances of `Socket` and can communicate freely with each other.

All of the above assumes the network is working properly, and appropriate values are specified for `host` and `port`. If communication fails for any reason, these statements will throw an `IOException`. Appropriate code must be written to handle such exceptions, e.g. notifying the user of the failure or trying again.

Once a connection is established, the exchange of communication may commence. From now on, both client and server can send messages to each other at any time. The connection is said to be *symmetric*, meaning that the client communicates with the server in the same way as the server communicates with the client.

Normally there will be two distinct *streams* of information: from server to client and from client to server. Each program uses an instance of InputStream to receive messages from the other program, and an instance of OutputStream to send messages to the other program. These classes are found in the package java.io, and their instances can be created as follows:

```
output = clientSocket.getOutputStream();
input = clientSocket.getInputStream();
```

When a message is sent from one program using its OutputStream, it may be read by the other connected program using its InputStream. However, InputStream and OutputStream deal with messages composed merely of bytes, the most primitive form of data. Programmers often want to exchange more sophisticated types of data without having to worry about how to translate them into a byte stream. To do this, Java provides a series of *filters* which convert the raw bytes into other forms. For example, DataOutputStream and DataInputStream allow direct transmission of the Java primitive types such as int and double. Another pair of filters, ObjectOutputStream and ObjectInputStream, allows the exchange of Java objects. For maximum flexibility, we will use this latter pair of classes in our client–server framework.

To send an object, Java uses a process called *serialization*. This is a technique by which every object is converted by an ObjectOutputStream into a binary form for transmission, and then reconstructed when it is received by an ObjectInputStream. Most objects can be serialized; the only requirements are that they be instances of classes that implement the interface java.io.Serializable, and that the data in their instance variables also be serializable. Serialization is also the mechanism used to save objects into a binary file.

In order to use an object stream, you must wrap it around a binary stream in the following manner:

```
output = new ObjectOutputStream(clientSocket.getOutputStream());
```

You can then send an object thus:

```
output.writeObject(msg);
```

In order to receive objects, you create an object input stream thus:

```
input = new ObjectInputStream(clientSocket.getInputStream());
```

and then arrange for the following statement to be executed in a loop:

```
msg = input.readObject();
```

The readObject method will wait until an object is received over the socket, or until an I/O error occurs. An I/O error will occur if the program at the other end of the connection is terminated.

3.6 The Object Client–Server Framework (OCSF)

In the next few sections we present a framework that can be used to develop any client–server system. We call this framework OCSF (Object Client–Server Framework) since it can be used to build a client–server system that exchanges Java objects. We will use the OCSF for the systems we develop in this book. In Chapter 6 we will extend the framework to make it more flexible.

You should attempt to understand completely how the OCSF functions. Not only will doing so ensure you understand the principles of frameworks and client–server systems in general, but it will also teach you about some of the subtleties of software design. Later in the book, some of the design issues raised here will be revisited.

To help you understand the framework, we provide a simple application in Section 3.9 that uses it. We also provide some project exercises where you change the application – modifying an existing application is one of the best ways to learn how it works.

The core of OCSF consists of three classes: one to implement the client and two to implement the server. The core classes are illustrated in Figure 3.7, along with their most important methods. The line with the asterisk connecting `AbstractServer` to `ConnectionToClient` indicates that there are many instances of `ConnectionToClient` associated with the server. The labels such as «control», «hook» and «slot» divide the methods into categories, which we will describe shortly.

In Chapter 6, we will discuss some additional classes that extend OCSF; there is no need to know anything about those to start working with OCSF.

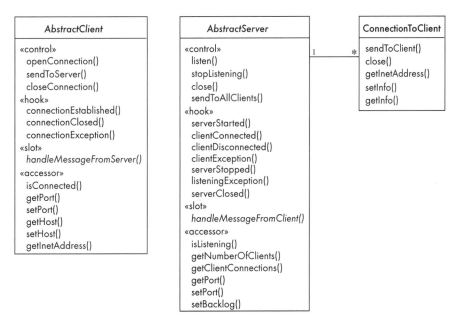

Figure 3.7   The essentials of the core OCSF classes

Programmers using OCSF never modify the framework's classes. Instead, a programmer should do the following to create an application:

■ Create *subclasses* of the abstract classes in the framework.

■ In these subclasses, write implementations of certain *slot* methods that are declared to be abstract in the framework classes.

■ Also in the subclasses, override certain methods that are explicitly designed to be overridden. These are the *hooks* of the framework.

■ In various parts of the application, call public methods that are provided by the framework. These public methods, which are the *services* of the framework, allow the application designer to control the client or server, and to find out information about them.

We will first discuss in detail the client side of the framework, and then the server side. In this chapter, your main objective should be to understand how to use the framework. To do that, you will have to understand how it works to some extent; however, you will probably obtain a more detailed understanding of that in later chapters.

Complete source code of the OCSF is found at www.lloseng.com.

3.7 Basic description of OCSF – client side

The client side of the OCSF consists of a single class `AbstractClient`. This is an abstract class that provides all of the facilities needed to connect and exchange objects with servers – with one exception: `AbstractClient` must be subclassed in order to implement the method `handleMessageFromServer` that takes appropriate action when a message is received from a server.

`AbstractClient` implements the `Runnable` interface. This is because we want the message waiting activity of its instance to run as a separate thread as described earlier. As an implementer of `Runnable`, `AbstractClient` has a `run` method which contains a loop that executes for the lifetime of the thread, receiving messages from the server and responding to them. We will discuss the internals of the `run` method a bit later.

The public interface of `AbstractClient`

The *public interface* to `AbstractClient` consists of the service methods that software developers who are using the class can access. In OCSF, as in other well-designed object-oriented systems, the public interface only provides a set of methods that can be called – it does not permit direct access to any variables.

The public interface of `AbstractClient` consists of three kinds of methods: a *constructor*, some methods that are used to *control* the client, and some methods used to *access* basic information about the client.

Public constructor. There is only one simple constructor in this class. It merely initializes variables representing the host and the port of the server to which the client will connect.

Public controlling methods. These methods provide services and do the bulk of the work of controlling the client. They are declared `final` so that they cannot be overridden by subclasses. The `final` declaration ensures that subclasses cannot create versions that contain bugs; however, it also means that subclasses cannot correct any design flaws in these methods. That puts a particularly strong responsibility for quality control into the hands of the framework's designers. The three key controlling methods are:

- `openConnection:` this connects, if it can, to a server at the host and port specified in the constructor (or subsequently using `setHost` and `setPort` described below). As soon as the connection to the server is established, this method starts the thread which will then run until the connection to the server is terminated.

- `sendToServer:` this sends a message to the server, if it can. The message can be any object.

- `closeConnection:` this stops the communication with the server and signals the thread to stop looping and hence terminate

All three of the above methods will throw an `IOException` if they fail – callers have to handle this in some way.

Utility accessing methods. These additional service methods are used to inquire about the state of the client or make minor changes to that state. They include:

- `isConnected:` allows callers to inquire whether the client is currently connected to a server.

- `getHostPort` and `getPort:` allow callers to inquire which host and port the client is connected to, or is prepared to connect to.

- `SetHost` and `SetPort:` allow callers to change the host and port of a disconnected client in preparation for the next call to `openConnection`.

- `getInetAddress:` provides some detailed information about the connection.

The callback methods of `AbstractClient`

In addition to the public interface, `AbstractClient` also contains several hook methods that are designed to be overridden by subclasses of the client, as well as one abstract slot method. The hooks and slots are called when particular events occur as the client operates. Methods like these are conventionally referred to as *callbacks*, since they are not called by the application code, but rather they represent *calls back* to the application code from methods in the framework.

Methods that may be overridden by subclasses (hooks). These may be overridden by subclasses and are called when various potentially 'interesting' events happen. If developers of subclasses of AbstractClient are interested in taking some action when these events occur, the developers can implement the methods. The default implementations do nothing.

- connectionEstablished: is called after a connection with a server is established.

- connectionClosed: is called whenever a connection with the server is terminated by the client.

- connectionException: is called when something goes wrong with the connection, such as when the connection is terminated by the server.

Method that *must* be defined in subclasses (slot). The only abstract slot method in AbstractClient is named handleMessageFromServer. This must be defined in subclasses and is called whenever a message is received from the server.

How an application developer should use AbstractClient

A developer who wants to design a client which uses the AbstractClient class need only do the following:

- Create a subclass of AbstractClient.

- In this subclass, implement the handleMessageFromServer slot method to do something useful with any messages coming from the server.

- Arrange for some code somewhere to create an instance of the new subclass of AbstractClient and to call openConnection.

  In almost all clients, the developer will also want to do the following:

- Arrange for some code somewhere to send messages to the server using the sendToServer service method. It is possible to have a client that only receives messages from a server, and hence does not call sendToServer, but that would be rather unusual.

- Implement the connectionClosed callback to do something intelligent, such as notifying the user, when the connection to the server is terminated normally.

- Implement the connnectionException callback to deal with abnormal disconnection.

  Not every application will need to use the other service methods, or override the other callback method (connectionEstablished).

A few details of the private internals of AbstractClient

Software developers do not, strictly speaking, need to know much more than the above to use AbstractClient. However, knowing a few details of how a class works can help a developer to diagnose problems and feel more comfortable using the class.

AbstractClient has the following instance variables:

- A Socket, clientSocket, which keeps all the information about the connection to the server.

- Two streams, an ObjectOutputStream (output) and an ObjectInputStream (input), that are used to transmit and receive objects using clientSocket.

- A Thread, clientReader, that runs using AbstractClient's run method.

- A boolean variable, readyToStop, used to signal when the thread should stop executing.

- Two variables storing the host and port of the server.

The thread starts running when openConnection calls start which in turn calls run. The loop inside run repeatedly waits for a message to come from the server by calling the readObject method of the ObjectInputStream. When a message is received, the run method then responds by calling the application's implementation of handleMessageFromServer.

Complete source code for AbstractClient is found on the book's web site. You may find it useful to study the code, following the above explanation. We suggest you do the exercises at the end of the chapter to test your understanding.

3.8   Basic description of OCSF – server side

The server side of OCSF is slightly more complex than the client side since it has two classes, not one. The two classes are needed because, as discussed in Section 3.4, the server has to implement both the thread that listens for new connections (AbstractServer) and the threads that handle the connections to clients (ConnectionToClient).

The public interface of AbstractServer

As with AbstractClient, there is a limited set of public methods (the API) that provide all the services of this side of the framework.

The public constructor. AbstractServer has only one constructor, which takes a port number on which the server will listen. The port number can be changed later, if needed.

The public controlling methods. Similarly to the client side, the AbstractServer has a set of methods that can be used by subclasses to perform useful functions.

- listen: this creates the serverSocket that will listen on the port that was specified in the constructor or by using setPort. It also starts this instance as a thread that will, in the run method, repeatedly wait for new clients to connect.

■ stopListening: this method signals to the run method controlling the thread to stop looping, and therefore terminate. No new clients will be accepted until the listen method is called again. Any connected clients can still communicate with the server because their connections are controlled by separate threads.

■ close: this does the same thing as stopListening, but goes further: it disconnects all connected clients and closes the server socket.

■ sendToAllClients: this attempts to send a message to all clients.

The methods listen and close can throw an IOException.

Utility accessing methods. These inquire about the state of the server or make modifications to that state.

■ isListening: determines if the server is listening for new clients.

■ getNumberOfClients: returns a count of the number of currently connected clients.

■ getClientConnections: returns an array of instances of ConnectionToClient (the array is declared as an array of Thread, but ConnectionToClient is a subclass of Thread, so that you can *cast* the elements of the array to ConnectionToClient). You can use this method to write services that do something with all clients, such as searching for clients that have a particular property. This is one of the most important service methods available to the developer of concrete subclasses.

■ getPort: finds out what port the server is listening on.

■ setPort: instructs the server to listen on the specified port *next time* listen is called; it does not change the port on which the server is currently listening.

■ setBacklog: sets the size of the queue length. If a client attempts to connect when this queue is full, the connection is refused. The queue can get full if large numbers of clients try to connect, and the server cannot accept them fast enough.

The callback methods of AbstractServer

These five methods are all called when important events occur.

Methods that may be overridden by subclasses. These may be overridden by subclasses and are called when events occur that may be interesting to concrete subclasses:

■ serverStarted: called whenever the server starts accepting connections.

■ clientConnected: called whenever a new client connects; it provides the instance of ConnectionToClient (described below) as an argument.

- **clientDisconnected:** called whenever the server disconnects a client using a call to the close method of ConnectionToClient. It provides the instance of ConnectionToClient as an argument.

- **clientException:** called whenever a client disconnects itself, or is disconnected as a result of a network failure.

- **serverStopped:** called whenever the server stops accepting connections as a result of a call to stopListening.

- **listeningException:** called whenever the server stops accepting connections due to some failure.

- **serverClosed:** called when the server closes down.

In the same way that the client had only one abstract method, the server has only one abstract method called handleMessageFromClient. This single slot method is the most important piece of code that a developer of a concrete subclass will write. When called by the framework, it provides as arguments the message received as well as the instance of ConnectionToClient corresponding to the client that sent the message.

The public interface of ConnectionToClient

For the period of time during which each client is connected, an instance of ConnectionToClient exists for that client. The currently existing instances of this class can be accessed using getClientConnections, as described above, as well as several of AbstractServer's callback methods. You use such objects to find out information about clients and to communicate with clients.

ConnectionToClient is a concrete class. Users of the framework can simply use its facilities – they do not have to subclass it. It provides five service methods that can be used by developers of concrete subclasses of AbstractServer. The first two of these can throw an IOException.

- **sendToClient:** the central method that is used to communicate with the client.

- **close:** causes the client to be disconnected.

- **getInetAddress:** obtains the Internet address of the client connection.

- **setInfo:** allows arbitrary information to be saved about this client. For example, the concrete server could give certain clients special privileges, which would be recorded using this method. More simply, this method could be used to record the client's user id.

- **getInfo:** allows the retrieval of any information that had been saved using setInfo.

How an application developer should use `AbstractServer` and `ConnectionToClient`

A developer who wants to create a server using OCSF needs to perform the following activities, which are almost identical to what a developer of a client needs to do:

■ Create a subclass of `AbstractServer`.

■ In this subclass, implement the slot method `handleMessageFromClient` to do something useful with any messages coming from the client.

■ Arrange for some code somewhere to create an instance of the new subclass of `AbstractServer` and to call the `listen` method.

In almost all servers, the developer will also want to do the following:

■ Arrange for code somewhere to send messages to clients, using the `getClientConnections` and `sendToClient` service methods. For a simple server, it might be possible to use `sendToAllClients` instead.

■ Implement one or more of the other callback methods to respond in intelligent ways to various events.

A few details of the private internals of `AbstractServer` and `ConnectionToClient`

You can design a server knowing only the above information; however, the following are a few of the internal details of the server side of OCSF. These details will help you form a better understanding of how it works.

■ The `setInfo` and `getInfo` methods make use of a Java class called `HashMap`. A `HashMap` can store an arbitrary object using some other arbitrary object as a key. The key can then be later used to retrieve the stored object.

■ Many of the methods in the server side of OCSF are *synchronized*. Synchronizing a method ensures that no other thread can access the object while it is running. Since there are many `ConnectionToClient` threads that could all make concurrent changes to the data maintained by the server, synchronization guarantees that critical operations are performed one at a time, ensuring the integrity of the data.

■ The collection of instances of `ConnectionToClient` maintained by `AbstractServer` is stored using a special Java class called `ThreadGroup`. This class takes care of automatically removing elements when a thread terminates.

■ The server must regularly take a temporary pause from listening to see if the `stopListening` method has been called; if not, then it resumes listening immediately. A design alternative would be to have the `stopListening` method force the listening thread to terminate; however, that would leave the `ServerSocket` in an unstable state. The method `setTimeout` can be used to set the interval between server pauses; it defines the maximum time that the server will take to stop the listening thread. The default value of 500 ms is suitable for most applications.

3.9   An instant messaging application using the OCSF

To illustrate the use of OCSF, we present here a simple client–server instant messaging system. We call this SimpleChat, and its source code can be found on the book's web site. The version presented here is Phase 1 of SimpleChat. Various project exercises found at the end of this and subsequent chapters ask you to add features to SimpleChat.

The server side of SimpleChat is particularly simple. All the server does is echo messages coming from clients to all the connected clients; thus the class is called EchoServer. EchoServer itself has no user interface; once started its process must be killed or it will run indefinitely.

As Figure 3.8 shows, EchoServer is simply a subclass of AbstractServer. The main method creates a new instance and starts listening for server connections by calling listen. To provide feedback, all the callback methods simply print out messages to the user's console. The main methods are underlined since they are static.

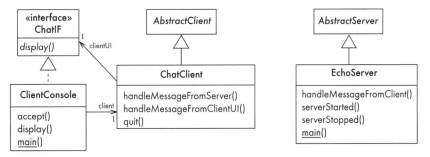

Figure 3.8   Extending the OCSF framework to build the SimpleChat application

The handleMessageFromClient method does one more thing: it calls sendToAllClients in order to echo any messages. The following is the code for handleMessageFromClient.

```
public void handleMessageFromClient (
  Object msg, ConnectionToClient client)
{
  System.out.println
    ("Message received: " + msg + " from " + client);
  this.sendToAllClients(msg);
}
```

On the client side, ChatClient is a subclass of AbstractClient that overrides one method, handleMessageFromServer. This method does nothing but arrange for messages to be displayed to the end-user, as discussed below. ChatClient also has two other methods that are called by the user interface.

The user interface of the client is carefully separated from the functional part of the client. A Java interface, ChatIF, is provided that specifies that any user interface must implement a single method, display. One class called ClientConsole implements this interface; some other class could be substituted in place of ClientConsole. For example, on the book's web site you will find a class called ClientGUI. This substitute class simply has to implement the display operation to work properly with ChatClient.

When the client starts, the main method in ClientConsole runs. This creates instances of ClientConsole and ChatClient (which runs as a second thread), and then calls a method called accept to await user input. The accept method runs in a loop until the program is terminated; it sends all input to the instance of ChatClient by calling its handleMessageFromClientUI. This in turn calls sendToServer. The code for handleMessageFromClientUI is written as follows:

```
public void handleMessageFromClientUI(String message)
{
  try
  {
    sendToServer(message);
  }
  catch(IOException e)
  {
    clientUI.display
      ("Could not send message to server. Terminating client.");
    quit();
  }
}
```

Communication coming from the server works as follows. The framework triggers a call to handleMessageFromServer. This in turn calls the display operation of ChatIF, which results in a call to the display method in the user interface class ClientConsole. The code for handleMessageFromServer is as follows.

```
public void handleMessageFromServer(Object msg)
{
  clientUI.display(msg.toString());
}
```

In the exercises at the end of the chapter, you will make some changes to Phase 1 of SimpleChat. In subsequent chapters, you will have the chance to make many other improvements and additions to its design. If you follow all the exercises, you will end up being able to transmit drawings in real time with the program.

3.10 Difficulties and risks when considering reusable technology and client–server systems

Software development organizations should design software that is reusable, and should reuse software whenever possible. In both cases, the goal is to reduce the large cost associated with developing the same thing over and over again. One important approach is to actively look for opportunities in any development project to design a framework instead of designing an entire application.

Unfortunately, there are some important risks involved in both reuse and reusability. Software engineers should always consider these issues as part of the risk management process we discussed in Chapter 1.

Risks when reusing technology

- **Poor quality reusable components**. You have to trust that the technology works properly, and that any problems will be fixed. Unfortunately, the designer of the reusable software might not have followed good software engineering practices, and you may discover major problems. The designer may not have the time to fix the technology, or the technology may be so poor that fixing it adds new problems.
  Resolution. Ensure the developers of the reusable technology follow good software engineering practices and are willing to provide active support.

- **Compatibility or availability not maintained**. Later versions of the technology might be changed in ways that are incompatible with how you have used it. Alternatively, the producer of the technology might go out of business or withdraw it from the market. You may therefore be forced to abandon the technology or modify your applications to stay compatible.
  Resolution. Avoid the use of obscure features of technology. Only reuse technology that others are also reusing. Mandate that reuse should be the rule, but allow exceptions in cases where developers can provide a clear justification.

Risks when developing reusable technology

- **Risk from an uncertain investment**. Developing reusable technology takes time away from developing applications and is therefore a calculated risk.
  Resolution. To ensure the investment pays off, carefully plan the development of the reusable technology, in the same manner as if it were a product for a client. Monitor the success or failure of the reusable software so that you can improve your investment decisions in future projects.

- **The so-called 'not invented here syndrome'.** A framework developed by one set of developers might not be used because others fear it might not be supported.
  Resolution. Build confidence in the reusable technology by guaranteeing support,

ensuring it is of high quality and responding to the needs of the users. (The users in this case are the software engineers who adopt the technology.)

■ **Competition**. Reusable technology might not end up being used if somebody else develops competing technology that gains wide acceptance. Being beaten by the competition is a risk in any business; however, with reusable software the competitive forces are often not financial in nature. Several groups may develop similar packages and one may be accepted for reuse merely because its developers are better known or 'market' it better.
Resolution. Ensure the reusable technology is as useful and as high quality as possible. Advertise the presence and advantages of your reusable software.

■ **Divergence**. Several development teams using the same framework may want to change it in different ways.
Resolution. Ensure that the framework is well tested and reviewed; if it is designed to be general enough, then it will be less likely to suffer from divergent changes.

Risks inherent in client–server or other distributed systems

■ **Security**. Distributed systems are particularly prone to security violations, due to the fact that information is transmitted over a network. Communications can be intercepted, or a denial-of-service attack can be implemented.
Resolution. Recognize that security is a big problem with no perfect solutions. Incorporate encryption, firewalls and similar protective measures into your designs.

■ **Need for adaptive maintenance**. If clients and servers are developed by different organizations, then the developers of clients are frequently forced to upgrade their clients whenever the server is changed.
Resolution. Ensure that all software is forward-compatible and backward-compatible with other versions of clients and servers. Achieving this requires designing the client–server protocols to be very general and flexible.

3.11 Summary

In this chapter we have studied reusable technology, which should be the basis for most software development projects. When developing software, you can reuse many kinds of things, ranging from the expertise of people who have worked on past projects up to complete applications. You should also strive to make anything you develop as reusable as possible.

An important type of reuse is reuse of frameworks. Frameworks are software systems that are not immediately usable, but can be quickly extended to build an application or part of an application, by providing essential details that are missing.

We studied in depth a client–server framework written in Java. The Object Client–Server Framework (OCSF) provides all the essential features of any

Network ethics

People who design and work with distributed systems must develop a heightened awareness of certain ethical issues.

With distributed systems, it is particularly easy to violate people's privacy. This can be done by simply gathering data about people as they use network-based programs, or else by actively intercepting communications. Both these activities should normally be considered unethical unless people have consented to the release of their private information, are able to withdraw that consent easily at any time, are able to examine and correct the information collected about them, and are aware of the method by which the information is collected.

Knowledge of how to develop distributed systems also brings with it knowledge of how to develop harmful programs such as viruses or Trojan horses, as well as how to 'hack' into systems. Some people take a perverse pride in using such knowledge; however, doing so is illegal and extremely unethical, no matter whether the knowledge is used for 'fun' or maliciously.

client–server system. On the server side it includes facilities for starting and stopping the server, maintaining a list of clients, sending messages to clients and responding to messages received from clients. On the client side, it provides facilities for connecting and disconnecting from a server, sending messages to the server, and responding to messages coming from the server.

We showed how it is possible to take this framework and implement only a few methods in order to create an instant messaging system we call SimpleChat.

3.12 For more information

Reuse

■ ReNewsWWW: http://frakes.cs.vt.edu/renews.html The Electronic Software Reuse and Re-engineering Newsletter on the World Wide Web

■ I. Jacobson, M. Griss, P. Jonsson, *Software Reuse: Architecture Process and Organization for Business Success*, Addison-Wesley, 1997

■ C. McClure, *Software Reuse Techniques: Adding Reuse to the System Development Process*, Prentice-Hall, 1997

Frameworks and product lines

■ M. E. Fayad, D. C. Schmidt and R. Johnson, *Implementing Application Frameworks: Object-Oriented Frameworks at Work*, Wiley, 1999

■ G. Rogers, *Framework-Based Software Development in C++,* Prentice Hall, 1997

■ D. F. D'Souza, A. C. Wills, *Objects, Components, and Frameworks with UML: The Catalysis(SM) Approach*, Addison-Wesley, 1999

■ The product line practice initiative: http://www.sei.cmu.edu/plp/

The Internet, networking etc.

■ The Living Internet: http://livinginternet.com. This web site gives an excellent overview about the Internet, including a discussion of IP addresses etc.

■ M. Hughes, M. Shoffner and D. Hamner, *Java Network Programming: A Complete Guide to Networking, Streams, and Distributed Computing*, 2nd edition, Manning Publications, 1999. http://nitric.com/jnp/

The client–server architecture

■ The Webopedia entry for this topic: http://webopedia.internet.com/TERM/c/client_server_architecture.html

■ The client–server newsgroup news:comp.client-server. http://groups.google.com/groups?&group=comp.client-server

Project exercises

The following series of exercises should ideally be followed in sequence. After completion of these exercises you will have built Phase 2 of SimpleChat. A complete implementation of Phase 2 is available on the book's web site.

E48 On the book's web site, you will find a set of 'test cases' for Phase 1 of the SimpleChat program. We will discuss test cases in much more detail in Chapter 10. For now, you can simply see them as a set of instructions that allow you to verify the functionality of the system. You can also use them to learn about the system. Pick ten Phase 1 test cases and execute them.

E49 This exercise will help you to become familiar with the internals of OCSF and Phase 1 of an instant messaging application we call SimpleChat. Modify the application to provide the following features (Remember: do not modify the OCSF framework):

Client side:

(a) *Currently, if the server shuts down while a client is connected, the client does not respond, and continues to wait for messages.* Modify the client so that it responds to the shutdown of the server by printing a message saying the server has shut down, and quitting. Design hint: look at the methods called connectionClosed and connectionException.

(b) *The client currently always uses a default port.* Modify the client so that it obtains the port number from the command line. Design hint: look at the way it obtains the host name from the command line.

Test that this works by connecting a client to a server using a different port from the default. If the port is omitted from the command line, then the default value should still be used.

Server side:

(c) *Currently the server ignores situations where clients connect or disconnect.* Modify the server so that it prints out a nice message whenever a client connects or disconnects. Hint: you will simply have to write code in EchoServer that overrides certain methods found in AbstractServer – study the AbstractServer description above to determine which methods you have to override.

E50 Make further modifications to the SimpleChat application, as follows:

Client side:

(a) *Currently, the client simply sends to the server everything the end-user types. When the server receives these messages, it simply echoes them to all clients.* Add a mechanism so that the user of the client can type commands that perform special functions. Each command should start with the '#' symbol – in fact, anything that starts with that symbol should be considered a command.

You should implement commands specified as follows:

(i) #quit causes the client to terminate gracefully. Make sure the connection to the server is terminated before exiting the program.

(ii) #logoff causes the client to disconnect from the server, but not quit.

(iii) #sethost <host> calls the setHost method in the client. Only allowed if the client is logged off; displays an error message otherwise.

(iv) #setport <port> calls the setPort method in the client, with the same constraints as #sethost.

(v) #login causes the client to connect to the server. Only allowed if the client is not already connected; displays an error message otherwise.

(vi) #gethost displays the current host name.

(vii) #getport displays the current port number.

Server side:

(b) *Currently, the server does not allow any user input.* Study the way user input is obtained from the client, using the ClientConsole class, which implements the ChatIF interface. Create an analogous mechanism on the server side. Design hint: you will have to add a new class you can call ServerConsole that also implements the ChatIF interface. Following your modifications, the following should be true:

(i) Anything typed on the server's console by an end-user of the server should be echoed to the server's console and to all the clients.

(ii) Any message originating from the end-user of the server should be prefixed by the string 'SERVER MSG>'.

(c) In a similar manner to the way you implemented commands on the client side, add a mechanism so that the user of the server can type commands that perform special functions. You should implement commands specified as follows:

(i) #quit causes the server to quit gracefully.

(ii) #stop causes the server to stop listening for new clients.

(iii) #close causes the server not only to stop listening for new clients, but also to disconnect all existing clients.

(iv) #setport <port> calls the setPort method in the server. Only allowed if the server is closed.

(v) #start causes the server to start listening for new clients. Only valid if the server is stopped.

(vi) #getport displays the current port number.

E51 Make further modifications to the SimpleChat application, as follows.

In Phase 1, clients are always anonymous. When a message is sent from a client, it is echoed to all the other clients, but nobody knows who sent it. In this exercise, you will implement a basic mechanism by which clients have a 'login id' that is known both to the client and the server.

Client side:

(a) Add a new 'login id' command line argument to the client. This should be the first argument, before the host name and port, because the host name and port are optional in the sense that if they are omitted, defaults are used. The login id should be mandatory; the client should immediately quit if it is not provided. Design hint: the login id should be stored in an instance variable in ChatClient. You might ask the question: why not put the instance variable in ClientConsole? The reason is to separate the user interface (how information is displayed and input) from the other aspects of the system.

(b) Whenever a client connects to a server, it should automatically send the message '#login <loginid>' (i.e. the string #login with the login id appended to it) to the server. Note that this use of the '#' is different from what we have seen so far: the #login is sent to the server; it is not handled by the client as was the case with #quit, #logoff etc.

Server side:

(c) Arrange for the server to receive the #login <loginid> command from the client. It should behave according to the following rules:

   (i) The #login command should be recognized by the server. Design hint: modify handleMessageFromClient so that it does more than just echo messages.

   (ii) The login id should be saved, so that the server can always identify the client. Design hint: use the setInfo method to set the login id and the getInfo method to retrieve it again later.

   (iii) Each message echoed by the server should be prefixed by the login id of the client that sent the message.

   (iv) The #login command should only be allowed as the first command received after a client connects. If #login is received at any other time, the server should send an error message back to the client.

   (v) If the #login command is not received as the first command, then the server should send an error message back to the client and terminate the client's connection. Hint: use the method called close found in ConnnectionToClient.

E52 Now that you have completed Phase 2 of SimpleChat, you can execute the test cases provided in the web site for Phase 2. You should execute all the test cases that are indicated to apply to Phase 2, along with a sample of test cases that are marked as relevant only to Phase 1. When testing, use your own server with somebody else's client and vice versa. If you have followed the instructions above consistently, then you should have no trouble doing this.

Developing requirements

4

In the previous two chapters, you learned about technologies that software engineers need to master before developing applications. Now, we can start thinking about the particular problem we wish to solve. We will first put effort into understanding the background of the problem, a process called domain analysis. Then we will look at the information you have to gather so that you can describe the problem and its proposed solution. Finally, we will discuss some techniques for gathering and analyzing that information.

In this chapter you will learn about the following

- Domain analysis: learning background knowledge so that you can communicate with users and make more intelligent decisions.

- Understanding the customer's problem and setting the scope for the project.

- What exactly is a requirement, as well as the various types of requirements.

- Requirements documents and what should be put in them.

- How to go about gathering requirements.

- How to model users' tasks using use case diagrams and detailed descriptions of use cases.

- How to review a set of requirements.

4.1 Domain analysis

Domain analysis is the process by which a software engineer learns background information. He or she has to learn sufficient information so as to be able to understand the problem and make good decisions during requirements analysis and other stages of the software engineering process. The word 'domain' in this case means the general field of business or technology in which the customers expect to be using the software.

Some domains might be very broad, such as 'airline reservations', 'medical diagnosis', and 'financial analysis'. Others are narrower, such as 'the manufacturing of paint' or 'scheduling meetings'. People who work in a domain and who have a deep knowledge of it (or part of it) are called *domain experts.* Many of these people may become customers or users.

To perform domain analysis, you gather information from whatever sources of information are available: these include the domain experts; any books about the domain; any existing software and its documentation; and any other documents you can find. The interviewing, brainstorming and use case analysis techniques discussed later in this chapter can help with domain analysis. Object-oriented modeling, discussed in Chapter 5, can also be of assistance.

As a software engineer, you are not expected to become an expert in the domain; nevertheless, domain analysis can involve considerable work. The following benefits will make this work worthwhile:

- **Faster development**. You will be able to communicate with the stakeholders more effectively, hence you will be able to establish requirements more rapidly. Having performed domain analysis will help you to focus on the most important issues.

- **Better system**. Knowing the subtleties of the domain will help ensure that the solutions you adopt will more effectively solve the customer's problem. You will make fewer mistakes, and will know which procedures and standards to follow. The analysis will give you a global picture of the domain of application; this will lead to better abstractions and hence improved designs.

- **Anticipation of extensions**. Armed with domain knowledge, you will obtain insights into emerging trends and you will notice opportunities for future development. This will allow you to build a more adaptable system.

It is useful to write a summary of the information found during domain analysis. The process of organizing and writing this summary can help you gain a better grasp of the knowledge; the resulting document can help educate other software engineers who join the team later.

We suggest that a domain analysis document should be divided into sections such as the following:

A. **Introduction**. Name the domain, and give the motivation for performing the analysis. The motivation normally is that you are preparing to solve a particular problem by development or extension of a software system.

B. **Glossary**. Describe the meanings of all terms used in the domain that are either not part of everyday language or else have special meanings. You must master this terminology if you want to be able to communicate with your customers and users. The terminology is likely to appear in the user interface of the software as well as in the documentation. You may be able to refer to an existing glossary in some other document, rather than writing a new glossary.

The section is best placed at the start of the domain analysis document so that you can subsequently use the defined terms.

C. **General knowledge about the domain**. Summarize important facts or rules that are widely known by the domain experts and which would normally be learned as part of their education. Such knowledge includes scientific principles, business processes, analysis techniques, and how any technology works. This is an excellent place to use diagrams; however, where possible, point the reader for details to any readily accessible books or other documents. This general knowledge will help you acquire an understanding of the data you may have to process and computations you may have to perform.

D. **Customers and users**. Describe who will or might buy the software, and in what industrial sectors they operate. Also, describe the other people who work in the domain, even peripherally. Mention their background and attitude as well as how they fit into the organization chart, and relate to each other.

E. **The environment**. Describe the equipment and systems used. The new system or extensions will have to work in the context of this environment.

F. **Tasks and procedures currently performed**. Make a list of what the various people do as they go about their work. It is important to understand both the procedures people are supposed to follow as well as the shortcuts they tend to take. If, for example, people are supposed to enter certain information on a form, but rarely do so, this suggests that the information is not useful. Tasks listed in this section may be candidates for automation.

G. **Competing software**. Describe what software is available to assist the users and customers, including software that is already in use, and software on the market. Discuss its advantages and disadvantages. This information suggests ideas for requirements, and highlights mistakes to avoid.

H. **Similarities across domains and organizations**. Understanding what is generic versus what is specific will help you to create software that might be more reusable or more widely marketable. Therefore, determine what distinguishes this domain and the customer's organization from others, as well as what they have in common.

Be careful not to write an excessive amount of detailed information. It is a waste of effort to duplicate the original source material; your domain analysis should simply include a brief summary of the information you have found, along with references that will enable others to find that information.

No serious software project should be undertaken without a sound domain analysis; a good knowledge of the domain of application considerably increases your chances of success. Many of the most successful software products have been developed by people who were actively working in the domain before they became software developers – such people have a better feel for what is really needed.

Once software engineers have a good grasp of the domain, they can move on to requirements analysis, which includes defining the problem to be solved and what software will be created to solve it. However, domain analysis should never really end: software engineers have the responsibility to continue improving their understanding as development proceeds. An extension to the system added for a subsequent release will often merit a domain analysis of its own sub-domain.

Example 4.1

Outline in one paragraph the information you would need to gather in order to perform domain analysis for an airline reservation system.

You would attempt to learn as much as possible about such things as how airline flights are scheduled; how fares are set and structured; and how ticketing and booking works in the customer's airline and other airlines. You would study how the various people in the airline reservation business, including travel agents and airline employees, do their jobs; what existing reservation systems are capable of doing and how they work; and what laws, regulations and other rules govern the industry. You would study the functionality of competing reservation systems, particularly the many web-based systems currently available.

Example 4.2

Imagine you are performing a domain analysis in order to develop a new and better telephone response and dispatch system for medical emergencies. The system will be used by operators and paramedics who respond to calls to the emergency number 911 (in North America) or 999 (in the UK). Summarize the information you would expect to learn. Structure your answer using the categories of information we suggest for a domain analysis document.

A. **Introduction**. The domain is 'Medical Emergency Dispatch'. You already know that the motivation for the domain analysis is to develop a new system that would improve upon existing systems. You would want to record the qualities that are valued in such systems; these presumably include accurate guidance to the paramedics, fast response time, flexibility, and, above all, saving lives.

B. **Glossary**. Much of the special terminology for this domain will be medical in nature, but there will also be terminology related to communications equipment, emergency vehicles and rescue equipment.

C. **General knowledge about the domain**. You should obtain statistics about the calls received and the types of cases handled; this will help you understand the level of performance the system must achieve. Other examples of information to learn include: what are the different categories of emergency situations, and how is each handled? how are addresses described (it is critically important that no mistake is made when communicating an address to an ambulance driver)? how do dispatchers decide whether police, fire-fighters or other special services should also be dispatched?

D. **Customers and users**. In this domain, everyone, including operators, drivers, paramedics and doctors in hospitals, has a clearly defined role. You should understand the knowledge they possess and what they need to learn during the process of handling an emergency. You might discover that some dispatch workers are opposed to the introduction of any new software – they might have developed considerable skill with the existing methods, and fear a new system will render their skills redundant, or even put them out of a job. Knowing this fact, you can take actions to address their concerns and thus avoid any political problems.

E. **The environment**. Study the computers and communications gear currently used. Your customers may be willing to upgrade generic hardware, but your system will have to work with specialized hardware that would be too expensive to replace.

F. **Tasks and procedures currently performed**. The procedures that are currently used by dispatchers and paramedics will help you decide the functions that you have to implement. These procedures are normally very well defined so that they can be followed without any decision-making delay even in a major crisis. Examples of procedures include: how decisions are made about which ambulance to dispatch to which address; how dispatchers and ambulance drivers decide upon a route, especially when traffic is heavy or blocked; how priorities are established in a disaster, when there are not enough ambulances; how communications are established among the dispatcher, the paramedics and doctors in hospitals; and how records of each call are logged. The study of these procedures will help you identify what aspects can be improved and how the software will become an asset to your customer. You will also have to learn about any standards, regulations and laws that may exist, so that the software can conform to them.

G. **Competing software**. You might discover that there is widely used and well-respected emergency management software on the market. You might come to realize that you have little chance of economically developing something that would be as good. In such a case, you would propose that your customer buy the widely used software. On the other hand, you might find that the market is under-developed, with many opportunities for a product like yours to excel. With extra effort you might be able to create a generic product, rather than a custom product, and sell it to many different municipalities.

H. **Similarities across domains and organizations**. The task of dispatching ambulances could be generalized as the problem of allocating the closest resource to a consumer. You might therefore consider developing a generic framework for this aspect of the problem.

Exercises

E53 Describe as many sources of information as you can think of, that should be consulted in order to perform a domain analysis for each of the following systems (see Appendix C for the descriptions of systems).

(a) The police information system.

(b) The household alarm system.

(c) The GPS automobile navigation system.

(d) The investments system.

(e) The woodworking design system.

E54 Write a short domain analysis for one of the systems listed in Exercise E53 using the format we proposed in this section. Record only the most important information a software engineer would need to know in order to develop your chosen system. Gather whatever information you can from several sources. Be resourceful in your hunt for information! Do not forget to consider including any general or specific knowledge you might already possess.

4.2 The starting point for software projects

When a development team starts work on a software project, their starting point can vary considerably. We can distinguish different types of project, based on whether or not *software* exists at the outset, and whether or not *requirements* exist at the outset. The four broad categories of starting point are illustrated in Figure 4.1.

	Requirements must be determined	Clients have produced requirements
New development	A	B
Evolution of existing system	C	D

Figure 4.1   Starting points for software projects

In projects of type A or B, the development team starts to develop new software from scratch – this is sometimes called *green-field* development, alluding to constructing a new building where none existed before. In cases C and D the team evolves an existing system, a rather more common situation.

In cases A and C, the development team has to determine the requirements for the software – they either have a bright idea for something that might sell, or else they are asked to solve a problem and have to work out the best way to solve it. In cases B and D, on the other hand, the development team is contracted to design and implement a very specific set of requirements. In these latter cases, the customer's organization has normally done the requirements analysis, perhaps using in-house software engineers or consultants specializing in requirements analysis.

Projects where the requirements are pre-specified should be handled carefully. If the customer has not done a good job of analysis and specification, the requirements are likely to be poor. For example, the customer may be proposing a system that is far too large, or that does not address a clear problem (we will discuss both of these issues later). As a software engineer, you have a professional responsibility to ensure that the requirements on which you base your work are of good quality, even when they were developed by others. You should evaluate such requirements yourself, and work with the customers to resolve any problems. You should not accept a contract where you are required to implement requirements with no changes allowed.

In the next few sections, we will largely be assuming that you are working on a project of type A or C and therefore have to develop your own requirements. However, the matters we discuss will also be helpful if you are reviewing requirements produced by others.

4.3   Defining the problem and the scope

Once you have learned enough about the domain, you can begin to determine the requirements. The first step in this process is to work out an initial definition of the *problem* to be solved.

A problem can be expressed as a *difficulty* the users or customers are facing, or as an *opportunity* that will result in some benefit such as improved productivity or sales. The solution to the problem will normally entail developing software, although you may decide that it is better to purchase software or to develop a non-software solution.

You should write the problem as a simple statement. Careful attention to the problem statement is important since, later on, the requirements will be evaluated based on the question: 'are we adequately solving the problem?'

A good problem statement is short and succinct – one or two sentences is best. For example, if you were developing a new student registration system, you might express the problem as follows: 'The system will allow students to register for courses, and change their registration, as simply and rapidly as possible. It will help students achieve their personal goals of obtaining their degree in the shortest reasonable time while taking courses that they find most interesting and fulfilling.'

If the problem is broad, or contains a long list of sub-problems, then the system will have a broad scope, and hence be more complex. An important objective is to narrow the scope by defining a more precise problem. In the above example, if we had stated: 'the system will automate all the functions of the registrar's office', that leaves open the possibility of including such features as fee payment, printing class lists and allocating rooms to courses.

One way to set the scope is to list all the sub-problems you might imagine the system attacking. To narrow the scope, you can then exclude some of these sub-problems – perhaps they can be left for another project. Figure 4.2 illustrates this.

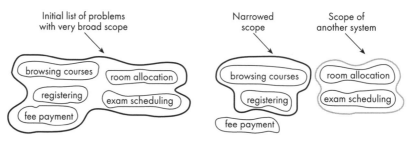

Figure 4.2   Narrowing the project's scope

Sometimes, an inappropriate choice of problem statement can result in a scope that is too narrow or completely wrong. To determine whether this is the case, think about what will be the user's ultimate *high-level goal* when they use the system, and the customer's high-level goal for having it developed.

In the university registration example you could consider a student's goal to be 'completing the registration process'. However, you can see that the student's higher-level goal might be, 'obtaining their degree in the shortest reasonable time while taking courses that they find most interesting and fulfilling'. This new goal sheds a different light on the problem; you might consider adding features to the system that would not otherwise have occurred to you, such as actively proposing courses based on an analysis of the student's academic and personal-interest profiles.

All the requirements gathering and analysis techniques described later in this chapter can help in defining the problem and hence the system's scope. Interviewing can give you the stakeholders' personal perspectives; brainstorming can generate lists of ideas from which you can extract a suitable problem or problems; use case analysis can give you a list of the possible things the system could do; and prototyping can give everybody a better perspective about what might be possible.

It is a good idea to define the problem and scope as early as possible, before getting deeper into analysis of the detailed requirements. This prevents you from working on unnecessary requirements. However, as with domain analysis, your perspective on the problem will improve as analysis continues, hence the problem statement may need to be refined several times.

Example 4.3	*Define the problem and scope for a system that handles university degree requirements and registrations. Then develop a requirements statement from this.*

A university registrar's office handles a large number of functions. Below, we have listed some of the functions that you might consider building into such a system.

The initial, overly broad, problem statement might be: 'to automate all the functions of the registrar's office'.

You would have extensive discussions with stakeholders, and then agree on a narrower problem statement such as the following: 'Helping university administrators manage lists of courses, degree requirements, registration and academic results. Helping students choose and register in courses in which they are interested that will lead to their degree.'

You can then determine which functions should be included in the system. The functions marked with a '++' will be included, while those marked with a '– –' will be excluded. Note that there will still have to be systems to handle the functions marked '– –', but these will be left to others to develop, or to a later project.

– – Fee payments and related accounting and billing

– – Applications for admission

++ Editing and querying the list of available courses, including their descriptions and lists of prerequisites

++ Editing and querying the requirements for obtaining a degree

++ Editing and querying the list of courses to be taught in a given semester

– – Scheduling the times that courses will be offered

– – Allocating courses or exams to rooms

++ Helping students determine which courses they could take by analyzing their degree requirements, the courses they have previously taken, their schedule, and their preferences

++ Registering students

++ Recording marks

++ Printing transcripts

Example 4.4	*You are asked to improve a data entry program used to enter a patient's personal information when he or she is first admitted to a hospital. Admission clerks have to enter each new patient's name, address, telephone number, and various other pieces of data. The customer tells you that the admissions clerks make an unacceptable number of mistakes that contaminate the database and cause administrative problems. You are told that the problem is lack of clarity in the*

user interface, which leads the clerks to put information in the wrong places. What, however, is the real problem and how might understanding this affect potential solutions?

The stated problem suggests that the solution is to clean up the user interface. However, the real problem is that many errors are made. Thinking about the real problem leads us to realize that a better solution might involve completely eliminating the data entry process, or at least reducing it. Perhaps some or all of each patient's information could be obtained from a database (e.g. one maintained by the government or insurance companies), or by scanning a patient's driver's license or some other document. Another issue to investigate is whether all the information typed by the clerks is actually needed – if they have to type less information, then maybe they will be able to spend more time checking the accuracy of the important information.

Example 4.5   *This is the inverse of the last example. This time, you are told by the customer that the problem is, 'the data-entry system is not "high-tech" enough'. Hence you are asked to write a system that scans drivers' licenses and other documents in order to enter a new patient's name and address accurately and quickly. What mistake could you be making if you accept this problem statement and proceed to do exactly what the customer asks?*

You should never accept a problem statement that merely says the technology lacks sophistication – simple technology is often perfectly adequate or even superior. The customers may not realize that software that accurately scans arbitrary documents and puts the relevant information in the correct fields will be difficult to write, and hence would be expensive. In fact there is a considerable risk that the accuracy achieved by this approach might be inadequate, and that much maintenance would be needed – for example as document formats change. Once again, you should base your analysis on the real problem – that clerks make too many errors. You might discover that your real focus should be on improving the user interface of the existing system.

Exercises

E55   Define a possible scope for the following systems. First, list a wide range of things that the system could do. Then narrow down the scope. To do this, select a minimal set of the most important features that you would implement in the first release of the system.

(a) A police information system.

(b) A system for real-estate agency.

(c) A system for a public library.

(d) A system for a car-rental agency.

E56 Give precise problem statements for the systems listed in E55. Remember to think about high-level goals.

4.4 What is a requirement?

> **Definition:** a *requirement* is a statement describing either 1) an aspect of what the proposed system must do, or 2) a constraint on the system's development. In either case, it must contribute in some way towards adequately solving the customer's problem; the set of requirements as a whole represents a negotiated agreement among all stakeholders.

Let us dissect this definition in order to better understand it:

■ *A requirement is a statement…*: this means that each requirement is a relatively short and concise piece of information, expressed as a fact. It can be written as a sentence or can be expressed using some kind of diagram. We will call a collection of requirements a requirements document.

■ *…an aspect of what the proposed system must do…*: most requirements say something about the tasks the system is supposed to accomplish. They do not describe the domain.

■ *…a constraint on the system's development…*: requirements often specify the quality levels required. They may also specify details such as the programming language to be used if this is truly important to the customer. They should, however, avoid discussing incidental aspects of the design.

■ *…contribute … towards adequately solving the customer's problem*: a requirement should only be present if it helps solve the customer's problem – as we discussed in Chapter 1, this is what software engineering is all about.

■ *…a negotiated agreement among all stakeholders…*: a statement about the system should not be declared to be an official requirement until all the stakeholders (users, customers, developers and their management) have reviewed it, have negotiated any needed changes, and have agreed that it is valid.

4.5 Types of requirements

Requirements can be divided into four major types: functional, quality, platform and process. Requirements documents normally include at least the first two types.

Functional requirements

Functional requirements describe what the system should do; in other words, they describe the *services* provided for the users and for other systems. The functional requirements should include 1) everything that a *user* of the system would need to know regarding what the system does, and 2) everything that would concern any *other system* that has to interface to this system. Details that go any deeper into how the requirements are implemented should be left out.

The functional requirements can be further categorized as follows:

- What *inputs* the system should accept, and under what conditions. This includes data and commands both from the users and from other systems.

- What *outputs* the system should produce, and under what conditions. Outputs can be to the screen or printed. They can also be transmitted to other systems, such as special I/O devices, clients or servers.

- What data the system should *store* that other systems might use. This is really a special kind of output that will eventually become an input to other systems. Data which is stored for the exclusive use of this system (e.g. the specifics of a file format used to temporarily back up some data) can be ignored until the design stage.

- What *computations* the system should perform. The computations should be described at a level that all the readers can understand. For example, you would describe a sorting process by saying that the result is to be ordered in ascending sequence according to the account number. You would not normally specify the particular algorithm to be used.

- The *timing and synchronization* of the above. Not all systems involve timing and synchronization – this category of functional requirements is of most importance in hard real-time systems that do such things as control hardware devices (e.g. telecommunications systems, systems that control power plants or factories, and systems that run automobiles and airplanes).

An individual requirement often covers more than one of the above categories. For example, the requirements for a word processor might say, 'when the user selects "word count", the system displays a dialog box listing the number of characters, words, sentences, lines, paragraphs, pages, and words per sentence in the current document.' This requirement clearly describes input (selecting 'word count'), output (what is displayed) and computation (counting all the necessary information, and computing the average words per sentence).

Example 4.6 *Summarize the functional requirements for an embedded software system that allows a user to control a microwave oven. The system as a whole consists of:*

❏ *A keypad, with the following buttons that deliver an interrupt to the software when they are pressed: 0 to 9, five power-level buttons ('hi', 'med-hi', 'med', 'med-low', 'low'), three temperature buttons ('frozen', 'refrigerated', 'room temperature'), and five action buttons ('AUTO-DEFROST', 'AUTO-REHEAT', 'START', 'CANCEL' and 'TIME OF DAY').*

❑ *A door sensor that delivers an interrupt to the software when the door is opened or closed.*

❑ *A steam sensor that can be queried by the software, and which indicates the amount of steam being released from the food.*

❑ *A digital LCD display on which the system can display output.*

❑ *A sound generator that the system can use to generate various tones.*

❑ *The cooking hardware (microwave emitter, fan and turntable). The software can run this at the five different power levels, and can turn it off.*

The following summarizes the main functional requirements. This is intended to illustrate the different categories of functional requirements, which we have marked in italics. It is not a complete requirements document; examples of more complete documents are found in Sections 4.11 and 4.12. There are a few deliberate weaknesses in these requirements, which are left for you to find in later exercises.

1. The system can be in the following modes (*conditions under which input and output can occur*):

   ❑ 'idle': this is entered when the system is switched on, when cooking is complete or when 'CANCEL' is pressed. This mode is exited when the system starts accepting input.

   ❑ 'accepting input': this is entered if the system was in idle mode and the user presses any button, except 'CANCEL' and 'START'. This mode is exited when the system enters 'cooking' mode, the user presses 'cancel', or the user completes the process of setting the time of day.

   ❑ 'cooking': this is entered if the door is closed, while the system is in 'suspended' or 'accepting input' mode, and the user then presses 'start'. This is exited when the user opens the door or presses 'cancel'.

   ❑ 'suspended': this is entered if the user opens the door while cooking. This mode is exited when the user presses 'cancel'; or closes the door and then presses 'start'.

2. The user specifies a valid cooking method in one of the following ways (*input*):

   ❑ By pressing a sequence of up to five digits indicating minutes and seconds. The last two digits are the seconds, the previous digits (if any) are the minutes. The user may optionally then press one of the power-level keys.

   ❑ By pressing 'AUTO-DEFROST' followed by an optional sequence of digits indicating the weight in pounds. If the user omits the weight, then the default is 1.

   ❑ By pressing 'AUTO-REHEAT' followed optionally by one of the temperature buttons. If the user omits the temperature, then the default is 'refrigerated'.

3. After specifying a cooking method, the user must press 'START' to initiate cooking (*input*).

4. The user sets the time of day by pressing 'TIME OF DAY' followed by four digits indicating the hours and minutes, followed by 'TIME OF DAY' again (*input*).

5. When in idle mode, the system displays the time of day using a 12-hour clock, without any 'a.m.' or 'p.m.' (*output*).

6. Each time the user presses a button, the system generates a tone. If the button is valid, the tone is high-pitched. If any button is pressed in an invalid sequence (e.g. the user presses 'START' while the door is open, or presses 'AUTO-DEFROST' followed by 'AUTO-REHEAT') the tone is low-pitched (*output and conditions for the output*).

7. When the system is in 'accepting input' mode, the system indicates on the display the buttons the user presses (*output – in a full document, more details would be needed*).

8. When the user specifies 'AUTO-DEFROST' cooking, the system computes the required heating time and power level from the entered weight of the food (*computation – in a full requirements document the formulas used would have to be specified*).

9. When the system enters 'cooking' mode, the system sends a signal to the cooking hardware to start cooking at the specified or computed power-level (*output*).

10. If the system is cooking, and 'AUTO-REHEAT' has been specified:

    ❏ The system stops cooking when it detects sufficient steam, indicating that the food is hot (*input and output – in a full requirements document more details of required steam levels would be required*).

    ❏ The system displays an estimate of the remaining cooking time from the initial temperature of the food, as specified by the user, and the amount of steam it detects. The system constantly updates this estimate (*computation and output*).

    ❏ As a safety measure, if the system has reached its time estimate and has not detected any increase in steam, then it stops cooking (*computation, timing and output*).

11. When the system is in 'cooking' mode and either a simple time-period or 'AUTO-DEFROST' has been specified:

    ❏ The system displays the power level and the cooking time remaining (*output*).

    ❏ The system stops cooking when the time remaining reaches zero (*timing and output*).

12. When the system is to stop cooking, it sends a signal to the cooking hardware to switch it off, and sounds three short high-pitched beeps (*output*).

Exercise

E57 Using the same format as Example 4.6, describe a set of functional requirements for systems that would solve the problem statements you devised in Exercise E56. If you find that a list of functional requirements is getting too extensive, you may further narrow the problem statement.

Quality requirements

Quality requirements ensure the system possesses quality attributes such as the five discussed in Chapter 1: usability, efficiency, reliability, maintainability and reusability. These requirements *constrain* the design to meet specified levels of quality.

One of the most important things about quality requirements is to make them *verifiable*. By this, we mean that it should be possible, after the system is implemented, to determine whether they have, in fact, been adhered to. The verification is normally done by measuring various aspects of the system and seeing if the measurements conform to the requirements.

The following are some of the main categories of quality requirements, although this is not an exclusive list.

- **Response time**. For systems that process a lot of data or use a network extensively, you should require that the system gives results or feedback to the user in a certain minimum time. For example, you might write that a result must be calculated in less than three seconds, or that feedback about the progress of a search must appear within one second. In Chapter 7, we will discuss usability guidelines for response time. Remember, however, that for hard real-time systems, response time requirements should be considered to be functional – the system would not work unless they are adhered to.

- **Throughput**. For number-crunching programs that may take hours, or for servers that continually respond to client requests, it is a good idea to specify *throughput*, in terms of computations or transactions per minute.

- **Resource usage**. For systems that use non-trivial amounts of such resources as memory and network bandwidth, you should specify the maximum amount of these resources that the system will consume. This allows others to plan hardware upgrades. For example, you could specify that no more than 50 MB of memory is to be used by the system, and that the system must consume less than 10% of the CPU's time when run on a 1.8GHz machine under a certain operating system.

> **Non-functional requirements**
> Quality, platform and process requirements used to be collectively called *non-functional* requirements. However, that term has fallen into disfavor and we have therefore stopped using it in this book.

■ **Reliability.** *Reliability* is measured as the average amount of time between failures or the probability of a failure in a given period. It is a good idea to set strong but realistic targets for this. For example, you might specify that a continuously running server must not suffer more than one failure in a six-month period. It is necessary to define what you mean by a failure: normally it means much more than just crashes; failures normally include any difficulties users have getting their work done which are attributable to defects.

■ **Availability.** *Availability* measures the amount of time that a server is running and available to respond to users. As with reliability, you should set a target for this. For example, you might specify that a server must be available over 99% of the time, and that no period of downtime may exceed 1 minute. Telecommunications systems have very rigorous availability criteria: for example, you might specify that such a system must not be down more than 10 minutes in its 20-year life-span. This is also often called '6-nines' availability, since it is equivalent to saying that the system must be up 99.9999% of the time.

■ **Recovery from failure.** Requirements in this category constrain the allowed impact of a failure. They state that if the hardware or software crashes, or the power fails, then the system will be able to recover within a certain amount of time, and with a certain minimal loss of data. For example, the requirements for a word processor might state: 'the system will allow users to continue their work after a failure with the loss of no more than 20 words of typing or 20 formatting commands.' Note that the detailed *procedure* for recovery from failure is a functional requirement.

■ **Allowances for maintainability and enhancement.** In order to ensure that the system can be adapted in the future, you should describe changes that are anticipated for subsequent releases. This constrains design and improves quality without adding explicit new functional requirements.

■ **Allowances for reusability.** Similarly to the previous category, it is desirable in many cases to specify that a certain percentage of the system, e.g. 40%, measured in terms of lines of code, must be designed generically so that it can be reused. This will help break the reuse vicious cycle discussed in the previous chapter.

Platform requirements

This type of requirement constrains the environment and technology of the system:

■ **Computing platform.** It is normally important to make it clear what hardware and operating system the software must be able to work on. Such requirements specify the *least* powerful platforms and declare that it must work on anything more recent or more powerful. For example, you might declare that certain software must run on any computer operating under Mac OS X version 10.2 or MS-Windows 98 or higher, with 128 MB of RAM or more, and 100 MB of free disk space. This is quite different from the resource usage constraint on memory above: a resource usage constraint specifies that the system *will not use* more than a certain amount of resources, whereas a platform constraint says it *is not guaranteed to run* if inadequate or incorrect resources are available.

■ **Technology to be used**. While it is wise to give the designers as much flexibility as possible in choosing how to implement the system, sometimes constraints must be imposed. Common examples are to specify the programming language or database system. Such requirements are normally stated to ensure that all systems in an organization use the same technology – this reduces the need to train people in different technologies. The company might have also spent considerable money on a certain technology and wants to get the best value for that money.

Process requirements

The final type of requirements constrains the project plan and development methods:

■ **Development process (methodology) to be used**. In order to ensure quality, some requirements documents specify that certain processes be followed; for example, particular approaches to testing. The details of the process should not be included in the requirements; instead a reference should be made to other documents that describe the process.

■ **Cost and delivery date**. These are important constraints. However, they are usually not placed in the requirements document, but are found in the contract for the system or are left to a separate project plan document, which we will discuss in Chapter 11.

In most cases, the boundaries between the functional requirements and other requirements types are clear. But sometimes it is unclear in which category a requirement should fit. For example, if you were designing a word processor you would likely build in an 'auto-save' feature so that, if the computer was turned off or crashed, very little work would be lost. The question is, is the auto-save feature a fundamental part of the word processor's functionality (a functional requirement), or is it a constraint on quality (a quality requirement)? You would probably conclude that it is a functional requirement.

Example 4.7   *Classify the following aspects of an airline reservation system into F for functional, Q for quality, PL for platform, PR for process, and X for 'should not be a requirement'. Also indicate the subcategory of requirement. For something that should not be a requirement, explain why not.*

■ How information about flights, passengers and bookings are entered. F: *Input.*

■ What information appears on tickets and reports. F: *Output.*

■ How fares are calculated. F: *Computation.*

■ What information must be stored in the database that travel agents and others access. F: *Data storage*.

■ The system should be designed such that it can be extended to handle a frequent-flier plan. Q: *Allowance for enhancement*.

■ The system must be available at all times. Only 2 minutes' downtime a week is to be permitted. Q: *Availability*.

■ The system must run on any Linux system. PL: *Computing platform*.

■ A merge-sort algorithm must be used to sort the flights by departure time. X: *This is a design issue*.

Exercises

E58 Classify the following requirements statements into F for functional, Q for quality, PL for platform, PR for process, and X for 'should not be a requirement'. Justify your answer. If you would need more information to provide the answer to one of these questions, indicate what else you would need to know.

(a) The system must use 128-bit encryption for all transactions.

(b) If the alarm system is ringing, then the elevators (lifts) will proceed to the ground floor, open their doors and suspend further operations.

(c) The student information system will provide output from all commands within one second.

(d) The system will be able to print to an LC-9 plotter.

(e) The system will use an array to hold the invoices.

(f) The system can read images of the following formats: JPEG, GIF, BMP.

(g) The system must use no more than 32 MB of RAM.

(h) The `java.util.Date` class should be used to handle dates.

(i) The JUnit framework should be used to test the system.

(j) The system must run under both Linux and Windows operating systems.

E59 The following requirements are stated in an unverifiable way. For each, indicate the kind of requirement it is, and rewrite it so that it is verifiable (make up some suitable details).

(a) A modern programming language must be used.

(b) A development process will be used that will ensure the system is of high quality.

(c) The http server will have high availability and throughput.

(d) The system must be produced at minimum cost.

(e) The automatic teller machine should be fast.

E60 Write a set of quality and platform requirements for the microwave oven system of Example 4.6.

E61 Add quality and platform requirements to the systems you worked on in Exercise E57.

4.6 Use cases: describing how the user will use the system

Use case analysis is a systematic approach to working out what users should be able to do with the software you are developing. It is one of the key activities in requirements analysis.

The first step in use case analysis is to determine the types of users or other systems that will use the facilities of this system. These are called *actors*. An actor is a *role* that a user or some other system plays when interacting with your system; each actor will need to interact with the system in different ways.

Most of the actors will be users; a given user may be considered as several different actors if they play different roles from time to time – that is, if they have different job functions. Other actors will be systems that automatically exchange information with your system. If you performed domain analysis, you will have already listed the different types of users

---

Example 4.8   *You are developing a system for managing the processes of a small town public library. List all the actors for this system.*

The actors might include the following: Librarian, Checkout Clerk, Borrower.

The second step in use case analysis is to determine the tasks that each actor will need to do with the system. Each task is called a *use case* because it represents one particular way the system will be used.

Definition: a *use case* is a typical sequence of actions that an actor performs in order to complete a given task.

When listing use cases, make sure you respect the system scope, as discussed in Section 4.3. In other words, only list use cases that actors will need to do when they are using the system to solve the customer's problem. You can also list a set of use cases to help define the system's scope.

Example 4.9   *List a minimal set of use cases for the following actors in a library system: Borrower, Checkout Clerk, Librarian, Accounting System.*

Borrower:

❏ Search for items by title.

❏ ... by author.

❏ ... by subject.

❏ Place a book on hold if it is on loan to somebody else.

❏ Check the borrower's personal information and list of books currently borrowed.

Checkout Clerk:

❏ All the Borrower use cases, plus

❏ Check out an item for a borrower.

❏ Check in an item that has been returned.

❏ Renew an item.

❏ Record that a fine has been paid.

❏ Add a new borrower.

❏ Update a borrower's personal information (address, telephone number etc.).

Librarian:

❏ All of the Borrower and Checkout Clerk use cases, plus

❏ Add a new item to the collection.

❏ Delete an item from the collection.

❏ Change the information the system has recorded about an item.

Accounting System (acting autonomously):

❏ Obtain the amount of overdue fines paid by borrowers.

Exercises

E62 For the following systems list the actors and, for each of these actors, list as many use cases as you can think of.

(a) A system to handle the functions of a mail-order company that manages a warehouse of goods, takes orders from customers by telephone, and ships goods overnight to customers.

(b) A system to handle electronic voting. The system will allow electors to vote for a specific number of candidates, and only vote once. At the end of the voting period, the system displays the result of the vote.

(c) A camping reservation system for multiple campgrounds. Campground managers register many details of their site in the system, including maps of camping locations and services available. Campers use the system to select and reserve a camping location.

(d) The microwave oven system of Example 4.6.

Building a use case model

So far, we have discussed the first two steps of use case analysis, listing the actors and listing the use cases. To build a complete *use case model*, we now need to describe the use cases in more detail. A use case model consists of a set of use cases, and optional descriptions or diagrams indicating how they are related.

How to describe a single use case

The following is how we suggest you describe a complete use case. Only the name and steps are essential – you may choose to provide a simplified use case description that omits the other components.

A. **Name.** Give a short, descriptive name to the use case. This should be a verb phrase describing the action the user will do with the system. It is also useful to include a number as a unique identifier for each use case.

B. **Actors.** List the actor or actors who can perform this use case. For example, in a library system both a borrower and a librarian can check out a book.

C. **Goals.** Explain what the actor or actors are trying to achieve. For example, in a library system, the goal of checking out a book would be to borrow the book in order to read it.

D. **Preconditions.** Describe the state of the system before the use case occurs by listing any conditions that must be true before an actor can initiate this use case. For example, to be able to check out a book, the book must be available and the client must not have any overdue fines.

E. **Summary.** Summarize what occurs as the actor or actors perform the use case.

F. **Related use cases.** List use cases that may be generalizations, specializations, extensions or inclusions of this one. Later, we will explain these relationships.

> **Use case versus task analysis**
> Use case analysis is similar to *task analysis*. Task analysis has been traditionally used to understand and improve the efficiency of the tasks that users perform, whether or not they are using a computer. User interface designers sometimes continue to use the term task analysis.

G. **Steps**. Describe each step of the use case using a two-column format, with the left column showing the actions taken by the actor, and the right column showing the system's responses.

H. **Postconditions**. What state is the system in following the completion of this use case.

In general, a use case should cover the full sequence of steps from the beginning of a task until the end.

A use case should describe the user's interaction with the system, not the computations the system performs. For example in a use case for withdrawing money from an automated teller machine, you would describe the fact that the user inserts his or her card, responds to various prompts by pressing some buttons, and then removes his or her card and money. You would not describe how communication with the bank is established or how the system computes any fees it charges. The latter information is clearly important, but it belongs in a different part of the functional requirements.

A use case should also be written so as to be as independent as possible from any particular user interface design. In Example 4.10, for example, instead of writing, 'Push the "Open…" button' as the first steps, we write 'Choose the "Open…" command'. The command could then be implemented as a button, a menu item, a keystroke or a voice command. Similarly, we have not specified whether the user types the file name or uses the mouse to select it from a list. Nor have we indicated what the 'File open' dialog looks like.

Example 4.10 *Describe in a simplified format a use case for opening a file in an application.*

Use case: Open file

Steps:

Actor actions	System responses
1. Choose 'Open…' command.	2. Display 'File open' dialog.
3. Specify filename.	
4. Confirm selection.	5. Remove dialog from display.

Example 4.11 *Briefly describe a use case for leaving a particular automated car park (parking lot).*

Use case: Exit car park, paying cash

Actors: Car drivers

Goals: To leave the parking lot after having paid the amount due.

Preconditions: The driver must have entered the car park with his or her car, and must have picked up a ticket upon entry.

Summary: When a driver wishes to exit the car park, he or she must bring his or her car to the exit barrier and interact with a machine to pay the amount due.

Related use case: Exit car park by paying using a debit card

Steps:

Actor actions	System responses
1. Drive to exit barrier, triggering a sensor.	2a. Detect presence of a car.
	2b. Prompt driver to insert his or her card.
3. Insert ticket.	4. Display amount due.
5. Insert money into slot.	6a. Return any change owing.
	6b Prompt driver to take the change (if any).
	6c. Raise barrier.
7. Drive through barrier, triggering a sensor.	8. Lower barrier.

Note that we have not dealt with the case where the user has not entered enough money at step 5. We will deal with this case later.

A use case should normally include only actions in which the actor interacts with the system. For example, when developing use cases for a library system, you would not include actions such as 'Get a book from the shelves' or 'Read the book'. However, if there is a manual task that must be done between two interactions with the computer, then this can be part of the use case; for example, 'Stamp the book with the due date' is a valid action in Example 4.12.

Example 4.12 *Describe in detail the 'Check out an item for a borrower' use case as performed by the checkout clerks at the circulation desk of a library. This is one of the use cases listed in Example 4.9.*

Use case: Check out an item for a borrower

Actors: Checkout clerk (regularly), chief librarian (occasionally)

Goals: To help the borrower to borrow the item if they are allowed, and to ensure a proper record is entered of the loan.

Preconditions: The borrower must have a valid card and not owe any fines. The item must have a valid barcode and not be from the reference section.

Steps:

Actor actions	System responses
1. Scan item's barcode and barcode of the borrower's card.	2. Display confirmation that the loan is allowed.

3. Stamp item with the due date.

4. Confirm that the loan is to be initiated.

5. Display confirmation that the loan has been recorded.

Postconditions: The system has a record of the fact that the item is borrowed, and the date it is due.

Exercise

E63 Write use case descriptions for the following activities:

(a) Paying a bill at an automatic teller machine.

(b) Creating a table in a word processor.

(c) Programming a microwave oven to turn on in five hours and heat some food.

(d) Read messages in a voice mail system.

(e) Programming a thermostat to set the day and night temperatures.

Use case diagrams

Use case diagrams are UML's notation for showing the relationships among a set of use cases and actors. They help a software engineer to convey a high-level picture of the functionality of a system.

It is not necessary to create a use case diagram for every system or subsystem. For a small system, or a system with just one or two actors, a simple list of use cases will suffice.

As Figure 4.3 shows, there are two main symbols in use case diagrams: an actor is shown as a stick person and a use case is shown as an ellipse. Lines indicate which actors perform which use cases. You do not actually need to write the word 'Actor' in each actor's name; however, we find it useful to do this when it helps prevent confusion with classes of the same names.

Exercise

E64 For the systems of Exercise E62, draw a use case diagram that shows which actors perform which use cases.

Extension, generalization and inclusion of use cases

You may want to develop a group of distinct but related use cases. For example, when an actor interacts with a system to achieve a particular goal, he or she may select different options, perform some action repetitively, provide different inputs, or answer too slowly causing a time-out error. Each variant or repetitive

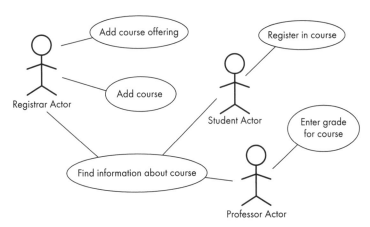

Figure 4.3 A simple use case diagram showing three actors and five use cases

pattern of interaction can be represented as a separate use case. Similarly, the system might have a special reaction when a file cannot be found. The use case modeler can use *extensions*, *generalizations* or *inclusions* to represent different types of relationships among use cases.

■ **Extensions** are used to make *optional* interactions explicit or to handle *exceptional* cases. A use case extension can, for example, describe what happens if an actor provides a wrong filename to access a given file or describes the extra interaction that occurs if the actor decides to browse in order to locate the required file instead of simply typing a filename. By creating separate extension use cases, the description of the basic use case remains simple. In the extension, you should indicate which step is the *extension point* – the point at which the extension changes the basic sequence.

■ **Generalizations** work the same way as in a class diagram and use the same triangle symbol: several similar use cases can be shown along with a common generalized use case. In Example 4,13, the general 'open file' use case has two sub use cases: 'open file by typing name', and 'open file by browsing'.

■ **Inclusions** allow you to express a *part* of a use case so that you can capture commonality between several different use cases. Even very different use cases can share a sequence of actions. For example, many different use cases might require an actor to specify a password, to browse through a list of items, or to open a file. Rather than repeating the details of such common interactions in multiple use cases, you can create a special use case that will be included in other use cases. Such a use case represents the performing of a lower-level task with a lower-level goal.

In practice, it can be difficult to decide whether to use specialization or extension. Although it is worth trying to understand the distinction, it is not worth wasting time in any particular model if you have trouble choosing between these constructs.

Example 4.13   *Describe related use cases that have to do with opening a file in an application.*

Use case: Open file

Related use cases:
    Generalization of:

      ❏ open file by typing name

      ❏ open file by browsing

Steps:

Actor actions	*System responses*
1. Choose 'Open…' command.	2. Display 'File open' dialog.
3. Specify filename.	
4. Confirm selection.	5. Remove dialog from display.

Use case: Open file by typing name

Related use cases:
    Generalization: Open file

Steps:

Actor actions	*System responses*
1. Choose 'Open…' command.	2. Display 'File open' dialog.
3a. Select text field.	
3b. Type file name.	
4. Click 'Open'.	5. Remove dialog from display.

Use case: Open file by browsing

Related use cases:
    Generalization: Open file
    Includes: Browse for file

Steps:

Actor actions	*System responses*
1. Choose 'Open…' command.	2. Display 'File open' dialog.
3. Browse for file (included use case).	
4. Confirm selection.	5. Remove dialog from display.

Use case: Attempt to open file that does not exist

Related use cases:
  Extension of: Open file by typing name (extension point: step 4: Click 'Open')

Actor actions	*System responses*
4. Click 'Open'.	4a. Indicate that file does not exist.
4b. Correct the file name.	
4c. Click 'Open'.	5. Remove dialog from display.

Use case: Browse for file (inclusion)

Steps:

Actor actions	*System responses*
1. If the desired file is not displayed, select a directory.	2. Display directory.
3. Repeat step 1 until the desired file is displayed.	
4. Select a file.	

The graphical notation for showing extension, generalization and inclusion is illustrated in Figure 4.4. The open triangle points to a generalization. The «extend» and «include» stereotypes show the other relationships between use cases.

Note that actors can also be arranged in a generalization hierarchy. In Figure 4.4, 'System Administrator' is a sub-actor of 'Ordinary User'. This means that all System Administrators can also act as ordinary users, and do such things as open files.

Exercises

E65 Write the following use cases, which are related to the 'Exit car park, paying cash' use case of Example 4.11.

(a) Exit car park by paying using a debit card.

(b) Attempt to exit car park without initially entering enough money.

(c) Exit car park.

E66 Draw a use case diagram showing the relationships among the use cases of the last exercise.

E67 Create a complete use case model for the systems you worked on in Exercises E55 to E57.

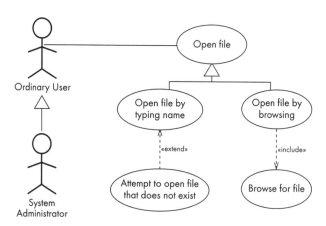

Figure 4.4   Extension, generalization and inclusion in a use case diagram

The modeling processes: choosing use cases on which to focus

You should identify all the use cases associated with the software product, but you have to put varying emphasis on them when actually developing the system. Often one use case (or a very small number) can be identified as *central* to the system. For example, in an airline reservation system, the central use case will be 'Reserve a seat on a flight'. Once identified, the system can be built around this particular use case.

There are also other reasons for focusing on particular use cases:

■ You may identify some use cases as *high risk* because you expect to have problems implementing them. For example, in the GPS-based Automobile Navigation Assistant (GANA) described in Section 4.11, you may identify 'Enter navigation mode' and 'Speak now' as high risk. These use cases will require exploratory prototypes, since it will be challenging to ensure that the voice output is easy to understand and is spoken to the user at the right time.

■ Some use cases will have high political or commercial value. For example, in an online stock exchange system, a use case in which the user can see, in real time, the evolution of the value of a given stock would not be essential – the users could do their jobs without it. Nevertheless, it might be given high priority because of its appeal when presenting the product prototype to potential clients.

Exercise

E68 For the following systems create a list of use cases and describe each of them in detail. Then identify the central ones, and any other ones that should be given high priority.

(a) A web-application to pay bills from your bank account.

(b) The GANA navigation system.

(c) A video-cassette recorder.

(d) A voice mail messaging system.

(e) A system to create digital photo albums on your computer.

E69 Identify the central use cases and the ones that should be given highest priority in the use case models you worked on in Exercise E67.

The benefits of basing software development on use cases

Use case analysis is an intuitive way to understand and organize what the system should do, since it is based on user tasks and expresses the tasks in natural language. It can also be used to *drive* the development process; in particular, use cases:

■ Can help to define the *scope* of the system – that is, what the system must do and does not have to do.

■ Are often used to plan the development process. The number of identified use cases is a good indicator of a project's size. Development progress can be measured in terms of the percentage of use cases that have been completed.

■ Are used to both develop and validate the requirements. If some piece of proposed functionality does not support any use case, then it can be eliminated. Users and customers can also understand requirements better if they are expressed in terms of use cases. The use cases therefore can serve as part of the contract between the customers and the developer.

■ Can form the basis for the definition of test cases (discussed in Chapter 10).

■ Can be used to structure user manuals.

However, use cases must not be seen as a panacea. There are three things to watch out for:

1. The use cases themselves must be validated, using the requirements validation methods to be discussed in Section 4.9. For example, it is important to make sure that the set of use cases is complete and that they are expressed consistently and unambiguously.

2. There are some aspects of functional requirements that are not covered by use case analysis. For example, only activities triggered by an actor will appear as use cases. An example of something not shown as a use case is the automatic cleaning of a database to remove outdated information. Although it is not a use case, this is still a functional requirement since it is important to the user that the outdated information be periodically purged.

3. You should be aware that when software requirements are derived from use cases, the software tends simply to mirror the way users worked *before* the software was developed. In other words, innovative solutions may not be considered. As an illustration of this last point, try to describe a use case for adjusting the wake-up time of an alarm clock. You will probably follow the procedure you use yourself to adjust your own clock, even though there might be more efficient and innovative ways to do it (for example, using speech recognition).

Scenarios

A scenario is an *instance* of a use case that expresses a specific occurrence of the use case with a specific actor operating at a specific time and using specific data. It can help to clarify the associated use case. It is also often simply called a *use case instance*.

Example 4.14 *Describe a concrete scenario corresponding to the 'Exit car park, paying cash' use case from Example 4.11.*

Steps:

Actor actions	System responses
Drives to the exit barrier.	Detects the presence of a car.
	Displays: 'Please insert your ticket'.
Inserts ticket.	Displays: 'Amount due $2.50'.
Inserts $1 into the slot.	Displays: 'Amount due $1.50'.
Inserts $1 into the slot.	Displays: 'Amount due $0.50'.
Inserts $1 into the slot.	Returns $0.50.
	Displays: 'Please take your $0. 50 change'.
	Raises barrier.
Drives through barrier, triggering sensor.	Lowers barrier.

4.7 Some techniques for gathering requirements

You can gather requirements from the same sources of information as you used for domain analysis: i.e. from the various stakeholders, from other software systems, and from any documentation that might be available.

In this section we list some structured techniques that are particularly effective at gathering (also known as *eliciting*) requirements. All of them can be used together to obtain a good set of requirements.

The first gathering technique, observation, is used to obtain subtle information that stakeholders may not think of telling you. The next three, interviewing, brainstorming and prototyping, are complementary techniques for actively asking for the opinions and knowledge of stakeholders as well as forcing the stakeholders to stretch their minds.

Users participate in all four of these techniques, therefore they feel personally involved in the project. This sense of involvement means that they will more readily accept the final system. In Chapter 7, we will focus on users and discuss other ways to make them feel personally involved.

Gathering requirements is an iterative process that must be combined with a process of *analyzing* the requirements to systematically organize and prioritize them. Building a use case model, as discussed in the last section, is a common approach to analysis. You can also analyze requirements with the help of other types of UML diagrams discussed in Chapters 5, 8 and 9. The analysis process can be done individually or in a group setting; often much analysis is done with users during the brainstorming and iterative prototyping sessions we will discuss shortly.

Whichever techniques you use, it is important to put adequate time and effort into the requirements process. Many projects have run into problems because the software engineers rushed the requirements stage and jumped into design or coding too early. Coding early can be fine as long as it is only rapid prototyping, not developing the final product.

Observation

You can read documents and discuss requirements extensively with users, but often only the process of observing the users at work will bring to light subtle details that you might otherwise miss. For example, in a retail application you may notice the manager bargaining with buyers over the price of certain items. In an interview, she may forget to tell you that this is something that ought to be automated.

In its simplest form, observation means taking a notebook and 'shadowing' important potential users as they do their work, writing down everything they do. You can also ask users to talk as they work, explaining what they are doing. In another variation, you can videotape the session so that you can analyze it in more detail later.

Observation, and analyzing the resulting information, can consume a large amount of time. Therefore it is best done only for the development of large systems with which potential users will be performing complex tasks.

Interviewing

Interviewing is a widely used technique. However, a well-conducted series of interviews can elicit much more information than poorly planned ad-hoc interviews. Unfortunately, despite it being an important skill, software engineers are rarely trained in conducting interviews; the guidelines below should help you perform this important step effectively.

Firstly, plan to have as many members of the software engineering team interview as many stakeholders as possible. Consider going beyond stakeholders, talking to users of competing products, marketing personnel, and people involved with other systems that may interact in any way with the proposed system.

Spread out the interviews over time, and allow yourself several hours for each interview, even if you do not expect to use that much time. Time between interviews will allow you to analyze what you have heard and to think of additional questions. Leaving plenty of time ensures that if the interviewee is providing lots of information, you can let him or her continue. For the most important stakeholders you should hold a series of interviews, going into more depth each time. This allows your knowledge and analysis to improve in the intervening period.

Prepare an extensive list of questions, although do not be disappointed if there is not enough time to have them all answered in a given interview. Brainstorming, described in the next section, is an excellent technique to generate a list of questions. The following are some types of questions you should not forget:

- Ask about **specific details** such as maximums and minimums, whether there are any exceptions to rules and what possible changes might be anticipated. For example, if you are told that there are exactly seven levels of management in an organization, you should find out what they are, and you should also ask whether this number is likely to change (even if the user says no, never design a system that is inflexible about a detail like this). Journalists are taught to ask the five W's: who, what, when, where and why; this suggestion applies to requirements interviews as well.

- Ask about the stakeholder's **vision for the future**. This question may elicit innovative ideas and suggest what flexibility should be built into the system. Some of the visionary ideas may, in fact, be easy to implement and should be considered immediately – customers and users not familiar with technology may think only of computerizing existing processes and may believe that more extensive changes are unattainable.

- If a customer or user presents concrete ideas for their view of the system, ask if they have any **alternative ideas**, or ask how they would feel about alternative ideas you have. This will help ascertain how flexible they are.

- Ask what would be a **minimally acceptable** solution to the problem. In requirements gathering, you will usually obtain far too many ideas; it is important to realize what customers and users consider to be their very basic needs – the basic needs may be surprisingly few in number. Without this information you may produce expensive facilities that are not used, often called *shelfware*.

- Ask for **other sources of information**. The stakeholder you are interviewing may have interesting documents or may know someone with useful knowledge.

■ Have the interviewee draw **diagrams**. The diagrams could show such things as the flow of information, the chain of command, how some technology works, or practically anything. Diagrams can be a focal point to stimulate improved information gathering.

An interviewer should cultivate *listening skills* and *empathy* for users and customers. Empathy is the ability to reach into the mind of the interviewee and really feel what they are feeling. Listening skills include patiently absorbing what the interviewee is telling you, and then paraphrasing it back to them, seeking confirmation so as to avoid misconceptions. Having empathy improves listening, because you will often find that users are telling you facts that are surrounded by emotional issues having to do with work frustrations, office politics etc. You have to be able to show the user you understand their feelings, and at the same time you have to be able to extract the facts and real needs from them.

Interviewing can be intimidating for some people. Customers and users can behave in annoying ways. There also can be significant communications problems if the two parties have quite different backgrounds. In order to avoid frustration, you have to make clear your level of knowledge: if the interviewee is talking about complexities you do not understand, ask her to tell you the basics. If she is explaining things you already know, summarize your knowledge so that she does not feel she needs to repeat it.

Analysis should not take place at early interviews – they should be used primarily for information gathering. In particular, if the user starts dictating exactly what they want to see in the system, do not give him or her the impression that, yes, you will deliver it. Instead, point out that the ideas are important, but that you will have to analyze them and discuss them with others.

Following the interview process, you should summarize the information you have found and share it with all the stakeholders, along with a request for comments. Doing so may stimulate the stakeholders to give you additional ideas.

Exercise

E70 Divide up into groups of three. Initially, one person will be the interviewee, one person the interviewer, and the third person will observe the process. Each person should first imagine a problem they have for which they desire a software solution and present this to their group-mates. Each person then takes a problem statement from another group member and prepares to conduct an interview by composing a list of questions. Each member takes his or her turn as interviewer, practicing the interview techniques described above, and taking detailed notes as he or she proceeds. Each interview should last about 10 minutes. After each interview, the observer gives feedback to the interviewer about the effectiveness of the questions.

Brainstorming

Brainstorming is an effective way to gather information from a group of people. The general idea is that the group sits around a table and discusses some topic with the goal of generating ideas. However, as with interviews, adding some structure to the brainstorming process can help elicit a larger amount of information. One of the keys to success is arranging for the brainstorming session to be led, or *moderated*, by somebody trained in the process.

The following is a suggested approach to organizing and running an effective brainstorming session:

1. Call a meeting with representation from all stakeholders. Effective brainstorming sessions can be run with five to 20 people.

2. Appoint an experienced moderator (also known as a facilitator) – that is, someone who knows how to run brainstorming meetings, and will lead the process. The moderator may participate in the discussions if he or she wishes.

3. Arrange the attendees around the periphery of a table and give them plenty of paper to work with.

4. Decide on a 'trigger question'. This is a key step in the process. A trigger question is one for which the participants can provide simple one-line answers that are more than just numbers or yes/no responses.

   Examples of trigger questions include the following: What features are important in the system? What future sources of data should we anticipate? What outputs should be produced by the system? What classes do we need in our domain model? What interview questions should we ask? What issues have we not considered? What are the risks or difficulties in this project? What trigger questions can we ask?

   The trigger question can be determined by the person who called the meeting, by the moderator, by a quick discussion, or by brainstorming followed by a vote.

5. Ask each participant to follow these instructions:

   (a) Think of an answer to the trigger question, no matter how trivial or questionable the answer is!

   (b) Write the answer down in one or two lines on a sheet of paper, *one idea per sheet*.

   (c) Pass the paper to the neighbor on your left (i.e. clockwise) to stimulate his or her thoughts.

   (d) Look at the answers passed from your neighbor to the right and pass these on to your left as well. Use the ideas you have read to stimulate your own ideas.

6. Continue step 5 until ideas stop flowing or a fixed time (5–15 minutes) passes.

7. Moving around the table, ask everybody to read out one of the ideas on the sheets that happen to be in front of them. If anyone seeks an explanation, the originator of the idea may comment briefly (although he or she may choose not to say anything in order to remain anonymous). The moderator, or a secretary, writes each idea on a flip-chart. Then, optionally, the whole group may briefly discuss the idea.

8. After a fixed time period, or after all ideas have been recorded on the flip-chart, the group may take a series of votes to prioritize them. For example, every person may be given a fixed number of votes that they can allocate to the answers they think are the most important.

The concept of passing ideas clockwise round the table is illustrated in Figure 4.5.

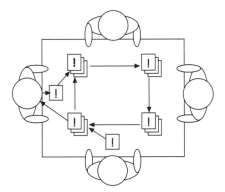

Figure 4.5   Phase 5 of structured brainstorming: passing ideas around the table to stimulate new ideas

The main advantage of brainstorming is that in a moderated group session, people are energized and tend to spontaneously invent many good ideas, stimulated by what others have said. There are two advantages of using a *structured* approach as described above. First, introverted or timid people can have their say effectively since anonymity can be assured. Sometimes, such people think their ideas are not very good because they lack self-confidence. Second, a lot of thinking goes on in parallel: during the first phase, everybody is thinking of their own ideas and writing them down concurrently. The session is therefore more productive than if everybody had to wait their turn to express their ideas.

Exercise

E71   Divide into groups of 7 to 12 people. Each group should then elect a moderator and hold a brainstorming session for 20 minutes, following the procedures defined above. A possible trigger question might be: 'what requirements could

JAD sessions

Joint Application Development (JAD) is a technique related to brainstorming. In JAD, the developers meet with customers and users in a secluded location for a period of three to five days. The entire time is spent working together to define the requirements. Activities can include regular brainstorming, and negotiation of specific wording. The participants can work together as one large group, or can divide up into smaller groups to work on specific issues. The final output should be a written requirements document.

An important rule is that nobody should be interrupted by any other activity; therefore JAD sessions must not be held near the offices of any of the participants. The participants often travel to a special location and stay in a hotel, as if going to a conference. Activities can take place in the evenings as well as in regular working hours.

The energy generated by intense JAD sessions can often shorten the period required to work out the requirements from several months to several days.

be implemented in the SimpleChat system, or some other system the group is developing?'

Prototyping

A prototype is a program that is rapidly implemented and contains only a small part of the anticipated functionality of a complete system. Its purpose is to gather requirements by allowing software engineers to obtain early feedback about their ideas.

The simplest kind of prototype is a *paper prototype* of the user interface. This is a set of pictures of the system that are shown to customers and users in sequence, to explain what would happen when the system runs. It can often be a very powerful tool for eliciting ideas and feedback, and requires very little effort to create.

Because paper prototypes are easy to create, they are ideal for *parallel development*. In parallel development, several software engineers independently create their own view of the system – the resulting prototypes are then evaluated and the best features of each become part of the system's requirements. It is possible to carry parallel development further than a paper prototype, but that takes more work.

The most common type of prototype is a 'mock-up' of the system's user interface, created using a *rapid prototyping language*. Rapid prototyping languages allows you to create code very quickly in order to display the important parts of a user interface; however, they have various weaknesses that limit their usefulness for creating the final version of complex systems. The weaknesses include inefficiency, and limitations on your ability to create robust and flexible designs.

Users can sometimes make actual use of a rapid prototype; however, there is often nothing much behind the user interface – it may not, for example, perform any computations, access any databases or interact with any other systems. You should modify a rapid prototype as many times as necessary in response to feedback from users. However, you will not have put effort into designing its architecture, therefore it will become hard to maintain, and will contain many bugs. Because of this you should not normally turn it directly into the final system; it should be used only as a requirements gathering tool.

In addition to prototyping the user interface, you may sometimes choose to prototype other aspects of a system, such as an algorithm or a database. As with all prototypes, the intent is to test and validate existing ideas, as well as to generate new ideas.

4.8   Types of requirements document

To perform good software engineering, it is always appropriate to write down requirements. The level of detail of the requirements can, however, vary significantly from project to project. At one extreme, there are documents that informally outline the requirements using a few paragraphs or simple diagrams. At the other extreme, there are specifications that contain thousands of pages of intricate detail. Unfortunately developers often err towards either extreme. Choosing the right level of detail requires careful balancing because too little detail can result in a system that does not adequately solve the problem, whereas too much detail can be a waste of time and can make the development process too inflexible.

Frequently, you have to produce several requirements documents, each describing a different part of the system or a different level of detail. When doing this, your strategy should be to make them all *complementary*. Each should refer to other documents as necessary, but there should not be redundancy between the documents. Redundancy leads to contradictions when changes are made in one place but not another.

Agile approaches to requirements

In agile development approaches you do not develop large requirements documents. Instead, two approaches are employed: *user stories* and *test-first development*.

A user story is similar to a use case, but has a looser structure; it describes some proposed software feature from the perspective of how the user will use it and should be limited to about three sentences. Development proceeds by choosing a very small number of user stories to implement in the next iteration. Ideally each iteration will take only a few days to develop.

The first stage of development in many agile approaches is to first develop test cases (discussed in Chapter 10). The series of test cases becomes the detailed specification of how a user story should be implemented.

Requirements documents for large systems are normally arranged in a hierarchy. There is a top-level document describing the overall system, its subsystems and how the subsystems interact. Then there are separate documents describing each subsystem, and sometimes each sub-subsystem. When we talk about 'the system', we are referring to whatever the current development team is working on, which may be a subsystem or a larger system. This notion of a hierarchy of requirements documents is illustrated in Figure 4.6.

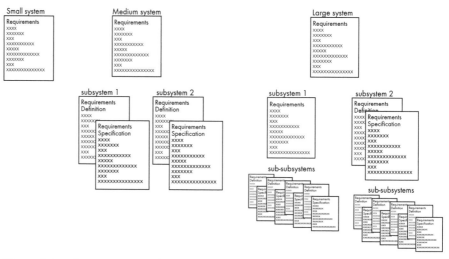

Figure 4.6   Hierarchies of requirements documents

How do you decide what type of document to produce and how much detail should be provided? The following factors can guide you as you make this decision:

■ **The size of the system**. A large system will need more detailed requirements for several reasons. First, there is simply more to say. Second, the system will need to be divided into subsystems so that different teams can work on each part – it then becomes essential that everybody have a clear idea of what everybody else is doing, and how the subsystems interconnect.

■ **The need to interface to other systems**. Even a small system will need to have well-described requirements if other systems or subsystems are going to use its services or communicate with it. For example, as discussed in the previous chapter, you have to specify the protocol with which clients and servers communicate, otherwise you will never be able to get them to work together.

■ **The target audience**. The requirements must be written at a high-enough level so that the potential users can read them. If the system is intended for the general population, it should omit jargon that would be understood by only a few people. On the other hand, the system might be intended for users with specific scientific or engineering backgrounds, in which case technical details from their domain can appear. Only if the system is strictly intended for use exclusively by other software engineers (perhaps it is a framework, or a class library) is it reasonable to include details down to the level of algorithms, data structures and procedures. Normally such a level of detail would only be found in a design document; however, in certain types of utility packages the distinction between requirements and design can become blurred.

■ **The contractual arrangements for development**. If you are arranging a contract by which a third party will develop software for you, then you will have to specify the requirements with considerable precision. Similarly, if you are developing requirements under contract, for a military client, for example, then you will have to follow specific rules regarding the format and detail to be provided.

■ **The stage in requirements gathering**. At an early stage in requirements gathering, it is important *not* to write large volumes of precise and detailed requirements – the risk that these will have to be completely rewritten is too great. An outline describing a system or subsystem in a few paragraphs or pages may be best at this stage. Once all the stakeholders agree with a short, informal statement of requirements, successive levels of detail can be added. Often it is best to develop a rough prototype, based on a very short statement of requirements, as the first iteration of a system. You should then experiment with the prototype, learning a lot of information about what is good and bad about it. You can then add more detail to the requirements as you develop the next iteration, which may be a more advanced prototype or a formal release of a polished system. You should think of this process of repeatedly prototyping as an integral part of the requirements gathering process.

■ **The level of experience with the domain and the technology**. If you are developing software in a well-known domain and using well-known technology, then you should be able to produce a complete requirements document before starting to design the system. However, if you are developing innovative software, then more caution is needed. You should certainly develop prototypes based on rough requirements to check out the validity of your ideas or the reliability of the technology. By technology, we mean such things as new programming languages, class libraries, frameworks, algorithms, hardware, databases or third-party software with which you will be interfacing.

■ **The cost incurred if the requirements are faulty**. Any system that, if it fails, could jeopardize safety or the environment must be precisely specified. Furthermore, those specifications should be subjected to rigorous analysis and review. Examples of such critical systems include those that control industrial processes, vehicles, telecommunications networks, medical equipment and many consumer devices. The safety risk involved with nuclear plants and automobiles is clear. Telecommunications networks failures can also pose a safety risk if people rely on them during emergencies. Software failures in consumer devices such as garage door openers or washing machines could lead to injury, fires or floods, not to mention severe financial penalties resulting from litigation. In addition to safety risks, some types of software failures can lead to extensive economic damage. A famous example is software that would not have operated in the year 2000 had it not been fixed – the requirements for software written in the 20th century should have specified 4-digit dates, instead of 2-digit dates.

As software evolves, requirements documents are often written describing incremental changes such as new *features* to be added to an existing system. Doing this repeatedly can cause maintenance difficulties. This is because, after a while, understanding the entire system will require reading the original requirements, which are now out of date, plus the requirements for all of the successive changes. To combat this problem, it is normally a good idea, when making changes, to update a document that describes general requirements for the entire system.

Requirements documents are given different names in different organizations. The term *requirements definition* normally refers to a less detailed, higher-level document, whereas the term *requirements specification* normally refers to a more detailed and precise document. You should, however, avoid being overly concerned about the precise names used for documents and follow the convention used in your company.

Exercise

E72 For each of the following systems, describe the kind of requirements documentation you think should be produced. Indicate the overall level of detail that should be provided, whether iterative refinement would be warranted, and whether a hierarchy of subsystem requirements would be a good idea. Justify your answers.

(a) Software controlling a manned spacecraft being sent to Mars.

(b) Software for managing the payroll at a large company.

(c) Software for the 'asteroids' computer game to be embedded in a cellular telephone.

(d) Software to find all the occurrences of a certain word or phrase in email you have sent or received.

4.9 Reviewing requirements

When developing requirements, software engineers should adhere to the guidelines listed below. Most of the guidelines apply to prototypes as

> **Design before requirements?**
> For a large system, you have to break it down into subsystems, and then develop requirements for each subsystem. This process of subdividing the system is part of *software architecture* – a design activity we will discuss in Chapter 9. This means that some aspects of design have to be interspersed among the requirements activities. The important thing to remember is to do the highest level of requirements analysis first.

well as to informal and formal requirements documents. Early prototypes or drafts of requirements should be reviewed by the author and stakeholders, and there may need to be several cycles of improvements and repeated review.

The review process normally culminates with a formal requirements review meeting at which all stakeholders are present. The stakeholders should have received the document well in advance in order for them to have read it. Ideally, most of the problems should have been eliminated by reviews of earlier drafts or prototypes, so that the formal review should not raise major controversies. However, if extensive changes are identified, then a further formal review may be needed once the changes are made.

Each individual requirement should be carefully reviewed. In order to be acceptable, a requirement should:

1. **Have benefits that outweigh the costs of development**. Cost–benefit analysis is an important skill in software engineering. You sum, in financial terms, the benefits of the requirement (such as improvements in productivity or sales) and compare this to the sum of the costs (development cost, hardware needed for users, training users, and ongoing maintenance, for example). Cost–benefit analysis can be performed with considerable attention to detail; however, a very rough estimate can often quickly show that a requirement will provide only a minimal benefit, but cost substantially more than this to develop. Such requirements should be immediately cut. In Chapter 11, we will discuss cost–benefit analysis in more detail and provide an example.

2. **Be important for the solution of the current problem**. Many ideas might be useful to implement, and might have benefits that outweigh their costs; unfortunately you have to ruthlessly weed out the less important ideas in order to reduce the total time required to develop the system, and to reduce risks by keeping the software from becoming overly complex. The less important ideas can be deferred for future consideration.

   One of the most important rules in software engineering is the 80–20 rule, which says that 80% of the user's problem can often be solved with 20% of the work. You should initially consider producing only that first 20% of the system. The 80–20 rule is also called the *Pareto principle*.

   Building a list of requirements that does more than needed is sometimes called 'gold-plating' or building a 'Cadillac system'.

3. **Be expressed using a clear and consistent notation**. Each requirement should be expressed using language that the customers can understand and should be consistent with the other requirements. Requirements are normally expressed in a natural language such as English, sometimes supplemented by a formal mathematical language, and often by some form of diagram. Whichever format is used, consistent style should be applied throughout the requirements document. We suggest that English sentences should use present tense, active voice, and express what the system is to do in response to various inputs. For example, rather than write: 'The pharmacist will enter the patient ID number and then the patient's

medication record will be displayed', write: 'When the pharmacist enters the patient ID number, the system displays the patient's medication record.'

4. **Be unambiguous**. It is typical to find that an English sentence can have more than one interpretation.

Often this is because words have several closely related meanings. For example, the following requirement has two ambiguities: 'When the user selects an aircraft, the system assigns it to the flight.' The first ambiguity has to do with the word 'aircraft': does this mean a specific plane, or does it mean a class of aircraft (e.g. Boeing 747s)? Secondly, what does the word 'flight' mean? Is the aircraft being assigned just for a particular day's departure, or is it being assigned in general to a flight number that departs every day at the same time?

5. **Be logically consistent**. You should check consistency with any standards, with other requirements in the document, with higher-level requirements and with the requirements for other subsystems. In a large system, it can be very hard to be sure that a requirement does not contradict some other requirement in some subtle way. In fact, considerable research effort is spent finding ways to automatically check requirements documents for consistency. However, since such tools require the document to be written using a mathematical language, and do not yet work very well for large systems, careful proofreading is the main way to proceed.

One of the most important ways to help ensure consistency is to avoid duplicating requirements. It is very common, for example, for a requirement to be stated in the introduction to a document, and then repeated in more detail in the body of the document. This is dangerous because if a change is made in one place, there is a tendency to forget to make the change in the other place. For this reason, the introductions and conclusions of requirements documents should not actually contain any requirements.

Another aspect of consistency is consistency of the functional requirements with the non-functional requirements and with the project plan. These are addressed in the next two points.

6. **Lead to a system of sufficient quality**. A requirement should contribute to a system that is sufficiently usable, safe, efficient, reliable and maintainable. It takes a good deal of expertise to judge whether requirements meet these needs – special analysis techniques can also be applied that we will not discuss in detail in this book. For example, to assess the safety of a critical system, formal mathematical proof techniques may be employed. To assess usability, the requirements can be validated against a checklist of good user interface design principles. As we will discuss in Chapter 7, to fully validate a system's usability you have to observe users actually working with a prototype.

7. **Be realistic with available resources**. A requirement is realistic if the development team has the expertise and technology to implement it on the required platform within the budget and time available. If there is any doubt about whether a requirement is realistic, further analysis is required. For example, if there is uncertainty about whether an efficient algorithm can be found to perform some computation, then experimental prototypes should be developed and tested before committing to make the computation a requirement.

8. **Be verifiable**. The requirements document will not only be the basis for a system's design, but also for testing the system. There must be some way that the system can be tested so as to clearly conclude whether or not the requirement has been correctly implemented. As we mentioned earlier, this issue is mostly a concern for quality and platform requirements. For example: 'the search result must be obtained rapidly' is not verifiable because it is too vague; readers will wonder what 'rapidly' means. A better requirement would be 'the first results of the search must appear in less than 1 second on average, and in less than 3 seconds 95% of the time.'

9. **Be uniquely identifiable**. It is important to be able to refer to each individual requirement. This is necessary in requirements review meetings so that people can indicate which requirement they want to discuss. It is also necessary in design documents to be able to say which requirement is being implemented by a given aspect of the design, a quality called *traceability* illustrated in Figure 4.7. The first step in making requirements identifiable is avoiding long paragraphs; ideally, each requirement should start a new paragraph. In some documents, each requirement is given a unique number – sometimes a hierarchical scheme is used, e.g. 4.7.12.3 means the third requirement in section 4.7.12. Numbering every single point makes the document cluttered, however, and leaving off the final number, and requiring people to count a small number of paragraphs, is often acceptable.

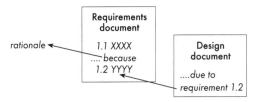

Figure 4.7   Providing traceability by giving justification for what is written, either as pointers to requirements or as rationale

10. **Not over-constrain the design of the system**. As we have mentioned before, a requirement should avoid indicating how it will be implemented, in order to give the designer as much freedom as possible to make decisions.

In addition to the above ten guidelines for individual requirements, there are several guidelines for requirements document as a whole:

11. **The document should be sufficiently complete**. We already discussed how a document could either give a high-level overview or be more detailed. However, at the chosen level of granularity, it should cover all of the functionality of the system or subsystem. It should also include all appropriate quality, platform and process requirements.

12. **The document should be well organized**. In particular, it should be carefully designed so that its structure can be easily understood; it can be quickly scanned, and any given requirement can be easily found. This means giving it a clear title and dividing it into sections with meaningful headings and subheadings.

13. **Reasoning should be clear**. Rationale should be provided for all requirements that involve a large amount of analysis, that are controversial or for which several alternatives are considered. Providing rationale serves several functions: it reduces the need for software engineers in the future to have to repeat your analysis when they make changes; it convinces the reader that you did in fact consider the alternatives; and it alerts the reader to the fact that the requirement may be controversial. Rationale provides traceability of the requirements to their justifications, as shown in Figure 4.7.

14. **The document should be agreed to by all the stakeholders**. Requirements should only be considered definitive when all the stakeholders agree they are to be implemented. The process of negotiation might result in trade-offs being made – a group of stakeholders may agree to a certain requirement only if a change is made to some other requirement. For example, one group may want to run the software on older computers. They may only agree to constrain the software to run only on new, fast computers if a web interface is added so that they can still see the output on their older computers.

We suggest that a complete requirements document should have sections covering the following types of information. Add a table of contents and an automatically generated index if the document is more than a few pages.

A. **Problem**. Provide a succinct description of the problem the system is solving.

B. **Background information**. Give information that will help readers understand the requirements. It should contain references to domain analysis documents, standards, and the requirements of related subsystems. In this section you can also discuss important issues you considered, and the rationale for your decisions (you can also place such rationale directly in sections D and E as long as those sections do not become cluttered with lengthy discussion).

C. **Environment and system models**. Provide the context in which the system runs and a global overview of the system or subsystem. Diagrams are very useful here. You should describe the hardware on which the system will run, and any other subsystems or software with which it will interact.

D. **Functional requirements**. As discussed earlier, describe the services provided to the user and to other systems. Describe inputs, outputs, computations and timing. Diagrams can again be useful.

E. **Quality, platform and process requirements**. As discussed earlier, describe any constraints that must be imposed on the design of the system.

Example 4.15   *Review the following short statement of functional requirements, pointing out any problems you find.*
*   **Requirements for a restaurant advisor system**. This system will allow people to choose a restaurant in a city. Users enter one or more of the following criteria, and then the system searches its database for suitable restaurants: food type, price range, neighborhood, size, service type (fast food, cafeteria, buffet, full service), smoking arrangements (none allowed, separately ventilated section, non-separately-ventilated section, allowed on outdoor patio only). The user can also specify a desired day and time-period, and the number of people in their party. The system will tap into the reservation database (of participating restaurants) and only display restaurants that have available space. After entering the criteria, the user clicks on 'search', and the system displays a list of matching restaurants. For restaurants that participate in the automated reservation system, the user can click on 'reserve' next to a selection in order to make a reservation.*

Some of the problems with the above requirements:

(i) Duplication of 'the system searches for suitable restaurants'/'the system displays matching restaurants'.

(ii) 'Food type', 'price range', 'neighborhood' and 'size' are inadequately defined. Are these taken from a fixed set of values, or does the database just contain free-form information? It will be hard for the user to search unless the values of these items are standardized.

(iii) There is ambiguity regarding the 'reservation database' and the 'automated reservation system'. Are these the same thing or not?

(iv) It appears that some of the listed restaurants are not in the reservation system/database. If the user specifies the desired day and time-period, and the number of people in the party, what does the system do with restaurants that are not 'participating'? Are they omitted from the list?

(v) Can the user select just one option or more than one option for 'type of food'? The same question applies to 'smoking arrangements' (the user may not care).

(vi) If the user selects 'reserve', there must presumably be some way for the system to record identifying information about the user, so that the restaurant knows who made the reservation. This is omitted.

It should be noted that the document was called a 'short statement of functional requirements', therefore we will hesitate to criticize the fact that it lacks quality requirements and rationale, or that it is just one large paragraph. However, its writers should take care of these matters as they add more detail for the next iteration.

Exercises

E73 The following are short statements of functional requirements for software applications. Review each of them, listing as many problems as you can. Justify your answers by referring to the guidelines. (This exercise is particularly effective when done in groups of two or three.)

(a) **Simple interest calculation program**. This is a handy utility for users who are considering borrowing or lending money. A window pops up when the program starts. This has three fields entitled: 'Principal:', 'Annual interest rate:' and 'Monthly interest payment:'. Whenever the user edits one of the fields the other two fields are automatically computed.

(b) **Dispatcher automation system**. This system helps speed up the process of ambulance dispatching. When an emergency call is received, an automated voice recognition system classifies the case into categories depending on the level of emergency. All urgent cases are transmitted to the ambulance dispatcher, who will receive the patient's record, a summary of the conversation with the operator, as well as the patient's address and medical details if known. The dispatcher uses the system to obtain the number of the closest available ambulance. The ambulance operator receives all the information about the case.

(c) **Inventory recording system**. This system runs on dedicated computers at the shipping and receiving gate of a warehouse. It is used by all warehouse staff. Whenever an item enters or leaves the warehouse, a staff member must record that fact in the system.

A window is always visible on the screen to record items entering the warehouse. This window has three fields, labeled 'Product code', 'Number' and 'Description'. Below these fields is an 'OK' key. To process an item, the staff member simply has to enter the product id and click 'OK', or press the 'return' key. The 'Number' field defaults to one.

If the clerk does not enter a product id, a dialog box appears with a list of valid product ids and their descriptions; the staff member selects a code from this list. The staff member can also type a description to add a product code.

When the item is successfully entered, the system prints out a sticker with a barcode on it. The staff member attaches the sticker to the item, and stores it in the warehouse. The system then clears the fields in the window so as to be ready to record the next item.

To remove an item from the warehouse, the staff member simply swipes the item's sticker past a barcode reader. The system then records that the item has been removed.

E74 Rewrite each of the statements of functional requirements in Exercise E73, solving each of the problems you found. Since you will have to add missing information, your requirements will become substantially longer and take the form of a requirements definition document. Therefore, pay attention to the organization of the document and follow the format and guidelines discussed in this section. We have provided example requirements documents in Sections 4.11 and 4.12 that you can use as templates.

E75 Review the functional requirements for the microwave oven system of Example 4.6, listing as many potential problems as you can.

E76 Review the requirements you wrote in Exercises E57 and E61.

4.10 Managing changing requirements

One of the most important things to realize about requirements is that they change. Just because you have written a requirements document, and have obtained approval of it by all the stakeholders, does not mean that you can confidently design and implement the system as specified. By the time the system is delivered, the users' and customers' needs will likely have evolved so that the requirements as documented no longer completely solve the customers' problem.

The following are some of the changes to anticipate:

■ **Business process changes**. Businesses regularly adjust the way they do things in order to better compete in the market or merely because they gain experience and decide that an alternative approach is better. Changes to business processes can also be prompted by such things as changes in laws, as well as growth or rearrangement of the company.

■ **Technology changes**. A new release of the operating system, or some other system with which your system interacts, may force you to reassess the requirements.

■ **Better understanding of the problem**. Even though everybody might be confident about the requirements when they are first approved, various stakeholders may discover problems when looking at them again several months later.

How do you measure requirements?

It is very important to be able to estimate the time it will take to develop a system as early as possible. Once one has developed requirements, it becomes possible to estimate size using a set of techniques called Function Point counting. We will discuss this and other cost estimation techniques briefly in Chapter 11.

Requirements analysis should therefore never really stop. The development team should continue to interact with the customers and users, asking them about their problems and their ideas and showing them prototypes of the system. Changes to the requirements should be made whenever the benefits of doing so outweigh the costs. Certain small changes, especially to the look and feel of the user interface, are usually quick and easy to make at relatively little cost. More large-scale changes have to be carefully assessed: forcing unexpected changes into a partially built system over and over again will probably result in a poor design and late delivery. On the other hand, the software that is delivered has to be useful. It is difficult to strike the right balance, but usually it is better to reject the more complex but less important requirements changes so as to not delay development excessively.

When dealing with changes to requirements it is very important to avoid *requirements creep*. This is what occurs when the changes are really enhancements in disguise. Remember we discussed earlier the importance of delivering the smallest possible system in the first release, minimally solving the customer's problem. Any changes to the requirements should if possible avoid making the system *bigger*, and they should only make it *better* if the benefits exceed the costs. Requirements creep has resulted in very significant cost overruns in projects – it is just too tempting to add a few new features to make customers happy. Unfortunately, 'a few new features' are often time-consuming to develop – so leave them to a future release.

A final aspect of managing requirements is keeping track of the different versions of requirements documents. Each time you change requirements, you should give the document a new version number. The changes in each new version should be highlighted to the reader using change bars (vertical bars shown in the margin of a page). You should also use some kind of archiving or configuration management system that stores older versions of documents. It can sometimes be important to be able to go back and look at decisions that were previously made, but subsequently changed.

4.11 GPS-based Automobile Navigation Assistant (GANA)

The following example requirements document is for an embedded system that will be installed in special-purpose hardware in cars.

Requirements for GANA software

A. **Problem**. GANA software will help drivers navigate by giving them directions to their destination.

B. **Background information**. See domain analysis document 1234 (not provided in this book).

C. **Environment and system models**. GANA software is to run on special GANA hardware, described separately in document 1234. As described in document 1234, the hardware provides the following to the software: a) GPS position information, b) a wireless Internet connection to a map database, c) position of a trackball, d) a color 10 cm by 10 cm LCD screen, e) six buttons at the bottom of the screen, and f) input from the car's other systems containing data about speed and turning of the steering wheel. This requirements document describes the software only.

D. **Functional requirements**.

1. The system uses GPS information to calculate which map to display. The system also integrates information about the car's speed and history of turns made in order to refine its accuracy about the vehicle's location.

2. The system has two main interaction modes: in *setup mode*, the user consults maps and specifies the destination; in *navigation mode*, the system assists the user to navigate to the destination.

3. **Setup mode**
   3.1 When the system is switched on, and the vehicle is stationary, it enters setup mode. If the vehicle is moving, the system enters navigation mode. For safety reasons the system cannot enter setup mode when the vehicle is moving.
   3.2 In setup mode, the system displays a map. The default map is in 1:25000 scale and is centered on the user's current position. At this scale, the map covers a square with 2.5 km sides (6.25 km^2). Maps are oriented so that true north is at the top.
   3.3 When the user's current position is within the visible part of the map, the system always indicates it with a red arrow. The arrow points in the direction the user is heading.
   3.4 The system also displays in orange (computed in real time) the shortest route (in estimated travel time) from the current position to the center of the map. It will not be possible to display the entire route if the current position is not displayed.
   3.5 When the user manipulates the trackball, the screen scrolls the map in the direction of rotation of the trackball, as if the user were grabbing the map.
   3.6 The LCD screen displays the labels 'Zoom Out', 'Zoom In', 'Go Current', 'Go Destination', 'Set Destination' and 'Navigate' above the six buttons (from left to right). The buttons work as follows:

   ❏ 'Zoom In' and 'Zoom Out' display new maps. The scale of the map appears at the top right of the screen. There may be a delay retrieving a map, in which case the system displays the message

'Retrieving map'. If the map or network is unavailable for any reason, the system displays: 'Sorry, map not available' near the top of the screen and continues to display the previous map.

❏ When the user presses 'Zoom In', the map scale is doubled so that a smaller region is displayed, with more local detail. The maximum scale is 1:3125 which means that the map covers an area with 312.5 m sides (about 100,000 m^2). If this scale is displayed, the 'Zoom In' button is inoperative and its label appears in light gray.

❏ When the user presses 'Zoom Out', the map scale is divided by 2 so that a larger region is displayed, with less local detail. The minimum scale is 1:102,400,000 which means that the map covers an area with sides of approximately 10,000 km (about 108 km^2 or enough to display entire continents). If this scale is displayed, the 'Zoom Out' button is inoperative and its label appears in light gray. Note that the scales are only approximate due to spherical aberration.

❏ When the user presses 'Set Destination', the location at the center of the screen (marked by the end of the orange route) is set as the destination. The shortest route from the current position to the destination is highlighted in red and is adjusted as the car moves.

❏ The shortest route to the set destination (red) is shown on top of the shortest route to the center of the screen (orange), and hence has precedence.

❏ When the user presses 'Go Current', the map jumps so that it is centered over the current location.

❏ When the user presses 'Go Destination', the map jumps so that it is centered over the destination. If no destination has been set, the destination defaults to the current location.

❏ When the user presses 'Navigate' or the vehicle starts moving, the system enters navigation mode described below.

4. **Navigation mode**

4.1 A detailed map is never displayed in navigation mode since the user would not be able to concentrate on driving while looking at the map.

4.2 If no destination has been set, the system just displays the name of the current highway or street and municipality in large type.

4.3 In addition, if a destination has been set, the system displays the following in as large a size as possible:

❏ An arrow pointing up if the driver should drive straight ahead, a left arrow if the driver should turn left, a right arrow if the driver should turn right and a U-turn symbol of the driver should turn around.

❑ A sentence describing what the user should do, in the following format: 'Turn <turning direction> at <turning landmark>, and head <heading direction> on <road identification> towards <next landmark>'. For example: 'Turn left at exit 25 and head north on highway 33 towards Newton'. The system computes the turning direction, turning landmark, heading direction, road identification, and the next landmark when these are available.

❑ The destination municipality (or address, if already within the municipality), the distance remaining, the expected time remaining and the expected arrival time.

4.4 The turning arrows and instructions are displayed as soon as possible, as long as they cannot be interpreted ambiguously. A left turn arrow, for example, would only appear when the driver must take the *next* left turn.

4.5 The system displays the labels 'Speak Now', 'Volume Up', 'Volume Down', 'Guide On', 'Guide Off' and 'Setup' above the six buttons (from left to right). The buttons work as follows:

❑ 'Speak Now' produces a computer-generated voice, reading the instructions that are on display. Every time the user presses the button, any reading in progress is canceled and the instructions are immediately read again starting from the beginning.

❑ 'Volume Up' and 'Volume Down' adjust sound output.

❑ 'Guide On' causes a computer-generated voice to automatically read the instructions one minute in advance of any required driver action, such as exiting the highway, being needed. 'Guide Off' cancels this function; the user would have to read the screen or press 'Speak Now'. In situations where navigational action is required more frequently than once a minute, the voice reads the next instruction as soon as the system detects that the driver has responded to the previous instruction.

❑ 'Setup' switches to setup mode if the car is stationary. If the car is not stationary, the 'Setup' button is grayed out and is inactive.

4.6 If the driver does not respond as expected to the instructions, and takes a different route, the system immediately calculates a new route.

E. **Quality requirements**.

1. The system will be robust in the case of failure of the Internet connection or failure to receive the GPS signal, maintaining whatever service it can.

2. The system will be designed in a flexible way such that changes in wireless Internet or GPS technology can be incorporated in future releases.

3. The system will be designed anticipating incorporation of input from an inertial navigation unit that would take over in cases where GPS signals fail.

Exercise

E77 Perform a requirements review of the GANA system described in this section.

4.12 Requirements for a feature of the SimpleChat instant messaging program

A. **Problem**. Sometimes a user wants to prevent messages received by a given client from appearing on his or her screen. This might be because the client's user is being deliberately annoying, or because the client's user is sending lots of public messages that are useful to other users but are not useful to the current user.

We therefore wish to add a facility to SimpleChat that will allow a given user to block messages coming from another specified user.

B. **Background information**. See the requirements for SimpleChat Phase 2 (exercises E49–E51 starting on page 104) for the system on which these requirements are based. The features described in these requirements are part of Phase 3.

Issues considered:

Issue 1: Can the user block more than one other user at a time?

Decision: *Yes; however, he or she will have to issue a sequence of block commands.*

Issue 2: The user needs some way of finding out if he or she has any blocking in progress, otherwise the user might forget that he or she had earlier established blocking.

Decision: *Add a command called* #whoiblock *that will list those clients I am blocking.*

Issue 3: It would be useful for a user to know if anyone is blocking messages that come from him or her.

Decision: *Add a command called* #whoblocksme *that will do this.*

Issue 4: Should the server be able to block messages?

Option 4.1: Do not allow the server to block messages.

Advantage: This would be simpler.

Option 4.2: The server should be able to block ordinary messages from clients, but not administrative messages such as #forward etc.

Advantage: This would prevent a malicious user from overwhelming the server's display.

Decision: *Choose option 4.2.*

Issue 5:   What types of messages should the user be able to block?

Option 5.1:   Block only private messages, but not public or channel messages.

Advantages: The user can always avoid public or channel messages by changing channel.

Disadvantages: Forcing the user to change channel is not really satisfactory – what if the user is interested in other messages on that channel?

Option 5.2:   Block private, public and channel messages.

Decision: *Choose option 5.2.*

Issue 6:   How should this feature interact with forwarding? The problem: imagine we have clients A, B and C, with A set to forward all messages to B.

Scenario 6.1: A blocks messages from C: should a message from C to A be forwarded to B as normal, or should it be blocked?

Decision: *Blocked.*

Scenario 6.2: B blocks messages from C (but A does not): should a message from C to A be forwarded to B, or should it be blocked?

Decision: *Blocked.*

Scenario 6.3: B blocks messages from A (even though A has forwarded incoming messages to B).

Option 6.3.1: Do not allow the blocking. However, this could be very annoying for B; after all, it is not B that requested the forwarding. Maybe the forwarding is just another harassment tactic of A.

Option 6.3.2: Allow the blocking but continue allowing forwarding. The problem with this is that the forwarding effectively allows A to circumvent B's block.

Option 6.3.3: Cancel the forwarding and establish a block.

Decision: *Choose option 6.3.3.*

Issue 7:   Does it make sense to block messages from myself?

Decision: *No.*

Issue 8:   Can a user block messages from the server?

Decision: *Yes.*

Issue 9:   How does a user unblock messages?

Decision: *The #unblock command with no arguments will cancel all blocking that a user has set up. The #unblock command with an argument will cancel blocking for messages from that user only.*

Issue 10: Any user could circumvent blocking by logging in using a different login ID (and automatically creating a password for the new login ID).

Option 10.1: Stop allowing users to create their own login IDs.

Advantages: Would solve this problem.

Disadvantages: Would make the system less useful in a chat environment.

Option 10.2: Status quo. Live with this problem.

Decision: *Choose option 10.2.*

Issue 11: Should it be possible to block users who are not even logged on; and should a block persist even if the blocked user logs off and logs on again?

Decision: *Yes, to both questions, because otherwise a user could circumvent the blocking by logging off and on.*

Issue 12: Should a block persist even if the blocking user logs off and logs on again?

Decision: *No. For simplicity, we require a user to re-establish any blocks that he or she desires.*

C. **Environment and system models**. This feature is to be added to Phase 3 of SimpleChat, at the same time as the forwarding and channels features are added (see the project exercises at the end of the chapter). There are no additional environmental considerations for these requirements.

D. **Functional requirements**:

1. General (applies to client and server alike)

   ❏ Commands. Each of these can be issued from the user interface of the client or server. If issued from the client UI they will be transmitted to the server unchanged.

   `#block <user>`

   ❏ Initiate blocking for any user named `<user>`, except self.

   ❏ Works whether `<user>` is connected or not.

   ❏ Displays a message on the originating UI that states:
   `Messages from <user> will be blocked.`

   ❏ An attempt to block messages to self will cause the following message to be displayed:
   `You cannot block the sending of messages to yourself.`

   ❏ An attempt to block messages from a user that does not exist will result in the following message being displayed:
   `User <user> does not exist.`

❏ Any number of these commands can be issued to block a series of users.

❏ `server` is a valid user for this command.

`#unblock {<user>}`

❏ If an argument is specified, terminates blocking for messages from `<user>` that had previously been established by the `#block <user>` command.

❏ When successful, displays the following on the originating UI:
`Messages from <user> will now be displayed.`

❏ If `#unblock <user>` is issued with no preceding `#block <user>` for the same user, then displays the following:
`Messages from <user> were not blocked.`

❏ When issued with no argument:

1. Cancels any blocking in effect.

2. If blocking had been active, displays the following messages for each previously blocked user:
`Messages from <user> will now be displayed.`

❏ If no blocking had been in effect, displays:
`No blocking is in effect.`

❏ `server` is a valid user for this command.

`#whoiblock`

❏ For each user for which this user has issued a `#block <user>` command, displays the following message:
`Messages from <user> are blocked`

❏ If no users are blocked, then displays:
`No blocking is in effect.`

`#whoblocksme`

❏ For each user that is blocking messages from this user, displays the message:
`Messages to <user> are being blocked.`

2. Operation:

2.1 If X blocks messages from Y, this has the following effects, irrespective of whether X or Y is client or server:

❏ Any simple message sent by Y will not reach X.

❏ Any **#private** X message sent by Y will not reach X.

❏ When Y issues the **#private** X command the following is displayed:
`Cannot send message because X is blocking messages from you.`

❏ If Y attempts to forward to X, using **#forward** X, the forwarding attempt will be rejected and the following message will be displayed:
`Cannot forward to X because X is blocking messages from you.`

❏ If Y is already forwarding to X, when the block is established, then forwarding will be terminated and the following messages will be displayed:

   ❏ On X (in addition to the message confirming the establishment of blocking):
   `Forwarding of messages from Y to you has been terminated.`

   ❏ On Y:
   `Forwarding to X has been canceled because X is blocking messages from you.`

❏ Unless additional blocking is in effect, all other messages will be unaffected.

2.2 Blocking persists no matter whether the blocked user logs off or on. However, if the originator of the blocking logs off, the blocking is terminated.

E. **Other requirements.** There are no additional quality, platform or process requirements for this feature. All such requirements of the base system still apply.

Exercise

E78 Perform a requirements review of the requirements for the SimpleChat features described above.

4.13 Difficulties and risks in domain and requirements analysis

■ **Misunderstanding and lack of understanding of the domain or the real problem.** The software developers may make invalid assumptions and hence create poor requirements or designs. Even customers or users who are 'experts' in the domain may not possess the kind of knowledge that can be easily communicated to others, and they may define their problem too broadly or too narrowly.
Resolution. Make good use of domain analysis, prototyping and other requirements gathering techniques to help bring to light any misunderstandings, and to help clarify the real problem.

■ **Requirements can change rapidly, resulting in requirements 'churn'.**
Requirements always change, and the rate of change is almost by definition
unpredictable. For example, if the requirements are dictated by the open
market, then the launch of competing products might necessitate changing the
requirements to stay competitive. Changes in requirements can result in
completed work being wasted, and can result in a deteriorating design if the
original design did not adequately anticipate the changes.
*Resolution. Use an incremental approach to development, build flexibility into the
design, regularly review the requirements and prototypes with the stakeholders,
and, above all, always respect the inevitability of change.*

■ **Attempting to do too much.** This occurs when inadequate boundaries have
been placed on the problem or the solution, or when those boundaries are not
respected (resulting in requirements 'creep').
*Resolution. Use incremental development, and carefully document the problem
boundaries at an early stage. Carefully estimate the time any proposed
requirement will take, using techniques discussed in Chapter 11. Defer major
changes to subsequent releases if possible.*

■ **It may be hard to reconcile conflicting sets of requirements.** Different
stakeholders may have very different views about what should be developed.
*Resolution. Use brainstorming and JAD sessions to help different stakeholders see
other points of view. Create prototypes of the competing visions; when users
actually compare different prototypes, they may change their preferences.*

■ **It is hard to state requirements precisely.** Natural languages, such as English,
are full of ambiguity. Even though everybody thought they had agreed, when
the system is built one group of stakeholders may complain that the system
does not do what they had expected.
*Resolution. Break requirements down into simple sentences and review them
carefully, looking for potential ambiguity. Early prototypes can also highlight any
misunderstandings embedded in the requirements.*

4.14 Summary

In this chapter we have discussed in detail the process of developing
requirements. It is important to keep developing the requirements throughout
the life of a software system to ensure that they continue to solve the customers'
problems.

We first discussed domain analysis, which enables software engineers to learn
enough about the domain so that they can effectively communicate with the
stakeholders.

We discussed the types of requirements: functional requirements are what the
system will do, while quality, platform and process requirements constrain the
design.

Next we discussed pinning down a statement of the problem and defining the system's scope. Doing this helps ensure that subsequent work is focused and is less subject to requirements creep.

We looked at various techniques for gathering and analyzing requirements, including brainstorming, interviewing, prototyping and use case analysis. These should all be used together. A prototype, in particular, should be seen as a tool for eliciting requirements. The first system you develop will almost always be thrown away – it is better that you plan to throw away a prototype, rather than be forced to throw away a system that you have spent much time developing.

Finally, we gave some guidelines for reviewing requirements documents: the requirements should be written consistently and clearly, solve the customers' problem, be cost effective, realistic, verifiable and not over-constrain the design. It is also important to consider quality, platform and process requirements as well as functional requirements.

4.15 For more information

The following are some resources about requirements. Many of the general software engineering resources from Chapter 1 also contain useful information about requirements. Use cases are covered by many of the books on UML listed in Chapter 5.

Books

- R. R. Young, *The Requirements Engineering Handbook*, Artech House, 2003

- I. Graham and L. Graham, *Requirements Engineering and Rapid Development: An Object-Oriented Approach*, Addison-Wesley, 1998

- S. Robertson and J. Robertson, *Mastering the Requirements Process*, Addison-Wesley, 2000

- D. Kulak and E. Guiney, *Use Cases: Requirements in Context*, 2nd edition, Addison-Wesley, 2003

- R. Thayer, M. Dorfman and S. Bailin (eds.), *Software Requirements Engineering*, 2nd edition, IEEE CS Press, 1997

- G. Kotonya and I. Sommerville, *Requirements Engineering*, Wiley, 1998

Web site

- The Requirements Engineering Specialists Group of the British Computer Society: http://www.resg.org.uk which has links to many other web resources on requirements.

Standards

There are many standards covering software engineering – the existence of standards is an important part of what makes software engineering an engineering discipline. The following IEEE standards cover requirements engineering. Organizations that produce standards make money by selling them, so you cannot, therefore, easily find current ones on the web; however, your library may subscribe to them. You can find information about them at www.standards.ieee.org/software/index.html.

■ IEEE Standard 830, *Recommended Practice for Software Requirements Specifications*

■ IEEE Standard 1233, *Guide for Developing System Requirements Specifications*

Project exercises

In the following two exercises, you will develop some requirements for extensions to the SimpleChat System that you worked on in Chapter 3. Then you will implement the requirements and test the resulting system. By implementing your requirements, you will develop a 'feel' for what constitutes a clear or unclear requirement. We have already presented guidelines for blocking features – you should use the same format in the first exercise.

E79 Develop both use cases and requirements for features to be added to the SimpleChat system that would solve the following problems. If you solve all these problems, you will have completed Phase 3 of SimpleChat.

(a) Anybody with a client program can connect to a server and start sending messages impersonating somebody else, since there is no password protection. Hint: there are two completely different solutions to this problem.

(b) There is no facility to send a private message to a particular user.

(c) It would be nice if instead of all connected users participating in the same global chat session, separate channels could be established. All messages in a channel would be broadcast to all other clients in that channel, but not to clients outside the channel.

(d) A user wants to have somebody else monitor her incoming messages while she is in a meeting.

E80 Implement the requirements you specified in Exercise E79.

In the following exercises we present a second project, the 'Small Hotel Reservation System'. As with the SimpleChat project, we propose that this be based on the Object Client–Server Framework presented in Chapter 3, and we will ask you to develop additional aspects of the project in each successive chapter. The main difference from SimpleChat is that this project will involve more complex object-oriented modeling and design.

We suggest you work in groups of three or four on this project.

The short description of functional requirements for this project is below. On the book's web site (www.lloseng.com) we present a fully worked-out example of a project similar to this. You may choose instead to base your project on one of the system descriptions in Appendix C.

The goal of this project is to create a system to manage the front-desk activities of the 'Interface Rapids Hotel'. You have been contracted to replace the existing paper-based system, since your customers believe an automated system will save money and help them to serve guests better. The system will be used to enter reservations as well as to check guests in and out of the hotel.

The hotel contains rooms in which guests can stay. Some hotel rooms adjoin others; that is, there are internal doors between them. Each hotel room is assigned a quality level (e.g. a larger room or a room with a view would be better than a smaller room without a view). Each room also has a certain number and type of beds, a room number, and a smoking/non-smoking status. Each quality level has a maximum daily rate, although the rate that a guest pays may be less.

When a hotel guest wishes to make a reservation, the hotel clerk asks him or her which nights he or she wants to stay and the type of room he or she wants. The system must verify if room(s) are available on those nights before allowing a reservation to be made.

The hotel needs to record basic information about each guest, such as his or her name, address, telephone number, credit card etc. A reservation can be canceled at any time but some fees (a percentage of the room price) may be charged if the cancelation is done too late.

When a guest checks in, a room is allocated to him or her until he or she checks out. When the customer requests a specific room, this can be allocated in advance at the discretion of the manager. The system must keep track of the guest's account, and print his or her bill.

E81 Perform a domain analysis about hotel reservations. This will help you to resolve certain ambiguities that might be present in the above statement of requirements.

E82 Develop a full requirements definition for the above problem. Among the techniques you should consider employing are the following: interview some people who run hotels, and take a look at existing front-desk systems; use brainstorming techniques to refine the requirements; perform use case analysis, to determine who the actors are and what tasks they must perform. As you do the above, narrow the problem statement, excluding features that will not be needed in the first release. Before you complete your requirements definition, make sure you hold a formal review.

Modeling with classes

5

UML class diagrams are one of the most important tools for both requirements analysis and design of object-oriented software systems. These diagrams show the classes, their attributes and operations as well as the various types of relationships that exist among the classes. In Chapter 2 we introduced some of the basics of class diagrams, including attributes, operations and generalizations. In Chapter 3, you saw some of those elements put together to represent the Object Client–Server Framework. In this chapter we will examine class diagrams in depth, using several additional examples.

In this chapter you will learn about the following

- How to properly use the most essential features of UML class diagrams: classes, associations, generalizations and interfaces.

- The basics of Object Constraint Language (OCL).

- Typical problems you will encounter when modeling with class diagrams.

- A step-by-step process for systematically developing class diagrams.

- Basic techniques for implementing class diagrams in Java.

5.1   What is UML?

The Unified Modeling Language (UML) is a standard graphical language for modeling object-oriented software. It was developed in the mid-1990s as a collaborative effort by James Rumbaugh, Grady Booch and Ivar Jacobson, each of whom had developed their own notation in the early 1990s. The 'U' in UML stands for 'unified', since its three developers combined the best features of the languages they had each previously developed. The custodian of the UML standard is the Object Management Group (OMG). In 2004 the OMG approved version 2.0 of UML.

UML contains a variety of diagram types, including:

- ■ Class diagrams, which describe classes and their relationships. These are the subject of this chapter.

- ■ Interaction diagrams, which show the behavior of systems in terms of how objects interact with each other. In Chapter 8, we will discuss two types of interaction diagrams: sequence diagrams and communication diagrams.

- ■ State diagrams and activity diagrams, which show how systems behave. We will also present these in Chapter 8.

- ■ Component and deployment diagrams, which show how the various components of systems are arranged logically and physically. We will cover these in Chapter 9.

UML, however, is much more than just a set of notations for drawing diagrams; it has the following additional interesting features:

- ■ The diagrams you create with it are intended to be interconnected to form a unified *model*; we will discuss this more in the next subsection.

- ■ It has a detailed *semantics*, describing mathematically the meaning of many aspects of its notations.

- ■ It has *extension* mechanisms, which allow software designers to represent concepts that are not part of the core of UML. We will show some examples of these mechanisms.

- ■ It has an associated textual language called *Object Constraint Language* (OCL) that allows you to formally state various facts about the elements of the diagrams. We will introduce this important topic by way of some examples.

The objective of UML is to assist in software development. It is not a *methodology*, because it does not describe, in a step-by-step way, how to do things. See the sidebar for a discussion of this term.

Why use a standard modeling language?

Some developers have been successful at developing small software systems without the use of diagrams or other features of modeling languages. However, as their systems become larger and larger, such developers have an increasingly difficult time seeing the 'big picture' and are liable to create poor designs and take much longer in their work.

Most systems are therefore documented with the use of diagrams. These provide views of structure and functionality that would be difficult to grasp by

'Methodology', 'Method' and 'Process'

Since the early 1970s, many books have been written describing how software engineers should go about developing software. The authors variously call their approaches *methodologies*, *methods*, *processes* or *development processes*. We prefer 'methodology' since the other terms can be used in several different ways.

Most methodologies describe detailed sequences of steps for performing analysis and design. Many of them require the use of a particular notation, and the production of documentation in particular formats. Most also describe aspects of project management, and many are supported by tools developed by the authors of the methodology, or by others. Some methodologies are publicly available in book form; others must be obtained, at great expense, by signing a contract with a consulting company.

It is generally a good idea for an organization to follow a specific methodology. By doing so, all members of the organization follow the same steps and use the same notations. They can communicate with each other, know what each other is doing, and co-ordinate their work.

The *Rational Unified Process* is one of the best known methodologies in wide use today. It was developed by the same group who developed UML and incorporates UML as its notation. Agile methodologies, such as eXtreme Programming, also have a wide following.

In the current book, our intent is to give you knowledge that will help you to understand and work in the context of any methodology.

looking at code or textual descriptions alone. In other words, diagrams provide *abstraction*.

A *model* goes beyond a mere set of diagrams. A model captures an inter-related set of information about the system: a diagram is simply one view of that information. Several diagrams can present the same information in slightly different ways, either with different notations or with different levels of detail. I can delete an element from a diagram, and keep it in the model; if I delete an element from the model it should disappear from all diagrams.

A model can lead software engineers to have insights about the system; they can analyze the model (manually or using tools) to discover problems and other properties of it. Simple diagrams generated from the model can also help communicate with clients and users. However, it is up to the modeler to generate these easy-to-understand views.

Employing UML, a well-defined *standard* modeling language, adds additional advantages:

■ Since it is a standard notation, everybody who looks at the model will be able to interpret it the same way.

■ There is a wide variety of tools available to build UML models and to enable simulation, animation and/or generation of code for all or parts of a system. For details of the most popular tools, see the 'For more information' section at the end of the chapter.

History of object orientation – methods and notations

In the 1980s, the object-oriented approach began to become widely accepted in the software community as a good way to cope with software complexity. At that time, however, object orientation was applied primarily at the programming level; there was no guidance to software engineers about how to analyze or design systems in an object-oriented way. As people continued to develop ever more complex software, systematic approaches to analysis and design were clearly needed.

At the end of the 1980s and the beginning of 1990s, the first object-oriented methodologies appeared. Each of these was published as a book and proposed its own notation for modeling.

Some of the most important contributors in this period were:

- Shlaer and Mellor, who proposed their recursive approach in 1989.
- Rumbaugh, and his colleagues, who published a book about the Object Modeling Technique (OMT) in 1991.
- Coad and Yourdon, who in 1991 proposed an approach based on prototypes.
- Jacobson, who in 1992 used his work experience to incorporate the idea of use cases into object-oriented development.
- Booch, a pioneer in object orientation, who presented his method in 1994.
- Martin and Odell, who also wrote a book describing their approach in 1994.

Unfortunately, the proliferation of methods and notations tended to cause considerable confusion. The initiative of combining their approaches was taken in 1994 by Rumbaugh and Booch at Rational Corporation (now part of IBM). In 1995, Jacobson joined the team to participate in defining what is now known as the Unified Modeling Language. These three UML developers are now sometimes called the Three Amigos.

In 1997 the Object Management Group (OMG) started the process of UML standardization, a process widely supported by industry. The UML standard is now used by most software engineers who are performing object-oriented analysis and design.

References to literature about UML and other earlier notations can be found at the end of the chapter.

5.2 Essentials of UML class diagrams

Class diagrams describe the data found in a software system. As you learned in Chapter 2, many of the classes in these diagrams correspond to things in the real world. For example, in an airline reservation system there would be classes such as Flight, Passenger and Airport.

The main symbols shown on class diagrams are:

- *Classes*, which represent the types of data themselves.

- *Associations*, which show how instances of classes reference instances of other classes.

- *Attributes*, which are simple data found in instances.

■ *Operations*, which represent the functions performed by the instances.

■ *Generalizations*, which are used to arrange classes into inheritance hierarchies.

We will start by explaining how to use these symbols properly. In later sections, we will discuss more advanced features of class diagrams as well as a step-by-step approach to drawing class diagrams. In the next chapter we will introduce common patterns found in class diagrams.

Classes

A class is represented as a box with the name of the class inside. As discussed in Chapter 2, the name should always be singular and start with a capital letter. When you draw a class in a class diagram, you are saying that the system will contain a class by that name, and that when the system runs, instances of that class will be created.

Optionally, the class diagram may also show the attributes and operations contained in each class. This is done by dividing a class box into two or three smaller boxes: the top box contains the class name, the next box lists attributes, and the bottom box lists operations. If you do not want to specify attributes or operations, then you simply omit the box.

Figure 5.1 illustrates how a class can be drawn at several different levels of detail. How much detail you show depends on the phase of development and on what you wish to communicate. In the leftmost example, only the class name is shown, indicating merely that the class exists. Additional detail is shown in the other four representations of the same `Rectangle` class. The most detail, including the type of attributes, whether the feature is public (+) or private (–), and the signature of operations, is shown in the rightmost example. When shown in full detail, an operation's signature is specified using the following notation: `operationName(parameterName: parameterType,...): returnType`.

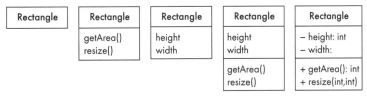

Figure 5.1   The `Rectangle` class at several different levels of detail

5.3   Associations and multiplicity

An *association* is used to show how instances of two classes will reference each other. The association is drawn as a line between the classes.

Symbols indicating *multiplicity* are shown at each end of the association. The multiplicity indicates how many instances of the class at this end of the association can be linked to an instance of the class at the other end of the

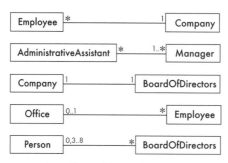

Figure 5.2   Examples of possible multiplicities

association. Figure 5.2 gives some examples of associations, showing their multiplicity.

A multiplicity of 1 indicates that there must be exactly one instance linked to each object at the other end of the association. For example, there can only be one Company associated with each Employee in Figure 5.2.

A very common multiplicity is *, which is normally read as 'many', and means any integer greater than or equal to zero. In Figure 5.2, for example, many employees can be associated with a company; one possibility being that a company has no employees. Although there is no theoretical upper bound, there is a practical upper bound that depends on the amount of memory and processing capacity available.

If there can be either zero or one object linked to an object at the other end of the association, then the multiplicity is said to be 'optional', and the notation 0..1 is used. So, for example, Figure 5.2 shows that there can be zero or one office per employee. In other words, it is optional that an employee is assigned to an office (some may work at home or in a job that does not require an office).

You can also specify the multiplicity to be an *interval*, which is shown as two dots between the lower and upper bound. An interval is also sometimes called a *range*. If, for example, you determine that a sailboat can have between 1 and 3 masts, then you would write 1..3 on the Mast end of the association. The 0..1 notation discussed above is a special case of an interval. If an interval has no upper bound, then you use the asterisk; therefore 0..* and * mean the same thing, while 1..* means 'at least one'.

The multiplicity can be a specific positive integer; and you can also specify several multiplicity values or ranges separated by commas. For example, imagine that the law in some jurisdiction states that a board of directors must have between three and eight members. Furthermore, if the board finds itself with insufficient members, then it is automatically dissolved and new elections must be held – during the election process, the board has zero members. The multiplicity of the final example in Figure 5.2 reflects this situation: there can be either zero, or between 3 and 8 persons on a BoardOfDirectors.

Specific multiplicities involving intervals or exact numbers greater than two are not common, and should only be specified after careful thought. For example, you might be tempted to specify that a person should always have *exactly* two parents. However, if you do so, then you are requiring that the system always have a record of everybody's two parents. Adhering strictly to such a rule would be impossible because not everybody knows who their parents are, and also because the system would have to know the parents of the parents, *ad infinitum*. A more reasonable multiplicity for parents might be 0..2.

If you do not specify the multiplicity of an association end, then it is said to be *undefined*. We strongly recommend never leaving a multiplicity undefined, since much of the meaning of a class diagram comes from the multiplicities. In some earlier versions of UML, leaving the multiplicity blank meant it should be interpreted as 'one' rather than undefined; you may see some older diagrams using this convention.

Labeling associations

Each association can be labeled, to make explicit the nature of the association. There are two types of labels, association names and role names. Figure 5.3 shows the same associations as in Figure 5.2, but with labels added.

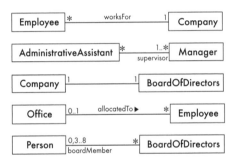

Figure 5.3   The associations of Figure 5.2, but with some association names and role names added

An *association name* should be a verb or verb phrase, and is placed next to the middle of the association. One class becomes the subject and the other class becomes the object of the verb. For example, the association between `Employee` and `Company` is called `worksFor`. You can read the association in one direction as, 'an employee works for a company'. The direction to read the association is normally obvious, but can be clarified by showing a little arrow (a filled triangle) next to the association name (as in the fourth association in Figure 5.3).

Another way of labeling an association is to use a *role name*. Role names can be attached to either or both ends of an association. A role name acts, in the context of the association, as an alternative name for the class to which it is attached. For example, in the association between `Person` and `BoardOfDirectors`, `boardMember` is a role name that describes the people who happen to be members of the board. You can read this association as, 'a board of directors has either zero or 3 to 8 persons as board members'.

If you omit both the association name and role names, then consider that an association's name is simply `has`, by default. This is not very informative, but in some cases it is adequate, since the meaning of the association might be clear by simply looking at the two classes. For example, in the association between `Company` and `BoardOfDirectors`, we have chosen not to add any label; the association would read, 'a company has a board of directors'.

A good rule of thumb when performing analysis is: add sufficient names to make the association clear and unambiguous. It is normally not necessary to add both role names and an association name to the same association. For example, we could have added a role name `employer` next to `Company` in the first association of Figure 5.3; however, the association name `worksFor` is sufficient. We could also have chosen here to use the role name instead of the association name.

Analyzing and validating associations

It is very common to make errors when creating associations – it is particularly easy to get the multiplicity wrong. Therefore you should get into the habit of reading *every* association in both directions to verify that it makes sense. Most importantly, you should always ask yourself whether a less restrictive multiplicity could also makes sense in some circumstances. By less restrictive, we mean using 'many' or 'optional' instead of 'one' or some other specific number.

In general, you should err on the side of being less restrictive so as to increase the flexibility of the system. For example, restricting the number of people who supervise an employee to 'one' would make it hard to introduce a 'matrix management' system, in which a person can have multiple supervisors. On the other hand, using 'many', as opposed to 'one', when it is not justified, will increase a system's complexity and reduce its efficiency.

The following points discuss three of the most common patterns of multiplicity, each of which is illustrated in Figures 5.2 and 5.3.

- **One-to-many**. A company has many employees, but an employee can only work for one company. You might argue that this is incorrect, since somebody might moonlight, working for several companies. However, company policy might explicitly disallow moonlighting in companies managed by our system. This multiplicity pattern correctly indicates that a company can have zero employees, as in the case of a 'shell' company. Finally, since it is not possible to be an employee unless you work for a company, the multiplicity at the `Company` end is correctly shown to be exactly one, not optional.

- **Many-to-many**. An administrative assistant can work for many managers, and a manager can have many administrative assistants. Of course, a one-to-one relationship would be typical between any particular administrative assistant and manager, but in general there are assistants who work for a group of managers, and managers who are so senior that they have a group of assistants. It is also the case that some managers might have zero assistants. An interesting question arises when you consider whether it is possible for an assistant to have, perhaps temporarily, zero managers. We have decided in Figures 5.2 and 5.3 not to allow this, and to require the system to ensure that at all times at least one manager supervises each administrative assistant.

■ **One-to-one**. For each company, there is exactly one board of directors. Also, a board is the board of only one company. A company must always have a board, and a board must always be of some company. What would happen if the board members all resigned? We would still say that the board exists, but temporarily has zero members.

The most common multiplicity pattern is one-to-many. The next most common is many-to-many. Together, these two patterns account for the vast majority of associations. Later on we will see how a many-to-many association can be split into two one-to-many associations.

One-to-one associations are less common. When you see such an association, you should ask yourself if in fact one or both ends should be changed to 'optional' or 'many'. The implication of a one-to-one association is that whenever you create an instance of one of the classes, you must simultaneously create an instance of the other; and when you delete one you must delete the other. If there is a true one-to-one association, you might also consider whether it is an aggregation, discussed later.

A common error is to create a one-to-one association between two classes, where the two classes should really be one. For example, in Figure 5.4 `Person` and `PersonInfo` should become a single `Person` class, with the attributes of `PersonInfo` transferred to `Person`.

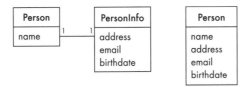

Figure 5.4   An inappropriate one-to-one association (left), and a corrected model showing a single class (right)

Figure 5.5 illustrates a possible multiplicity pattern involving three classes. Let's look in detail at its semantics. We can tell that for each `Booking` there must always be exactly one `Passenger`, but each `Passenger` can have any number of `Bookings` (i.e. on different flights and dates). Similarly, for each `Booking` there must always be exactly one `SpecificFlight`, but each `SpecificFlight` can have any number of `Bookings` (up to the capacity of the aircraft, of course).

We will read and analyze the left association in Figure 5.5 in the following two directions:

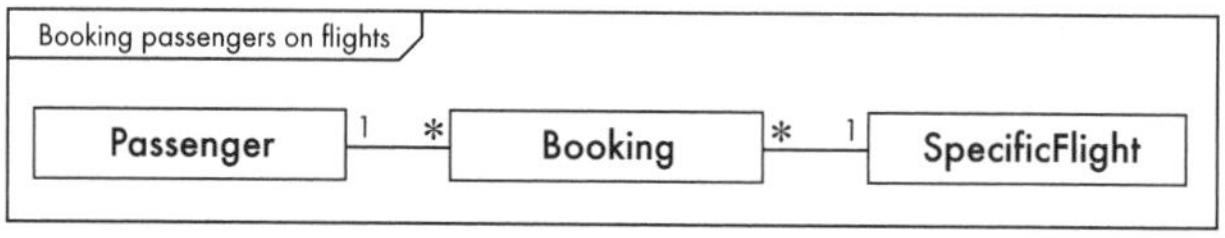

Figure 5.5   **Associations related to booking passengers on a flight**

■ 'A `Booking` is always for exactly one `Passenger`'

This means there could never be a booking with zero passengers. Does this seem correct? Yes. After all, it would not make sense to have a booking if we did not know who the booking was for. From this information we can also conclude that to create a `Booking`, either we must have *previously* created the `Passenger`, or else we must create it at the same time as the `Booking`.

The above association also implies that a `Booking` could never involve more than one `Passenger`. Is this really what we mean when we think of a booking? The answer is not so clear and hence requires careful thought. You might imagine an entire family sharing a single `Booking` to fly to some vacation spot. On the other hand, the alternative shown in Figure 5.5 is that each member of the family has his or her own `Booking`. This alternative provides more flexibility since it allows any member of the family to change itinerary without affecting the others.

> **Diagram frames and labels**
> Figure 5.5 has a *frame* around it, with a label 'Booking passengers on flights' in the top-left corner. This is an optional feature that any UML 2.0 diagram may possess. We have shown it here to illustrate its use; we will leave it off all other diagrams in this book.

■ 'A `Passenger` can have any number of `Bookings`'

This statement says that a passenger could have no bookings at all. Does this seem reasonable? Again, to answer this might need further requirements analysis. One possibility is that we might not want to waste space storing information about a passenger who does not have any bookings – hence we may decide always to *delete* a passenger if he or she has just one booking and cancels it. If this is our decision, then the multiplicity can be changed from * to 1..*. If we make this change, then whenever we add a new passenger, we will have to add their first booking simultaneously.

On the other hand, it might be convenient to be able to add some passengers to the system and then later on to go back and add bookings. Therefore we will conclude that allowing a `Passenger` to exist without a `Booking` is acceptable and leave the multiplicity at *.

Can a passenger have more than one booking? Yes, since it is easy to imagine somebody arranging a whole series of flights.

Exercises

E83   Discuss other multiplicities that could have been considered in Figure 5.5.

E84   Create two or three classes linked by associations to represent the situations below. Take care to specify appropriate multiplicity, as well as labels for the associations. If there is more than one reasonable alternative, explain the advantages and disadvantages of each.

(a) Racing with vehicles and drivers.

(b) A video rental shop, where you must purchase a membership before renting anything.

(c) A landlord renting apartments to tenants.

(d) A student taking courses in a school.

(e) A professor teaching courses in a university.

(f) An author writing books distributed by publishers.

(g) A repertory theater company planning presentations of various plays.

E85 Explain the consequences of the associations in Exercise E84 in terms of the creation and destruction of instances. Think about the order in which instances can be created or destroyed.

E86 For each of the associations you created in Exercise E84, write a few sentences showing how you would read the association in both directions.

Association classes

In some circumstances, an attribute that concerns two associated classes cannot be placed in either of the classes. For example, imagine the association shown in Figure 5.6, in which a student can register in any number of course sections, and a course section can have any number of students. In which class should the student's grade be put?

Figure 5.6   A many-to-many association. The 'grade' attribute can be put in neither class

If you put the grade in the `Student` class, then a student could have only one grade, not one per course section. If you put the grade in the `CourseSection` class, then a course section could have only one grade, not one per student. The grade is therefore not a property of either class.

The solution to this problem is to create an *association class* to hold the grade. As shown in the left half of Figure 5.7, an association class is connected to its association by a dashed line. In this example, the new class is called `Registration`; in general, an association class should be named using a noun that reflects the meaning of the association; the association name is then no longer needed.

Aside from being attached to an association, an association class is no different from any other class. In particular, it can have subclasses and other associations connected to it.

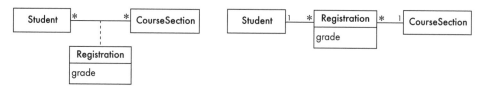

Figure 5.7   A many-to-many association with an association class, and an equivalent diagram using two one-to-many associations

Any time you see a many-to-many association, you should consider whether an association class is needed.

The diagram in the left half of Figure 5.7 can be transformed into the diagram in the right half, which uses only one-to-many associations. Any pair of classes, linked by a many-to-many association with an association class, can be transformed in this manner. Pay special attention to the positions of the 'many' multiplicities before and after the transformation.

Both halves of Figure 5.7 would be implemented the same way. Sometimes, though, the left version is clearer since it emphasizes the importance of the relationship between Student and CourseSection. At other times, the right version can be easier to read, since no special notation is needed.

Note that Figure 5.5 can also be transformed such that it uses an association class, since it follows the pattern in the right half of Figure 5.7.

The fact that an association class has two many-to-one associations means that to create an instance, you must already have instances of the two associated classes.

Reflexive associations

It is possible for an association to connect a class to itself. Two examples of this are found in Figure 5.8. A course can require other *prerequisite* courses to be taken first. If two courses cover nearly the same material, taking one of them may preclude a student from taking the other, and vice versa – such courses are said to be *mutually exclusive*. The first association is *asymmetric*, since the roles of the classes at each end are clearly different. The second, on the other hand, is *symmetric*. To make the meaning clear, you should label an asymmetric reflexive association using role names instead of an association name.

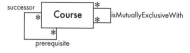

Figure 5.8   Two examples of reflexive associations

Exercise

E87 Add association classes to the three many-to-many associations in Figure 5.9.

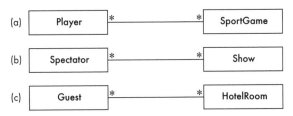

Figure 5.9   Three many-to-many associations for Exercise E87

E88 Add association classes to the two many-to-many associations in Figure 5.8. Show the attributes that might be found in these association classes.

E89 Apply the transformation shown in Figure 5.7 to your answer to the previous exercise.

Links as instances of associations

In the same way that we say an object is an instance of a class, we say that a *link* is an instance of an association. Each link connects two objects – an instance of each of the two classes involved in the association. For example, in Figure 5.5, there will be one link of the Passenger-to-Booking association for every Booking.

Directionality in associations

Associations and links are by default *bi-directional*. That is, if a Driver object is linked to a Car object, then the Car is also implicitly linked to that Driver. If you know the car, you can find out its driver – or if you know the driver, you can find out the car.

It is possible to limit the navigability of an association's links by adding an arrow at one end. For example, Figure 5.10 shows two classes that might exist in a calendar application. The user of this application can associate any number of written notes with any day. An instance of class Day would need to know about the instances of Note associated with it; but it is not expected that if you have a Note, there will be any need to determine the Day to which it belongs.

Figure 5.10   A unidirectional association

Decisions about directionality should normally be deferred to later phases of development, when the detailed design is created. Making associations unidirectional can improve efficiency and reduce complexity, but might also limit the flexibility of the system.

5.4 Generalization

We discussed generalization in Chapter 2, and presented several examples. You will remember that they are represented using a small triangle pointing to the superclass. They must follow the isa rule, and several other rules as well. Here, we will present some more issues to consider when creating generalizations.

Avoiding unnecessary generalizations

A common mistake made by beginners is to overdo generalization. Figure 5.11 shows a taxonomy of different types of products that might be sold by a music store. However, to justify the existence of each class, there must be some operation that will be done differently in that class. In the case of Figure 5.11, it would be hard to imagine that there would need to be different methods written for most of the classes. For example, `JazzRecording`, `ClassicalRecording` and `BluesRecording` would not differ with regard to how they are sold, nor with regard to what kinds of information clients can find out about them.

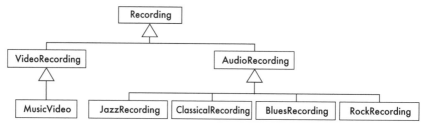

Figure 5.11 A hierarchy of classes in which there would not be any differences in operations. This should be avoided

A better way to model the information in Figure 5.11 is to create a class diagram such as that in Figure 5.12 (a). Most of the classes from Figure 5.11 now become *instances* of `RecordingCategory`, and the hierarchy itself becomes a hierarchy of instances, as shown in Figure 5.12 (b). In fact, Figure 5.12 (b) is an example of an *object diagram* – we will discuss these further shortly.

Handling multiple generalization sets

A *generalization set* is a labeled group of generalizations with a common superclass; the label describes the criteria used to specialize the superclass into two or more subclasses. It is clearest to unite all the generalizations in a set using a *single* open triangle. You place the label next to the open triangle.

Two examples of generalization sets, as used in a zoology program, are shown in Figure 5.13. Animals can be divided up by *habitat* into aquatic and land animals, or by *type of food*, into carnivores and herbivores.

> **Discriminators**
> In earlier versions of UML, generalization set labels were called *discriminators*. That term is now obsolete.

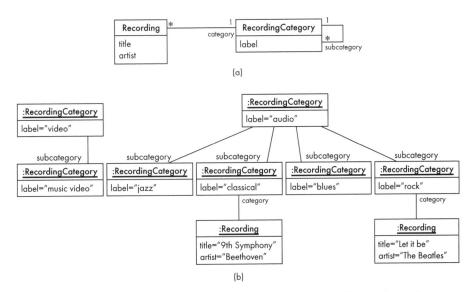

(a)

(b)

Figure 5.12   (a) Modeling a taxonomy of products using a single class, and (b) an object diagram generated from this

Figure 5.13   Two generalization sets

The label of a generalization set will typically be an attribute that has a different value in each subclass. As discussed above, there must also be other differences in the features of the subclasses in order to justify their existence – these differences could be attributes, operations or associations. For example, a Carnivore may have a prey association, an attribute describing its huntingStrategy, and operations to manipulate this data.

Situations like Figure 5.13, where there is more than one possible generalization set sharing the same superclass, pose interesting modeling challenges. If you were to include both generalization sets in the same model, then a problem would arise in implementation environments such as Java: if an animal was an AquaticAnimal, it could not also be a Carnivore. Figure 5.13 would therefore make it hard to represent aquatic carnivores such as sharks. This problem leads us to search for a way to enable animals to have all possible combinations of habitat and type of food.

One solution, shown in Figure 5.14, is to create a higher-level generalization set (here habitat), and then to have generalization sets with duplicate labels at a lower level in the hierarchy. The drawback to this is that all the features associated with the second generalization set would also have to be duplicated. For example, you would have to provide a `prey` association for both `AquaticCarnivore` and `LandCarnivore`. Another problem with this solution is that the number of classes can grow very large. If you wanted to add omnivores, you would have to add both `AquaticOmnivore` and `LandOmnivore`. Figure 5.14 therefore is not an ideal solution.

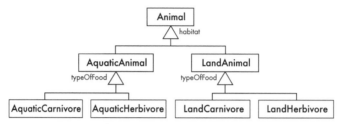

Figure 5.14   Allowing different combinations of features by duplicating a generalization set label at a lower level of the hierarchy. Duplication like this should be avoided

Another possible solution, using *multiple inheritance*, is shown in Figure 5.15. This approach uses even more classes and generalizations but avoids duplication of features. However, multiple inheritance generally adds too much complexity. This example illustrates one reason why it should normally be avoided; a second reason is that multiple inheritance does not exist in Java.

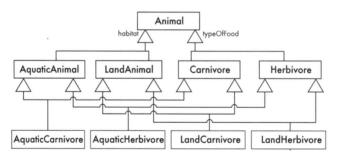

Figure 5.15   Allowing different combinations of features by using multiple inheritance. This is complex and should be avoided

In the next chapter, we will discuss the *player–role* pattern, which provides a superior solution to the problem of multiple generalization sets.

Avoiding having objects change class

Another issue that can arise when creating generalizations is avoiding the need for objects to change class. In general, an object should never need to change class. In most programming languages, changing class is simply not possible; therefore you have to completely destroy the original object and create a new instance of the second class. This is complex and error prone because you have to copy all the instance variables and make sure that all links that connected to the old object now connect to the new one.

The need for an object to change class is illustrated in Figure 5.16. It is clear that during his or her studies, the attendance status of a student can change from full-time to part-time and vice versa. You do not want to model this situation in your system by destroying a PartTimeStudent and creating a FullTimeStudent, or the opposite, each time the student's status changes. For this reason Figure 5.16 is a poor model. A possible solution is simply to make attendanceStatus an attribute of Student and to omit the two subclasses completely. The problem with this is that we lose the advantage of polymorphism for any operations that would differ in PartTimeStudent and FullTimeStudent. The player–role pattern, discussed in the next chapter, can again provide a better solution.

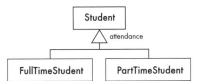

Figure 5.16   A situation in which objects will need to change class from time to time. Generalizations of this type should be avoided

Exercise

E90   Draw a class diagram corresponding to the following situations.

(a) An organization has three categories of employee: professional staff, technical staff and support staff. The organization also has departments and divisions. Each employee belongs to either a department or a division Assume that people will never need to change from one category to another.

(b) A grocery store has some items sold by weight, and some per unit. Some items are taxable, while others are not. Some items have special prices when sold in groups (e.g. 3 for $2). Finally, some items have special prices if you have certain 'membership cards'. There could be several different membership prices on the same item, but you can only use one membership card per purchase.

(c) A media player that can handle sound, images and sequences of images. Each type of media requires a 'plugin', although some plugins can handle more than one type of media.

5.5 Object diagrams

Class diagrams tell us what classes will exist in a given system, but they are quite abstract. Sometimes it can be hard to visualize the relationships among the objects that will exist at run-time.

An *object diagram* shows an example configuration of objects and links that may exist at a particular point during execution of a program. Objects are shown as rectangles, just like classes; the difference is that the name of the class is underlined and preceded by a colon, `:Employee`, for example. You can also give a name to each instance before the colon, as in `Pat:Employee`, or even omit the class name entirely if it is clear from the context, such as `Pat:`.

A link between two objects is shown as a simple line. You can imagine that each of the two objects contains a pointer to the other object joined by the link. The reality can be a little more complex than this, but while we are doing analysis, a simple vision suffices.

It is important to understand the relationship between a class diagram and an object diagram. A class is an abstract representation of all the instances of that class that can *ever* exist. Similarly, an association represents all the links between two classes that can ever exist. It should be clear from this that while we put multiplicity symbols on associations, we *never* put them on links.

We say that a given object diagram is *generated* by a class diagram. This means that it contains instances and links of the classes and associations present in the class diagram. It also means that the numbers of links among instances are consistent with the multiplicity of that class diagram. A class diagram can generate an infinite number of object diagrams.

We have already used an object diagram in Figure 2.2 to represent examples of instances, including their attributes.

Figure 5.17 shows object diagrams generated from two of the class diagrams of Figure 5.3.

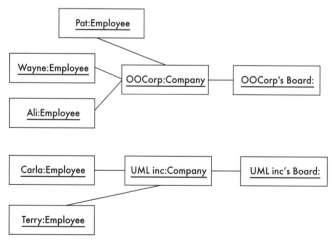

Figure 5.17   Object diagrams generated from class diagrams

Odds and ends about object diagrams

Object diagrams are sometimes called instance diagrams. There has been a tendency for some people to speak about object diagrams when they mean class diagrams. The term 'instance diagram' prevents this confusion even though it is not standard UML.

Most tools for drawing UML diagrams do not provide facilities for drawing object diagrams. This is because class diagrams contain an abstract view of the system that is much more information-rich and is always necessary, whereas object diagrams are less commonly used, and then only to analyze specific scenarios.

Associations versus generalizations in the context of object diagrams

It is a common mistake for beginners to think of generalizations as special associations. This misconception arises because both generalizations and associations connect classes together in a class diagram.

However, the differences between the two concepts are profound.

■ An association describes a relationship that will exist between *instances* at run-time.

■ A generalization describes a relationship between *classes* in a class diagram.

An object diagram can never contain a generalization, and can only contain links generated by associations, not the associations themselves.

When you show an object diagram generated by an association, you show instances of *both* classes joined by that association. On the other hand, when you show an object diagram generated by an inheritance hierarchy, you show a *single* instance of one of its concrete classes. That single instance will contain values of the attributes defined in its class, as well as those attributes inherited from superclasses. In other words, an instance of any class should also be considered to be an instance of each of that class's superclasses.

Exercise

E91   Draw a class diagram that could generate the object diagram shown in Figure 5.18. Make reasonable choices for multiplicity.

E92   Write a sentence describing a specific situation, with actual instances, for the class diagrams of Exercise E84. Then draw the corresponding object diagram. Make sure that each diagram is compatible with its underlying class diagram.

E93   Draw an example object diagram compatible with the class diagrams of Exercise E90.

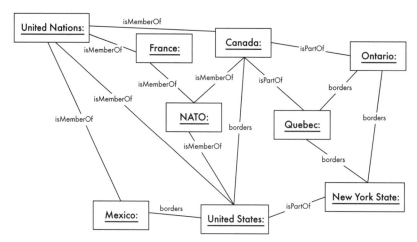

Figure 5.18   Object diagram for Exercise E91

5.6   More advanced features of class diagrams

The notations described in Sections 5.2 to 5.4 are the most important aspects of class diagrams. In this section, we describe additional features for adding more specific information to the diagrams. It is important to be able to understand the meaning of these features in class diagrams, but most modeling, especially at the analysis level, can be done without them.

Aggregation

Aggregations are special associations that represent 'part–whole' relationships. The 'whole' side of the relationship is often called the *assembly* or the *aggregate*.

As Figure 5.19 shows, aggregations are specified using a diamond symbol, which is placed next to the aggregate. This symbol is a shorthand notation that saves you from having to write an association name such as `isPartOf` or its inverse `hasParts`. Many aggregations are one-to-many, but this is not a requirement.

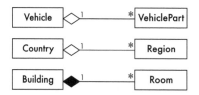

Figure 5.19   Some examples of aggregation. The third example is a strong aggregation called a composition

When to use an aggregation instead of an ordinary association has always been a source of confusion. As a general rule, you can mark an association as an aggregation if the following are true:

- You can state that the parts 'are part of' the aggregate, or the aggregate 'is composed of' the parts.

- When something owns or controls the aggregate, then they also own or control the parts.

For example, the parts of a vehicle are clearly in an aggregation relationship with the vehicle. The other two associations in Figure 5.19 are also legitimate aggregations. On the other hand, the members of a club are not in an aggregation relationship with the club. It might sometimes be possible in English to say that a person is part of a club, but the owner of the club does not own the members.

A *composition* is a strong kind of aggregation in which if the aggregate is destroyed, then the parts are destroyed as well. A composition is shown using a solid (filled-in) diamond, as opposed to an open one. The parts of a composition can never have a life of their own; they exist only to serve the aggregate. For example, as shown in the bottom example of Figure 5.19, the rooms of a building cannot exist without the building. In ordinary aggregations, on the other hand, the parts can exist on their own. For example, the engine can be taken out of one vehicle and placed in another, or a region can secede from one country and become independent.

A one-to-one composition often corresponds to a complex attribute. You can therefore show it as an attribute or, if you want to emphasize the details of the composed class, you can show it as a composition. Figure 5.20 illustrates a situation where an attribute has been expanded into an associated class. Such compositions are normally unidirectional, as shown here.

Figure 5.20   The address of an employee represented as an attribute or as a composition

Unlike other associations, UML allows aggregations to be drawn as a hierarchy, as shown in Figure 5.21. The use of such hierarchies in valid models is quite rare, however. Figure 5.21 is a much less flexible way to model vehicle parts than the first diagram, Figure 5.19. This is because Figure 5.19 can more easily accommodate new types of vehicles that have different configurations of parts.

Marking a part–whole association as an aggregation using the diamond symbol is optional. Leaving it as an ordinary association is not an error, whereas

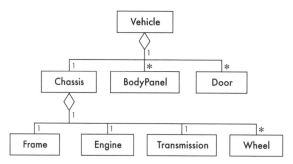

Figure 5.21   An aggregation hierarchy

marking a non-aggregation with a diamond is an error and can cause confusion. Therefore, as a general rule of thumb: when in doubt, leave it out.

An advantage of explicitly identifying aggregation is that it provides useful information to the designer. In particular, the designer can improve the encapsulation of the system by arranging for the part objects to be *hidden* inside the aggregate object. Methods in the system would be able to perform most operations on the aggregate, without needing to know about the existence of the parts. For example:

■ An operation to register the sale of a vehicle would only need to record the new owner of the aggregate. There would be no need to also record the new owner of all the parts, since if any subsequent query were made about the ownership of a part, the part could simply return the owner of the aggregate.

■ An operation to delete an aggregate could automatically delete the parts.

■ An operation to change the thickness of the outline of a shape might work by simply changing the thickness of all of the line segments that compose the shape.

The last two examples illustrate a mechanism called *propagation* that is often present in aggregations. Under this mechanism, an operation in an aggregate is implemented by having the aggregate perform that operation on its parts – in other words, the operation is propagated to the parts. At the same time, this process often results in the features of the parts being propagated back to the aggregate. For example, the weight of an aggregate could be obtained by summing the weights of its parts.

In a sense, we can say that propagation is to aggregation as inheritance is to generalization. However, the major difference is that inheritance is an implicit mechanism, whereas propagation has to be programmed when required.

Example 5.1   *Justify the use of a composition to represent the association between a polygon and its line segments, as in Figure 5.22.*

Figure 5.22   Composition example for Example 5.1

The justification is as follows:

■ A polygon is composed of line segments.

■ An object that manipulates a polygon also manipulates the line segments.

■ When the polygon is translated or scaled, the line segments are also translated or scaled.

■ The perimeter of the polygon is computed as the sum of the lengths of all the line segments.

■ Removing a line segment from a polygon would mean that the polygon is no longer a polygon, therefore the polygon must have complete control to prevent such a change.

■ The line segments are deleted when the polygon is deleted.

Exercise

E94   For each of the following associations, indicate whether it should be an ordinary association, a standard aggregation, or a composition.

(a) A telephone and its handset.

(b) A school and its teachers.

(c) A book and its chapters.

Interfaces

As discussed in Chapter 2, an *interface* is similar to a class, except it lacks instance variables and implemented methods. It normally contains only abstract methods although it may also contain class variables. We can say that an interface describes a *portion of the visible behavior* of a set of objects.

In UML, there are two ways to specify interfaces, both of which are shown in Figure 5.23:

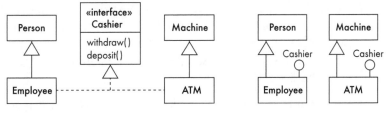

Figure 5.23   Two ways of showing the cashier interface

■ As a small circle (like a lollipop), labeled with the name of the interface.

■ As a class rectangle, with the expression «interface» at the top, and (optionally) a list of supported operations. The «interface» notation is an example of a *stereotype* in UML. A stereotype is a way to use some of the standard UML notation (here a class box) to represent something special (here an interface). Note that the « and » symbols are called *guillemets*; they should preferably be written using the special characters available in most fonts, not using pairs of less-than or greater-than signs.

In some programming languages, interfaces are simply created using superclasses containing only abstract methods. But interfaces should not be confused with generalizations since the basic relation is not the same. We have already mentioned that generalization is characterized by an isa relationship between a subclass and a superclass. In the case of interfaces, the relationship between the implementing class and the interface can be described as 'can-be-seen-as'.

Figure 5.23 shows classes representing bank employees and automatic teller machines; both can be seen as a sort of cashier. That is, it is possible to interact with one or the other in order to deposit or withdraw money. However, although Employee and ATM share common operations, they have different superclasses. This means that they cannot be put in the same inheritance hierarchy; therefore an interface called Cashier is used.

A key advantage of using interfaces is that they reduce what is called the *coupling* between classes. We will discuss this in detail, with an example, in Chapter 9.

Constraints, notes and descriptive text

Very often, in a class diagram, you want to say more than the graphical UML notation readily allows. There are three ways in which you can add additional information to a UML diagram:

■ **Descriptive text and other diagrams**. It is highly recommended to embed your diagrams in a larger document that describes the system more fully. Such text can explain aspects of the system using any notation you like. It is best not to repeat what is shown in the UML diagrams, but you can highlight and expand on important features, and give rationale for why certain decisions were made.

■ **Notes**. In contrast to the descriptive text described above, a note is a small block of text embedded in a UML diagram. The box has a 'bent corner'. The note can explain a detail, and acts like a comment in a programming language. Figure 5.24 shows an example note, explaining the purpose of the class LinearShape.

■ **Constraints**. A constraint is like a note, except that it is written in a formal language that can be interpreted by a computer. In a UML diagram, a

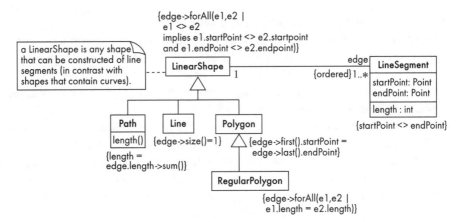

Figure 5.24   Constraints and notes on polygons and points

constraint is shown in curly brackets (also called 'braces'). A constraint expresses a logical statement that should evaluate to **true**. UML allows constraints to be written in any language supported by a given tool; however, the recommended language is *Object Constraint Language (OCL)*. We will discuss OCL in more detail next.

5.7   The basics of Object Constraint Language (OCL)

OCL is a formal language designed to enhance the modeling capabilities of UML. It was originally designed exclusively to specify constraints in UML models; the latest version, however, can also be used to specify such things as navigation paths that allow you to formulate queries for information in UML models.

We will focus here on its original use for modeling constraints, and will give examples you can emulate in order to write the most common kinds of constraints. Although we will only discuss its use in class diagrams, OCL can also be used in other types of UML diagram where constraint specification is required. If you wish to learn more, you can consult a more advanced book, or else the OCL specification itself, available from the Object Management Group.

OCL is a *specification* language, not a full programming language. The OCL statements we will look at simply specify logical facts (constraints) about the system that must remain **true**. OCL statements need not themselves be compiled and executed; however, designers must ensure that the code they write always respects the constraints imposed by each OCL statement. Automatic code generators must also ensure that code adheres to what the OCL statements say. A constraint cannot have any side effects; it can only compute a Boolean result and cannot modify any data.

OCL statements in class diagrams can specify what the values of attributes and associations must be. They can also state the preconditions and post-conditions of operations, although we will not discuss that usage here.

Formal methods, first order logic, Z and OCL

A *formal method* is an approach to software engineering in which everything is specified in *logic*, and mathematical techniques are used to verify the logic. Also, where possible, the logic is automatically processed to demonstrate that important properties of the software, such as safety requirements, are true. The type of logic normally used is called *first order logic*, although extensions to this exist. Concepts from *set theory* are also employed.

There is an 'opinion war' going on between those who feel formal methods rarely pay off in practice, and those who feel that judicious or even extensive use of formal methods (using a good notation) should be promoted since it will result in much better software.

Historically, logic has been written using a notation called *predicate calculus*. Z, pronounced 'zed', is a syntax for logic and set theory designed at Oxford University for software specification. For many years it is been one of the most popular notations for formal methods since it incorporates important abstractions missing from predicate calculus.

However, ordinary practitioners often find Z intimidating, partly because it uses a wide variety of special characters. *OCL* was developed by IBM as a logic notation that incorporates powerful abstractions while at the same time reading more like the programming languages that software engineers are used to. OCL is part of the UML set of standards managed by the OMG, and is in fact used to specify much of UML itself. Almost everything written in Z can be translated very directly into OCL; we therefore predict that in the long run OCL will become the dominant notation for formal methods.

The simplest OCL statements can be built out of the following elements:

- References to role names, association names, attributes and the results of operations

- The logical values `true` and `false`

- Logical operators such as `and`, `or`, `=`, `>`, `<` or `<>` (not equal)

- String values such as: `'a string'`

- Integers and real numbers (the latter having a decimal point)

- Arithmetic operations `*`, `/`, `+`, `-`

For example, the following constraint is found in Figure 5.24:

- `{startPoint <> endPoint}` constrains the two ends of a `LineSegment` to be different.

You can also navigate from class to class using a dot to separate components. For example, in `LinearShape`, to refer to the length of the edges you can refer to `edge.length`.

When you refer to the 'many' end of an association, the result is a collection of objects. You can refer to special OCL properties of a collection itself using the `->` operator, as in:

- `{edge->size() = 1}` constrains the number of edges in a line always to equal one.

■ `{length = edge.length->sum()}` constrains the length of a `Path` to be equal to the sum of all the separate values of `edge.length`.

A collection is most often a mathematical set; however, if the special constraint `{ordered}` is present on the association, then the collection is a *sequence*. In that case you can refer to special properties such as the first and last elements, as in:

■ `{edge->first().startPoint = edge->last().endPoint}` which constrains a `Polygon` to be a closed loop.

You can make logical statements about all the values in a collection using the `forall` operator. The following expression also uses the `implies` operator, which works as an if-then statement.

■ `{edge->forAll(e1,e2 | e1 <> e2`
    `implies e1.startPoint <> e2.startpoint`
    `and e1.endPoint <> e2.endpoint)}`

The above statement can be interpreted in English as follows. Take all possible pairs of edges, e1 and e2. (All possible pairs can result in two identical edges, since either member of a pair can be any element in the set.) If the members of a pair of edges are different, then they must have a different start point and a different end-point.

OCL expressions do not have to be written directly on a diagram. In order to avoid clutter, you can write them separately and specify a context for each expression, as indicated in the following:

```
context LineSegment inv:
    startPoint <> endPoint
```

In this expression, `inv` means that the statement is an *invariant* (always true) of the class `LineSegment`.

Exercises

E95 Write, in English, as many constraints as you can think of about shapes, that have not been expressed in Figure 5.24. Take at least three of these and write them in OCL.

E96 Write constraints using OCL that express the following constraints:

(a) In Figure 5.12(a), a subcategory must be different from its super-category.

(b) In Figure 5.8, none of the mutually exclusive courses can also be successors or prerequisites.

(c) In Figure 5.8, a successor cannot also be a prerequisite.

Aspects of UML class diagrams we have not covered

We have covered the most important elements of UML class diagrams – enough for you to create most models. There are, however, many details we have not covered. To learn about these, you should consult a book that describes UML in more depth, or the UML 2.0 specification from the OMG. The following are some of the features of class diagrams you may want to learn about first because you may see them in models you need to understand:

■ Qualifiers. These are attributes that are shown in a special box at the far end of an association. The value of the attribute is a unique identifier, controlled by the class to which it is attached.

■ A notation (a dashed box overlapping the top-left of a class) to represent *templates* such as those found in C++ or now Java 1.5. These are also known as *parameterized classes* or *generic classes*.

■ Showing *dependencies* among classes using a dashed line. Dependencies can include one class calling the methods in another, or being a friend of another (allowing access to its private methods).

■ The UML *metamodel*: a class diagram that describes the elements of UML itself.

■ Ternary or N-ary associations. These are associations involving more than two classes. It is always possible to convert these into a series of binary associations. We therefore do not recommend using them.

5.8 A class diagram for genealogy

In this section we will present a modeling problem that has some interesting issues to consider. Imagine you are developing a genealogy system, in which you have to model various human relationships, particularly those between parents and children in a genealogical tree.

The first observation to make is that Child and Parent should *not* be two distinct classes, since one person can both be the parent of someone and the child of someone else. It must be the case, then, that child and parent are *roles* in an association between instances of a class called Person.

Starting with this observation, we can draw the somewhat naïve initial class diagram shown in Figure 5.25(a). The fact that the parents of a child must be of opposite sex is specified here using an OCL constraint. The constraint says that for all pairs of Person objects playing the parent role, the sex of one must not equal the sex of the other.

Figure 5.25(a), however, does not allow the system to keep track of marriages, which are important to genealogists. The two parents of a person are not necessarily married, and married people may have no children. Therefore Figure 5.25(b) adds an extra association showing the marriage relation explicitly. This association contains two constraints that specify the sex attribute possessed by the husband and wife.

However, there are still some severe problems with Figure 5.25(b), which are fixed in Figure 5.25(c):

■ A person may have multiple marriages, and also children with several different partners over the course of his or her life. This problem is solved by making the

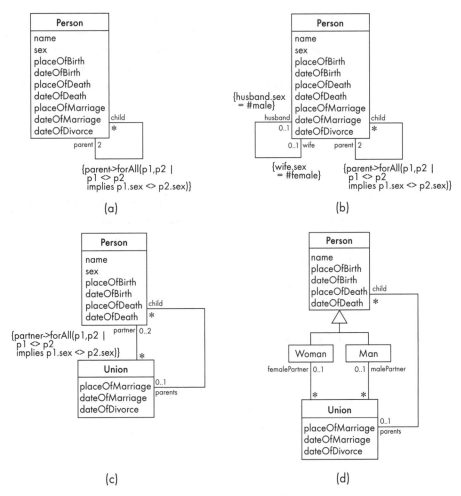

Figure 5.25 Alternatives for a genealogical class diagram – the first two are unacceptable since they have major problems

husband–wife association into an association class. We call it `Union`, and create a new role of `Person` called `partner`, since there may be no formal marriage. `Marriage` could in fact be a subclass of `Union`. The attributes `placeOfMarriage`, `dateOfMarriage` and `dateOfDivorce` are now put into the `Union` class; previously they would have been duplicated in both instances of `Person`.

■ In Figure 5.25(b), a person was required to have exactly two parents. In Figure 5.25(c), the `parents` role of the child–parent association is made optional since there may be no record of a person's parents; this is often the case when researching historical genealogical information. In addition, the `partner` role allows for only zero or one partner to be known, although information such as the date of marriage might be.

Note that Figure 5.25(c) has an interesting configuration: there are two separate associations, with quite different meanings, between `Person` and `Union`.

Figure 5.25(d) is similar to Figure 5.25(c), except that two subclasses of Person have been added. This allows for the removal of a constraint, but is otherwise of minimal benefit. The sex attribute of person is now removed. A polymorphic operation would now have to be provided that has different methods in Woman and Man. These methods might both return constant values, either "female" or "male".

Exercises

E97 Using Figure 5.25(d), describe how the following operations of class Person would be performed. You do not need to write code; simply describe how the available information would be used to compute the result.

(a) getSiblings

(b) getHalfSiblings

(c) getStepSiblings

(d) isMarried

(e) getNumberOfMarriages

E98 Write OCL constraints expressing the following facts about Figure 5.25(d):

(a) You cannot die before you are born.

(b) The date of a marriage always precedes the date of that marriage's divorce.

E99 Give the advantages and disadvantages of Figure 5.25(d), as opposed to Figure 5.25(c).

E100 A possible variation of Figure 5.25(c) would be to create a class Marriage that is a subclass of Union.

(a) Describe the two classes Union and Marriage in terms of their associations and attributes.

(b) What would be the advantages and disadvantages of this change, as opposed to Figure 5.25(c)?

E101 Extend the genealogical example to handle the following situations:

(a) Adoption and adopting parents.

(b) Same-sex unions (but still ensuring that the biological parents of a child must be of opposite sex).

5.9   The process of developing class diagrams

So far in this chapter we have discussed the syntax of class diagrams, and have raised some issues about what constitutes a good or bad model. You may, however, be left wondering: where do I start, and what steps should I take to ensure I build an effective model? This section provides some guidance on this issue.

Class diagrams versus entity-relationship diagrams

Database designers have for many years used a notation called Entity Relationship Diagrams (ERDs). This notation has much in common with UML's class diagrams; in fact, the developers of OMT, a predecessor to UML, took many ideas from ERDs. In ERDs, the 'entities' are similar to classes and the 'relationships' are similar to associations. Relationships are shown using a large diamond symbol, which is one of the features that makes them substantially more bulky than class diagrams. Also, standard ERDs do not show operations. Traditional ERDs did not show inheritance either, but Extended ERDs (EERDs) do.

ERDs are still widely used in the database community, although many database designers prefer now to use UML class diagrams. Those who prefer to continue using ERDs do so because the database community has developed many ERD tools and considerable expertise at using both the notation and the tools.

Models of the domain, versus models of the system

You can create class diagrams or other UML models at different stages in the software engineering process and with different purposes and levels of detail. Three types of model are listed in Table 5.1.

First, you can create informal class diagrams while performing domain analysis – these constitute part of what we call an *exploratory domain model*. Such diagrams represent what you have learned about the various entities and relationships in the domain; they help in understanding that domain. They are not, however, intended to model the software you will develop. They normally have some classes, associations and attributes that are outside the scope of the system. Also, in an exploratory domain model, you would not normally be concerned with operations and polymorphism, nor with many of the modeling principles we have discussed so far, such as avoiding multiple inheritance.

During requirements analysis or the early stages of design you will need to develop a model that also contains domain classes, associations and attributes. But this time, the model represents data that will actually be manipulated and stored by the system. We call this the *system domain model*; most of the class diagrams discussed so far in this chapter can be considered to be of this type. When we say 'domain model' we are referring by default to the system domain model, not the exploratory one. The classes in this model become real software modules and the instances of most of these classes normally end up being stored

Table 5.1   Class diagrams developed at different phases of the software engineering process

Type of model	Contains elements that represent things in the domain	Models only things that will actually be implemented	Contains elements that do not represent things in the domain, but are needed to build a complete system
Exploratory domain model: developed in domain analysis to learn about the domain	Yes	No	No
System domain model: models those aspects of the domain represented by the system	Yes	Yes	No
System model: includes classes used to build the user interface and system architecture	Yes	Yes	Yes

persistently in some kind of database. Instances are typically loaded from and saved in the database as the program runs.

The system domain model, however, omits many classes that are needed to build a complete system; in fact it can contain less than half the classes of the system. The complete system model includes the system domain model, but also adds classes representing the following:

- User interface classes such as windows, menus, commands and forms.

- Classes representing aspects of the system's architecture such as clients, servers, files and databases.

- Utility classes that make parts of the system more reusable, easier to maintain or easier to connect to other systems.

Instances of the user interface and architectural classes are normally created when a program is started, and then discarded when a program terminates. Most of these classes tend to be directly reused from class libraries, or else represent subclasses of library classes.

Generally, the system domain class diagram should be developed in such a way that it can be used independently of a particular set of user interface classes or architectural classes. This point is illustrated by Figure 5.26, which is a package diagram – a type of diagram we will discuss in Chapter 9. The domain model classes are in one package, but this package can be used in conjunction with different UI packages or architectural frameworks.

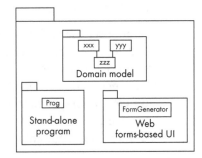

Figure 5.26 Two different systems which use the same domain model

A suggested sequence of activities

You would be modeling in a disorganized way if you simply wrote down whatever occurred to you, and then filled in gaps until you were finished. If you do this you will find yourself going backwards and forwards adding different things to your model, never quite sure how close you are to being finished. You will tend to work slowly and leave out important details.

You could, on the other hand, take a rigid approach in which you would start by determining a *complete* list of classes, then determine *all* the associations, then fill in *all* the attributes, etc. However, it is very hard to complete one step before moving on to the next. Almost all experienced modelers find that working on one aspect of a model gives them ideas about all the other aspects. Therefore, if you follow a rigid approach, you will also tend to leave out important details.

Following an intermediate approach, which is neither disorganized nor overly rigid, seems to be best. You do need to have a starting point, and that starting point should be identifying an initial set of classes. However, you will certainly add and delete from this set as work progresses. We will discuss creating the initial set of classes shortly.

You also need to have in mind a general path to follow after identifying the initial classes. However, it is also important to feel free to come back to earlier steps when you realize you forgot something, and to jump ahead to record your inspirations when you have them.

We therefore suggest that you work in the following sequence, unless seized by inspiration to work in a different sequence:

- Identify a first set of candidate **classes**.

- Starting with the most important classes, add any **associations** and **attributes** that clearly will be needed.

- Work out the clearest **generalizations**.

- List the main **responsibilities** of each class. These are simple statements of functions to be performed by each class; we will discuss them below.

- Based on responsibilities, decide on specific **operations** that are needed.

- **Iterate** over the entire process, examining the model to see if you need to add or delete classes, associations, attributes, generalizations, responsibilities or operations. In particular, you will want to ensure that all associations, attributes and operations are needed to fulfill some responsibility, and that there is sufficient information to fulfill every responsibility. You will also want to see if you can apply any of the **design patterns** discussed in the next chapter. In addition, you will want to identify any suitable **interfaces**.

- Repeat the previous step as needed until the model is satisfactory.

We will explain the steps of the above sequence, with examples, in the coming subsections.

Should you decide upon attributes or responsibilities first?

There are several points of view about the sequence in which you should decide upon the elements of a class diagram.

Some people prefer to decide upon responsibilities before attributes. The holders of this point of view believe that attributes represent the private state of objects, which should be hidden inside each class, and that responsibilities are more abstract. In this approach, determining responsibilities first will help you determine the attributes later on.

A different point of view is that when you are deciding upon attributes, you are really deciding upon abstract responsibilities for holding information, which are among the most important responsibilities.

Whichever viewpoint you hold, the process of revisiting the analysis steps performed earlier means that either approach will work.

People who promote both of the above points of view agree on one thing: you should not decide on *instance variables* (concrete implementations of attributes) until the final stages of modeling, because these really do represent the private state of objects.

Identifying classes

There are two ways to identify classes:

- When developing a domain model, you tend to *discover* classes. They may be found in source material such as requirements descriptions, interview notes, or the results of brainstorming sessions.

- When you work on the user interface or the system architecture, you tend to *invent* classes that are needed to solve a particular design problem. You may also sometimes invent classes when creating a domain model; for example, you might invent a generalization whose superclass has a name not normally used in the domain. To illustrate this, in Figure 5.24 the class LinearShape was invented to represent all those shapes (Polygons, Lines and Paths) that are composed of line segments – even though people normally do not use the term 'linear shape' when they talk.

Reuse should always be a concern when identifying classes. If you are building your system using a framework, then your model will contain many classes from that framework. If you are building your system as an extension to an existing system, then you will incorporate many of the classes from the original system. You may also be able to look at similar systems to obtain useful insights about the current application.

A simple technique for discovering the initial set of domain classes for a system is to look at source material such as a description of requirements. From this, you extract the *nouns* and *noun phrases*. A noun phrase is simply a string of nouns, or a noun modified by one or more adjectives. Once you have picked potential nouns or noun phrases, you can choose class names by following the principles described in Section 2.2 (on page 31).

From the initial set of class names you should make sure there are no nouns or noun phrases that:

- Are redundant (i.e. two names for the same class).

- Clearly represent instances (although their class may have to be included).

- Are vague or highly general terms, which do not convey specific information about the proposed software. For example, 'the *organization's purpose*', 'the *user's goal*', 'the *information* this *application* will represent'.

- Correspond to classes that are not needed for this application or this type of model. For example, in a domain model, you would eliminate classes that represent commands or menus in the user interface. As a rule of thumb, a class is only needed in a domain model if you have to store or manipulate instances of it in order to implement a requirement.

A common difficulty is deciding whether to keep classes in a domain model that represent *types of users* or other actors. You would only keep such classes if storing and manipulating this information is actually part of the domain. In a security or instant messaging system, for example, it would probably be part of the domain; whereas in a drawing program it would not. But what about a system for managing corporate accounts? The corporate accounting database would not itself store information about the various users of such a system who might, for example, be managers, administrative assistants, accountants and purchasers. However, some part of the system will clearly need to store information about them in order to permit security checks. The answer here is that there should probably be two separate subsystems, each with its own domain model: one for the accounting records and one for access permission.

You might choose to be fairly liberal in the process of building the initial list of classes, keeping most classes that seem to be possible candidates. You could on the other hand be stricter, only keeping a class if you are definite it will be needed. We suggest the liberal approach since it allows you to be more spontaneous. You can easily eliminate classes later.

| Example 5.2 | *Using the description of the Airline system from Appendix C, list the nouns and noun phrases that might end up being classes in a system domain model. For those nouns that should not become classes, explain why not.* |

Nouns that are put on an initial list of classes include: `Flight`, `Passenger`, `Employee`.
Other nouns or noun phrases that we choose not to include in the initial list of classes:

❏ 'Ootumlia Airlines', 'Java Valley', 'Ootumlia'. These are instances.

❏ 'Reservation system'. This is not a class because it is part of the system, not the domain information represented by the system.

❏ 'Sightseeing Flight'. Rejected in favor of `Flight`, since the latter is more general and therefore makes the system more flexible.

❏ 'Seat'. Appears to be an attribute of `Flight`.

❏ 'Crew'. This word implies the entire crew, when we really want to store information about individual members of that crew. We could have created a class `CrewMember`, but `Employee` seemed more flexible – allowing us to use the class in future for people who are not actually crew members.

❏ 'Schedule'. This is a word that describes a complex bundle of information that would be better represented by classes such as `Flight`, and the attributes and associations of those classes.

❏ 'Future'. This is a noun, but it is not part of the system to be developed.

❏ 'Frequent Flier Plan'. This is not part of the current scope.

Exercise

E102 This exercise is based on the short program descriptions, as found in Appendix C. Determine the nouns and noun phrases that might, in the end, become classes. While making your list, choose good names for each of the potential classes.

(a) Bank account management system.

(b) Election management system.

(c) Geographical information system.

(d) Investments system.

(e) Manufacturing plant controller.

(f) The woodworking design system.

Identifying associations and attributes

Once you feel you have a good initial list of classes, it is time to turn your attention to identifying associations and attributes.

The best way to do this is to start with the class or classes that you think are most central and important to the system. For each of these, decide on the clear and obvious data it must contain and its relationships to other classes. Then work outwards towards the classes that are less important.

As you add an association or attribute, make sure it is relevant to the application – that it will be needed to implement some requirement. For example, you might be tempted to add many different attributes to a class `Person`: `name`, `height`, `weight`, `dateOfBirth`, `educationLevel` etc. But do you really need all this information in your application? If there is no requirement to manipulate certain information, then representing that information in your model adds unnecessary complexity.

As you are adding attributes and associations, follow the principles of good modeling discussed in the earlier sections of this chapter. For example, analyze each association to make sure its multiplicity is correct.

Tips about identifying and specifying valid associations

To find out whether an association should exist, ask yourself if one class *possesses, controls, is connected to, is related to, is a part of, has as parts, is a member of,* or *has as members* some other class in your model. You will often find statements of these types by scanning the document from which you extracted the original list of classes.

As you add each association, remember to specify the multiplicity at both ends and label it clearly.

An association is only legitimate if its links will survive beyond the execution of any particular operation. Associations in domain models will normally be stored in a database. So, if you do not think that the information captured by an association will need to be stored, then perhaps the association should be eliminated.

A common mistake is to represent actions as if they were associations. For example, imagine you had classes `LibraryPatron` and `CollectionItem` (where a `CollectionItem` might be a book, video recording, etc.) You might initially think that `borrow` and `return` should be associations between these two classes. On the surface this seems reasonable since you might want to keep a record of each of these actions. However, the correct way to model this information is to use a separate class `Loan`, as shown in Figure 5.27.

Tips about identifying and specifying valid attributes

Attributes can be identified by looking at the description of the system and searching for information that must be maintained about instances of each class.

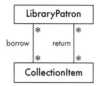

Bad, due to the use of associations | Better. The `borrow` operation creates a
that are actions | `Loan`, and the `return` operation sets the
`returnedDate` attribute

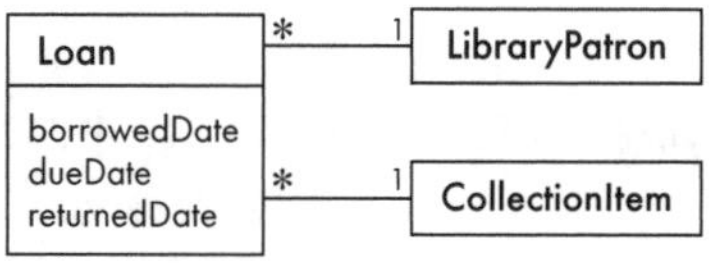

Figure 5.27   Avoiding using associations to represent actions

Several of the nouns you may have originally identified, but rejected as classes, may now become attributes.

Remember that an attribute should generally be a simple variable – typically an integer or string. It can also be a one-to-one composition as shown in Figure 5.20.

An attribute should not normally represent a variable number of things (i.e. it should not have a plural name). For example, as shown in Figure 5.28, **addresses** is not a good name for an attribute of **Person**, even though there might be a home address, work address and shipping address. It is also not good to have many duplicate attributes as shown in the middle diagram. In situations like this it is best to create an association to a separate **Address** class as shown on the right.

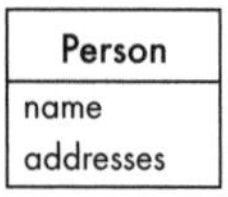

Bad, due to   Bad, due to too many   Good solution. The type indicates whether it
a plural attribute   attributes, and the   is a home address, business address etc.
                        inability to add more
                        addresses

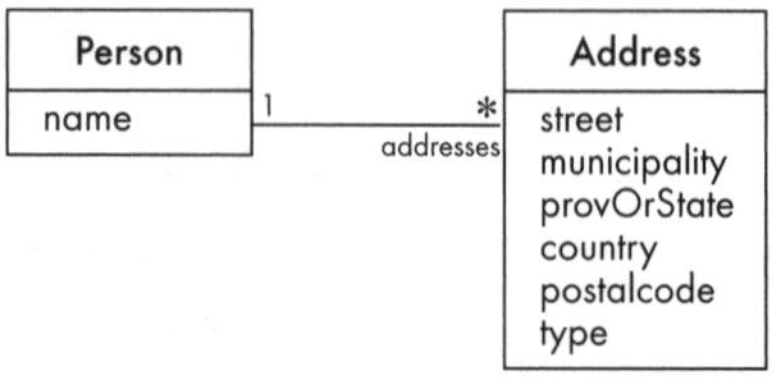

Figure 5.28   Alternatives for handling multiple addresses

An attribute should not have an implicit internal structure. For example, if in your application you will need to obtain the first name of a person, then you should not use a single attribute to represent the name. If you did this, then the application would have to parse the attribute to extract the first name, which is error-prone. Instead you should have separate `firstName` and `lastName` attributes.

In general, if a subset of a class's attributes forms a coherent reusable group (such as an address), then you should consider creating a distinct class containing these attributes. This will make your system simpler, more flexible and easier to use.

Example 5.3   *Continuing from Example 5.2, add an initial set of associations and attributes to the classes you identified. Add and delete classes as necessary.*

A central class at which to start identifying associations and attributes is `Flight`. The problem description informs us that there is a schedule of numbered flights; from this we can infer that a flight has a `date`, a `time` and a `flightNumber`. However, we notice that every day the flights that leave at the same time have the same flight number. Therefore it makes sense to split `Flight` into two classes we will call `RegularFlight` (containing the time and flight number for flights that regularly depart at the same time of day) and `SpecificFlight` (that departs on a particular day, and on which passengers are booked). The association between these classes is one-to-many. We do not need to name the association explicitly since the default 'has' appears adequate. (This approach does not allow us to deal well with charter flights, but we leave that as an exercise.)

We now move on to understand how passengers are booked. There is clearly a many-to-many relationship between `Passenger` and `SpecificFlight` but, as discussed earlier in Section 5.3, we need to add a `Booking` association class; this will contain the `seatNumber`.

Each `Passenger` has a name, but we will also assign him or her a number in case names are identical, and to allow for the anticipated frequent-flier plan.

The phrase 'who supervises whom' implies that `Employee` needs a reflexive association with a `supervisor` role. The phrase 'what everyone does' implies an attribute `jobFunction`.

The class diagram so far is shown in Figure 5.29.

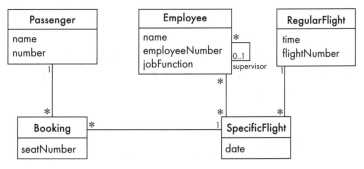

Figure 5.29   First attempt at a class diagram for the airline system

Exercise

E103 For the system(s) you worked on in the last exercise, identify an initial list of attributes and associations. Add or delete classes as necessary. Draw a preliminary class diagram.

Identifying generalizations and interfaces

There are two ways to identify generalizations: bottom-up and top-down. The bottom-up approach groups together similar classes, creating a new superclass, whereas the top-down approach divides up a complex class, creating new subclasses.

To use the bottom-up approach, you look for classes that have features in common. In general, if you find two or more classes that have similar attributes, associations or operations then you should consider creating a common superclass.

For example, for any system in which there are different types of person, you will probably find that they all have attributes to store the name, telephone number and address. These attributes should therefore be placed in the common superclass.

Sometimes the common features do not have the same name. The left part of Figure 5.30 shows a case where there are two types of customers: instances of `Company` and instances of `Person`. Despite the fact that the attributes and associations have different names, we can still see that they are really the same, hence we should create a common superclass `LegalEntity`, as shown in the right part of Figure 5.30. This will possess renamed attributes and a single association.

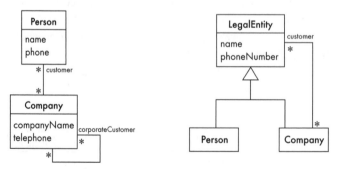

Figure 5.30 Creating a generalization of two classes which have similar features, but the names of the features are different. The left diagram is the original version; the right diagram is the improved version

Instead of creating a superclass, it might be better (or necessary) in some cases to create one or more interfaces. This would be typical if you will sometimes need to declare a variable that can contain instances of several classes, yet:

■ The classes are very dissimilar except for having a few operations in common, or

■ One or more of the classes already have their own superclasses, or

■ You want to limit the operations that can be performed on the variable to just those available in an interface.

For example, in the SimpleChat system there is a class called `ClientConsole`. If we wanted to add another type of user interface, such as `ClientGUI`, then we might be tempted to create a common superclass called `ClientUI`. However, this would prevent us from giving `ClientGUI` some other superclass – in fact we will want to make `ClientGUI` a subclass of `Frame`.

Example 5.4 *Continuing from Example 5.3, add any obvious generalizations, making whatever other changes become necessary.*

Classes `Passenger` and `Employee` clearly share common information. However simply making a superclass called `Person` does not suffice since it is possible for a person to be both an employee and a passenger – an instance can only be of one class. Therefore we introduce a class called `PersonRole` and an association that allows each Person to have up to two roles. The result is shown in Figure 5.31.

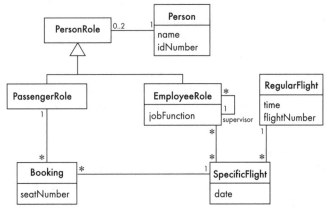

Figure 5.31   Airline system class diagram after adding a generalization

Exercises

E104   For the system(s) you worked on in the previous two exercises, identify any generalizations or interfaces. This may lead you to add or delete classes, associations and attributes. Modify your class diagram(s) accordingly.

E105   For the sets of potential classes listed in Exercise E12, build a complete class diagram with associations and attributes as well as generalizations.

Allocating responsibilities to classes

A *responsibility* is something that the system is required to do. The prime responsibility of performing each functional requirement must be attributed to one of the classes, although other classes will likely collaborate with it to help perform the task.

In general, it is important to distribute the responsibilities among the classes so that no one class has an unfair share, and hence becomes unduly complex. If a class has too many responsibilities then you should examine it to see whether it can be split into several distinct classes. Also, all the responsibilities of a given class should be clearly related to each other and to the attributes and associations of the class.

If a class has no responsibilities attached to it, then it is probably useless. On the other hand, when a responsibility cannot be attributed to any of the existing classes, then a new class should be created.

A good way to determine responsibilities is to perform use case analysis as discussed in Chapter 4. Another good source of information about responsibilities is to look for verbs and nouns describing *actions* in the system description.

There are several categories of responsibilities that can be found in a wide variety of classes:

■ **Setting** and **getting** the values of attributes. It is good practice to make attributes themselves private and to create public methods where necessary to allow access to them. This allows the class to have more control over its attributes – it can ensure that they are given only valid values. It also allows you to change the internal design of the class without affecting how users of the class interact with it. For some classes, all the responsibilities fall into this category. A `Date` class, for example, might have no other responsibility than holding the day, month and year of a date, and allowing access to the values of these attributes.

■ **Creating** and **initializing** new instances. Often, the primary responsibility for creating an instance of a class is given to some other class. (That other class has to call the constructor of the class being instantiated.) Sometimes, however, responsibility is placed directly in the class whose instance is being created (implemented as a static operation). There is often a need for several classes to collaborate in this type of responsibility, as we will discuss in the next section.

■ **Loading** to and **saving** from persistent storage.

■ **Destroying** instances. Like the process of creating instances, this also often requires collaboration with other classes.

■ **Adding** and **deleting** links of associations, such as recording that a particular professor will teach a certain course. Responsibilities of this kind are similar to manipulating attributes. However, they are more complex since there is the need to collaborate with other classes to ensure that the bi-directional nature of most associations is maintained properly. We will discuss this in more detail in the next section.

■ **Copying**, **converting**, **transforming**, **transmitting** or **outputting**. Many applications have responsibilities of these types, which require changing the information to some other form. A common example is the `toString` method in Java, which creates a `String` representation of an object.

■ **Computing** numerical results, such as the fine on an overdue library book.

■ **Navigating** and **searching**. For example, in Figure 5.30, there might be a need for capabilities to look up a particular customer by name, or to find all the customers that match a certain criteria.

■ **Specialized work** needed by the particular application that does not fit in any of the above categories.

When listing responsibilities, many skilled modelers will omit all but the last three categories – and it is extremely common to omit the first category. This is because the presence of such responsibilities can largely be inferred from the class diagram. However, taking this loose approach leaves uncertainty about where some responsibilities will be put – the modelers have to mentally decide where to place omitted responsibilities when identifying operations.

Example 5.5 *Create a list of responsibilities for the Airline system discussed in Examples 5.2 to 5.4. Allocate each responsibility to a class and discuss your reasoning for the allocation. Finally, update the class diagram as necessary.*

The following are a few of the responsibilities derived from the system description, with an indication of in which classes they might be put. It is clear when creating this list of responsibilities that the airline system description is rather too brief – forcing us to deduce the presence of unstated requirements.

■ Creating a new `RegularFlight`. This could be a class (static) responsibility of the `RegularFlight` class. But we prefer, as much as possible, to give responsibilities to instances. We will therefore introduce a new class called `Airline` (shown in Figure 5.32) that will have this responsibility. There will probably be only one instance of `Airline`.

■ Searching for a particular `RegularFlight`. In order to do this, we need a class that maintains a collection of all the instances of `RegularFlight`. That class will be `Airline`, which will therefore have this responsibility.

■ Modifying the attributes of a `RegularFlight`. Each class should normally modify its own attributes; this responsibility should therefore go in `RegularFlight`.

■ Creating a `SpecificFlight`. We choose to put `RegularFlight` in charge of this, since the new `SpecificFlight` will be an occurrence of a particular `RegularFlight` that already exists at the time this responsibility is initiated.

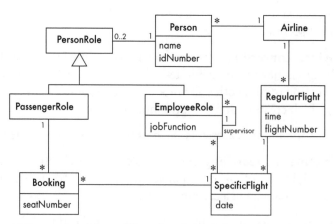

Figure 5.32   Airline system after adding the **Airline** class

■ Canceling a `SpecificFlight`. This can be put in `SpecificFlight`.

■ Booking a `PassengerRole` on a `SpecificFlight`. This could go in either `PassengerRole` or `SpecificFlight`. It could also go in `Booking`, but we prefer not to put it there since the appropriate Booking is not yet created by the time this responsibility is initiated. We choose to give this responsibility to `PassengerRole`, since in the real world it is the passengers who initiate bookings.

■ Canceling a `Booking`. This should be put in `Booking`.

Exercises

E106   For the system(s) you worked on in Exercises E102 to E104, determine the responsibilities of each class. Update your class diagrams as necessary.

E107   Determine the responsibilities for each of the classes in the genealogical example, Figure 5.25(c).

A paper-and-pencil technique to rapidly develop a class diagram

A useful technique for prototyping class diagrams involves the use of small cards, or pieces of paper such as sticky notes. As you identify classes, you write their names on the cards. You can add and delete cards as the technique progresses. The cards are often called CRC (Class–Responsibility–Collaboration) cards.

As you identify attributes and responsibilities, you list them on the cards as well. The fact that each card has limited space encourages you to not make any of the classes excessively complex. If you cannot fit all the responsibilities on one card, this suggests you should split the class into two related classes.

Tagged values

Figure 5.33 shows the use of a UML feature called *tagged values*. You can attach information to any UML element. In this case we have attached 'id' tags to each operation. The 'id' indicates the responsibility using a letter from 'a' to 'e' as its first character.

You can move the cards around freely on a whiteboard to arrange them into a class diagram. Draw lines between cards to represent associations and generalizations.

The above technique allows you to rapidly rearrange the class diagram, quickly repositioning classes without having to redraw them. A good software tool can also be used for this, but low-tech paper-and-pencil techniques can often be faster than manipulating the software's user interface. The paper-and-pencil approach is especially effective in a brainstorming environment, where several people can be working together to move around the various classes.

Identifying operations

Operations are needed to realize the responsibilities of each class – there may be several operations per responsibility, but one will be in charge.

The operation that is in charge of fulfilling the responsibility will normally be declared `public`. It becomes part of the interface of the entire subsystem. Other methods that collaborate to perform the responsibility will be as private as possible.

The following are situations in which several classes must collaborate to implement some typical responsibilities of a given class. We will look at the operations required to implement these responsibilities, and will use the class diagram shown in Figure 5.33 as an illustration.

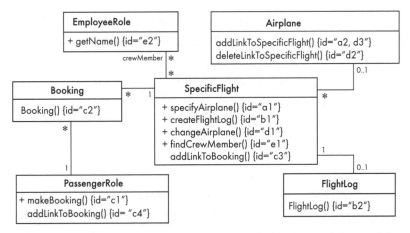

Figure 5.33 Classes and operations that collaborate to perform responsibilities of class `SpecificFlight`. The public operations are shown with a + symbol

(a) **Making a bi-directional link between two existing objects**; e.g. adding a link between an instance of `SpecificFlight` and an instance of `Airplane`.

a1. (public) The instance of SpecificFlight makes a unidirectional link to the instance of Airplane, and then calls operation a2.

a2. (non-public) The instance of Airplane makes a unidirectional link back to the instance of SpecificFlight.

(b) **Creating an object and linking it to an existing object**; e.g. creating a FlightLog, and linking it to a SpecificFlight.

b1. (public) The instance of SpecificFlight calls the constructor of FlightLog (operation b2); then, when it is complete, makes a unidirectional link to the new instance of FlightLog.

b2. (non-public) Class FlightLog's constructor, among its other actions, makes a unidirectional link back to the instance of SpecificFlight.

(c) **Creating an association class, given two existing objects**; creating an instance of Booking, for example, which will link a SpecificFlight to a PassengerRole.

c1. (public) The instance of PassengerRole calls the constructor of Booking (operation c2).

c2. (non-public) Class Booking's constructor, among its other actions, makes a unidirectional link back to the instance of PassengerRole, makes a unidirectional link to the instance of SpecificFlight, and calls operations c3 and c4.

c3. (non-public) The instance of SpecificFlight makes a unidirectional link to the instance of Booking.

c4. (non-public) The instance of PassengerRole makes a unidirectional link to the instance of Booking.

(d) **Changing the destination of a link**; e.g. changing the Airplane linked to a SpecificFlight, from <u>airplane1:</u> to <u>airplane2:</u>.

d1. (public) The instance of SpecificFlight deletes the link to <u>airplane1:</u> makes a unidirectional link to <u>airplane2:</u>, calls operation d2, and then calls operation d3.

d2. (non-public) <u>airplane1:</u> deletes its unidirectional link to the instance of SpecificFlight.

d3. (non-public) <u>airplane2:</u> makes a unidirectional link to the instance of SpecificFlight.

(e) **Searching for an associated instance**; e.g. searching for a crew member associated with a SpecificFlight that has a certain name.

e1. (public) Create an Iterator over all the crewMember links of the SpecificFlight, and for each of them call operation e2, until it finds a match.

e2. (may be public) The instance of EmployeeRole returns its name.

These types of collaborations are applicable in many different systems.

Notice that it would be very harmful for any of the non-public methods to be called directly – they would end up only performing part of a complete responsibility, leaving the system in an unstable state.

Exercises

E108   Add operations to the examples you worked on in Exercises E102 to E104 and E106.

E109   Add operations to the genealogical example of Figure 5.25(c), which you also worked on in Exercise E107.

E110   Use the techniques described in this section to extend the airline system. Your extended system should include the requirements listed below. You should produce a single class diagram showing classes, attributes and generalizations. Do not show operations yet.

(a) Flights fly from one airport terminal to another, but may also have several intermediate stops. A passenger can be booked on one or more of the legs of a flight.

(b) Passengers can query the system to determine at what times flights are available from their desired origin city to their desired destination city (they do not care about which terminal or airport is used by the airline).

(c) Flights have scheduled departure and arrival times, but they can be late, therefore they have actual departure and arrival times as well.

(d) The airline may add charter flights that are not regularly scheduled.

(e) The airline publishes prices that apply between any pair of cities to which it flies. Business class, regular and seat-sale fares are available.

(f) Passengers buy tickets and are charged the prices in effect when their tickets were booked. Each ticket involves a complete itinerary, composed of a sequence of one or more legs. The fare type is not necessarily the same for each leg of the flight.

(g) Passengers are automatically part of a frequent-flier plan. They accumulate points based on the distance they flew and their fare type (business class or not).

E111   (a) Determine the responsibilities needed to implement the requirements listed in the previous exercise (omitting the responsibilities that merely involve setting and getting attributes).

(b) Determine all the operations needed to implement the responsibilities – specifying in which classes they belong.

5.10 Implementing class diagrams in Java

So far in this chapter we have been talking strictly about modeling. We want now, however, to take a brief foray into the detailed design stage in order to give you a taste of how to implement your models. We believe that to become a good modeler, you have to develop an understanding of how your model will be concretized as a real system.

On the book's web site (www.lloseng.com) you can find a complete implementation of the Airline system discussed in the last section. Below, we will briefly discuss some aspects of its Java implementation, leaving you to study the code in order to understand other details.

The implementation of some aspects of class diagrams is rather straightforward:

■ Attributes are generally implemented as instance variables. You have to choose an appropriate class, but normally it will be a class from the standard Java library such as `String`.

■ Generalizations are implemented using the `extends` keyword, and interfaces are implemented using the `implements` keyword.

Implementing associations, however, takes a bit more thought because there are several ways to do it. However, once you learn to implement a few associations you will find yourself using the same general structure of the code over and over again. In what follows, we will suggest typical ways to implement associations as objects in a running Java program. More sophisticated techniques are needed when objects have to be loaded from a database.

Associations are normally implemented using instance variables. You divide each two-way association into two one-way associations so that each associated class has an instance variable representing the other end of the association.

To implement a one-way association where the multiplicity at the other end is 'one' or 'optional', you declare a variable whose type is that class. Therefore `SpecificFlight` from Figure 5.33 would have declarations of the following instance variables:

```
private TerminalOfAirport destination;
private Airplane airplane;
private FlightLog flightLog;
```

Some of the declarations in other classes would include:

■ in `Booking`: `SpecificFlight specificFlight` ;

■ in `FlightLog`: `SpecificFlight specificFlight` ;

To implement a one-way association where the multiplicity at the other end is 'many', you use a collection class such as `ArrayList`. Therefore, `SpecificFlight` would have declarations:

```
private List crewMembers; // of EmployeeRole
private List bookings;
```

The following shows the code needed to implement a responsibility in
RegularFlight to create a new SpecificFlight. This follows the pattern of
responsibility (b) from the last section.

```
class RegularFlight
{
  private List specificFlights;
  ...
  // Method that has primary responsibility
  public void addSpecificFlight(Calendar aDate)
  {
    SpecificFlight newSpecificFlight;
    newSpecificFlight = new SpecificFlight(aDate, this);
    specificFlights.add(newSpecificFlight);
  }
  ...
}


class SpecificFlight
{
  private Calendar date;
  private RegularFlight regularFlight;
  ...
  // Constructor that should only be called from
  // addSpecificFlight
  SpecificFlight(
    Calendar aDate,
    RegularFlight aRegularFlight)
  {
    date = aDate;
    regularFlight = aRegularFlight;
  }
}
```

To implement an association where the multiplicity at the other end has a small,
fixed upper bound, you can use a regular array. An example is the 0..2
multiplicity in the association between PersonRole and Person in Figure 5.31.
Remember that if you do this you should make sure you are not limiting the
flexibility of the system.

Person would declare the following instance variable:

```
private PersonRole[] roles = new PersonRole[2];
```

5.11 Difficulties and risks when creating class diagrams

The following is the key difficulty to anticipate when creating class diagrams in an industrial context:

■ **Modeling is a particularly difficult skill.** Many people who are excellent programmers nevertheless have considerable difficulty thinking at the level of abstraction needed to create effective models. Also, since education programs have not traditionally focused on it, software developers often have significantly less knowledge about modeling than about design and programming. Taken together, these mean that software projects are at risk from models that are incomplete, incorrect or insufficiently flexible.
Resolution. Ensure that members of the team have adequate training in modeling. Have an experienced modeler as part of every team. Review all models thoroughly.

5.12 Summary

In this chapter we introduced UML, the Unified Modeling Language. Then we showed you how to create class diagrams, one of the most important types of diagrams in UML. Class diagrams model classes and how they are related.

Very careful analysis is required to create good class diagrams. A good starting point is to take a description of the problem, or a statement of requirements, and look for the nouns in it. Once you have created a basic list of classes, it is best to start arranging your model starting with the classes that are the most central or important to the system.

Class modeling can proceed by creating an initial set of associations among the classes, and adding attributes and generalizations. You then assign responsibilities to the classes and derive operations from these responsibilities. This whole process should be performed iteratively.

Any class diagram should be subjected to detailed review. A key thing to ensure is that all generalizations are valid – that is, they follow the *isa* rule and everything in the superclass makes sense in subclasses. Other common types of error are poor naming of elements of the diagrams and incorrect multiplicity.

Creating good class diagrams is a central skill in modern software engineering, but it takes time to become an expert. We suggest practicing with many examples, and implementing your models. The process of implementation – actually getting a system to run – will help you heighten your awareness of potential flaws.

5.13 For more information

The following are some of the many available resources about UML:

UML in general

- Cetus Links on UML: http://www.cetus-links.org/oo_uml.html is a very extensive list of resources

- OOTips: http://www.ootips.org, a site that consolidates information about OO technologies from various sources

- The UML Bibliography: http://www.db.informatik.uni-bremen.de/umlbib

- G. Booch, J. Rumbaugh and I. Jacobson, *The Unified Modeling Language User Guide*, Addison-Wesley, 1998

- J. Rumbaugh, I. Jacobson and G. Booch, *The Unified Modeling Language Reference Manual*, Addison-Wesley, 1998

- I. Jacobson, G. Booch and J. Rumbaugh, *The Unified Software Development Process*, Addison-Wesley, 1999

- M. Fowler, *UML Distilled: A Brief Guide to the Standard Object Modeling Language*, 3rd edition, Addison-Wesley, 2003

- J. Warmer and A. Kleppe, *The Object Constraint Language: Getting Your Models Ready for MDA*, 2nd edition, Addison-Wesley, 2003

- The Object Management Group: home of the UML Specification: http://www.omg.org

Object-oriented development processes

- P. Kruchten, *The Rational Unified Process, An Introduction*, 2nd edition, Addison-Wesley, 2000. Discusses the most popular UML-based methodology

- S. Shlaer and S. Mellor, *Object-Oriented Systems Analysis: Modeling the World in Data*, Yourdon Press, 1989

- J. Rumbaugh et al., *Object-Oriented Modeling and Design*, Prentice Hall, 1991. A classic book that presents the OMT notation, a predecessor of UML, along with a development method that focused on class diagrams

- P. Coad and E. Yourdon, *Object Oriented Analysis*, Yourdon Press, 1991. This places the emphasis on entity-relation diagrams

- G. Booch, *Object-Oriented Analysis and Design With Applications*, Addison-Wesley, 1994. A detailed methodology that was also an important predecessor of UML

- J. Martin, and J. Odell, *Principles of Object Oriented Analysis and Design*, Prentice Hall, 1992

- I. Jacobson, *Object-Oriented Software Engineering: A Use Case Driven Approach*, Addison-Wesley, 1994. Introduces use case analysis; another UML predecessor

Tools for creating UML models

- IBM Rational Software: http://www.ibm.com/software/rational

- Together by Borland: http://www.borland.com/together/

- Objects By Design maintains a list of UML modeling tools at http:/www.objectsbydesign.com/tools/umltools_byCompany.html

- ObjectPlant: a good basic shareware tool for the Macintosh. http://www.arctaedius.com/ObjectPlant/

- Argo UML: an open source shareware project run by Tigris. http://argouml.tigris.org. Argo UML actively helps you to draw UML diagrams by suggesting things that you should do; its developers call this 'cognitive support'. Argo UML is written in Java; you can therefore study and modify its source code if you wish

Project exercise

Since the SimpleChat system has a very simple class diagram, there are no exercises for that project in this chapter.

The following problem will allow you to make further progress on the Small Hotel Reservation System project.

E112 Create a class diagram of the 'Small Hotel Reservation System'. Base your analysis on the requirements you developed in the last chapter. Your diagram should have any necessary classes, associations, generalizations and attributes. Write the main use cases of this system and determine the main responsibilities of each class. We will consider the operations later when we study system interactions in Chapter 8.

Using design patterns

6

In the previous chapter, we looked at UML class diagrams. This chapter continues the study of the static view of software by looking at typical patterns found in class diagrams. These patterns recur in many designs; by learning and using them you are reusing the collective experience of many software developers.

In this chapter you will learn about the following

- The structure and format used to describe patterns.

- Patterns used to help ensure separation of concerns in a class diagram: Abstraction–Occurrence, Observer, and Player–Role.

- A pattern used to create hierarchies of instances: General Hierarchy.

- The Delegation pattern in which a method simply calls another method in another class, but which can significantly improve the overall design of a system.

- Patterns in which you use delegation to gain access to facilities in one or more other classes: Adapter, Façade and Proxy.

- Patterns that help protect other objects from unanticipated access: Immutable and Read-Only Interface.

- A pattern that enables you to create application-specific objects in a framework: Factory.

6.1   Introduction to patterns

As you gain experience in object-oriented software development, you will begin to notice that many parts of your models or designs reappear, with only slight changes, in many different systems or subsystems. These recurring aspects are called *patterns*. Many of them have been systematically documented for all software developers to use.

> **Definition:** a *pattern* is the outline of a reusable solution to a general problem encountered in a particular context.

In this chapter we will restrict our attention to patterns used in modeling and design; but people have also developed patterns for many other human tasks, such as doing business, diagnosing mechanical problems or taking better photographs. In Chapter 9, we will look at architectural patterns, which are used at the very highest level of software design.

A good pattern should be as general as possible, containing a solution that has been proven to solve the problem effectively in the indicated context. The pattern must be described in an easy-to-understand form so that people can determine when and how to use it. Studying patterns is an effective way to learn from the experience of others.

Each pattern should have a name; it should also have the following information:

- **Context:** the general situation in which the pattern applies.

- **Problem:** a sentence or two explaining the main difficulty being tackled.

- **Forces:** the issues or concerns that you need to consider when solving the problem. These include criteria for evaluating a good solution.

- **Solution:** the recommended way to solve the problem in the given context. The solution is said to 'balance the forces'; in other words, it has a good combination of advantages, with few counterbalancing disadvantages.

- **Antipatterns:** (optional) solutions that are inferior or do not work in this context. The reason for their rejection should be explained. The antipatterns may be valid solutions in other contexts, or may never be valid. They often are mistakes made by beginners.

- **Related patterns:** (optional) patterns that are similar to this pattern. They may represent variations, extensions or special cases.

- **References:** acknowledgements of those who developed or inspired the pattern.

A pattern should normally be illustrated using a simple diagram and should be written using a narrative writing style.

In the following sections, we present a sample of the most useful patterns that you can apply when you perform modeling and design using UML class diagrams. You will recognize some of them from the discussions in the last chapter. Here, however, we will describe them in a more formal way. Our list of patterns is by no means exhaustive – you should see the references at the end of the chapter to learn about the wide variety of patterns that are available.

The first three of the patterns described below we call *modeling patterns*, since they appear in domain models long before any software design occurs. The rest

Patterns and the patterns community

The word 'pattern' has a well-understood meaning in ordinary English: it refers to a set of instructions, or a model or an example from which things are made or matched.

The architect Christopher Alexander developed the notion of patterns for use in architecture and design. The software engineering community has adopted his meaning of the term.

Alexander defines patterns as 'a three-part rule, which expresses a relation between a certain context, a problem and a solution'.

Patterns are an excellent way to document design understanding, and to pass that understanding on to others who are learning how to design. By thinking about relevant patterns as they design, designers can work more rapidly and produce higher-quality work because they are reusing the experience of others.

The exact format you use to write patterns varies from author to author, but most authors include the same kind of information that we include. A group of interrelated patterns form a *pattern language*.

There is a 'patterns community' within software engineering. This is a loose but large collection of people who believe in the usefulness of patterns, as well as in certain philosophies regarding their development. Among the important philosophies of the patterns community are:

- Patterns represent well-known knowledge. In other words, no pattern could ever be patented because it must be in common use (note the use of a completely unrelated word 'patent' that sounds similar; for more on patents, see the sidebar in the risks section of Chapter 11). People do not *invent* patterns – a pattern is a literary work describing common practice.
- Patterns should be in the public domain, where possible; people should be encouraged to improve the pattern to make it more usable.
- When patterns are written or modified, they should be reviewed in a public setting by a group of the author's peers.
- Patterns should be written for the public good. A pattern that describes how to do something unethical, for example, would not be acceptable to the community.

of the patterns are *design patterns* since they involve details that would normally be deferred until the design stage.

6.2 The Abstraction–Occurrence pattern

Context This modeling pattern is most frequently found in class diagrams that form part of a system domain model.

Often in a domain model you find a set of related objects that we will call *occurrences*; the members of such a set share common information but also differ from each other in important ways.

Examples of sets of occurrences include:

- All the episodes of a television series. They have the same producer and the same series title, but different story-lines.

■ The flights that leave at the same time every day for the same destination. They have the same flight number, but occur on different dates and carry different passengers and crew.

■ All the copies of the same book in a library. They have the same title and author. However, the copies have different barcode identifiers and are borrowed by different people at different times.

Problem What is the best way to represent such sets of occurrences in a class diagram?

Forces You want to represent the members of each set of occurrences without duplicating the common information. Duplication would consume unnecessary space and would require changing all the occurrences when the common information changes. Furthermore, you want to avoid the risk of inconsistency that would result from changing the common information in some objects but not in others. Finally you want a solution that maximizes the flexibility of the system.

Solution Create an «*Abstraction*» class that contains the data that is common to all the members of a set of occurrences. Then create an «*Occurrence*» class representing the occurrences of this abstraction. Connect these classes with a one-to-many association. This is illustrated in Figure 6.1.

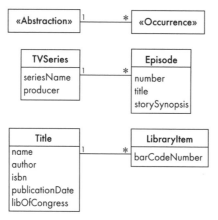

Figure 6.1 Template and examples of the Abstraction–Occurrence pattern

Examples You might create an «Abstraction» class called TVSeries; an instance of this might be the children's series 'Sesame Street'. You would then create an «Occurrence» class called Episode. Similarly, you might create an «Abstraction» class called Title which will contain the author and name of a book or similar publication. The corresponding «Occurrence» class might be called LibraryItem. These examples are illustrated in Figure 6.1.

Another example of the Abstraction–Occurrence design pattern is the pair consisting of RegularFlight and SpecificFlight in the airline system, as shown in Figure 5.29.

Antipatterns These antipatterns are examples of real mistakes made by beginners.

One inappropriate solution, shown in Figure 6.2(a), is to use a single class. This would not work, because information would have to be duplicated in each of the multiple copies of a book. For example, the different copies of *Moby Dick* can be borrowed by different people; there would, therefore, have to be separate 'Moby Dick' instances, listing the same name, author and ISBN.

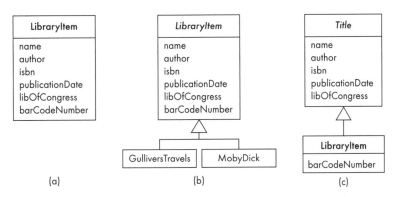

Figure 6.2 Inappropriate ways to represent abstractions and occurrences

Another very bad solution, shown in Figure 6.2(b), is to create a separate subclass for each title (i.e. a class `GulliversTravels` and another class `MobyDick`). Information such as name, author, etc. would still be duplicated in each of the instances of each subclass. Furthermore, this approach seriously restricts the flexibility of the system – you want to be able to add new books without having to program new classes.

Figure 6.2(c) shows another invalid solution: making the abstraction class a *superclass* of the occurrence class. This would not solve the original problem presented in this pattern, since, although the attributes in the superclass are inherited by the subclasses, the *data* in those attributes is not. For example, even though there is a `name` attribute defined in the superclass `Title`, we would still have to set the value of this attribute in every instance of `LibraryItem`.

Related patterns When the abstraction is an aggregate, the occurrences are also typically aggregates. The result is the Abstraction–Occurrence Square pattern, illustrated in Figure 6.3.

References This pattern is a generalization of the Title–Item pattern of Eriksson and Penker (see the 'For more information' section at the end of the chapter).

Exercise

E113 Apply the Abstraction–Occurrence pattern in the following situations. For each situation, show the two linked classes, the association between the classes, and the attributes in each class.

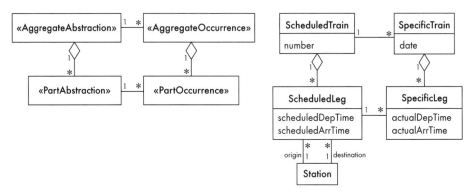

Figure 6.3   The Abstraction–Occurrence Square pattern

(a) The issues of a periodical.

(b) The copies of the issues of a periodical.

(c) The repeats and re-runs of the same television program.

(d) Models of electronic appliances and the individual appliances.

6.3   The General Hierarchy pattern

Context This modeling pattern occurs in many class diagrams. You often find a set of objects that have a naturally hierarchical relationship. For example, the relationships between managers and their subordinates in an organization chart, or the directories (also known as folders), subdirectories and files in a file system.

Each object in such a hierarchy can have zero or more objects above them in the hierarchy (superiors), and zero or more objects below them (subordinates). Some objects, however, cannot have any subordinates – for example the staff members in an organization chart (as opposed to the managers) or the files in a file system (as opposed to the directories).

Problem How do you draw a class diagram to represent a hierarchy of objects, in which some objects cannot have subordinates?

Forces You want a flexible way of representing the hierarchy that naturally prevents certain objects from having subordinates. You also have to account for the fact that all the objects share common features.

Solution Create an abstract «*Node*» class to represent the features possessed by each object in the hierarchy – one such feature is that each node can have superiors.

Then create at least two subclasses of the «Node» class. One of the subclasses, «*SuperiorNode*», must be linked by a «*subordinates*» association to the superclass; whereas at least one subclass, «*NonSuperiorNode*», must not be. The subordinates of a «SuperiorNode» can thus be instances of either «SuperiorNode» or «NonSuperiorNode».

The multiplicity of the «subordinates» association can be optional-to-many or many-to-many. If it is many-to-many, then the hierarchy of instances becomes a lattice, in which a node can have many superiors. The 'optional' allows for the case of the top node in the hierarchy, which has no superiors.

Examples In Figure 6.4, there are three kinds of employee in an organization, but only managers can supervise subordinates. Similarly, only directories can contain other file system objects. In a user interface, some objects (such as panels) can contain others; this is illustrated in Figure 6.5. As a final example, in Figure 5.30 a company can have customers, who in turn have other customers, and are the customers of other companies – the result is a network of customer/service-provider relationships.

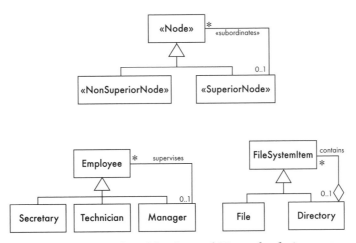

Figure 6.4   Template and examples of the General Hierarchy design pattern

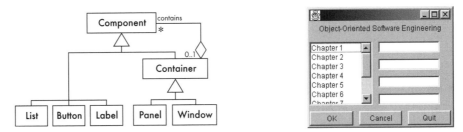

Figure 6.5   Component classes whose instances form a hierarchy in a user interface. The example shows a frame, composed of a label (top), a list (left) and two panels. The first panel (on the right) is in turn composed of four text fields. The other panel (at the bottom) contains three buttons

Antipatterns A common beginner's mistake is to model a hierarchy of categories using a hierarchy of classes, as illustrated in Figure 5.11. This mistake is made because beginners are taught about inheritance hierarchies, and then immediately think that every hierarchy should be an inheritance hierarchy.

Related The Reflexive Association, discussed in Section 5.3, can be considered to be a
patterns pattern. Figures 5.8, 5.12(a) and 5.25(a) show that hierarchies of objects can be
modeled using asymmetric reflexive associations. Doing so, however, does not
allow for the special «NonSuperiorNode» classes that occur in the context of the
General Hierarchy pattern.

  The *Composite* pattern is a specialization of the General Hierarchy pattern. In
the Composite pattern, the association between «SuperiorNode» and «Node» is
an aggregation. A Composite is a recursive container; that is, a container that
can contain other containers. This is the case with directories in a file system
(Figure 6.4) as well as instances of GUIComposite (Figure 6.5).

References The Composite pattern is one of the 'Gang of Four' patterns. See the book by
Gamma, Helm, Johnson and Vlissides in 'For more information'.

Exercises

E114 Figure 5.21 shows a hierarchy of vehicle parts. Show how this hierarchy might
be better represented using the General Hierarchy pattern (or more precisely,
by the Composite pattern).

E115 Revisit Exercise E91. Did you use the General Hierarchy pattern? If not, then
redo the exercise, showing a hierarchy of various levels of government. Imagine
that municipalities are the lowest levels of government.

E116 An expression in Java can be broken down into a hierarchy of subexpressions.
For example, (a/(b+c))+(b-func(d)*(e/(f+g))) has (a/b+c)) as one of its higher-
level subexpressions.

 (a) Using the General Hierarchy or Composite pattern, create a class diagram
  to represent expressions in Java. Hints:

  (i) A higher-level expression might have more than two parts.
  (ii) The parts of a higher-level expression are connected by operators; how
   can these be represented?
  (iii) Think about what the «NonSuperiorNodes» must be.
  (iv) Some expressions are surrounded by parentheses, while others need
   not be; how can this be represented?

 (b) Using your class diagram from part (a), create an object diagram for the
  example above.

6.4 The Player–Role pattern

Context This modeling pattern can solve modeling problems when you are drawing
many different types of class diagram. A *role* is a particular set of features

associated with an object in a particular context. An object may *play* different roles in different contexts.

For example, a student in a university can be either an undergraduate student or a graduate student at any point in time – and is likely to need to change from one of these roles to another. Similarly, a student can also be registered in his or her program full-time or part-time, as shown in Figure 5.16; in this case, a student may change roles several times. Finally, an animal may play several of the roles shown in Figure 5.15, although in this case the roles are unlikely to change.

Problem How do you best model players and roles so that a player can change roles or possess multiple roles?

Forces It is desirable to improve encapsulation by capturing the information associated with each separate role in a class. However, as discussed in Chapter 5, you want to avoid multiple inheritance. Also, you cannot allow an instance to change class.

Solution Create a «*Player*» class to represent the object that plays different roles. Create an association from this class to an abstract «*Role*» class, which is the superclass of a set of possible roles. The subclasses of this «Role» class encapsulate all the features associated with the different roles.

If the «Player» can only play one role at a time, the multiplicity between «Player» and «Role» can be one-to-one, otherwise it will be one-to-many.

Instead of being an abstract class, the «Role» can be an interface. The only drawback to this variation is that the «Role» usually contains a mechanism, inherited by all its subclasses, allowing them to access information about the «Player». Therefore you should only make «Role» an interface if this mechanism is not needed.

Examples Figure 6.6 shows how an Animal or a Student can take on several roles to solve the problems posed by Figures 5.14 and 5.15.

The example in the middle of Figure 6.6 shows that an object can have a varying number of roles. An animal could be aquatic, land-based or both. Note that we could also have used a role class to record whether an animal is a carnivore, herbivore or omnivore; however, since this information remains the same for the life of an animal, we can just use ordinary subclasses.

The bottom example in Figure 6.6 shows that you can have two separate «Role» superclasses. In this case, a student is characterized by his or her attendance status (full-time or part-time) and by whether he or she is a graduate or undergraduate. Both of these types of status can change during the life of a Student object. The Player–Role pattern with two one-to-one associations makes it possible to create a full-time undergraduate student, a part-time graduate student or any other combination.

The Player–Role pattern is also used in the airline system to allow a person to be both a passenger and an employee. This is illustrated in Figure 5.31.

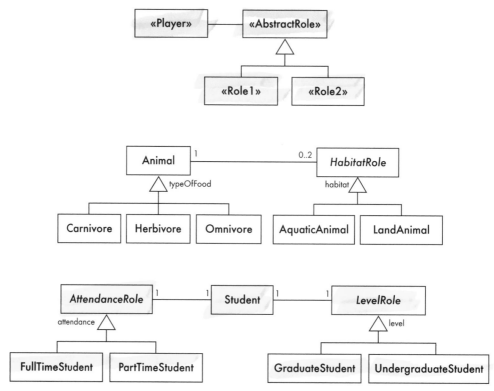

Figure 6.6   Template and examples of the Player–Role design pattern

Antipatterns   One way to implement roles is simply to merge all the features into a single «Player» class and not have «Role» classes at all. This, however, creates an overly complex class – and much of the power of object orientation is lost.

   You could also create roles as subclasses of the «Player» class. But, as we have already discussed, this is a bad idea if it results in the need for multiple inheritance or requires an instance to change class.

Related   The Abstraction–Occurrence pattern has a similar structure to the Player–Role
patterns   pattern: the player has many roles associated with it, just like the abstraction has many occurrences. However, the semantics of the two patterns is quite different. A key distinction is that in the Abstraction–Occurrence pattern, an abstraction is, as the name says, abstract, while its occurrences tend to be real-world things such as copies of books. The inverse is true in the Player–Role pattern: the player is normally a real-world entity (e.g. a person) while its roles are abstractions.

References   This pattern appears in the OMT book by Rumbaugh et al. (1991), referred to in the 'For more information' section of Chapter 5. At the time that book was written, however, the term 'pattern' had not yet taken on its current use.

Exercise

E117   Draw a class diagram, applying the Player–Role pattern in the following circumstances.

(a) Users of a system have different privileges.

(b) Managers can be given one or more responsibilities.

(c) Your favorite sport (football, baseball, etc.) in which players can play at different positions at different times in a game or in different games.

6.5   The Singleton pattern

Context   In software systems, it is very common to find classes for which you want only one instance to exist. Such a class is called a *singleton*.

For example, the `Company` or `University` classes in systems that run the business of that company or university might be singletons. Another example is the `MainWindow` class in a graphical user interface for systems that can only have one main window open.

Problem   How do you ensure that it is never possible to create more than one instance of a singleton class?

Forces   If you use a public constructor, you cannot offer the guarantee that no more than one instance will be created.

The singleton instance must also be accessible to all classes that require it, therefore it must often be public.

Solution   In a singleton class, create the following:

- A private class variable, often called `theInstance`. This stores the single instance.

- A public class method (static method), often called `getInstance`. The first time this method is called, it creates the single instance and stores it in `theInstance`. Subsequent calls simply return `theInstance`.

- A private constructor, which ensures that no other class will be able to create an instance of the singleton class.

Example   In an employee management system (Figure 6.7), the `Company` class might be the central class that encapsulates several important features related to the system as a whole. The Singleton implementation ensures that only one instance of this important class can exist. The public class method `getInstance` makes this instance globally accessible.

Note   The Singleton pattern should not be overused, since the singleton instance is effectively a global variable, and the use of global variables should be minimized.

References   The Singleton pattern is one of the 'Gang of Four' patterns.

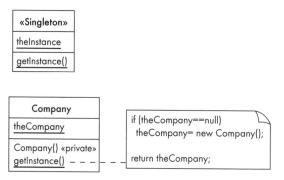

Figure 6.7   Template and example of the Singleton design pattern

Exercise

E118   Discuss how the Singleton pattern could be generalized to the case where a class could be limited to have a maximum of N instances.

6.6   The Observer pattern

Context   When you create a two-way association between two classes, the code for the classes becomes inseparable. When you compile one, the other one has to be available since the first one explicitly refers to it. This means that if you want to reuse one of the classes, you also have to reuse the other; similarly, if you change one, you probably have to change the other.

Problem   How do you reduce the interconnection between classes, especially between classes that belong to different modules or subsystems? In other words, how do you ensure that an object can communicate with other objects without knowing which class they belong to?

Forces   You want to maximize the flexibility of the system to the greatest extent possible.

Solution   Create an abstract class we will call the «*Observable*» that maintains a collection of «*Observer*» instances. The «Observable» class is very simple; it merely has a mechanism to add and remove observers, as well as a method `notifyObservers` that sends an `update` message to each «Observer». Any application class can declare itself to be a subclass of the «Observable» class. This is illustrated in Figure 6.8.

  «Observer» is an interface, defining only an abstract `update` method. Any class can thus be made to observe an «Observable» by declaring that it implements the interface, and by asking to be a member of the observer list of the «Observable». The «Observer» can then expect a call to its `update` method whenever the «Observable» changes.

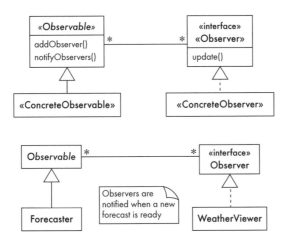

Figure 6.8   Template and example of the Observer design pattern

Using this pattern, the «Observable» neither has to know the nature or the number of the classes that will be interested in receiving the update messages, nor what they will do with this information.

Examples Java has an Observer interface and an Observable class. The Java mechanism is a specific implementation of this pattern.

In order to obtain a weather forecast, a system has to perform a long sequence of calculations. Suppose that these computations are under the control of a Forecaster object, as shown in Figure 6.8. When a new forecast is ready this object notifies all interested instances. The Forecaster is therefore the observable object. One observer might be a user interface object responsible for displaying the weather forecast. Another observer might use weather forecasts to plan the schedule of some workers – the workers might do one set of tasks on rainy days and another set on sunny days.

The Observer pattern is widely used to structure software cleanly into relatively independent modules. It is the basis of the MVC architecture presented in Chapter 9. It is also used in an additional layer of the OCSF framework as presented in Section 6.14.

Antipatterns Beginners tend to connect an observer directly to an observable so that they both have references to each other. We pointed out earlier that this means you cannot plug in a different observer.

Another mistake is to make the observers subclasses of the observable. This will not work because then each observer is at the same time an observable. It is not therefore possible to have more than one observer for an observable.

References The Observer pattern is one of the 'Gang of Four' patterns. It is also widely known as Publish-and-Subscribe (the observers are *Subscribers* and the observable is a *Publisher*).

Exercises

E119 Look at the Java documentation and explain the similarities or differences between the mechanism behind the `ActionEvent` and `ActionListener` classes and the Observer pattern.

E120 Use the Observer pattern to model a small system where several different classes would be notified each time an item is added or removed from an inventory.

6.7   The Delegation pattern

Context You need an operation in a class and you realize that another class already has an implementation of the operation. However, it is not appropriate to make your class a subclass and inherit this operation, either because the isa rule does not apply, or because you do not want to reuse *all* the methods of the other class.

Problem How can you most effectively make use of a method that already exists in the other class?

Forces You want to minimize development cost and complexity by reusing methods. You want to reduce the linkages between classes. You want to ensure that work is done in the most appropriate class.

Solution Create a method in the «Delegator» class that does only one thing: it calls a method in a neighboring «Delegate» class, thus allowing reuse of the method for which the «Delegate» has responsibility. By 'neighboring', we mean that the «Delegate» is connected to the «Delegator» by an association. This is illustrated in Figure 6.9.

Normally, in order to use delegation an association should already exist between the «Delegator» and the «Delegate». This association may be bidirectional or else unidirectional from «Delegator» to «Delegate». However, it may sometimes be appropriate to create a new association just so that you can use delegation – provided this does not increase the overall complexity of the system.

Delegation can be seen as providing selective inheritance.

Examples As shown in Figure 6.9, a `Stack` class can be easily created from an existing collection class such as `LinkedList`. The `push` method of `Stack` would simply call the `addFirst` method of `LinkedList`, the `pop` method would call the `removeFirst` method and the `isEmpty` method would delegate to the method of the same name. The other methods of the `LinkedList` class would not be used since they do not make sense in a `Stack`.

The bottom example in Figure 6.9 shows two levels of delegation in the airline system. `Booking` has a `flightNumber` method that does nothing other than delegate to the method of the same name in its neighbor, `SpecificFlight`. This in turn delegates to `RegularFlight`.

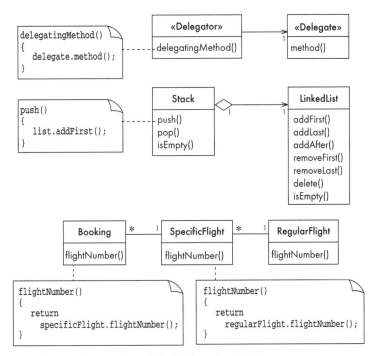

Figure 6.9   Template and examples of the Delegation design pattern

Antipatterns   The Delegation pattern brings together three principles that encourage flexible design:

(a) favoring association instead of inheritance when the full power of inheritance is not needed;

(b) avoiding duplication of chunks of code; and

(c) accessing 'nearby' information only. Violation of any of these principles should be avoided, as explained below.

Instead of using delegation, it is common for people to overuse generalization and *inherit* the method that is to be reused – for example, making `Stack` a subclass of `LinkedList`. The biggest problem with this is that some of the methods of `LinkedList`, such as `addAfter`, do not make sense in a `Stack`, yet they would be available.

   Instead of creating a single method in the «Delegator» that does nothing other than call a method in the «Delegate», you might consider having many different methods in the «Delegator» call the delegate's method. For example, all the methods in `Booking` could independently call `specificFlight.flightNumber()`. Unfortunately, this would create many more linkages in the system. It would be better to ensure that only *one* method in the «Delegator» calls the method in the «Delegate». Otherwise, when you make a change to the method in the «Delegate», you may have to change all of the calling methods.

The Law of Demeter

A fundamental principle of the Delegation pattern is that a method should only communicate with objects that are neighbors in the class diagram. This is a special case of the 'Law of Demeter', which was formulated by a team from Northeastern University in Boston.

The Law of Demeter says, in short, 'only talk to your immediate friends'. In software design, this means that a method should only access data passed as arguments, linked via associations, or obtained via calls to operations on other neighboring data. The rationale is that this limits the impact of changes, and makes it easier for software designers to understand that impact. If each method only communicates with its neighbors, then it should only be impacted when those neighbors change, not when changes occur in more distant parts of the system.

The Law of Demeter was named after Demeter, the ancient Greek goddess of agriculture, because its developers were interested in 'growing' software incrementally. Adhering to the Law of Demeter should make incremental development much easier.

Finally, you want to ensure that in delegation a method only accesses neighboring classes. For example it would not be good for Booking's `flightNumber` method to be written as:

```
return specificFlight.regularFlight.flightNumber();
```

This is bad because the further a method has to reach to get its data, the more sensitive it becomes to changes in the system. Maintenance becomes easier if you know that a change to a class will only affect its neighbors.

Related patterns The Adapter and Proxy patterns, discussed below, both use delegation.

References The Delegation pattern is mentioned in the book by Grand (see 'For more information' at the end of the chapter).

Exercise

E121 Find as many situations as you can where the Delegation pattern should be applied in Figure 5.25(c).

6.8   The Adapter pattern

Context You are building an inheritance hierarchy and you want to incorporate into it a class written by somebody else – that is, you want to reuse an existing unrelated class. Typically the methods of the reused class do not have the same name or argument types as the methods in the hierarchy you are creating. The reused class is also often already part of its own inheritance hierarchy.

Problem How do you obtain the power of polymorphism when reusing a class whose methods have the same function but do not have the same signature as the other methods in the hierarchy?

Forces You do not have access to multiple inheritance or you do not want to use it.

Solution Rather than directly incorporating the reused class into your inheritance hierarchy, instead incorporate an «*Adapter*» class, as shown in Figure 6.10. The «Adapter» is connected by an association to the reused class, which we will call the «*Adaptee*». The polymorphic methods of the «Adapter» *delegate* to methods of the «Adaptee». The delegate method in the «Adaptee» may or may not have the same name as the delegating polymorphic method.

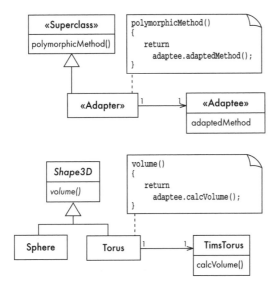

Figure 6.10   Template and example of the Adapter design pattern

Other code that accesses facilities of an «Adapter» object will be unaware that it is indirectly using the facilities of an instance of the «Adaptee».

Instead of being part of an inheritance hierarchy, an «Adapter» can be one of several classes that implement an interface.

Example As shown in Figure 6.10, imagine you are creating a hierarchy of three-dimensional shapes. However, you want to reuse the implementation of an equivalent class called `TimsTorus`. You do not want to modify the code of `TimsTorus`, since it is also being used by others; therefore you cannot make `TimsTorus` a subclass of `Shape3D`. You therefore make `Torus` an «Adapter». Its instances have a link to an instance of `TimsTorus`, and delegate all operations to `TimsTorus`.

Adapters are sometimes called *wrappers*. The Java wrapper classes `Integer`, `Float`, `Double` etc. are adapters for the Java primitive types.

A variation of the Adapter design pattern is used in an extended version of the OCSF framework, as explained in Section 6.14.

Related patterns The Adapter pattern is one of several patterns that make it easier to use other classes. Other patterns discussed below that do this are:

- **Façade:** provides a single class to make it easy to access a whole subsystem of classes.

- **Read-Only Interface:** provides an interface that prevents changing instances of another class.

- **Proxy:** provides a lightweight class that makes it unnecessary to always have to deal with a heavyweight class.

References The Adapter pattern is one of the 'Gang of Four' patterns.

Exercise

E122 Explain whether or not the `MouseAdapter` class defined in Java is an implementation of the Adapter pattern.

6.9 The Façade pattern

Context Often, an application contains several complex packages. A programmer working with such packages has to manipulate many different classes.

Problem How do you simplify the view that programmers have of a complex package?

Forces It is hard for a programmer to understand and use an entire subsystem – in particular, to determine which methods are public. If several different application classes call methods of the complex package, then any modifications made to the package will necessitate a complete review of all these classes.

Solution Create a special class, called a «Façade», which will simplify the use of the package. The «Façade» will contain a simplified set of public methods such that most other subsystems do not need to access the other classes in the package. The net result is that the package as a whole is easier to use and has a reduced number of dependencies with other packages. Any change made to the package should only necessitate a redesign of the «Façade» class, not classes in other packages.

Example The airline system discussed in Chapter 5 has many classes and methods. Other subsystems that need to interact with the airline system risk being 'exposed' to any changes that might be made to it. We can therefore define the class `Airline` to be a «Façade», as shown in Figure 6.11. This provides access to the most important query and booking operations.

References This pattern is one of the 'Gang of Four' patterns.

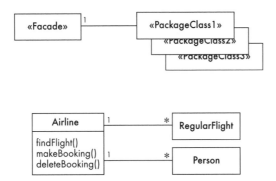

Figure 6.11   Template and example of the Façade design pattern

Exercise

E123   Suppose that you want to be able to use different database systems in different versions of an application. To facilitate interchanging databases, you create a Façade interface plus Façade classes associated with each specific database system. Draw the class diagram that corresponds to this.

6.10 The Immutable pattern

Context An immutable object is an object that has a state that never changes after creation. An important reason for using an immutable object is that other objects can trust its content not to change unexpectedly.

Problem How do you create a class whose instances are immutable?

Forces The immutability must be enforced. There must be no loopholes that would allow 'illegal' modification of an immutable object.

Solution Ensure that the constructor of the immutable class is the *only* place where the values of instance variables are set or modified. In other words, make sure that any instance methods have no *side effects* by changing instance variables or calling methods that themselves have side effects. If a method that would otherwise modify an instance variable *must* be present, then it has to return a new instance of the class.

Example In an immutable `Point` class, the `x` and `y` values would be set by the constructor and never modified thereafter. If a `translate` operation were allowed to be performed on such a `Point`, a new instance would have to be created. The object that requests the `translate` operation would then make use of the new translated point.
In Figure 2.8, imagine there was a method `changeScale(x,y)` in an immutable version of class `Circle`. This would return the same object if `x` and `y` were both 1.0, a new `Circle` if `x` and `y` were both equal, and a new `Ellipse` otherwise. Similarly, the `changeScale(x,y)` method in an immutable `Ellipse` class would

return a new `Circle` if the `changeScale(x,y)` would result in the semi-major axis equaling the semi-minor axis.

Related The Read-Only Interface pattern, described next, provides the same capability
patterns as Immutable, except that certain privileged classes are allowed to make changes to instances.

References This pattern was introduced by Grand (see 'For more information' at the end of the chapter).

Exercise

E124 Imagine that all the classes in Figure 2.8 were immutable. What other methods might be added to the system that would return instances of a *different* class from the class in which they are written?

6.11 The Read-Only Interface pattern

Context This is closely related to the Immutable pattern. You sometimes want certain privileged classes to be able to modify attributes of objects that are otherwise immutable.

Problem How do you create a situation where some classes see a class as read-only (i.e. the class is immutable) whereas others are able to make modifications?

Forces Programming languages such as Java allow you to control access by using the `public`, `protected` and `private` keywords. However, making access public makes it public for both reading and writing.

Solution Create a «*Mutable*» class as you would create any other class. You pass instances of this class to methods that need to make changes.

Then create a public interface we will call the «*ReadOnlyInterface*», that has only the read-only operations of «Mutable» – that is, only operations that *get* its values. You pass instances of the «ReadOnlyInterface» to methods that do not need to make changes, thus safeguarding these objects from unexpected changes. The «Mutable» class implements the «ReadOnlyInterface».

This solution is shown in Figure 6.12.

Example Figure 6.12 shows a `Person` interface that can be used by various parts of the system that have no right to actually modify the data. The `MutablePerson` class exists in a package that protects it from unauthorized modification.

The Read-Only Interface design pattern can also be used to send data to objects in a graphical user interface. The read-only interface ensures that no unauthorized modifications will be made to this data. We present this usage in the description of the MVC architecture in Chapter 9.

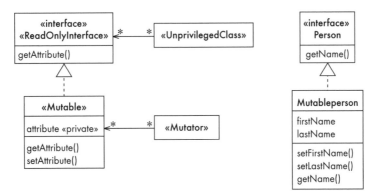

Figure 6.12   Template and example of the Read-Only Interface design pattern

Antipattern   You could consider making the read-only class a subclass of the «Mutable» class. But this would not work since whole point of this pattern is that you want a single class with different sets of access rights.

References   This pattern was introduced by Grand (see 'For more information' at the end of the chapter).

Exercise

E125   Create a read-only version of the `SpecificFlight` class shown in Figures 5.32 and 5.33. The purpose of this would be so that you could pass instances to other subsystems safely.

6.12 The Proxy pattern

Context   This pattern is found in class diagrams that show how aspects of the architecture of a system will be implemented.

Often, it is time-consuming and complicated to obtain access in a program to instances of a class. We call such classes *heavyweight* classes. Instances of a heavyweight class might, for example, always reside in a database. In order to use the instances in a program, a constructor must load them with data from the database. Similarly, a heavyweight object may exist only on a server: before using the object, a client has to request that it be sent; the client then has to wait for the object to arrive.

In both the above situations, there is a time delay and a complex mechanism involved in creating the object in memory. Nevertheless, many other objects in the system may want to refer to or use instances of heavyweight classes.

It is very common for all the domain classes to be heavyweight classes. Sets of instances of these must also be managed by heavyweight versions of the collection classes used to implement associations (such as `ArrayList` or `Vector`).

Problem How can you reduce the need to load into memory large numbers of heavyweight objects from a database or server, when not all of them will be needed?

A related problem is this: if you load one object from a database or server, how can you avoid loading all the other objects that are linked to it?

Forces You want all the objects in a domain model to be available for programs to use when they execute a system's various responsibilities. It is also important for many objects to persist from run to run of the same program.

However, in a large system it would be impractical for all the objects to be loaded into memory whenever a program starts. Memory size is limited; it takes a long time to load a database into memory; and only a small number of the objects in the database will actually be needed during any particular run of a program. Keeping all objects in memory would also make it difficult for multiple programs to share the same objects.

It would be ideal to be able to program the application *as if* all the objects were located in memory. The details of how the objects are actually stored and loaded should be *transparent* to the programmer. This provides for separation of concerns: some programmers can worry about loading and saving of objects, while others can be concerned with implementing the responsibilities of the domain model.

Solution Create a simpler version of the «HeavyWeight» class. We will call this simpler version a «Proxy». The «Proxy» has the *same interface* as the «HeavyWeight», therefore programmers can declare variables without caring whether a «Proxy» or its «HeavyWeight» version will be put in the variable. This is illustrated in Figure 6.13.

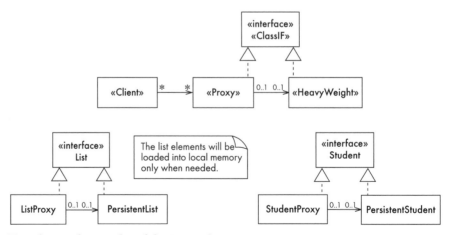

Figure 6.13   Template and examples of the Proxy design pattern

The «Proxy» object normally acts only as a placeholder. If any attempt is made to perform an operation on the proxy then the proxy *delegates* the operation to the «HeavyWeight». When needed, the «Proxy» undertakes the expensive task of obtaining the real «HeavyWeight» object. The proxy only needs to obtain the «HeavyWeight» once; subsequently it is available in memory and access is therefore fast.

Some proxies may have implementations of a limited number of operations that can be performed without the effort of loading the «HeavyWeight».

In some systems, most of the variables manipulated by the domain model actually contain instances of «Proxy» classes.

Examples In Figure 6.13, a software designer may declare that a variable is to contain a `List`. This variable would, however, actually contain a `ListProxy`, since it would be expensive to load an entire list of objects into memory, and the list might not actually be needed. However, as soon as an operation accesses the list, the `ListProxy` might at that point create an instance of `PersistentList` in memory. On the other hand, the `ListProxy` might be able to answer certain queries, such as the number of elements in the list, without going to the effort of loading the `PersistentList`.

Now, imagine that the `PersistentList` was actually a list of students. These objects might *also* be proxies – in this case, instances of `StudentProxy`. Again, instances of `PersistentStudent` would only be loaded when necessary.

The Proxy pattern is widely used in many software architectures. We will discuss it again in the context of the Broker architectural pattern in Chapter 9.

Antipatterns Instead of using proxy objects, beginner designers often scatter complex code around their application to load objects from databases.

A strategy that only works for very small systems is to load the whole database into memory when the program starts.

Related patterns The Proxy pattern is one of several patterns that obtain their power from delegating responsibilities to other classes, hence it uses the Delegation pattern.

References The Proxy pattern is one of the 'Gang of Four' patterns.

Exercise

E126 Discuss the advantages of using an image-proxy when manipulating the photos in a digital photo album application. What operations could conceivably be performed by the proxy without loading the heavyweight image into memory?

6.13 The Factory pattern

Context You have a reusable framework that needs to create objects as part of its work. However, the class of the created objects will depend on the application.

Problem How do you enable a programmer to add a new application-specific class «ApplSpecificClass» into a system built on such a framework? And how do you arrange for the framework to instantiate this class, without modifying the framework?

Forces You want the benefits of a framework, but retain the flexibility of having the framework create and work with application-specific classes that the framework does not yet know about.

Solution The framework delegates the creation of instances of «ApplSpecificClass» to a specialized class «ApplSpecificFactory». The «ApplSpecificFactory» implements a generic interface «Factory» defined in the framework. The «Factory» declares a method whose purpose is to create some subclass «AppSpecificClass» of a class we will call «GenericClass». This is illustrated in Figure 6.14.

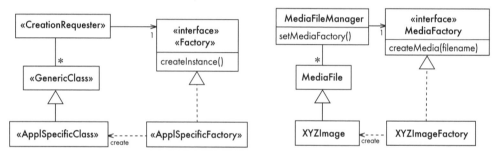

Figure 6.14   Template and example of the Factory design pattern

Example As is shown in right-hand diagram of Figure 6.14, suppose you have a framework with a class called MediaFile, whose subclasses will represent the contents of various types of audio-visual media files. You want to create a subclass of this, XYZImage, to represent your new media format; and you need to ensure the framework class MediaFileManager can instantiate this. You therefore create a factory class, XYZImageFactory, whose sole job is to create instances of XYZImage. This implements the MediaFactory interface. You initiate the system to create XYZImages by calling the setMediaFactory method of MediaFileManager; this creates a link to an instance of XYZImageFactory. Each time the MediaFileManager needs to create a new MediaFile object, it calls the createMedia method as implemented by XYZImageFactory; this then creates a new XYZImage.

Antipatterns You could get rid of the factory and instead modify the framework code in MediaFileManager to force it to always instantiate XYZImage directly. However, this would only be possible if you have access to the source of the framework; and would not work if you needed to be able to work with several different «Factory»–«ApplSpecificClass» pairs. As a general principle, modifying a framework should always be considered forbidden.

References The Factory pattern is one of the 'Gang of Four' patterns.

Exercises

E127 In a given game, carnivore and herbivore animals are created at random instants by the game engine. Depending on the country selected by the user, a factory for the appropriate carnivores and herbivores is loaded (e.g. one that will create lions and gazelles in Kenya, but cougars and beavers in Canada). Draw the class diagram to represent this idea.

E128 Find the design pattern that would be most appropriate for the following problems:

(a) You are building an inheritance hierarchy of products that your company sells; however, you want to reuse several classes from one of your suppliers. You cannot modify your suppliers' classes. How do you ensure that the facilities of the suppliers' classes can still be used polymorphically?

(b) You want to allow operations on instances of RegularPolygon that will distort them such that they are no longer regular polygons. How do you allow the operations without raising exceptions?

(c) Your program manipulates images that take a lot of space in memory. How can you design your program so that images are only in memory when needed, and otherwise can only be found in files?

(d) You have created a subsystem with 25 classes. You know that most other subsystems will only access about 5 methods in this subsystem; how can you simplify the view that the other subsystems have of your subsystem?

(e) You are developing a stock quote framework. Some applications using this framework will want stock quotes to be displayed on a screen when they become available; other applications will want new quotes to trigger certain financial calculations; yet other applications might want both of the above, plus having quotes transmitted wirelessly to a network of pagers. How can you design the framework so that various different pieces of application code can react in their own way to the arrival of new quotes?

E129 The Iterator interface, as defined in Java, is an implementation of what is called the 'Iterator' design pattern. Study the Java documentation describing Iterator, then using the format discussed in this chapter, write a description of the Iterator pattern, with sections that define its context, problem, forces and solution.

E130 (Advanced) In order to improve the access to information stored in a database, several applications use the concept of a cache. The basic principle is to keep in local memory objects that would normally be destroyed, because it is expected that these objects will be requested again later on. In this way, when they are indeed required again, access to them is very fast.

(a) Create a design pattern that describes this idea. Use the format presented in this chapter.

(b) Scan the literature on design patterns and look for the Cache Management design pattern. Compare it with the solution you proposed.

6.14 Enhancing OCSF to employ additional design patterns

The Object Client–Server Framework (OCSF) presented in Chapter 3 provides a simple way to set up a client–server application rapidly. In this section, we introduce additional features of OCSF and show how the use of design patterns can greatly increase flexibility. As with the basic classes of OCSF, code for the extensions discussed here is available on the book's web site (http://www.lloseng.com).

Client connection factory

The first extension to the basic framework is the addition of a *Factory* to handle client connections. To understand the usefulness of this mechanism, let us first review client connection management on the server side. Each time a new client connects to the server, a `ConnectionToClient` object is created. This object defines a thread that manages all communication with that particular client. All messages received from the client are passed on to the `handleMessageFromClient` method in a subclass of `AbstractServer`. This method is *synchronized* so that if two `ConnectionToClient` threads need to access the same resource (e.g. an instance variable of the server) then they won't interfere with each other – only one call to `handleMessageFromClient` will execute at a time.

However, there are some circumstances when you might want to allow developers to create application-specific subclasses of `ConnectionToClient`:

■ You might not like having all message handling processed sequentially in the synchronized `handleMessageFromClient` in the server object. Instead you might want to have client message handling take place in a version of `handleMessageFromClient` in a special subclass of `ConnectionToClient`. This could still be synchronized if you like, but it would be synchronized on the `ConnectionToClient` object in order that the processing of messages from different clients could be done concurrently.

■ You might want to have different `handleMessageFromClient` methods in different subclasses of `ConnectionToClient`. A different subclass of `ConnectionToClient` could, for example, be created to handle clients in your local area network, as opposed to clients somewhere else on the Internet.

To enable the server class to instantiate an application-specific subclass of `ConnectionToClient`, OCSF provides an optional Factory mechanism. There are two keys to this. The first key is an interface called `AbstractConnectionFactory` (see Figure 6.15). You create an application-specific factory class that implements the createConnection method in this interface. Your factory class will in turn create instances of your own subclass of ConnectionToClient. The second key is the method setConnectionFactory found in AbstractServer. Your server class calls this to ensure that whenever a new client attempts to connect, your factory will be directed to instantiate your subclass of ConnectionToClient to handle the connection.

To use the OCSF factory mechanism, you therefore need to do the following:

1. Create your subclass of ConnectionToClient. Its constructor must have the same signature as ConnectionToClient, and it must call the constructor of ConnnectionToClient using the super keyword. Your class will also normally want to override handleMessageFromClient; if this method returns true, the version of handleMessageFromClient in your server class will *also* be subsequently called.

2. Create your factory class that simply defines a method for the createConnection operation of the AbstractConnectionFactory interface. Typically, the method would look like this:

```
protected ConnectionToClient createConnection(
    ThreadGroup group, Socket clientSocket,
    AbstractServer server) throws IOException
{
    return new Connection(group,clientSocket,server);
}
```

3. Arrange for the server make the following call before it starts listening:

```
setConnectionFactory(new MyConnectionFactory());
```

Observable layer

A second extension to the OCSF framework is the addition of an Observable layer. We will describe the client side, but the server side works the same way.

In the basic OCSF, a message received by a client is processed by the subclass of AbstractClient that implements the handleMessageFromServer abstract method. Each time a new application is developed, therefore, the AbstractClient class must be subclassed.

The Observer pattern provides an alternative mechanism for developing a client. Any number of «Observer» classes can ask to be notified when something 'interesting' happens to the client – the arrival of a message or the closing of a connection, for example. We would therefore like to have a subclass of AbstractClient that is an «Observable». Unfortunately, since Java does not permit multiple inheritance, we cannot make it a subclass of the Observable class itself. Instead, we use the Adapter pattern, as shown in Figure 6.15.

The extended OCSF has the class ObservableClient. This has exactly the same interface as AbstractClient, except that it is a subclass of Observable. It is also an adapter: it delegates methods such as sendToServer, setPort, etc. to instances of a concrete subclass of AbstractClient called AdaptableClient. Designers using ObservableClient never need to know that AdaptableClient exists.

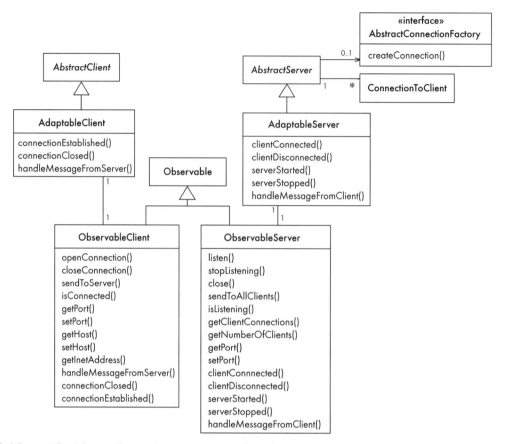

Figure 6.15   The Object Client–Server Framework with extensions to employ the Observable and Factory design patterns

Implementation of the Observable layer

The following are some of the highlights of the implementation of the client side:

■ The class `AdaptableClient`, as the concrete subclass of `AbstractClient`, provides the required concrete implementation of `handleMessageFromServer`. It also provides implementations of the hook methods `connnectionClosed` and `connectionEstablished`. All that these three callback methods do is delegate to the `ObservableClient`. Their structure is as follows:

```
callbackMethod()
{
  observable.callbackMethod();
}
```

■ There is always a one-to-one relationship between an `AdaptableClient` and an `ObservableClient`. Instances of both these classes must exist.

■ All the service methods in ObservableClient (such as openConnection) simply delegate to the AdaptableClient. They have the following structure:

```
serviceMethod()
{
  return adaptable.serviceMethod();
}
```

■ The method handleMessageFromServer in ObservableClient is implemented as follows:

```
public void handleMessageFromServer(Object message)
{
  setChanged();
  notifyObservers(message);
}
```

■ The other callback methods in ObservableClient, such as the hook method connectionClosed, do nothing. A designer could elect to create a subclass of ObservableClient which might implement connectionClosed like this:

```
public void connectionClosed()
{
  setChanged();
  notifyObservers("connectionClosed");
}
```

The server side is implemented analogously, except that the instance of ConnectionToClient could also be sent to the observers.

Some important advantages of using the Observable layer of OCSF are:

1. Different types of messages can be processed by different classes of observer. For example, different parts of a user interface might update themselves when specific messages are received; they would ignore the other messages.

2. Programmers using the ObservableClient or ObservableServer need to know very little about these classes. There is thus a better separation of concerns between the communication subsystem (OCSF) and different application subsystems.

Exercise

E131 In the Observable layer of OCSF, the classes ObservableClient and ObservableServer are similar to adapters in the sense that their main function is to delegate to the adaptable classes. In what way do they differ from true adapters? You can look at the design presented above to answer this, but it may also help if you study the source code.

Using the Observable layer

In order to connect a class to the observable layer of OCSF, the procedure is as follows:

1. Create the application class that implements the `Observer` interface (note that this is not a subclass of any of the framework classes).

2. Register an instance of the new class as an observer of the `ObservableClient` (or `ObservableServer`). Typically, you would do this in the constructor, in the following manner:

```
public MessageHandler(Observable client)
{
  client.addObserver(this);
  ...
}
```

3. Define the `update` method in the new class. Normally a given class will react only to messages of a particular type. In the following example, our application class is only interested in messages that are of class `SomeClass`.

```
public void update(Observable obs, Object message)
{
  if (message instanceOf SomeClass)
  {
    // process the message
  }
}
```

If `message` is a `String`, a condition in the `if` block could be added to determine what to do with the message.

6.15 Difficulties and risks when using design patterns

The following are the key difficulties to anticipate when designing and using design patterns:

■ **Patterns are not a panacea**. Whenever you see an indication that a pattern should be applied, you might be tempted to apply the pattern blindly. However, this can lead to unwise design decisions. For example, you do not always need to apply the Façade pattern in every subsystem; adding the extra class might make the overall design more complex, especially if instances of many of the classes in the subsystem are passed as data to methods outside the subsystem. *Resolution. Always understand in depth the forces that need to be balanced, and when other patterns better balance the forces. Also, make sure you justify each design decision carefully.*

■ **Developing patterns is hard**. Writing a good pattern takes considerable work. A poor pattern can be hard for other people to apply correctly, and can lead them to make incorrect decisions. It is particularly hard to write a set of forces effectively.

Resolution. Do not write patterns for others to use until you have considerable experience both in software design and in the use of patterns. Take an in-depth course on patterns. Iteratively refine your patterns, and have them peer reviewed at each iteration.

6.16 Summary

Applying patterns to the process of creating class diagrams helps you to create better models. Patterns help you to avoid common mistakes and to create systems that are simpler and more flexible.

Some of the more important patterns that occur in domain models include Abstraction–Occurrence, General Hierarchy and Player–Role. Observer, Adapter and Factory are patterns that frequently occur in complete system class diagrams. Immutable, Façade and Proxy are typically applied when the modeler is moving towards a more detailed stage of design.

The patterns can also be categorized according to the principles they embody. The Delegation pattern is a fundamental pattern that prevents excessive interconnection among different parts of a system. Abstraction–Occurrence, Observer and Player–Role also help increase separation of concerns. Adapter, Façade and Proxy help the developer to reuse the facilities of other classes. Immutable and Read-Only Interface help protect objects from unexpected changes.

6.17 For more information

The following are some of the many available resources about patterns:

- The Patterns Home Page: http://www.hillside.net/patterns/ – an extensive list of resources about patterns

- A reference source for design patterns in Java: http://www.fluffycat.com/java/patterns.html

- Brad Appleton's description of patterns: http://www.cmcrossroads.com/bradapp/docs/patterns-intro.html

- E. Gamma, R. Helm, R. Johnson and J. Vlissides, *Design Patterns: Elements of Reusable Object-Oriented Software*, Addison-Wesley, October 1994. This book is the most widely cited book about patterns. Its authors are often referred to as the 'Gang of Four'

- C. Alexander, *A Pattern Language*, Oxford University Press, 1977. The classic book by the originator of the patterns movement

■ H-E. Eriksson and M. Penker, *Business Modeling with UML: Business Patterns at Work*, Wiley, 2000

■ M. Grand, *Patterns in Java Volume 1: A Catalog of Reusable Design Patterns Illustrated with UML*, 2nd edition, Wiley, 2002

■ W. H. Brown, R. C. Malveau, H. W. McCormick III and T. J. Mowbray, *Antipatterns: Refactoring Software, Architectures, and Projects in Crisis*, Wiley, 1998. A summary of many of the key mistakes that software developers and managers make

Project exercises

E132 Summarize the advantages and disadvantages of:

(a) The observable layer of OCSF.

(b) Creating a subclass of `ConnectionToClient` (and instantiating it using the factory).

E133 Draw an object diagram showing an instance of a subclass of `AbstractServer` with a `ConnectionFactory` that has created three instances of two different subclasses of `ConnectionToClient`

E134 Modify the SimpleChat system so that it uses the Observable layer of the OCSF. The number of changes you make should be minimized, and the external interface to the system should not change. When you complete this exercise, you will have completed Phase 4 of SimpleChat.

E135 Examine your class diagram for the Small Hotel Reservation System from Chapter 5.

(a) Determine which patterns, if any, you already applied, without knowing it.

(b) See if you can improve your class diagram by applying one or more of the patterns discussed in this chapter.

Focusing on users and their tasks 7

The vast majority of software is developed for human beings to use. In this chapter we will show you how to design software for users and how to keep users involved in the process of design. In fact, we will show that if you do not involve users, it will be very hard for you to develop usable software.

In Chapter 4, we showed you the first steps towards involving users in software engineering: one such step is requirements analysis which includes interviewing, brainstorming and use case analysis. In this chapter we will introduce the concept of *user-centered design*. We will also show you how to create and evaluate designs so as to ensure that they are usable – usability is one of the important software qualities that we discussed in Chapter 1.

In this chapter you will learn about the following

- Characteristics of users that every software engineer should understand.

- Various ways of working with users to ensure that a software system has both the required functionality and the required usability.

- Some basic principles for the design of simple graphical user interfaces (GUIs), involving windows, menus, icons and pop-up dialogs.

- How to evaluate user interfaces.

- How to implement basic GUIs in Java.

Users and eXtreme Programming
One of the tenets of the agile method, eXtreme Programming, mentioned in Chapter 1, is that there should at all times be a user representative present and working with the developers.

7.1 User-centered design

During the 50-year history of computing, software developers have often failed to involve users adequately in the development process. For example, during requirements analysis, they have tended to communicate with customers and management, but have often ignored the users. They have then designed, implemented, tested and installed the software, and finally said to the users: 'It's ready to use!' A typical response from the users to this is, 'No, it's not! This lacks functions we need to help us get our work done, it's hard to understand and it's time-consuming to use.' In situations like this, the software is either not used or has to be extensively, and expensively, modified.

User-centered design (UCD) is the term used to describe approaches to software development that focus on the needs of users. Software development approaches that incorporate UCD can help ensure that extensive and expensive modifications are not needed.

Ways to make software development user centered

Many different activities can contribute to making a development process user centered. The following are some of the most important:

- **Understand your users**. Knowing the characteristics of your users allows you to design a system that matches their level of knowledge, their abilities and their preferences. We will discuss this in the next section.

- **Design software based on an understanding of the users' tasks**. Software needs to facilitate the user's work. Performing use case analysis, as discussed in Chapter 4, is the recommended way to ensure this occurs.

- **Ensure users are involved in decision-making processes**. Rather than involving users to a limited extent in requirements analysis, it is better to involve them extensively throughout development. Users cannot be expected to participate in detailed low-level internal design decisions. However, they should be involved in all decision making that relates to the requirements and to the user interface design.

- **Design the user interface following principles of good usability**. Following well-researched UI design principles and guidelines naturally leads you to think about users and their needs. We will study some important usability principles in Section 7.4.

- **Have users work with and give their feedback about prototypes, online help and draft user manuals**. One of the best ways to ensure that users are involved is to develop software iteratively and to involve users in the evaluation of prototypes and user documents. We will look at evaluation of user interface prototypes in Section 7.5.

The importance of focusing on users

User-centered design techniques can significantly improve the quality of the software. They can also reduce the cost to produce, operate and maintain it. Here are some of the clear benefits:

- **Reduced training and support costs**. Large amounts of money are spent both training users to use software and running help desks which support users who have difficulties. If software is designed so that it is more intuitive to use, then its users will need less training and help.

- **Reduced time to learn the system**. Even if users do not take training courses, they still have to invest time to learn how to use the software. The time users spend learning software is a *hidden* cost that cannot be as easily measured as the cost of training courses and help desks. UCD techniques are particularly effective at reducing these hidden costs.

- **Greater efficiency of use**. Another hidden cost is the amount of time that users take to do their work with the system, once they have learned how to use it. UCD techniques can highlight a system's inefficiencies and help to make it faster to use. For example, you might discover that users have to enter unnecessary data, type too many keystrokes, or constantly open and close dialog boxes. Helping users speed up their work can save their employers large amounts of money.

- **Reduced costs by only developing features that are needed**. Without UCD, developers will likely add features that are little used, and hence become 'shelfware'. Development of these features is a waste of money and time. In Chapter 4, we discussed the importance of cutting unnecessary features from requirements; UCD helps you choose which features to keep.

- **Reduced costs associated with changing the system later**. Without UCD, important features will likely be omitted, hence they will have to be added later. If the software is not flexible and maintainable, this is expensive; but even if the missing features can be easily added, the delay will cost money.

- **Better prioritizing of work for iterative development**. UCD techniques permit developers to understand which features should be developed for the first release, and which can be delayed until later. UCD can therefore ensure that the most important features reach the users sooner, and hence the users can start reaping the benefits sooner too.

- **Greater attractiveness of the system means that users will be more willing to buy and use it**. Many systems have *discretionary* patterns of use – users may be able to use competing software or to avoid using any software at all. Benefits from the software can only be achieved if the software is *attractive* to users. UCD techniques can help developers learn what qualities are likely to make users actively choose to use the software.

Exercise

E136 Think of a reasonably complex piece of software with which you have experience (e.g. an operating system, word processor or spreadsheet). Answer the following questions about that system:

(a) Do typical users require training to use this software to its full capacity? Is there anything in the software that could be improved so that less training would be needed? Remember that, as a computing student or professional, you probably have considerable experience with a variety of different software packages; you can therefore figure out a new program much more easily than the average person.

(b) What aspects did you find most difficult to learn when you learned the software? Are there any aspects of the system that you deferred learning because they appeared too complex?

(c) Do you ever find yourself wishing that you could use the software more quickly? What could be improved about the software that would allow you to work faster?

(d) Are there any features that you never use? Do you think that removing the features might make the system easier to use? Or, conversely, do you take comfort in knowing that the features are available, in case you should ever need them?

7.2 Characteristics of users

The first activity that you should perform as part of user-centered design is to understand your users. In Chapter 4, we pointed out that this is something you should start to do in domain analysis, and as the first step of use case analysis.

The following are some of the characteristics that can vary from user to user. As you design software, think about how these characteristics apply to your particular users.

■ **Goals for using the system**. Different types of users have different job functions or roles, and therefore have different goals. These goals will lead the users to want different features, and to place different levels of importance on each feature. Understanding goals is critical to defining the problem to be solved, as discussed in Chapter 4, and to choosing an appropriate set of use cases.

■ **Potential patterns of use**. For some users, using the system may be optional. The task they would use the system for may not be an essential part of their work, or they may have some alternative way of doing the task. Other users might have no choice but to use the system. Some users may only use the system occasionally – they will therefore have to relearn it every time they want to use it.

■ **Demographics**. Demographic variables, such as the age ranges of your users, their educational background, their language and culture, and their geographical location, will all have an influence on the software design. For example, software that is used by adults in their employment will have different characteristics from software that is to be used by children. Special attention will have to be paid if the software is to be used equally by both groups, in the case, for example, of a web search engine.

■ **Knowledge of the domain and of computers**. If the users of software are experts in a domain, then the software does not have to provide explanations of concepts and terminology that should be known by those experts. For example, a diagnosis assistant to be used by physicians could assume that its users understand basic anatomy. On the other hand, software that is to be used by the population at large must be significantly simpler to use, providing explanations of all terms that are not in common use. Also, software that is to be used by people who are experienced computer users can be more complex than software that is to be used by people who have little knowledge of computers.

■ **Physical ability**. You cannot assume that all users can see and hear. Others may have difficulty using a keyboard or a mouse. You must therefore ensure that the software can interact with devices that help people with disabilities to use it. Some disabilities are quite subtle, such as color-blindness: if you rely on people seeing colors, your application becomes unusable by many people.

■ **Psychological traits and emotional feelings**. There are many psychological factors that should be taken into account when designing a system. Many of these relate to the capabilities of human memory and attention (how well humans can focus on a task). For example, a large percentage of the population has to think in order to distinguish right from left – these people (one of the authors included) tend to make mistakes if asked to do so in stressful conditions. Some people have emotional reactions to particular color combinations or imagery. Others might feel a personal attachment to 'the way they used to do things'. Finally, people vary in how easily they get frustrated, or whether they will tend to explore a system out of interest, rather than merely using it to get their task done. We recommend that a psychology course should be part of the basic training of a software engineer.

Exercise

E137 Imagine you are planning to develop the following types of software projects. What different kinds of users should you anticipate? Consider each of the issues mentioned above.

(a) An air-traffic control system.

(b) The GANA GPS-based navigation system discussed in Chapter 4.

Correctly distinguishing left from right in an interface can be critical

On 8 January 1989, British Midland Flight 92 had just taken off from Heathrow, heading towards Belfast. Unfortunately, the *left* engine started emitting smoke and lost power. A Boeing 737 is capable of flying with just one engine. However, the cockpit indicators did not give a strong enough indication about which engine was in trouble; the pilots mistakenly thought the *right* engine had the problem and shut it down instead. Flying with one engine shut down and the other in trouble, the plane crashed while attempting to make an emergency landing. Of the 126 people on board, 47 died. Many people believe that an improved cockpit user interface could have averted this disaster. For more details, see http://pw2.netcom.com/~asapilot/92.html.

(c) A microwave oven.

(d) A payroll system.

7.3 The basics of user interface design

As with many other areas of software engineering, user interface design is the topic of entire books, some of which are listed in the 'For more information' section at the end of this chapter. It has been left out of many general software engineering books because it has historically been seen as a separate discipline. In the early days of computing, user interfaces were much simpler, and the bulk of software design work went into databases and algorithms. In today's world, the user interface is often the most complex part of the system to design. It can take over half of all development effort and is the part that is most likely to cause users to perceive a lack of quality.

User interface design is therefore an essential skill that all software engineers should possess. In this section and the next, we want to highlight some of the most important things that every software developer should know about this topic.

User interface design should be performed in conjunction with other software engineering activities. Prior to UI design, you should have done some domain analysis and made a first attempt at defining the problem. You can then employ use case analysis to help define the tasks that the UI must help the user perform. Next you can begin an iterative process of user interface prototyping in order to address the set of use cases that you have identified. During the prototyping process you will refine both the UI and the use cases. Eventually, results of the prototyping process will enable you to finalize the requirements for the delivered system.

We will present various UI design guidelines in the next section. However, no matter how many guidelines a group of software engineers follow, it would be very arrogant of them to believe they could develop a perfect user interface on their own. The iterative prototyping process must involve extensive discussion with, and evaluation by, both users and other user interface designers. We will discuss techniques to do this in Section 7.5.

Usability versus utility

The overall *usefulness* of a software system can be considered on two quality dimensions:

■ Does the system provide the raw functionality to allow the users to achieve their goal? In other words, does it store the right data, allow the right operations and do the right calculations? This quality of a system is often called its *utility*.

■ Does the system allow the users to learn and to use the raw capabilities easily? This is *usability*.

Both utility and usability are essential. It is possible to have one without the other, but such a system would be useless. For example, you could imagine a system with very powerful computational capabilities but which is extremely difficult for its users to understand. At the same time, you can imagine a system that is easy to use, but which does not do the correct calculations or store the data a user needs. Both systems would be rejected, for different reasons.

Both utility and usability must be measured in the context of particular types of user (i.e. particular actors). Users with one set of tasks to perform will judge the utility differently from users with different sets of tasks to perform. Also, users with different levels of computer experience and different patterns of use will perceive usability differently. Power users of computers will be able to quickly learn software of considerable complexity, and will then insist that the software allows them to do their job as rapidly as possible. However, users who only occasionally use the software, or are less computer literate, will be more concerned with how easy it is to learn.

Aspects of usability

Usability can be divided into four separate aspects: learnability, efficiency of use, error handling and acceptability.

Learnability is a measure of the speed with which a new user can become proficient with the system. Learnability can be improved in two ways: by having fewer things to learn, or by making the learning process more intuitive. Beginners will perceive a system to be easier to learn if the complex features are hidden from them initially. This can be done by having separate 'beginner' and 'expert' interfaces. The expert interface might, for example, have additional menu items, fields and buttons. It is common to describe learnability in terms of learning curves, illustrated in Figure 7.1. For example, a user might be able to learn the most important 20 functions of the system in 3 days if the system is simple and intuitive, in 7 days if the system is simple but non-intuitive, and in 11 days if the system is complex and non-intuitive.

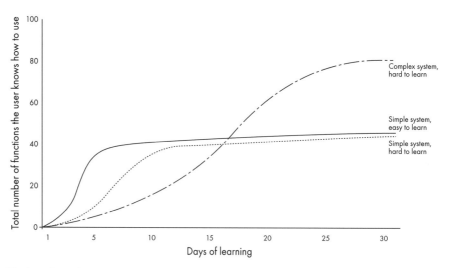

Figure 7.1   Various learning curves

Efficiency of use is concerned with how fast an expert user can do his or her work using the system. Suitable metrics for this are: the total number of instances of a small task that a user can do per hour, or the total time required to do a certain large task.

Whereas efficiency of use and learnability consider *ordinary* use, the effectiveness of a system at handling errors is concerned with *abnormal* situations. A system is better at error handling if it *prevents* the user from making errors, if it helps the user to *detect* errors, and if it helps the user to *correct* errors. The following are suitable metrics for these three aspects of error handling:

- Error prevention: Compute the number of error messages that appear per hour of use; a lower number is better.

- Error detection: Count the number of errors a user notices, and divide this by the total number of errors the user makes. Note that some errors, such as navigating to the wrong place, do not result in error messages; these may or may not be noticed by the user.

- Error correction: For each error the user makes, measure the time that elapses from when the user detects the error, to when the user has corrected the error. To compute the percentage of time spent correcting errors, sum the time spent correcting all errors and divide the result by the time spent using the application.

Acceptability measures the extent to which users *like* the system. A system may be learnable and efficient to use, but if users do not like it they will resist using it. Acceptability is a purely subjective phenomenon to which many factors contribute. Various other aspects of usability contribute to it, as does the graphic design.

Basic terminology of user interface design

User interface designers use specific terms that you should understand:

Dialog The word *dialog* (also sometimes spelled *dialogue*) is used generically to describe the back-and-forth interaction between user and computer. The terms dialog or *dialog box* are used to mean a specific window with which a user can interact, other than the main UI window.

Control or widget These words are used interchangeably to describe specific components of a user interface. Typical widgets include menus, lists, input fields and scroll bars.

Affordance The *affordance* is the set of operations that the user can do at any given point in time. Examples of operations include typing into an input field, clicking on a button or selecting an item from a menu. Clicking a button or selecting a menu item are *commands* because they cause the system to perform some computations. UI designers say 'a button affords clicking' if clicking on it would cause some action to occur.

State At any stage in the dialog, the system is displaying certain information in certain widgets, and has a certain affordance. Taken together, these are the system's *user interface state*. The UI state usually changes when the user issues a command. It also changes when the system itself notifies the user of some happening, such as the completion of an earlier command or the arrival of a message.

Mode A *mode* is a situation in which the UI restricts what the user can do – that is, it restricts the affordance. For example, if a dialog appears saying 'Do you really want to delete a file?' and all the user can do is click 'Cancel' or 'OK', then the system is in a mode.

Modal dialog A *modal dialog* is one in which the system is in a very restrictive mode. The user cannot interact with any other window until he or she has dismissed the modal dialog. The most restrictive type of modal dialog has a single 'OK' button to dismiss the dialog. A *non-modal dialog* is a separate window with which the user can choose to interact, but is not forced to. Palettes and toolbars are examples of non-modal dialogs.

Feedback Whenever the user does something, the response from the system is called *feedback*. Feedback includes displaying a message, changing a color or displaying a dialog.

Encoding techniques These are ways of representing information so as to communicate it to the user. Tables 7.1 and 7.2 list some of the most common encoding techniques, along with their advantages and disadvantages.

Table 7.1   Ways of encoding information to be transmitted using sound. Unless backed up by visual cues, these are inaccessible to deaf people

Medium	Uses and advantages	Problems
Spoken words	Essential when there is no screen or only a small screen (e.g. a telephone system). Important for blind people who otherwise must rely on tools that convert text into Braille	Can be overheard, violating privacy. Sequential, therefore the user has to request replay if he or she misses a part. Slower for most users than reading text
Music	Can convey mood. Can add attractiveness	Does not usually convey meaning. People have different tastes in music
Abstract sounds (e.g. beeps)	Can give useful feedback about actions that are taking place	Can be hard to interpret
All of the above	Attract attention rapidly at onset, even if the person is not looking at the screen	Can be distracting and annoying

7.4   Usability principles

In this section, we discuss twelve principles that you should apply when designing and evaluating a user interface. After we list the principles, we will give an example of a user interface that violates many of these principles, as well as an improved version of the same system.

The twelve principles

Usability Principle 1: Do not rely only on usability guidelines – always test with users

Each situation is different and there are exceptions to the principles in this section. You should therefore ask the opinions of users and evaluate how they use prototypes. Evaluation is the topic of Section 7.5.

Usability Principle 2: Base UI designs on users' tasks as expressed in use cases

Perform a first iteration of use case analysis and then design the UI based on this. As you evaluate your prototype UI, you will have to go back and revise your use case model as well as your UI.

Usability Principle 3: Ensure the sequences of actions to complete a task correctly are as simple as possible

Make sure users can move from step to step easily as they perform their tasks. You want the user to have to read the smallest amount of text, to navigate the least, to type the least and not to be led into making errors. In particular, make sure the user does not have to select menu items repeatedly to complete a single task. Also, avoid sequences of modal dialogs, since they slow users

Table 7.2   Ways of encoding information to be transmitted visually. Except for text, which can be spoken or converted to Braille, these are generally inaccessible to blind people

Medium	Uses and advantages	Problems
Text written in a language the user can read	Has unlimited ability to express meaning. Simple to generate and display. Accessible by blind people using Braille translators	Takes a lot of space. Writing clearly and unambiguously is hard. Not usable by young children or the illiterate. Hard for users to scan quickly
Fonts (including font family, as well as bold, italics and size attributes)	Add emphasis to text, and reinforce its structure, thus simplifying and highlighting information	Using too many fonts results in confusion and a cluttered appearance. Decorative or unusual fonts can be distracting
Icons (simple and abstract graphics, each representing a specific action or object)	Allow many commands or objects to be listed in less space than is possible with text. Users can scan the screen to find an icon faster than they can scan to find particular text	Notoriously difficult for users to interpret or distinguish. Require artistic skill to create
Diagrams (convey objects and their relationships)	Can communicate or summarize complex concepts or mechanisms more easily than other techniques	Can be hard for users to interact with or interpret. Can be expensive to generate automatically
Photographs and hand-drawn images of reality	Can help users better appreciate reality	Can take a lot of space on screen and can slow response time due to downloading
Animations and video	Provide high impact communication of complex information. Entertaining and hence attractive for users	Bandwidth-intensive, hence reduce response time. Sequential, requiring replay if users miss parts. Users cannot quickly scan them. Expensive to produce. May be annoying
Purely decorative graphics	Make the interface attractive and helps to emphasize its organization	Can be distracting or annoying
Colors	Draw attention to specific items. Convey organization (items colored similarly are related). Makes the UI more attractive. Users can almost instantly notice a small spot of color on the screen	Users cannot distinguish among large numbers of colors. Some color combinations clash. Color-blind people cannot see differences in hue. Some colors (e.g. bright red) can be distracting if overused
Grouping, bordering and organizing in columns or tables	Help to convey the organization of information and reduce its perceived complexity	No problems
Flashing	Rapidly draws attention to items	Distracting and annoying. Fast flashing can cause epileptic seizures and migraine headaches

down and give them the feeling that the computer is in control of the interaction.

Usability Principle 4: Ensure that the user always knows what he or she can and should do next, and what will happen when he or she does it

At any one time there are usually several things that a user can do next – i.e. the system affords several possible actions. Perhaps the user can click on one of several icons, select one of several menu items, or type data into one of several fields. When designing the UI, take note of all these things the user should be able to do; make sure that the user can clearly see how to do all the things that are possible, and 'gray out' those options that are temporarily not available. Make the things the user will want to do most often stand out; they could be larger, in a separate box, or colored more brightly. The consequences of each action should also be clear.

> **The importance of analyzing the task and interacting with users**
>
> One of the reviewers of this book relates the following story. Some designers had put considerable work into developing a new graphical user interface to control an existing piece of hardware more easily. The UI team were excited about the way the system would give the hardware operators easy access to all sorts of information. However, when they showed the system to the users, one of them said, 'Well, I guess that's nice, but all we need to do is press "Start" and "Stop".'

Usability Principle 5: Provide good feedback, including effective error messages

When a change of state occurs, make sure it is clearly visible to the user. Some specific guidelines are:

- If some operation is taking more than a few seconds, provide a progress bar so that the user knows what is going on.

- Always keep the user informed about where he or she is located among the various windows and pages.

- Communicate clearly to the user when something goes wrong, regardless of whether the problem arises from the user making a mistake, or from a problem with the system itself. Error messages should be informative, telling the user the exact thing that has gone wrong and exactly how to correct the problem, if that is possible.

Example 7.1   *Imagine you are maintaining a program that has to write some data to a specific file. Whenever the program fails to write to the file, for any reason, it currently displays the message: "Error 34 writing file". Describe how this message could be improved.*

1. The message number should not be shown, since this is disconcerting for the user to see.

2. The message should state which file (including which directory) could not be written.

3. The message should tell the user the reason or reasons why it could not write the file. These might include: the existing file is write-protected (for everybody or for specific users), the directory is write-protected, the file system is inaccessible (if it is on a network), the file is locked by another program, there is not enough space to write the file, or the disk appears to be damaged.

4. The message should give the user as much information as possible to help him or her to solve the problem. Such information might include: a) the name and login ID of user who has permission to write to the file or directory, b) the name and process ID of the program that is locking the file, and c) how much space must be freed before there is enough space to write the file.

Usability Principle 6: Ensure that the user can always get out, go back or undo an action

Users will always make mistakes; they will issue incorrect commands or navigate to somewhere they had not intended to go. Therefore you must ensure, where possible, that the user can back out of any action.

In particular, make sure that users can easily undo any operation, even if it has resulted in changes to data. Also make sure that they can easily exit any dialog box and cancel any operation in progress. Providing both these facilities helps users to recover from mistakes, and ensures that they are not afraid of experimenting with the system.

Occasionally it is not possible to undo an action – for example, formatting a disk. If such an action may have serious consequences, you should warn users *before* they perform the action, and ask them to confirm that they really want to do it.

Usability Principle 7: Ensure that response time is adequate

Response time is the time that elapses from when a user issues a command (by selecting a menu item, clicking on an icon etc.) to when the system provides sufficient results that the user can continue his or her work. Response time can be a problem when processing large volumes of information or transmitting data over a network.

Users' perceptions of what is acceptable are determined largely by other applications they use. If your application runs more slowly than users are accustomed to, then users will have a sense that the system is wasting their time.

Operations such as the popping up of menus and echoing of input should appear instantaneous to users. Most other operations should take a second or less, so that the user's train of thought is not interrupted. A few operations may be allowed to take up to about 10 seconds if the user understands that they are naturally time-consuming. An example is loading a complex web page over a slower network connection. Unfortunately, many web sites force users to download excessively large images.

If an operation is to take more than about 10 seconds then warn users in advance. This gives them the opportunity to choose not to perform the operation, and reduces their annoyance with any delay.

When you evaluate a user interface, work on the slowest hardware that end-users are likely to encounter. We suggest assuming that some users will be working with computers that are up to three years old.

Usability Principle 8: Use understandable labels and other encoding techniques

Everything that appears on the screen should be easily understandable to users. This includes all feedback, all elements of the affordance (e.g. buttons) as well as other information for the user. Refer to Tables 7.1 and 7.2 to select encoding techniques. Also:

- Avoid technical jargon and acronyms.

- Employ technical writers to compose text and graphic designers to create graphics.

- Label items so that their meaning is obvious. You can place captions underneath them or provide pop-up labels that appear when the user moves the mouse over them.

Usability Principle 9: Ensure that the UI's appearance is neat and uncluttered

A very common error among UI designers is to provide users with too much to look at. This distracts users, slows them down and makes it harder for them to learn the system. Web pages are especially prone to information overload, particularly with the presence of advertisements.

Messiness of the layout and graphic design can also be distracting, and results in the user taking longer to figure out how to use the interface.

To achieve a neat, uncluttered UI:

- Only display essential information, but provide a way for the user to request additional information.

- Avoid having large numbers of dialogs that each display only a small amount of information: the user may become lost trying to navigate your system.

- Highlight information that belongs together using boxes, colors and fonts. For example, place a box around related items in a form, and use horizontal lines to separate related items in a menu.

- Avoid using too many different colors, fonts or graphics.

- Line up labels and input fields so that users can more quickly read what they have to enter.

Usability Principle 10: Consider the needs of different groups of users

Earlier, we pointed out that there are different types of users, each with their own needs. You should accommodate the needs of the following categories of people:

■ *People from different locales.* A locale is an environment where the language, culture, laws, currency and many other factors may be different. Table 7.3 lists some of the things that differ among locales. When designing a UI, it is important to internationalize it, which means ensuring that it can be easily adapted to different locales. Adapting the system to a particular locale is called *localization.*

■ *People with disabilities.* People have many kinds of disabilities. To accommodate blind people, ensure that your application works with programs that convert text to Braille or speech. For example, when displaying an image in a web page, use an 'alt' html tag that describes what the image shows. To accommodate deaf people, ensure the system has visual output that conveys the same information as the sound. To accommodate physically disabled people, ensure that your application can interact with software that permits voice input.

■ *Beginners versus experts.* In complex applications, provide a simple mode for beginners, and a fully functional mode for experts. The expert mode would have more icons and fields as well as more items in menus.

Also, consider providing a 'preferences' dialog, to enable users to tailor the system to their particular needs.

Localization and internationalization in Java and in operating systems

Operating systems have to display locale-specific information. This means that you can query the operating system to obtain such information when programming a user interface. However, different operating systems store different types of locale information.

Java has its own class called `Locale` that it uses to format numbers, etc. You can use this as a basis for decisions about locale-specific UI features. Java sets the default locale based on what is set in the operating system. However, many of the issues listed in Table 7.3 are not automatically managed by Java.

Java has classes called `Calendar` and `DateFormat` which allow for the use of the calendars of specific cultures, and a class called `TimeZone` which deals with the difference between Universal Time Co-ordinated (UTC or GMT) and local time.

Usability Principle 11: Provide all necessary help

Ensure that users can easily and quickly access relevant and easy-to-understand help about anything they are trying to do. It should be the objective of UI design to make the system good enough such that users will rarely need to access the help, but it is nevertheless essential to have online help as a backup.

Table 7.3　　Some types of information that can differ among locales

Locale-dependent feature	Issues the UI designer needs to be aware of
Language	Different languages use different amounts of space, different character sets, different fonts, and run in different directions. Employ a skilled technical translator and ensure he or she runs the system in both languages to verify it
Character set and fonts	Unicode can handle most world character sets, but you also have to ensure that appropriate fonts are available
Direction for reading text	Text in some languages runs left to right or top to bottom. Laying out screens so that they can automatically accommodate this is a challenge
Collating sequences (sort order of words)	Some languages order characters with accents or diacritics at the end of an alphabet, whereas others order them as if the accent or diacritic were absent. Often, the sort order for names in phone books is special
The order and components of peoples' names.	Family name comes first in some cultures, last in some, and is non-existent in others. In some cultures, a person's legal name differs from their commonly used name. Salutations such as Mr and Dr vary widely
Currency and format for displaying currencies	An application may use more than one currency at once. The number of decimal places and the magnitude of values may differ widely. The language somebody uses may not correspond to the currency they use
Time zones	Time-zone abbreviations are not used consistently. Daylight savings time starts and ends on different dates in different places, or may not exist at all
Format for dates, times and numbers	There are many ways of writing dates, times and numbers. Even though the international standard is YYYY/MM/DD, this is often not followed
Calendars and holidays	Although international business is based on the Gregorian calendar, the calendars of particular cultures and religions are also used in some places
Formats for phone numbers, addresses, postal codes, credit card numbers, etc.	You should almost never require a specific format for these items since they differ so widely and can change at any time. Allow free-form input of whatever the user wants to type. A common error is not to allow sufficient characters, or not to allow extensions to be recorded for telephone numbers
Laws and business practices	You have to accommodate different ways of calculating taxes, performing accounting, or keeping records. Patents and other regulations might place restrictions on designs
Icons and metaphors	Icons and other encoding techniques can invoke different impressions in people of different cultures

When you develop help, remember that users are often frustrated when they seek help. Be sure, therefore, that the help system does not increase this frustration.

Focus on help that guides the user through the steps of a task. But avoid help that explains all the details at once. Integrate help with the application, making it context sensitive. For example, allow the user to point to some aspect of the UI, or to an error message, and obtain an explanation of it.

Ensure that the help can be easily searched, and that searches retrieve relevant help.

Usability Principle 12: Be consistent

Once users learn how to use one application or dialog, it is a big advantage to them if other applications and dialogs work the same way. Be consistent, therefore, within your own application, make your application follow the standards of the operating system on which it runs, and consider mimicking aspects of other applications. However, ensure that you are not infringing copyrights or patents, and avoid duplicating weaknesses.

An example user interface

Figure 7.2 shows parts of a user interface that has several problems. Figure 7.3 shows the same system after improvements have been made. Before reading on, see how many problems you can find in Figure 7.2.

Here are some of the specific problems found in Figure 7.2, and the corresponding improvements made in Figure 7.3.

■ The instructions in Figure 7.2(a), 'To sign up, use the Edit menu' violate Principle 3. Forcing the user to select a menu item in order to start entering information is more complex than is necessary. In Figure 7.3, the user simply has to click on the 'Start' button.

■ Although the Edit menu of Figure 7.2(a) shows that the user can add three different kinds of information, there is no indication about the order in which the information should be filled in. Nor is it clear how to finish the sign-up process. These problems violate Principle 4, since the user will not know what to do after completing each step. Figure 7.3, on the other hand, uses a 'wizard' interface: the user can step through the various steps by clicking on 'Next>>', which is prominently visible. Figure 7.3 also numbers each step, which is useful feedback, better conforming to Principle 5.

■ In Figure 7.2(a), one of the menu items is 'Add Addresses…'. The intent is to allow the user to specify more than one address (e.g. home, work etc.), but this is not clear. Also, in Figure 7.2(b) there is a field labeled 'type' that is supposed to contain the type of address (home, work, etc.), but the user will probably not understand what to put there. These are both violations of Principles 4 and 8, which require clear instructions and labels. In Figure 7.3, on the other hand, a

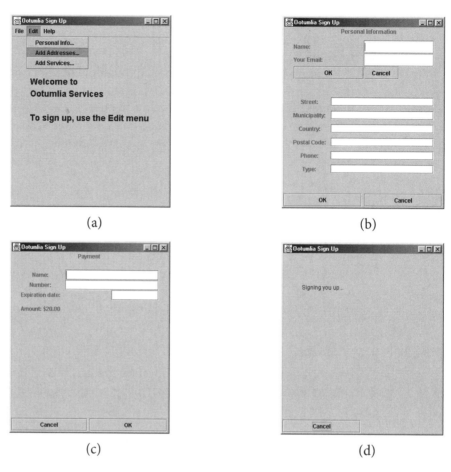

(a) (b)

(c) (d)

Figure 7.2   Parts of the user interface of an Internet Service Provider sign-up application that has several usability problems

'tabbed dialog' is used that makes it clearer to the user how to add several addresses.

■ In Figure 7.2 there appears to be no way a user can delete a secondary address once he or she has added it. This violates Principle 6, which states that all actions should be undoable. The '<<Prev' button and the tabbed dialog make it much easier for users of Figure 7.3 to change any data they have input.

■ Figure 7.2(b) and (c) are modal dialogs, since they only have 'OK' and 'Cancel' buttons. This is another violation of Principle 3. Figure 7.3's 'wizard' interface is preferable.

■ Figure 7.2(b) has two sets of 'OK' and 'Cancel' buttons. The user will not understand the reason for this, violating Principles 4 and 8. They also add clutter, violating Principle 9. The duplicate buttons have been removed in Figure 7.3.

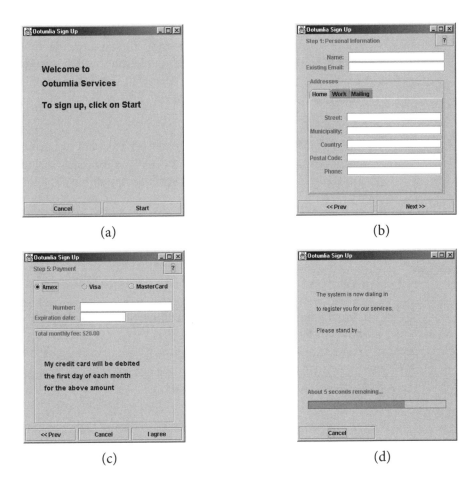

Figure 7.3   Views of the ISP sign-up application that has improvements compared with Figure 7.2. It uses a 'wizard' approach as well as tabbed dialogs

■ In Figure 7.2(b), the 'OK' button is on the left, and the 'Cancel' button is on the right. This the reverse of what normally appears, violating Principle 12. It is also likely to lead the user to press the 'Cancel' key accidentally, violating Principle 3. In Figure 7.3, the button the user would be most likely to select is always located at the bottom-right corner.

■ The layout of Figures 7.2(b) and (c) is messy and inconsistent, violating Principles 9 and 12. In Figure 7.3, all the labels are right justified, and all the input fields line up with each other.

■ Figure 7.2(c) has a field labeled 'Name' which is ambiguous and violates Principles 4 and 8. Most users would assume the field is asking for the person's name, but why is system asking for it again? The intent is that the user enters the type of credit card (Visa, MasterCard, etc.) but this is very obscure. Figure 7.3(c) allows the user to select the card type making this much clearer.

■ The feedback about the amount owing in Figure 7.3(c) is better than that of Figure 7.2(c), since it is clear that the amount is a *monthly* payment (Principle 5). Also, the user is clearly told that by clicking on 'I agree' he or she is agreeing to payment; it is not clear that this will occur by pressing 'OK' in Figure 7.2(c). This violates Principle 4.

■ The feedback provided in Figure 7.2(d) is very weak, violating Principle 5. Figure 7.3(d) gives the user much clearer feedback about what is going on as the system connects to the remote site. The feedback includes a progress bar and an estimate of the number of seconds remaining.

■ In Figure 7.2, there is no clear way to access help, violating Principle 11. Figures 7.3(b) and (c) have '?' buttons to provide this capability.

Exercises

E138 Describe the error messages that will need to be displayed in each of the panels shown in Figure 7.3.

E139 You are asked to design the GUI for a software application that can convert audio files from one format to another.

(a) Use the twelve usability principles to draw a paper prototype of this GUI.

(b) Describe how you have adhered to each of the twelve usability principles.

(c) Obtain an application that does the same thing and compare your GUI to this one. There are free applications available on the Internet.

E140 Imagine your goal is to develop a web-based application to access your voice messaging system (or your answering machine). This application can allow you to select messages, play them, drag messages to other applications, etc.

(a) Create a use case model for this application.

(b) Draw the interface of this application. Pay attention to the layout; specify all labels you would use; propose icons or other encoding techniques to make your interface more usable.

E141 Draw a paper prototype of the user interface for the GANA system, whose requirements were presented in Chapter 4. Base your prototype on the textual description of the UI given in the requirements document, and the use cases you developed in Exercise E68(b). You will have to fill in some details not explicit in the textual description, such as the size and shape of buttons etc.

7.5   Evaluating user interfaces

No matter how well a designer adheres to the principles discussed in the last section, usability can only be assured by careful evaluation. In this section, we describe two approaches to evaluation that can be combined to produce a highly usable system.

Evaluation versus quality assurance

In Chapter 10, we will discuss inspection and testing of software — two quality assurance processes. These two processes are used to uncover defects resulting, in general, from violation of requirements.

Heuristic evaluation and usability testing, as discussed here, are analogous to the above but focus on one particular quality: usability. However, there is an important difference: most of the usability defects found do not represent violation of explicit requirements in fact, the recommendations for change resulting from these processes really are *new* requirements — requirements that couldn't be known until you have a system to evaluate. Evaluating usability therefore cannot be left until you think the design and coding are finished.

Heuristic evaluation

Heuristic evaluation involves systematically examining the system, looking for *usability defects* – aspects of the design that might pose problems for users. Heuristic evaluation is the most popular of several techniques that are collectively called *usability inspection*. Usability inspection should be performed on all software; it can be done by regular members of the software engineering team, and by usability experts if they are available.

You can perform a heuristic evaluation of a paper prototype, a finished system, or any intermediate version. It is best to ask two or three people to do each evaluation independently in order to maximize the number of defects found.

Use the following steps when you perform a heuristic evaluation:

1. Pick some use cases to help focus the evaluation. Focus initially on the most important ones.

2. For each window, page or dialog that appears during the execution of the use cases, study it in detail to look for possible usability defects: violations of the principles and guidelines (the heuristics) discussed in the previous section. Be as critical as you can; if you think something has a chance of being a problem for some user, then consider it a defect. It is better to raise a concern about something that is actually not a problem than to ignore something that is.

3. When you discover a usability defect, write down the following information:

   ❏ A short description of the defect. You may need to include a screen snapshot if the nature of the problem might not be obvious.

❏ Your ideas for how the defect might be fixed.

Your purpose in recording this information is to communicate with other software engineers who will be fixing the defect. You can also learn what to avoid when you next design a user interface.

Exercises

E142 Find an application that performs each of the following tasks. Perform a heuristic evaluation based on each task in order to find the situations where it violates the twelve usability principles described in the last section. Describe each of the defects you find, and suggest how it could be fixed.

(a) A facility for drawing a graph, in a spreadsheet or statistical application. Evaluate changing the graph format (e.g. scatter, bar or line), changing x- and y-axis labels, changing the scale of the axes and adding extra data points.

(b) Facilities for creating a table in a word processor. Evaluate converting text into a table, balancing the widths of columns and making the format of a table look like those in this book.

E143 Download three freeware applications designed to perform the same task. Perform a heuristic evaluation of each. Select the best and worst one and explain why you ranked them this way.

E144 Work in groups of two or three to do the following. First, each member of the group should independently perform a heuristic evaluation of the paper prototype you developed in Exercise E139 or E140. Then the group members should get together and study each other's lists of defects. Determine how many were found by only one person, how many were found by two people and how many were found by all three (if you have three members). This exercise should demonstrate that having more than one evaluator is important.

E145 Perform a heuristic evaluation of the GANA UI that you drew in Exercise E141. Update your GUI if necessary; also, indicate any requirements that should be changed based on your UI review.

Usability testing: evaluation by observation of users

No matter how much work a software engineer puts into user interface design and heuristic evaluation, some usability problems will exist. It is therefore essential to carefully and systematically observe users as they use a prototype of the system, in order to discover these problems.

Some strategies for usability testing include:

■ Select users corresponding to each of the most important actors. Remember that a user may have more than one role. Also, try to select people who are both beginners and experts in the domain, as well as people who are experts and non-experts in terms of their experience with computers. You will likely learn different things from observing different types of users; and you will help ensure that the system is suited to different types of users.

■ Select the most important use cases for each of the actors you selected in the last step, and determine specific tasks for the users to follow. Each task should be a concrete scenario of one of the use cases.

■ Write sufficient instructions about each of the scenarios so that the users know what goal they should try to achieve. Record these on small cards so that you can hand them to the users one at a time.

■ Arrange evaluation sessions with users well in advance, and leave plenty of time for each session. Sessions lasting more than an hour are too tiring. A good length is 20–30 minutes. Work with one user at a time.

■ At the beginning of the session explain the purpose of the evaluation. In particular, explain to the users that the objective is to evaluate the software, not them. Also, make sure that the users understand that their participation is optional, that they can withdraw at any time, and that whatever happens will be kept confidential.

■ Preferably make a video recording of each session. It is very difficult to notice and record all the details of interactions while observing them live. Studying a video later will often bring to light important information. However, video recording can be intimidating to users and may make the logistics of the session harder to manage. If you do record sessions, then test the camera and look at a sample recording in advance to make sure the screen is sufficiently readable. When you look at the recording, you need to be able to understand what the user is doing (you may not be able to completely read all the text on the screen). Also make sure that the sound is clearly audible.

■ Converse with the users as they are performing the tasks. Ask them what they are thinking, what they think the system's feedback means, and why they perform various actions. Encourage them to think out loud.

■ When the users finish all the tasks, de-brief them. This means ask for their overall impressions and recommendations.

■ Analyze any difficulties experienced by the users, no matter how small. There could be times when they had to seek help, times when they made mistakes, or times when they had to think or explore before figuring out what to do.

■ Formulate your recommendations for changes to the system that will avoid repetition of the difficulties.

Ethics of usability testing

Whenever you observe users as part of the process of studying software, you need to ensure that you adhere to certain ethical principles. Users may be nervous about participating, may feel an obligation to perform well, may worry about what their manager or others will think about their mistakes, and may become frustrated with the system.

First, ensure that the users fully understand the purpose of the study and are made to feel at ease. They must know that they are volunteers and can stop for any reason. Second, respect their confidentiality: do not involve managers or other people in the process. Furthermore, as soon as your recommendations for changing the UI have been understood by the developers, all records that mention the names of (or show pictures of) individual users should be erased.

If you are performing user studies as part of a *research* activity (i.e. not just for product development), then even stricter ethical guidelines apply. In such situations, users should be asked to sign an 'informed consent' form that clearly specifies their rights, since they are now acting as 'research subjects'.

Exercise

E146 Working in groups of two or three, conduct a usability testing session of some reasonably complicated web site that interests you. You can each take turns being the user.

E147 Download two freeware applications designed to perform the same task and ask two users to use both of them. Follow the usability testing approach described above. Produce a list of recommendations that would improve the usability of each of these applications.

7.6 Implementing a simple GUI in Java

After designing the UI abstractly, and evaluating paper prototypes, it is time to implement it. Java provides two main frameworks for implementing user interface designs: Swing and the Abstract Window Toolkit (also called AWT). AWT is considerably simpler, although rather more limited. Other organizations provide additional frameworks: for example the SWT (Standard Widget Toolkit) is used in the Eclipse environment (www.eclipse.org).

Due to the volume of details that we would have to provide, and the fact that GUI libraries change frequently, we will not discuss how to construct a Swing or SWT-based GUI. However, the basic principles of GUI design in Java remain the same no matter what GUI library you use.

Under the AWT, building a graphical user interface relies on the use of three main elements:

1. `Component`. These are the basic building blocks of any graphical interface. Important subclasses are `Button`, `TextField`, `TextArea`, `List`, `Label`, and `ScrollBar`.

2. `Container`. The role of these is to contain the components that constitute the GUI; the main subclasses are `Frame`, `Dialog` and `Panel`. In Java, a `Frame` is an independent window, with a title and border. A `Dialog` is also a window, but is owned by another window. A `Panel` is designed to be included in another `Container`, even another `Panel`. It therefore also acts as a `Component`. `Panels` are used to compose complex GUIs.

3. `LayoutManager`. These are classes that define the way `Components` are laid out in a `Container`. The simplest layout manager is the `GridLayout` that divides a `Container` into a grid where all `Components` occupy equal-sized rectangles. Another useful layout manager is the `BorderLayout`. This time, the `Container` is divided into five areas, designated as Center, North, South, East and West. When a `Container` with a `BorderLayout` is resized, the West and East regions grow vertically only, while the North and South regions grow horizontally only. The Center area grows in both directions.

As an illustration, let us examine how a graphical interface for the SimpleChat program (Phase 1) can be built. The resulting GUI is shown in Figure 7.4.

Figure 7.4 Simple graphical user interface (GUI) for Phase 1 of SimpleChat

The first step consists of creating the main window by defining a subclass of `Frame`. All the widgets that compose the window will be attributes of this class.

```java
public class ClientGUI extends Frame implements ChatIF
{
    private Button closeB =    new Button("Close");
    private Button openB =     new Button("Open");
    private Button sendB =     new Button("Send");
    private Button quitB =     new Button("Quit");
    private TextField portTxF = new TextField("12345");
    private TextField hostTxF = new TextField("localhost");
```

```
private TextField message = new TextField();
private Label portLB =      new Label("Port: ", Label.RIGHT);
private Label hostLB =      new Label("Host: ", Label.RIGHT);
private Label messageLB =   new Label("Message: ", Label.RIGHT);
private List messageList =  new List();
```

Note that this class also implements the ChatIF interface, as required by the ChatClient class.

In order to add a title to the Frame, to define its size and to make it visible, the constructor contains the following lines:

```
public ClientGUI(String host, int port)
{
  super("Simple Chat");
  setSize(300,400);
  setVisible(true);
```

The window is composed of a List, which is meant to display all the received messages, as well as a series of other widgets located at the bottom of the window. These are laid out using a BorderLayout, with the List at the Center and the remaining widgets in the South region. However, since only one Component can be placed in the South region, a Panel called bottom is created to contain all the widgets. The following lines, also in the constructor, accomplish this:

```
setLayout(new BorderLayout(5,5));
Panel bottom = new Panel();
add("Center", messageList);
add("South", bottom);
```

The bottom panel uses a GridLayout of 5 lines and 2 columns to lay out its Components, as follows:

```
bottom.setLayout(new GridLayout(5,2,5,5))
bottom.add(hostLB);
bottom.add(hostTxF);
bottom.add(portLB);
bottom.add(portTxF);
bottom.add(messageLB);
bottom.add(message);
bottom.add(openB);
bottom.add(sendB);
bottom.add(closeB);
bottom.add(quitB);
  ...
}
```

When a message is received, the ChatClient instance calls the display method of the associated ChatIF. The message thus received by the ClientGUI is displayed in the List widget as follows:

```
public void display(String message)
{
  messageList.add(message);
  messageList.makeVisible(messageList.getItemCount()-1);
}
```

When a user wants to send a message, he or she has to type the message into the TextField named message and then push the 'Send' button. The send method that actually sends the message is written as follows:

```
public void send()
{
  try
  {
    client.sendToServer(message.getText());
  }
  catch (Exception ex)
  {
    messageList.add(ex.toString());
    messageList.makeVisible(messageList.getItemCount()-1);
    messageList.setBackground(Color.yellow);
  }
}
```

We must arrange for the above method to be called whenever the user pushes the 'Send' button. This can be achieved by creating what Java calls an ActionListener. ActionListener is in fact an interface with only one abstract operation called actionPerformed. This operation will be called each time a user pushes the associated button. To associate a Button with an ActionListener you must proceed as follows (these lines are normally located in the constructor of the Frame):

```
sendB.addActionListener(new ActionListener()
{
  public void actionPerformed(ActionEvent e)
  {
    send();
  }
});
```

These lines introduce a feature of Java called an anonymous class – refer to a Java manual for more details on this technique. The basic idea is that we are creating a class which implements the ActionListener interface without explicitly naming the new class. We merely give a definition to the abstract method actionPerformed, defined in that interface. The sendB button is now associated with an ActionListener that has an actionPerformed method. That method in turn calls the send method described earlier. The net effect of this is that when you push the 'Send' button, the send method is automatically called.

The complete code for this class and additional examples of AWT GUIs are available on our web site (www.lloseng.com).

7.7 Difficulties and risks in user-centered design

■ **Users differ widely**. This means that different types of user will want to perform different use cases. Users will also have different perceptions of what is a good user interface and what is not. In addition, users will want to use the system in different locales.
Resolution. Make sure you account for differences among users when you design the system. Design it for internationalization. When you perform usability studies, try the system with many different types of users.

■ **User interface implementation technology changes rapidly**. Vendors deliver new and changed class libraries for UI design more frequently than they change the core of a programming language.
Resolution. Stick to simpler UI frameworks that are widely used by others; make sure, however, that they have sufficient power for your needs. Avoid fancy and unusual UI designs, and especially the design of new controls, because they will be more sensitive to changes.

■ **User interface design and implementation can often take the majority of the application development effort**. UI design is often thought to be easy and is therefore not explicitly budgeted for as part of the software engineering process.
Resolution. Make UI design an integral part of the software engineering process, allocating time for many iterations of prototyping and evaluation. Remember that you can save a lot of time by designing the UI using very simple prototypes.

■ **Developers often underestimate the weaknesses of a GUI**. Many software developers have not been trained in user interface design. Others tend to feel over-confident about a UI because they personally understand it.
Resolution. Ensure all software engineers have training in UI development. Always test with users. Study the UIs of any software you use so that you learn to appreciate what constitutes a good and bad UI.

7.8 Summary

In this chapter we have looked at aspects of software development that relate to users: involving users in the development process, and developing user interfaces.

User-centered design is the term given to a variety of software development approaches and techniques that collectively focus on the user. It has been widely recognized that developing software without a user focus results in software that has poor usability.

The USS Vincennes disaster

The *USS Vincennes* was patrolling the Persian Gulf, when operators noticed an aircraft on their combat control system's screen. Unfortunately, in order to determine the altitude and other information about the plane, they had to look at a separate monitor. Under stress, the operators associated the wrong information with the plane they saw. They believed it was a military plane that was threatening them, and shot it down. Actually, it was an Iran Air passenger plane – 290 people lost their lives.

If the designers of the system had followed the principles discussed in this book, this tragedy might never have occurred. If they had performed use case analysis user-centered design, they would have realized that essential information about a plane should be immediately accessible on the combat control system's screen.

User interface design should be performed once you have a clear idea of the use cases. You should follow design principles such as:

- keep the sequences of action simple;

- ensure that the user knows what step to take next;

- provide feedback; ensure response time is adequate;

- use good techniques for encoding information, such as appropriate fonts and colors;

- keep the UI uncluttered;

- ensure the system can be used by different types of users;

- provide help;

- be consistent.

Evaluating user interfaces can be done in two main ways: by inspecting them to verify that they adhere to UI design principles (heuristic evaluation), and by systematically observing users as they use the system (usability testing).

7.9 For more information

The following are some sources of information about user interfaces and usability.

Web sites about usability

- The User Interface Hall of Shame http://digilander.libero.it/chiediloapippo/ Engineering/iarchitect/shame.htm is a valuable site including some truly hilarious examples of bad user interface design from real applications. Every software engineer should visit and learn from this site

- useit.com: http://www.useit.com is Jakob Nielsen's personal web site is a very rich source of information related to usability. Jacob Nielsen is probably the best-known author and speaker in the field of user interface design

- Usable Web: http://www.usableweb.com has many links about designing usable web sites

- The Usability Professionals Association: http://www.upassoc.org.

Books about user interfaces and usability

- D. J. Mayhew, *The Usability Engineering Lifecycle: A Practitioner's Handbook for User Interface Design*, Morgan Kaufmann, 1999

- J. Nielsen, *Usability Engineering*, Academic Press Professional, 1994. Discusses techniques for evaluating user interfaces

- J. Nielsen, *Designing Web Usability: The Practice of Simplicity*, New Riders, 2000. Contains numerous color pictures of web sites and large numbers of design guidelines

- J. Johnson, *GUI Bloopers: Don'ts and Do's for Software Developers and Web Designers*, Morgan Kaufmann, 2000

- S. Fowler, *GUI Design Handbook*, McGraw Hill, 1997. http://www.books.mcgraw-hill.com/computing/authors/fowler.html

- D. Norman, *The Design of Everyday Things*, Basic Books, 2002

Project exercises

E148 Working in teams of three or four, develop a graphical user interface for the client side of Phase 4 of the SimpleChat system (the version developed in the project exercises of the last chapter). The result of your work will be Phase 5. Use the guidelines presented in this chapter. In particular, undertake the following activities:

(a) Have each person in the team independently create a paper prototype that contains his or her best ideas about how the user interface should appear. Doing this should take no more than about half an hour.

(b) Have each person present his or her paper prototype to the other members of the group. The group members should first point out the good ideas of the prototype, and then give constructive criticism. The creator of the prototype should write down the ideas.

(c) Working together, the group should then take the best ideas from the paper prototypes and develop a new unified paper prototype. Be careful, however, not to add too many features.

(d) Now, using AWT or a GUI building tool, develop Java code to implement your interface, replacing the `ConsoleChat` class.

(e) Evaluate your user interface by arranging for several members of some other group to use it. Take note of any problems they encounter, and update your interface to reduce the problems.

E149   On the book's web site, you will find a class called `DrawPad`. Associated with this there is a class called `StartDraw` that allows you to create an instance of `DrawPad` and draw some simple lines and curves using the mouse. Without changing `DrawPad` at all, add a feature to SimpleChat that will allow you to communicate with other users of SimpleChat by drawing pictures. This would work by having two clients simply open `DrawPads` and start drawing. The drawing actions should be transmitted as commands via the server. The result of your work will be Phase 6 of SimpleChat.

E150   The SimpleChat system is not internationalized. Its most severe problem is that all the displayed messages are hard-coded in English. Design and implement an internationalized version of SimpleChat that obtains all the displayed messages from a message file. Arrange for the system to determine the locale from the operating system, and then select an appropriate message file. Hint: you can number each message (but do not display numbers to end-users). You will need to develop a way to embed parameters in messages.

E151   Develop a prototype user interface for the Small Hotel Reservation System, as follows. If possible, involve users from the hotel industry.

(a) Do some parallel design of paper prototypes. Then pick the best features of each paper prototype to create a final version.

(b) Review your prototype, following the guidelines discussed in this chapter. Change it as necessary.

(c) Use a rapid prototyping tool to create a partially functional prototype based on your paper prototype. This prototype will not actually manipulate any data and it will not, therefore, make use of the object model you have developed.

(d) Have people use your prototype. Observe the difficulties they have. Change the prototype as necessary.

Modeling interactions and behavior

8

In Chapters 5 and 6 we showed you how to use class diagrams to build a static model of objects in a software system.

In this chapter, we look at how to model system dynamics, focusing on two aspects: interactions and behavior. An interaction model shows a set of actors and objects interacting by exchanging messages. A behavior model shows how an object or system changes state in reaction to a series of events.

In this chapter you will learn about the following

■ Two types of UML interaction diagram used to model detailed scenarios of system execution: sequence diagrams and communication diagrams.

■ State and activity diagrams, two other UML diagram types that are used to model the possible behavior of a system.

8.1 Interaction diagrams

Interaction diagrams are used to model the dynamic aspects of a software system – they help to visualize how the system runs. They show how a set of actors and objects communicate with each other to perform the steps of a use case, or of some other piece of functionality. The set of steps, taken together, is called an *interaction*.

Interaction diagrams can show several different types of communication. These include messages exchanged over a network, simple procedure calls, and commands issued by an actor through the user interface. Collectively, these are referred to as *messages*.

The following elements can be found in an interaction diagram:

■ **Instances of classes or actors**. As discussed in Chapter 5, instances of classes (i.e. objects) are shown as boxes with the class and object identifier underlined. Actors are shown using the same stick-person symbol as in use case diagrams, introduced in Chapter 4.

■ **Messages**. These are shown as arrows from actor to object, or from object to object. One of the main objectives of drawing interaction diagrams is to better understand the sequence of messages.

Since you need to know the actors and objects involved in an interaction, you should normally develop a class diagram and a use case model before starting to create an interaction diagram.

Two kinds of diagrams are used to show interactions: *sequence diagrams* and *communication diagrams*. Both contain similar information about an interaction, although sequence diagrams have notations that make them somewhat more powerful. Sequence diagrams explicitly show the sequence of events on a time line, whereas communication diagrams are more compact.

Sequence diagrams

A sequence diagram shows the sequence of messages exchanged by the set of objects (and optionally an actor) performing a certain task. Figure 8.1 gives an example.

The objects are arranged from left to right across the diagram – an actor that initiates the interaction is often shown on the left. The vertical dimension represents time. The top of the diagram is the starting point, and time progresses downwards towards the bottom of the diagram. A vertical dashed line, called a *lifeline*, is attached to each object or actor. The lifeline becomes a box, called an *activation box*, during the period of time that the object is performing computations. The object is said to have *live activation* during these times.

A message is represented as an arrow between activation boxes of the sender and receiver. You give each message a label; it can optionally have an argument list and a response. The complete syntax is as follows:

```
response:=message(arg,...)
```

Figure 8.1 shows how the classes work together to allow a student actor to register in a course; the corresponding class diagram is shown in Figure 8.2.

There are three objects and one actor involved in this interaction. A `Student` object and a `CourseSection` object exist initially; a `Registration` object is created as the interaction proceeds. A creation message is shown using a dashed line with the label `create`. Note the different types of arrowheads used by the create message and the others; it is important to use the correct arrowheads to conform to UML 2.0 syntax.

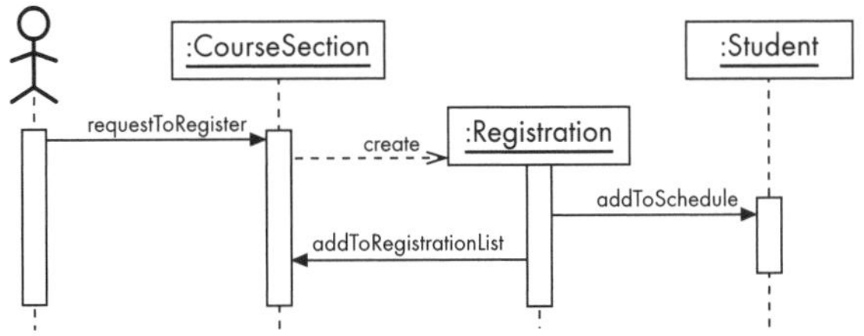

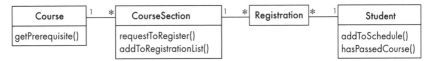

Figure 8.1   A simple sequence diagram showing the student registration process

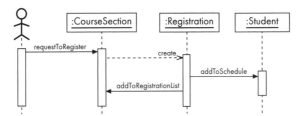

Figure 8.2   Class diagram for the sequence diagrams shown in Figures 8.1, 8.3 and 8.4

The objects that exist initially should be lined up along the top of the diagram. Since the `Registration` is created later, its box appears further down, at the time when it is created. Unfortunately, many tools can only draw diagrams in which all the objects appear at the top, as shown in Figure 8.3. However, the create message still makes it clear when the object is created.

Figure 8.3   Sequence diagram similar to Figure 8.1 as it would have to be drawn by most tools, which require all objects to be listed along the top of the diagram

The actor initiates the interaction via the user interface; the user interface sends a `requestToRegister` message to the `CourseSection`, which in turn creates a `Registration`. The `Registration` object then asks the `Student` to add it to the list of courses the student is taking, and also asks the `CourseSection` to add it to the list of registered students.

The labels on the messages in Figure 8.1 correspond to operations in Figure 8.2. The reception of a message by an object causes one of its methods to be run. Sequence diagrams are therefore useful for identifying the operations that have to be included in each class.

Often, when an actor interacts with a system, a corresponding object will exist that contains information about that actor. In Figure 8.1, the actor shown on the far left is most likely a student, whose corresponding object is shown on the far right. Both are abstractions of the same reality, but should not be confused.

As with class diagrams, interaction diagrams can be drawn at various levels of detail. The level of detail you choose depends on what you wish to communicate. For example, Figure 8.4 provides more detail than is presented in Figure 8.1.

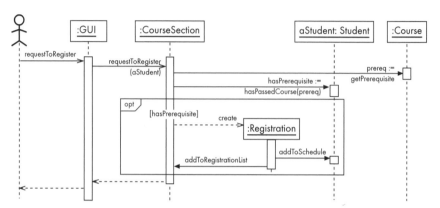

Figure 8.4   **A sequence diagram showing more detail about the student registration process including an optional combined fragment**

■ Figure 8.1 showed the user directly interacting with a CourseSection object. In reality, the user interacts with the user interface, which in turn interacts with the rest of the data in the system. Figure 8.4 shows this more clearly.

■ Figure 8.4 gives the arguments and return values of certain messages. For example, the requestToRegister message has aStudent as an argument. This same object is also the destination of two messages, therefore the second-to-right object has been labeled aStudent:Student to make this clear.

■ Figure 8.4 makes use of a *combined fragment* marked 'opt'. A combined fragment is a subsequence of an interaction that is special in some way, and is shown within a box. The 'opt' label means that it may or may not occur. A Boolean *condition*, written within square brackets, describes the circumstances when it will occur. In this case, the condition is written over the :CourseSection lifeline, and indicates that the subsequence in the combined fragment will only occur if the hasPrerequisite variable (the return value of the previous message) is true.

■ Sometimes a message is sent, but the reply to that message is sent back after considerable delay. A dashed line from the CourseSection to the GUI in Figure 8.4 indicates when the reply to the original requestToRegister message is sent.

In some cases, a sequence of messages must be repeated – in other words *iteration* must occur. You show iteration using a combined fragment marked 'loop', as is illustrated in Figure 8.5. The number of times to loop is specified using the syntax `min..max`. In Figure 8.5 the `getSubtotal` message will be sent to `numPurchase` different `Purchase` objects. The class diagram for this example is given in Figure 8.6.

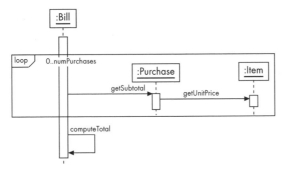

Figure 8.5   A sequence diagram showing a loop fragment

Figure 8.6   Class diagram for Figure 8.5

Figure 8.5 also shows the case of a message being sent from an object to itself. A sequence diagram can show the destruction of an object using a big **X** symbol on a lifeline. For example, Figure 8.7 shows what might happen when a booking in the airline system is canceled. The corresponding class diagram is Figure 5.32.

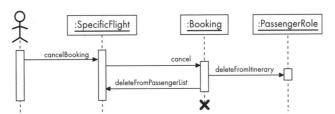

Figure 8.7   Illustration of deleting an object in a sequence diagram

Exercises

E152   Draw sequence diagrams representing the following interactions:

(a) A client searches for a book in a library. He or she then asks to borrow the book. If a copy of this book is available, a loan object is created.

(b) To obtain the cousins of an individual, you must determine his or her two parents. You then obtain the siblings of these parents. For each of these siblings, you obtain their children (refer to Figure 5.25(c)).

(c) A client wishes to open a new account at a bank branch. To do so, his instance of class `Client` must first be retrieved from the central bank server. For a new client, an instance of `Client` must be created. An instance of `BankAccount` is then created using the `Client` object. A deposit must then immediately follow, to complete the account creation process.

Communication diagrams

A communication diagram shows several objects working together. It appears as a graph with a set of objects and actors as the vertices.

A communication diagram is very much like an object diagram except that, as we will discuss below, it shows *communication* links instead of links of associations. It also has much in common with a sequence diagram, except that lifelines, activation boxes and combined fragments are absent. Instead, you draw a communication link between each pair of objects involved in the sending of a message; the messages themselves are attached to this link.

You represent a message using an arrow, labeled with the message name and optional arguments. You specify the order in which messages are sent by prefixing each message using some numbering scheme.

Figures 8.8 and 8.9 show examples of communication diagrams describing the same interactions as the sequence diagrams of Figures 8.1 and 8.4.

Figure 8.8   A communication diagram representing the same interaction as the sequence diagram of Figure 8.1

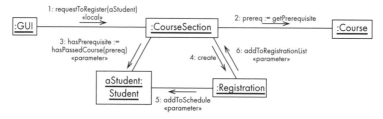

Figure 8.9   A communication diagram corresponding to the sequence diagram of Figure 8.4

Communication links can exist between two objects whenever it is possible for one object to send a message to the other one. Several situations can make this possible:

■ The classes of the two objects are joined by an association. This is the most common case. In Figure 8.9, message 2 is sent over such a link. If all messages are sent in the same direction, then probably the association can be made unidirectional.

■ The receiving object is stored in a *local* variable of the sending method (but the objects are not yet joined by an association). This can happen when the receiving object is created in the sending method, such as in message 4 of Figure 8.9, or when some computation returns an object that is only kept in a local variable. In message 1 of Figure 8.9 we tag such a message with the stereotype «local».

■ A reference to the receiving object has been received as a parameter of an earlier message to the sender. In Figure 8.9, we tag such messages with the stereotype «parameter». For example, in message 3 the `Student` was previously passed as a parameter to the `CourseSection`.

■ The receiving object is *global*. This is the case when a reference to an object can be obtained using a public static method (e.g. using the Singleton pattern). The stereotype «global» could be used in this case. Note that the use of global data should be minimized, as we will discuss in Chapter 9.

■ The objects communicate over a network. The stereotype «network» could be used to show this.

Exercises

E153 Draw a communication diagram corresponding to Figure 8.5.

E154 Draw communication diagrams for the interactions described in Exercise E152.

How to choose between using a sequence or a communication diagram

Since sequence and communication diagrams contain much the same information, you have to decide which of the two you should draw. Sequence diagrams are often the better choice in the following four situations:

■ You want the reader to be able to easily see the order in which messages occur.

■ You want to build an interaction model from a use case. Use cases already have a sequence of steps; sequence diagrams expand on these to show which objects are involved.

■ You need to show details of messages, such as parameters and return values. Doing so on communication diagrams can result in clutter.

■ You need to show loops, optional sequences and other things that can only be properly expressed using combined fragments.

On the other hand, you may prefer a communication diagram when you are deriving an interaction diagram from a class diagram. This is because communication diagrams are effectively object diagrams with communication links instead of association links. Communication diagrams can in fact be used to help validate class diagrams – a communication diagram might suggest, for example, that you should add a new association in order to make the interaction possible.

Communication diagrams, patterns and collaborations

A communication diagram can be used to represent aspects of a design pattern – such as those discussed in Chapter 6. Figure 8.10(a) shows the two steps involved in the main interaction of the Proxy pattern. First, a client object makes a request to a «Proxy» object. Then, if the «HeavyWeight» is needed and is not already loaded, the «Proxy» causes it to be loaded, before returning the result to the client. Compare this to Figure 6.13.

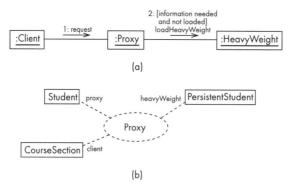

Figure 8.10   Using a communication diagram and a collaboration symbol to represent the Proxy design pattern

The *collaboration* between the classes involved in an interaction can be represented in a class diagram using a dashed ellipse, as shown in Figure 8.10(b). Dashed lines link the ellipse to classes that fulfill the various roles of the collaboration. Here, for example, PersistentStudent has the role of «HeavyWeight». This notation is particularly convenient for showing the classes fulfilling the roles in a design pattern.

8.2   State diagrams

A *state diagram*, also known as a *state machine diagram*, is another way of expressing dynamic information about a system. It is used to describe the externally visible behavior of a system or of an individual object.

At any given point in time, the system or object is said to be in a certain *state*. It remains in this state until an *event* occurs that causes it to change state. Being

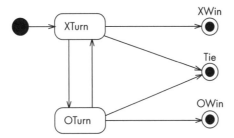

Figure 8.11   State diagram of a tic-tac-toe (noughts and crosses) game

in a state means that it behaves in a specific way in response to any events that occur. You represent a state using a rounded rectangle that contains the name of the state. Figure 8.11, for example, contains two such states.

Several different types of event can cause the system to change from one state to another. In each state, the system behaves in a different way. A *transition* represents a change of state in response to an event, and is considered to occur instantaneously – that is, to take no time. You draw a transition using an arrow connecting two states. You can also show a label on a transition; this represents the event that causes the change of state.

There are two other special symbols that can appear on a state diagram:

■ A black circle represents the *start state*. When the system or object starts running, it immediately takes a transition from the start state to a regular state. There should be only one start state in each top-level state diagram, and there should be only one unlabelled transition pointing out of the start state.

■ A black circle with a ring around it represents an *end state*. The system or object finishes its work when such a state is reached. There can be more than one end state in a state diagram. The symbol is supposed to resemble a target.

In addition, there are several other pieces of notation that can be placed inside states and on transitions to describe their behavior more precisely. We will discuss these in the context of examples below.

Figure 8.11 represents the game of tic-tac-toe, also known as noughts and crosses. Since player X always goes first, the initial transition from the start state points to the 'X Turn' state. From then on, the game alternates between 'X Turn' and 'O Turn' states, until the game ends. There can be three possible outcomes of the game, represented by the three end states: X can win, O can win or there can be a tie. The 'Tie' end state can be reached from both 'X Turn' state and 'O Turn' state.

Notice that there is more than one transition leading out of both 'X turn' and 'O turn' states. In this situation, the system will take the transition that corresponds to the *first* occurring event: a move resulting in a win, a tie or continued play. In the remainder of this chapter we will use event labels of various kinds to make clear what causes each transition.

Elapsed-time transitions

The event that triggers a transition can be a certain amount of elapsed time. Figure 8.12(a) illustrates the use of such *elapsed-time* transitions to model a simple traffic signal.

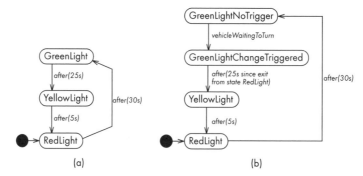

(a)   (b)

Figure 8.12   State diagrams of a simple traffic light, illustrating elapsed-time transitions

There are three main states in Figure 8.12(a), corresponding to the three colors of the traffic signal at point 1 of Figure 8.13. The initial state has a transition to 'RedLight' state to indicate what happens when the system starts up. After startup, the system indefinitely rotates among green, yellow and red, therefore there is no end state.

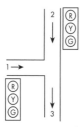

Figure 8.13   Street layout for the traffic signals of Figure 8.12

The red light only stays on for 30 seconds, at which time the green light comes on. The green light stays on for 25 seconds, at which time the system moves to the 'YellowLight' state. After five more seconds the yellow light gives way to the red light again. Note that the traffic signal at point 2 of Figure 8.13 would have the same state diagram, except that when it goes green, the signal at point 1 would go red, and vice versa.

Figure 8.12(b) extends the above scenario by showing a slightly different pattern for the signal at point 2. In this case, traffic moving from point 2 to 3 always has a green light unless a vehicle arrives at point 1 and triggers a sensor. When the sensor at point 1 is triggered, the system moves to 'YellowLight' state, but only after the traffic coming from point 2 has had at least 25 seconds of green light. An extra state 'GreenLightChangeTriggered' is used to model this latter situation. Without this state and its outgoing transition, a steady series of

Traffic lights work differently in different locales

You might notice that the traffic light state diagram of Figure 8.12 does not work in quite the same way as your local traffic lights do. For example, in many countries, just before the light goes green, the red and yellow lights come on simultaneously to let drivers know they should prepare to move. The timing of lights and the rules for the triggering of sensors can differ at each intersection. Designing a generic and internationalized traffic light system would therefore require considerable domain analysis.

vehicles arriving at point 1 would prevent the light at point 2 from staying green long enough for traffic to flow.

Transitions triggered by a condition becoming true

Figure 8.14 gives an example of a state diagram containing transitions that are made whenever certain conditions become true. A condition can be distinguished from an event name since it contains a Boolean operator. The two conditions in this figure are `classSize >= minimum`, and `classSize >= maximum`.

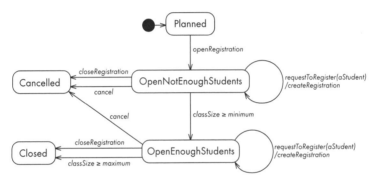

Figure 8.14   State diagram of a CourseSection class

The figure shows the behavior of instances of the `CourseSection` class shown in Figure 8.2. When it is first created, a `CourseSection` is in 'Planned' state and is not yet ready to receive students. When registration is opened, the system moves to 'OpenNotEnoughStudents' state.

In this state, the `CourseSection` can accept requests to register, but the course will not actually be taught until the class size reaches a certain minimum. The object evaluates the `classSize >= minimum` condition every time anything occurs that could make the condition `true`; as soon as it becomes `true`, a transition is taken to 'OpenEnoughStudents' state.

If requests to register continue while in 'OpenEnoughStudents' state, the object will eventually exceed a predefined maximum number of students, at which time it automatically moves to 'Closed' state. The course section can also be explicitly closed by a `closeRegistration` event, indicating that the registration deadline has passed. If there are not enough students, closing a course section has the same effect as canceling it.

There is no end state (the target symbol) because we will keep a permanent record of the course section, whatever happens.

The `requestToRegister` transitions in Figure 8.14 shows that a transition can lead from a state back to the same state. Also, the `/createRegistration` notation designates an *action*; this is discussed in the next subsection.

Exercises

E155 Enhance Figure 8.11 to show the conditions that should be present to determine when the system should transition to each of the end states ('X Win', 'O Win' and 'Tie') or to the regular states 'X Turn' and 'O Turn'.

E156 Given the state diagram in Figure 8.14, in what state would the system be in after the following sequences of events? Assume that `minimum` is set to 3 and `maximum` is set to 5.

(a) `openRegistration`, `requestToRegister` (repeated twice), `cancel`.

(b) `openRegistration`, `requestToRegister` (repeated 8 times in total), `closeRegistration`

E157 Enhance Figure 8.14 to handle the following situations:

(a) The course section can be canceled when in any state, except after it has been taught.

(b) A student can drop out at any time, except after the course section has been taught.

E158 Figure 8.12(b) shows the state diagram for a sensor-activated light at point 2 of Figure 8.13, where the light remains green until the sensor is triggered by traffic wishing to move from point 1 to point 3. Show the corresponding diagram for point 1 (where the light remains red until the sensor is triggered).

E159 Draw a state diagram for a four-way intersection (also known as a crossroads). There will be several different signals controlling the different directions of flow. You have to consider which lights are on at any given time. In the basic case, the signals facing north will look the same as the signals facing south, and the signals facing east will appear the same as those facing west. Thus the system as a whole can have the following states, where NS means north and south, and EW means east and west: 'NSRed-EWGreen', 'NSChanging-EWYellow', ` 'NSGreen-EWRed' and 'NSYellow-EWChanging'.

E160 Enhance your answer to the last exercise by considering a set of traffic signals for an intersection with turning lanes controlled by separate turning signals. You may want to study a real intersection to understand what states can occur.

E161   Model a simple vending machine that can be in four states: 'Waiting', 'Receiving
Money', 'Returning Money', and 'Delivering Item'.

Activities and actions in state diagrams

You can represent two kinds of computations using state diagrams. These
computations are called *activities* and *actions*.

An activity is something that occurs over a period of time and takes place
while the system is in a state. The system may take a transition out of the state
in response to completion of the activity. However, if some other transition is
triggered first, then the system has to terminate the activity as it leaves the state.

An activity is shown textually within a state box by the word 'do' followed by
a '/' symbol, and a description of what is to be done. When you have details such
as actions in a state, you draw a horizontal line above them to separate them
from the state name.

Figure 8.15 shows a jukebox with just two states. In 'ProposeSelection' state,
the system waits for the user to press a button, selecting some music. In the
'MusicPlaying' state, the system plays the chosen music until it comes to an end.
The system then takes a transition back to 'ProposeSelection' state.

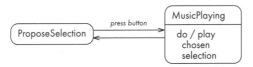

Figure 8.15   State diagram for a jukebox, illustrating an activity in a state

An *action* is something that takes place effectively *instantaneously* in any of
the following situations:

■ When the system takes a particular *transition*.

■ Upon entry into a particular state, no matter
which transition causes entry into that state.

■ Upon exit from a particular state, no matter
which transition is being taken.

An action should take place with no
noticeable consumption of time; therefore it
should be something simple, such as sending
a message, starting a hardware device or
setting a variable.

An action is always shown preceded by a
slash ('/') symbol. If the action is to be
performed during a transition, then the
syntax is event/action. If the action is to be

Action semantics

UML allows you to specify
actions using whatever notation
you find suitable. However, the
UML specification describes
over 40 classes of action that
you can represent in models.
Some examples are actions to:
send a message, change a variable, create or destroy an
object, and create or destroy a
link.

performed when entering or exiting a state, then it is written in the state box with the notation `enter/action` or `exit/action`.

Figure 8.16 illustrates the use of actions in the state diagram for a garage door opener. Upon entry into each state, a particular action occurs that has an effect on the garage door motor: the motor controller can be told to start the motor running forwards (opening the door), to start the motor running in reverse (closing the door), or to stop the motor. For example, whenever the garage door becomes completely open, it enters 'Open' state; the action taken when this occurs is to stop the motor.

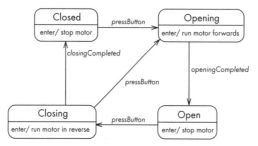

Figure 8.16   State diagram for a garage door opener, showing actions triggered by entry into a state

Normally the controller cycles around the four states in a clockwise manner, a button being used to initiate opening or closing. When closing the door, however, there is a safety mechanism: if the button is pressed while the door is closing, the motor is immediately thrown into the forwards direction, causing the door to start opening again.

Figure 8.17 shows another example of the use of actions. This is a partial state diagram of a tape recorder. In this case, there is an exit action that stops the recording process no matter what causes the 'Recording' state to be exited. In addition, the `startOfTape` transition has a `stop` action that occurs during the transition to the 'Wait' state.

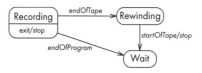

Figure 8.17   Partial state diagram for a tape recorder showing an action on a transition and an action on exiting a state

Figure 8.17 is clearly incomplete, since there is no transition out of 'Wait' state. An important part of validating a state diagram is to ensure that each state has at least one outgoing transition, and at least one incoming transition. You should also make sure that it is possible to get from any state to any other state, otherwise the system can reach what is called 'livelock'. We will discuss this concept in Chapter 10.

Nested substates and guard conditions

A state diagram can be nested inside a state. The states of the inner diagram are called *substates*.

Figure 8.18 shows a state diagram of an automatic transmission; at the top level this has three states: 'Neutral', 'Reverse' and a driving state, which is not explicitly named. The driving state is divided into substates corresponding to the three gears that the system automatically chooses. The advantage of the nesting is that it shows compactly that the driving substates are all very similar to each other – in particular, that they can all transition to 'Neutral' at any time, upon the user's command. The start symbol inside the driving state shows that it by default starts at the 'First' substate. However, the user can also manually select 'First' or 'Second' to force the transmission to move into, and stay in, these substates.

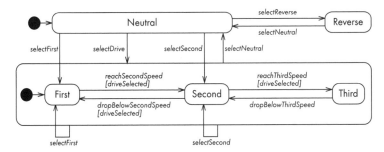

Figure 8.18   State diagram for a car's automatic transmission showing substates

The notation `reachSecondSpeed[driveSelected]` illustrates the use of a *guard condition*. The system will only respond to the indicated event (`reachSecondSpeed`) if the condition in square brackets is true. In Figure 8.18, this is used to prevent the transmission from changing gear if the driver had manually selected first or second gear. A guard condition differs from the type of condition we saw in Figure 8.14: a guard condition is only evaluated when its associated event occurs.

Figure 8.19 shows how we have converted Figure 8.14 to use nested substates. Now we need to show only one `cancel` transition and one `requestToRegister` transition. Note that the 'Planned' state has a transition that points directly to the 'NotEnoughStudents' substate, and both the transitions to the 'Closed' state comes directly from the inner 'EnoughStudents' state. Finally, note that we have added an activity to the 'Canceled' state that deletes all registrations.

Exercises

E162   There is a missing transition in Figure 8.18. Study the diagram, and see if you can find it (do not add any new states or event types).

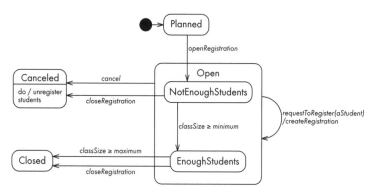

Figure 8.19   A version of the course section example from Figure 8.14, showing the effect of nested states

E163   Modify the diagram shown in Figure 8.18 so that it correctly incorporates the 'Park' control of an automatic transmission.

E164   There are several other subtleties of nested states that we will not discuss here. One of the important skills of a software engineer is to be able to look up information directly from documentation. Go to the OMG web site and find the official specification of the latest version of UML. Use this to learn about the 'history' state and how to use it in the context of nested state diagrams.

E165   Draw state diagrams for the following situations:

(a) Modify the jukebox diagram shown in Figure 8.15 so that it has an 'AcceptingMoney' state. The correct amount of money must be accepted prior to the user selecting the music.

(b) Create a state diagram for the microwave oven system described in Example 4.6.

(c) Expand Figure 8.17 to model the general operation of a VCR. It can be in at least the following states: 'Off', 'StandbyForAutomaticRecording', 'AutomaticRecording', 'ManualRecording', 'PlayingTape', 'Showing TV Channel', 'Rewinding', and 'FastForwarding'. Tape operations can only occur if a tape has been inserted. Automatic recording occurs when the VCR is programmed to record a program at a certain time, and for a certain period of time.

(d) Create a state diagram to model the steps involved in programming a VCR to record a program at a certain time. Study a real VCR to understand the possible states. The events are buttons pressed on the VCR's remote control or console. This diagram represents the behavior of part of the user interface of the VCR, whereas Exercise E165(c) represents the behavior of the functional layer.

8.3 Activity diagrams

An activity diagram is like a state diagram, except that it has a few additional symbols and is used in a different context. In a state diagram, most transitions are caused by *external* events; however, in an activity diagram, most transitions are caused by *internal* events, such as the completion of an activity.

An activity diagram is used to understand the flow of work that an object or component performs. It can also be used to visualize the interaction between different use cases.

One of the strengths of activity diagrams is the representation of concurrent activities. Concurrency is shown using forks, joins and rendezvous, all three of which are represented as short lines, at which transitions can start and end.

- A *fork* has one incoming transition and multiple outgoing transitions. The result is that execution splits into two concurrent threads.

- A *join* has multiple incoming transitions and one outgoing transition. The outgoing transition will be taken only when all incoming transitions have been triggered. The incoming transitions must be triggered in separate threads.

- A *rendezvous* has multiple incoming and multiple outgoing transitions. Once all the incoming transitions are triggered, the system takes all the outgoing transitions, each in a separate thread.

An activity diagram also has two types of nodes for branching within a single thread. These are represented as small diamonds:

- A *decision node* has one incoming transition and multiple outgoing transitions, each with a Boolean guard in square brackets. Exactly one of the outgoing transitions will be taken.

- A *merge node* has two incoming transitions and one outgoing transition. It is used to bring together paths that had been split by decision nodes.

Figure 8.20 shows an example activity diagram for the process of registering in a course section. The first thing that occurs is the reception of the registration request. Once this processing is complete, the system immediately takes the outgoing transition and forks the processing into two concurrent threads.

The concurrent thread on the right is responsible for checking whether a course is full or not. The outcome of its computations is either that the course is not full, in which case execution proceeds to the join, or else the course is full, in which case the whole activity diagram terminates.

The concurrent thread on the left, meanwhile, checks whether the student is allowed to register. First it checks if the student has the prerequisites for the course; if this check is affirmative, the thread proceeds to the join via a merge node. Otherwise a second check is performed, to see if the student has special permission that can override the lack of prerequisites. If this second check is

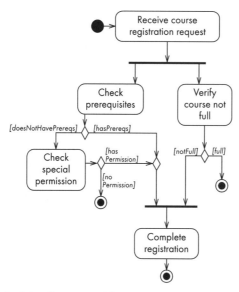

Figure 8.20   Activity diagram of the registration process

affirmative, the thread proceeds to the join via the merge node, otherwise registration is disallowed and the whole activity diagram terminates.

Either concurrent thread may reach the join first, at which time it will wait for the other. It may be the case that neither thread, or only one thread, ever reaches the join, due to the course being full or registration being disallowed. However, if both threads reach the join, then they are replaced by a single thread that performs the final activity – completing the registration.

In Figure 8.20, the entire process comes to an end as soon as any of the end states is reached. This implies that even if one thread is waiting at the join, it will be terminated if the other thread reaches an end state.

While state diagrams typically show states and events concerning only one class, activity diagrams are most often associated with several classes. The partition of activities among the existing classes can be explicitly shown in an activity diagram by the introduction of *swimlanes*. These are boxes that form columns, each containing activities associated with one or more classes.

Figure 8.21 shows how the activities of Figure 8.20 can be allocated to two different classes.

8.4   Implementing classes based on interaction and state diagrams

Drawing the diagrams discussed in this chapter for every class, interaction and activity would take too much time. However, you should certainly use these diagrams for the parts of your system that you find most complex.

For example, a state diagram is useful when different conditions will cause the instances of a class to respond differently to the same event. This is particularly true when behavior is distributed across several use cases.

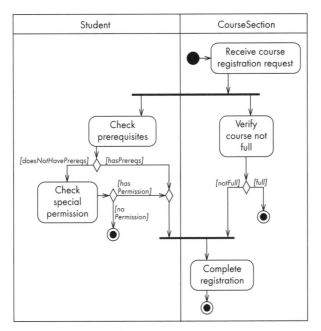

Figure 8.21   Activity diagram with swimlanes

In this section we will give an implementation of the CourseSection class found
in Figure 8.2. Our intent is to show you how interaction and state diagrams help
you create a correct implementation.

First, consider how we have implemented the state diagram from Figure 8.19.
An object's state can be determined from the values of variables open and
closedOrCanceled, as well as how many students are registered. An object can
determine which state it is in by evaluating the following expressions:

■ 'Planned':

```
closedOrCanceled == false
   && open == false
```

■ 'Open' (accepting registrations):

```
open == true
```

■ 'NotEnoughStudents' (substate of 'Open'):

```
open == true
   && registrationList.size() < course.getMinimum()
```

■ 'EnoughStudents' (substate of 'Open'):

```
open == true
   && registrationList.size() >= course.getMinimum()
```

■ 'Canceled':

```
closedOrCanceled == true
```

```
&& registrationList.size() == 0
```

■ 'Closed' (course section is too full, or being taught):

```
closedOrCanceled == true
  && registrationList.size() > 0
```

Calls to operations openRegistration, closeRegistration, cancel and requestToRegister are used to implement the events of the same names. Note that these events can cause different transitions, depending on the state of the object.

Two transitions are triggered by conditions becoming true. Method requestToRegister has to explicitly check if it should trigger the conditional transition to 'Closed'.

In Figure 8.19, two transitions are taken when a variable called classSize reaches certain thresholds. This variable is not present in the implementation – instead registrationList.size() is used. This is an example of refinement between the modeling phase and the implementation phase.

The method unregisterStudents is used to implement the action in the 'Canceled' state. This must be called by any method that can cause a transition into that state (i.e. cancel and closeRegistration).

Next let us consider how the sequence diagram from Figure 8.4 is implemented. Most of the code for this is found in the requestToRegister method. Two of the messages are also found in the constructor of class Registration, which is not shown here.

The following is the code for CourseSection, incorporating the decisions we have discussed above. Note that the complete class would also contain other methods we have not discussed.

```
public class CourseSection
{
  // The many-1 abstraction-occurrence association (Figure 8.2)
  private Course course;

  // The 1-many association to class Registration (Figure 8.2)
  private List registrationList;

  // The following are present only to determine the state
  // (as in Figure 8.19). The initial state is 'Planned'
  private boolean open = false;
  private boolean closedOrCanceled = false;

  public CourseSection(Course course)
  {
    this.course = course;
    registrationList = new LinkedList();
  }

  public void openRegistration()
```

```
  {
    if(!closedOrCanceled) // must be in 'Planned' state
    {
      open = true; // to 'OpenNotEnoughStudents' state
    }
  }

  public void closeRegistration()
  {
    // to 'Canceled' or 'Closed' state
    open = false;
    closedOrCanceled = true;
    if (registrationList.size() < course.getMinimum())
    {
      unregisterStudents(); // to 'Canceled' state
    }
  }

  public void cancel()
  {
    // to 'Canceled' state
    open = false;
    closedOrCanceled = true;
    unregisterStudents();
  }

  public void requestToRegister(Student student)
  {
    if (open) // must be in one of the two 'Open' states
    {
      // The interaction specified in the sequence diagram of
      // Figure 8.4
      Course prereq = course.getPrerequisite();
      if (student.hasPassedCourse(prereq))
      {
        // Indirectly calls addToRegistrationList
        new Registration(this, student);
      }

      // Check for automatic transition to 'Closed' state
      if (registrationList.size() >= course.getMaximum())
      {
        // to 'Closed' state
        open = false;
        closedOrCanceled = true;
      }
```

```
      }
    }

    // Private method to remove all registrations
    // Activity associated with 'Canceled' state.
    private void unregisterStudents()
    {
      Iterator it = registrationList.iterator();
      while (it.hasNext())
      {
        Registration r = (Registration)it.next();
        r.unregisterStudent();
        it.remove();
      }
    }

    // Called within this package only, by the constructor of
    // Registration to ensure the link is bi-directional
    void addToRegistrationList(Registration newRegistration)
    {
      registrationList.add(newRegistration);
    }
  }
```

Exercise

E166 In the above code, what happens if you are in 'Planned' state and
`closeRegistration` or `cancel` is called? Update the state diagram, as required, to
reflect the implementation. Discuss the implications of this kind of change.

8.5   Difficulties and risks in modeling interactions and behavior

- ■ **Dynamic modeling is a difficult skill, particularly because in a large system
there are a very large number of possible paths a system can take, and
because it is hard to choose which classes to allocate to each behavior.** We
already mentioned in Chapter 5 that static modeling is a difficult skill.
Modeling the dynamics and behavior requires at least as much skill.
*Resolution. The general resolution of this difficulty is the same as for static
modeling: ensure that skilled developers lead the process and ensure that all
aspects of your models are properly reviewed. Also, work iteratively: develop
initial class diagrams, use cases, responsibilities, interaction diagrams and state
diagrams; then go back and verify that all of these are consistent, modifying them
as necessary. Drawing different diagrams that capture related, but distinct,
information will often highlight problems. In safety-critical systems it is
important to use tools that can help you animate, analyze and verify your models.*

8.6 Summary

In this chapter we have discussed various ways to represent the behavior of systems. The types of UML diagrams we studied can be used to design and understand what happens in a system during the passage of a period of time. As with other modeling notations, these diagrams can be analyzed to uncover defects and can serve to communicate designs to others.

Interaction diagrams come in several flavors, including sequence diagrams and communication diagrams. Both of these show the order in which several objects communicate with each other. This communication is shown as a series of messages that may be implemented as procedure calls or as communication over a network. Sequence diagrams show time on the vertical axis, as well as a series of objects on the horizontal axis. Communication diagrams show similar information in a more compact way.

State and activity diagrams show the states in which objects or systems can be found, as well as what causes them to change state. State diagrams are used primarily to show what happens when external events occur, while activity diagrams primarily show internal transitions caused by completion of computations. Activity diagrams can also show separate threads initiated by forks and coming together in joins or rendezvous.

8.7 For more information

Aside from general UML books and web sites, there are relatively few up-to-date practical resources targeting the specific topics discussed in this chapter – software interaction and behavior. However, you can search the web for such topics as 'state diagram' or 'sequence diagram' to uncover many examples of their use. The following are references that will help you dig a little deeper.

- D. Harel and M. Politi, *Modeling Reactive Systems with Statecharts: The STATEMATE Approach*, McGraw-Hill, 1998. http://www.wisdom. weizmann.ac.il/~harel/books.html. David Harel has had more influence over the development of state diagrams than anyone else

- S. Shlaer and S. Mellor, *Object Lifecycles: Modeling the World in States*, Yourdon Press, 1992

- The Use Case Maps web site. This shows a completely different way to model the behavior of systems. http://www.usecasemaps.org

- The SDL Forum Society: http://www.sdl-forum.org/. This organization is the custodian of SDL (Specification and Description Language) as well as Message Sequence Charts, which are similar to sequence charts. UML 2.0 incorporated many ideas from Message Sequence Charts

■ Petri Nets World: http://www.daimi.au.dk/PetriNets/. Petri nets are a classical way of expressing behavior. The notation in UML for forks, joins and rendezvous has its origins with Petri nets

Project exercises

E167 In Chapter 3, the OCSF was partly explained using interaction, state and activity diagrams. You should now be able to fully understand these diagrams. Before you do the following exercises, study Figures 3.2 to 3.5 as a review.

E168 Draw interaction diagrams to model the sequences of messages involved in the three most important SimpleChat use cases you developed in Exercise E79.

E169 Draw detailed state diagrams for

(a) `ConnectionToClient` in the OCSF framework.

(b) A client in Phase 5 of SimpleChat, which can be in various states that have to do with connecting to servers, logging in, forwarding of messages, etc. Hint: you may want to draw separate state diagrams for different aspects of the client's operation.

E170 Based on your use cases and requirements for the Small Hotel Reservation System from Chapter 4, your UI design from the last chapter, as well as your class diagrams from Chapters 5 and 6, do the following:

(a) Create a list of responsibilities that must be implemented in the Small Hotel Reservation System for the three most important use cases.

(b) Develop interaction diagrams that will help you work out how the various classes will need to collaborate to perform each of the responsibilities, and how to allocate the responsibilities to classes.

(c) Create any state diagrams that you believe will help you to better understand the behavior of objects over their life-span.

(d) Update your use cases, user interface design, and class diagram to reflect whatever you have learned from this exercise. Describe the rationale for each change.

Architecting and designing software

9

In earlier chapters you have seen how to gather requirements and build models of software systems. We have also looked at how to design the external functionality of the system – the user interface. In this chapter, we will look at general principles of design, as well as various patterns that can be used to construct the high-level architecture of a system. We will place particular emphasis on communicating design decisions to others.

In this chapter you will learn about the following

- Design as a series of design decisions.

- Various approaches and types of design, including top-down design starting with the architecture, and bottom-up design starting with utilities.

- Design principles that lead to maintainable software, such as 'divide and conquer', striving for high cohesion and low coupling, as well as using good abstractions to hide details, thus simplifying the system.

- How to perform design while keeping portability, reuse, reusability and testability in mind.

- Evaluating trade-offs among alternatives, and applying basic cost–benefit analysis when making design decisions.

- Software architectures for high-level design.

- How to write a good design document.

9.1 The process of design

We start this chapter by taking a very high-level view of design, attempting to answer the following questions. What exactly is design? What general approaches do designers use? What types of design are there?

Design as a series of decisions

> **Definition:** in the context of software, *design* is a problem-solving process whose objective is to find and describe a way to implement the system's functional requirements, while respecting the constraints imposed by the quality, platform and process requirements (including the budget and deadlines), and while adhering to general principles of good quality.

A designer is faced with a series of *design issues*, which are sub-problems of the overall design problem. Each issue normally has several alternative solutions, also known as design *options*. The designer makes a *design decision* to resolve each issue – this process involves choosing what he or she considers to be the best option from among the alternatives. To make each design decision, the software engineer uses all the knowledge at his or her disposal, including:

- knowledge of the requirements;
- knowledge of the design as created so far;
- knowledge of the technology available;
- knowledge of software design principles and 'best practices'; and
- knowledge about what has worked well in the past.

Once a decision is made, new issues are raised.

Sometimes there is no suitable choice to resolve a given issue. In that case, the designer may have to go back and revise previous decisions, or else propose that the requirements be changed.

There may not be a single best alternative when dealing with a particular design issue. Several different alternatives may have opposite advantages and disadvantages, with no clear 'winner'. For example, a thin-client system might result in software that is simpler, whereas a fat-client system might result in software that makes more efficient use of CPU and network resources. Both might seem equally good.

Also, when evaluating alternatives, different designers have different knowledge and ideas, therefore they will tend to reach different conclusions. As a result, two designers will rarely come up with exactly the same solution.

The space of possible designs that could be achieved by choosing different sets of alternatives is often called the *design space*. Figure 9.1 illustrates this idea. The

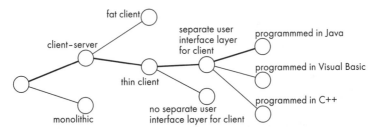

Figure 9.1   Part of a design space, showing alternative designs resulting from different choices when making design decisions. The lines represent options; the bold path is the set of decisions made

final software product is the result of all the design decisions made; different sets of decisions lead to a different product.

You should try to explore different paths through design space – investigating the consequences of choosing different alternatives when major issues arise. In Chapter 7, we recommended employing parallel design to do this. In parallel design, several different designers create their own designs. Following parallel design, you analyze the resulting designs to determine which combination of choices seems best for the final product.

We also showed you the process of selecting among alternative designs in Chapter 2, where several exercises asked you to choose among alternative designs of the `PointCP` class. In Chapter 5, we studied alternative ways of modeling problems using class diagrams.

Although there might be several ways to produce a good quality system, some design issues are critical. For these critical decisions, bad choices will lead to a poor system. For example, imagine that very early on in your design you chose not to separate the user interface from the rest of the system. Such a decision would greatly constrain your ability to achieve a flexible, maintainable design. For example, it would become much harder to provide a web-enabled version of your system or to internationalize it.

Each design decision should be recorded, along with the reasoning that went into making the decision (known as the *design rationale*). The entire record of the series of decisions becomes a design document. We will discuss the structure of design documents later in this chapter.

Parts of a system: subsystems, components and modules

It is now time to define some important terms that will help in further discussion. These terms are often used interchangeably, but in this book we will give them the meanings below. The first two terms, *component* and *module*, describe concrete, implemented parts of a system.

Component any piece of software or hardware that has a clear role and can be isolated, allowing you to replace it with a different component with equivalent functionality. Many components are designed to be reusable, but in other cases they will perform special-purpose functions (e.g. providing the user interface for a particular system). A framework, discussed in Chapter 3, is a kind of component. Other components include source code files, executable files, dynamic link libraries (DLLs) and databases. Some components, such as source files, only exist at compile time; other components, such as certain data files, may only exist at run time.

Module a component that is defined at the programming language level. For example, methods, classes and packages are modules in Java. The modules in the C programming language are files and functions.

The next two terms describe entities that may be implemented in different ways and are therefore more abstract than components and modules.

System a logical entity, having a set of definable responsibilities or objectives, and consisting of hardware, software or both. A system can have a specification that is then implemented by a collection of components. The notion of system can be extended beyond hardware and software to include also people, business processes, organizations, or natural phenomena that work together to achieve something. We will, however, use the more restricted meaning unless otherwise stated. A system continues to exist, even if its components change over the course of time, or are replaced by equivalent components.

Subsystem a system that is part of a larger system, and which has a definite interface. Java uses packages to implement subsystems; individual classes may also implement particular low-level subsystems.

In software engineering, the requirements analysis process determines the responsibilities of a system. The specification process determines the interface of any component built to implement a system. The design process determines how components will be implemented.

Figure 9.2 is a domain model that shows how the above terms are related. Note that you may find these terms used in slightly different ways in other books. Later on in this chapter we will discuss UML's notation for components.

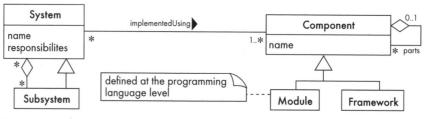

Figure 9.2 Domain model explaining the concepts of system, subsystem, component and module as used in this book

Note that for much of the discussion that follows, we talk about designing modules. However, the points we make would be the same if we talked in the context of larger-scale components, or more abstract subsystems.

Top-down versus bottom-up design

There are several fundamentally different sequences with which you can make design decisions. In *top-down design*, you start with the very high-level structure of the system. You then gradually work down towards detailed decisions about low-level constructs. Examples of high-level issues that are approached first in top-down design include the software architecture and the kind of database that will be used. After many higher-level decisions are made, you finally arrive at detailed decisions such as the format of particular data items, and the individual algorithms that will be used.

The inverse approach, *bottom-up design*, involves first making decisions about reusable low-level utilities and then deciding how these will be put together to create high-level constructs.

A mix of top-down and bottom-up design is normally used. Top-down design is almost always needed to give the system a good structure. On the other hand, some bottom-up design helps ensure that you create reusable components that can be used in several places in the overall system.

We will revisit the distinction between top-down versus bottom-up in the next chapter, in the context of testing.

Special types of design

There are many different aspects of software design, including:

- *Architecture design*: the division of software into subsystems and components, as well as the process of deciding how these will be connected and how they will interact, including determining their interfaces. We will talk more about this later in the chapter. Architecture design is commonly referred to as 'software architecture', although the latter term can also refer to the documentation produced, and the whole field of study.

- *Class design*: the design of the various features of classes such as associations, attributes, interactions and states. We discussed essential aspects of this in Chapters 5 and 8.

- *User interface design*, discussed in Chapter 7.

- *Database design*: the design of how data is persistently stored so that it may be accessed by many programs and users, over an indefinite period of time.

- *Algorithm design*: the design of computational mechanisms.

- *Protocol design*: the design of communications protocols – the languages with which processes communicate with each other over a network.

Each of these types of design is the subject of specialized books.

9.2   Principles leading to good design

In this section we introduce you to general principles you should apply whenever you are designing software. Applying these principles diligently will result in designs that have many advantages over designs in which the principles were not applied.

Some overall goals we want to achieve when doing good design are:

- Increasing profit by reducing cost and increasing revenue. For most organizations, this is the central objective. However, there are a number of ways to reduce cost, and also many different ways to increase the revenue generated by software.

- Ensuring that we actually conform to the requirements, thus solving the customers' problems.

- Accelerating development. This helps reduce short-term costs, helps ensure the software reaches the market soon enough to compete effectively, and may be essential to meet some deadline faced by the customer.

- Increasing qualities such as usability, efficiency, reliability, maintainability and reusability. These can help reduce costs and also increase revenues.

Design Principle 1: Divide and conquer

The divide and conquer principle dates back to the earliest days of organized human activity. Trying to deal with something big all at once is normally much harder than dealing with a series of smaller things. Military campaigns are waged this way: commanders try to avoid fighting on all fronts at once. Cars are also built using the divide and conquer strategy: some people design the engines while others design the body, etc. Furthermore, the task of assembling the car is also divided into smaller, more manageable chunks – each assembly-line worker will focus on one small task.

In software engineering, the divide and conquer principle is applied in many ways. We have already seen how the process of development is divided into activities such as requirements gathering, design and testing. In this section we will look at how software systems themselves can be divided.

Dividing a software system into pieces has many advantages:

- Separate people can work on each part. The original development work can therefore be done in parallel.

- An individual software engineer can specialize in his or her component, becoming expert at it. It is possible for someone to know everything about a small part of a system, but it is not possible to know everything about an entire system.

- Each individual component is smaller, and therefore easier to understand.

- When one part needs to be replaced or changed, this can hopefully be done without having to replace or extensively change other parts.

- Opportunities arise for making the components reusable.

  A software system can be divided in many ways:

- A distributed system is divided up into clients and servers.

- A system is divided up into subsystems.

- A subsystem can be divided up into one or more packages.

- A package is composed of classes.

- A class is composed of methods.

Exercise

E171 In Exercises E55 to E57 and E61, you were asked to create requirements for four systems. Divide each of these into separate subsystems.

Design Principle 2: Increase cohesion where possible

The cohesion principle is an extension of the divide and conquer principle – divide and conquer simply says to divide things up into smaller chunks. Cohesion says to do it intelligently: yes, divide things up, but keep things together that belong together.

A subsystem or module has high cohesion if it keeps together things that are related to each other, and keeps out other things. This makes the system as a whole easier to understand and change.

Listed below are several important types of cohesion that designers should try to achieve. Table 9.1 summarizes these types of cohesion, starting with the most desirable.

Functional cohesion This is achieved when a module only performs a single computation, and returns a result, without having side effects.

A module lacks side effects if performing the computation leaves the system in the same state it was in before performing the computation. The result computed by the module is the only thing that should have an effect on subsequent computations.

The inputs to a functionally cohesive module typically include function parameters, but they can also include files or some other stream of data. Whenever exactly the same inputs are provided, the module will always compute the same result. The result is often a simple return value, but can also be a more complex data structure.

Modules that update a database or create a new file are not functionally cohesive since they have side effects in the database or file-system respectively. Similarly, a module that interacts with the user is not functionally cohesive:

Table 9.1 The different types of cohesion, ordered from highest to lowest in terms of the precedence you should normally give them when making design decisions

Cohesion type	Comments
Functional	Facilities are kept together that perform only *one computation* with no *side effects*. Everything else is kept out
Layer	*Related services* are kept together, everything else is kept out, and there is a *strict hierarchy* in which higher-level services can access only lower-level services. Accessing a service may result in side effects
Communicational	Facilities for operating on the *same data* are kept together, and everything else is kept out. Good classes exhibit communicational cohesion
Sequential	A set of procedures, which work in sequence to perform some computation, is kept together. *Output from one is input to the next*. Everything else is kept out
Procedural	A set of procedures, which are called *one after another*, is kept together. Everything else is kept out
Temporal	Procedures used in the *same general phase* of execution, such as initialization or termination, are kept together. Everything else is kept out
Utility	*Related utilities* are kept together, when there is no way to group them using a stronger form of cohesion

prompting the user is a kind of output, therefore it violates the rule that the only output of a functionally cohesive module is the result returned at the end of execution.

The following are some examples of modules that can be designed to be functionally cohesive:

- A module that computes a mathematical function such as sine or cosine.

- A module that takes a set of equations and solves for the unknowns.

- A module in a chemical factory that takes data from various monitoring devices and computes the yield of a chemical process as a percentage of the theoretical maximum.

A functionally cohesive module can call the services of other modules, but the called modules must preserve the functional cohesion. For example, a module that computes a mathematical function can certainly call modules that perform other mathematical functions.

There are several reasons why it is good to achieve functional cohesion:

■ It is easier to understand a module when you know that all it does is generate one specific output and has no side effects.

■ Due to its lack of side effects, a functionally cohesive module is much more likely to be reusable.

■ It is easier to replace a functionally cohesive module with another that performs the same computation. Being able to make such easy replacements greatly assists maintenance. In the case of a non-functionally cohesive module that has side effects, you would have to verify that any replacement also has precisely the same side effects. Even if the side effects were carefully documented, doing such verification is time-consuming and error-prone. Furthermore, maintainers often fail to pay attention to the presence of side effects.

Layer cohesion This is achieved when the facilities for providing a set of related *services* to the user or to higher-level layers are kept together, and everything else is kept out.

To have proper layer cohesion, the layers must form a hierarchy. Higher layers can access services of lower layers, but it is essential that the lower layers do not access higher layers. This is illustrated in Figure 9.3.

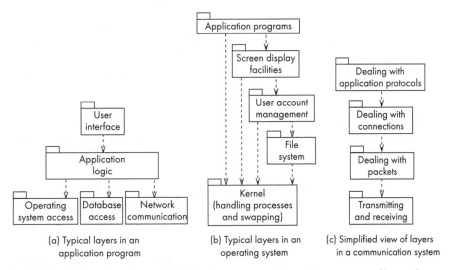

Figure 9.3 Examples of the use of layers. Higher layers can call on the services of lower layers, but not the other way around

An individual service in a layer may have functional cohesion. However, this is not necessary – side effects are allowed, and are often essential.

The set of related services that could form a layer might include:

■ services for computation;

- services for transmission of messages or data;

- services for storage of data;

- services for managing security;

- services for interacting with users;

- services to access the operating system;

- services to interact with the hardware.

For example, if a system is to interface with a particular sound card, then a module should be created specifically to interact with that card. Furthermore, all the code for directly accessing the card should be in this module, and the module should do nothing else except interact with the card.

The set of procedures or methods through which a layer provides its services is commonly called an *application programming interface* (API). The specification of the API must describe the protocol that higher-level layers use to access it, as well as the semantics of each service, including the side effects.

Advantages of layer cohesion are:

- You can replace one or more of the top-level layers without having any impact on the lower-level layers.

- You know you can replace a lower layer with an equivalent layer, because you know it does not access higher layers. To do this, however, you have to replicate all aspects of the API, so that upper layers will continue to work the same way.

We will revisit the notion of layers when we discuss architectural patterns, in Section 9.6.

Communi-cational cohesion This is achieved when modules that access or manipulate certain data are kept together (e.g. in the same class) – and everything else is kept out. One of the strong points of the object-oriented paradigm is that it helps ensure communicational cohesion – provided the principles of object orientation discussed in Chapters 2, 5 and 6 are properly followed.

The term 'communicational' is used for historical reasons. You can remember it by thinking of the following: All the procedures that 'communicate' with the data are kept together.

For example, a class called Employee would have good communicational cohesion if all the system's facilities for storing and manipulating employee data were contained in this class, and if the class did not do anything other than manage employee data.

As another example of communicational cohesion, imagine a module that updates a database, and a second module that keeps a history log of the changes to the database. Since both database and log file are representations of the same data, both modules should be kept together in a higher-level module or subsystem.

A communicationally cohesive module can be embedded in a layer. In other words, part of a layer's API can involve manipulating a particular class of data. The objects manipulated by the layer may be returned to higher layers in response to calls to the API.

The big advantage of communicational cohesion is the same key advantage we ascribed earlier in this book to object orientation: when you need to make changes to the data, you will find all the code in one place.

You should not sacrifice layer cohesion to achieve communicational cohesion: for example, even though objects may be stored in a database or on a remote host, a class must only load and save objects using the services in the API of lower layers.

Figure 9.4 shows several examples of communicationally cohesive modules (marked with a 'C'). These exist inside layers (marked 'L') and call on services in their own layer as well as lower layers. The services they call on may be in modules with other types of cohesion.

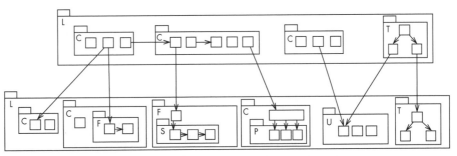

Figure 9.4   Cohesive modules, nested inside each other, using the services of other modules. The modules are labeled using the first letter of the type of cohesion they represent

Sequential cohesion   This is achieved when a series of procedures, in which one procedure provides input to the next, are kept together – and everything else is kept out. This is illustrated in Figure 9.4 by the module marked 'S'.

Your objective should be to achieve sequential cohesion, once you have already achieved the other types of cohesion listed above. Methods in two different classes might provide inputs to each other and be called in sequence; but they would each be kept in their own class, since communicational cohesion is more important than sequential cohesion.

As an example of sequential cohesion, imagine a text recognition subsystem. One module is given a bitmap as input and divides it up into areas that appear to contain separate characters. The output from this is fed into a second module that recognizes shapes and determines the probability that each area corresponds to a particular character. The output from that is fed into a third module that uses the probabilities to determine the sequence of words embedded in the input. If all these modules were grouped together, then the result would have sequential cohesion.

Procedural cohesion This is achieved when you keep together several procedures that are used one after another, even though one does not necessarily provide input to the next. It is therefore weaker than sequential cohesion. In Figure 9.4, the module marked 'P' is procedurally cohesive.

For example, in a university registration system, there would be a module to perform all the steps required to register a student in a course. The facilities for doing separate activities, such as adding a new course, would be in other modules.

Temporal cohesion This is achieved when operations that are performed during the same phase of the execution of the program are kept together, and everything else is kept out. This is weaker than procedural cohesion and is illustrated in Figure 9.4 by the modules marked 'T'.

For example, a designer would achieve temporal cohesion by placing together the code used during system start-up or initialization, so long as this did not violate one of the other forms of cohesion listed above. Similarly, all the code for system termination, or for certain occasionally used features, could be kept together to achieve temporal cohesion.

There may be a temporally cohesive module in a layer whose job is to initialize the services of that layer. The module would be called at startup time, and not at any other time.

Although it would be temporally cohesive, it would be a violation of communicational cohesion to create a module that *directly* initializes the static variables of several different classes or the services of different layers. However, it would be permissible to have a temporally cohesive module that *calls* the initialization procedures of other modules.

Utility cohesion This is achieved when related utilities that cannot be logically placed in other cohesive units are kept together. A utility is a procedure or class that has wide applicability to many different subsystems and is designed to be reusable. A utility module is marked 'U' in Figure 9.4.

For example, the `java.lang.Math` class has utility cohesion. Where possible, it would be better to put mathematical functions in classes on whose instances they are applied; however, `java.lang.Math` allows the grouping together of functions that have no obvious single home.

Exercises

E172 Categorize the following aspects of a design by the types of cohesion that they would exhibit if properly designed:

(a) All the information concerning bookings is kept inside a particular class, and everything else is kept out.

(b) A module is created to convert a bitmap image to the JPEG format.

(c) A separate subsystem is created that runs every night to generate statistics about the previous day's sales.

(d) A data processing operation involves receiving input from several sources, sorting it, summarizing information by input source, sorting according to the input source that generated the most data and then returning the results for the use of other subsystems. The code for these steps is all kept together, although utilities are called to do operations such as sorting.

E173 What is wrong with the following designs from the perspective of cohesion, and what could be done to improve them?

(a) There are two subsystems in a university registration system that do the following. *Subsystem A* displays lists of courses to a student, accepts requests from the student to register in courses, ensures that the student has no schedule conflicts and is eligible to register in the courses, stores the data in the database and periodically backs up the database. *Subsystem B* allows faculty members to input student grades, and allows administrators to assign courses to faculty members, add new courses, and change a student registration. It also prints the bills that are sent to students.

(b) In an electronic commerce application, a module is created to add books to the 'shopping basket' and perform such operations as computing the total amount the customer owes. A second module adds 'special reward' merchandise to the shopping basket; this module also displays the contents of the shopping basket on the screen and sends an email to the user telling him or her what he or she bought.

E174 Describe the kinds of cohesion present in the SimpleChat system.

Design Principle 3: Reduce coupling where possible

Coupling occurs when there are interdependencies between one module and another. Figure 9.5 illustrates the concept of a tightly coupled and loosely coupled system.

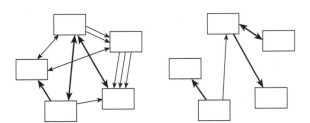

Figure 9.5   Abstract examples of a tightly coupled system (left) and a loosely coupled system (right). The boldness of the arrows indicates the strength of the coupling

In general, the more tightly coupled a set of modules is, the harder it is to understand and, hence, change the system. Two reasons for this are:

■ When interdependencies exist, changes in one place will require changes somewhere else. Requiring changes to be made in more than one place is problematic since it is time-consuming to find the different places that need changing, and it is likely that errors will be made.

■ A network of interdependencies makes it hard to see at a glance how some component works.

Additionally, coupling implies that if you want to reuse one module, you will also have to import those with which it is coupled. This is because the coupled components need each other in order to work properly.

Below, we list some of the many different ways by which modules can be coupled, and some of the ways to reduce the coupling. The types of coupling are summarized in Table 9.2.

To reduce coupling, you have to reduce the *number* of connections between modules and the *strength* of the connections. Some of the types of coupling listed in Table 9.2 are particularly strong and should always be avoided.

Content coupling This occurs when one component *surreptitiously* modifies data that is *internal* to another component. Content coupling should always be avoided since any modification of data should be easy to find and easy to understand.

Java is designed so that the worst kinds of content coupling (e.g. those involving manipulation of pointers) cannot be easily achieved. However, there are still some unfortunate tricks that Java programmers can play.

A form of content coupling occurs whenever you modify a public instance variable in a way that designers did not intend. To reduce content coupling you should therefore *encapsulate* all instance variables by declaring them `private`, and providing get and set methods. If you do this, you then have confidence that the only places where the variable is accessed and modified are in these methods. The set methods can ensure that only valid changes are made to the variables.

A worse form of content coupling, which is much harder to detect, occurs when you directly modify an instance variable *of* an instance variable. For example, in the following code, class `Arch` has a method called `slant`; this surreptitiously modifies the y value of the `Point` at the end of its `baseline` instance variable.

```
public class Line
{
  private Point start, end;
  ...
  public Point getStart() {return start;}
  public Point getEnd() {return end;}
}
```

Table 9.2   Different types of coupling. You should reduce coupling where possible, but the types at the top are the strongest and hence the most important to avoid

Coupling type	Comments
Content	A component *surreptitiously modifying internal data* of another component. Always avoid this
Common	The use of *global variables*. Severely restrict this
Control	One procedure *directly controlling another* using a flag. Reduce this using polymorphism
Stamp	One of the *argument types* of a method is one of your *application classes*. If it simplifies the system, replace each such argument with a simpler argument (an interface, a superclass or a few simple data items)
Data	The use of *method arguments that are simple data*. If possible, reduce the number of arguments
Routine call	*A routine calling another*. Reduce the total number of separate calls by encapsulating repeated sequences
Type use	The use of a *globally defined data type*. Use simpler types where possible (superclasses or interfaces)
Inclusion/ import	*Including a file or importing a package*. Eliminate when not necessary
External	A *dependency exists to elements outside the scope* of the system, such as the operating system, shared libraries or the hardware. Reduce the total number of places that have dependencies on such external elements

```
public class Arch
{
  private Line baseline;
  ...
  void slant(int newY)
  {
    Point theEnd = baseline.getEnd();
    theEnd.setLocation(theEnd.getX(),newY);
  }
}
```

The content coupling occurs here even though the instance variables are private, and `baseline`, an instance of `Line`, is supposedly immutable (`Line` has no `setStart` or `setEnd` methods). It is surreptitious because the `Line` is changed without 'knowing' it is changing.

Part of the problem is that this code does not adhere to the delegation pattern (and the law of Demeter) as discussed in Chapter 6: the slant method is not accessing a neighboring object (the Line) but a more distant object (the Point).

Two things must be done to combat this form of content coupling:

1. Make moving the end of a Line *explicit*, by adding a moveEnd method to it. The slant method should call this. However, this is not enough since programmers could still bypass the moveEnd method.

2. Make the Line class truly immutable. To do this it is necessary to use immutable classes for its instance variables. If you do this, then you eliminate the possibility of surreptitious modification. You will notice that the PointCP class discussed in Chapter 2 was immutable.

Common coupling This occurs whenever you use a global variable – all the modules using the global variable become coupled to each other, and to the module that declares the variable. The coupling occurs because changes to the variable's declaration will affect all the code that uses the variable. Also, changes to the way one module uses a variable will often have an effect on how the other modules should interpret the variable.

The word 'global', as used here, can mean that the variable is visible to all procedures and objects in the system. However, a weaker form of common coupling occurs any time a variable can be accessed by all instances of a subset of the system's classes (e.g. a Java package).

In older programming languages, the use of global variables was widespread; the name 'common' comes from the Fortran language in which it is the keyword used to declare global data. In Java, public static variables serve as global variables.

The use of common coupling should be minimized, since it shares many of the disadvantages of content coupling. Occasionally, a case can be made to create global variables that represent system-wide default values – the argument for this is that it would be more complex to force a large number of routines to pass around such information as their parameters. However, most of these system-wide values are actually constants (i.e. declared final), and not variables. For example, the java.lang.Math package has the constants PI and E.

As is the case with content coupling, common coupling can be reduced by encapsulation. For each global variable, create a module that has specially designated public methods that can be called to get or set the data. The internal representation of the data can then be more easily changed and it can be protected from inappropriate changes made by 'rogue' code; also, the set method can verify that changes are valid.

Encapsulation reduces the harm of global variables, but there is still some undesirable coupling, therefore avoid having too many such encapsulated variables. Note that the Singleton pattern, discussed in Chapter 6, provides encapsulated global access to an object; therefore avoid having too many singletons.

Control coupling This occurs when one procedure calls another using a 'flag' or 'command' that explicitly controls what the second procedure does. The following is an example:

```
public routineX(String command)
{
  if (command.equals("drawCircle")
  {
    drawCircle();
  }
  else
  {
    drawRectangle();
  }
}
```

The method `routineX` will have to change whenever any of its callers adds a new command. It should also probably be changed if any of its callers deletes a command, otherwise it will have code that is said to be 'dead'.

Control coupling can often be reduced by simply having the callers of `routineX` directly call methods such as `drawCircle` or `drawRectangle`. But the use of polymorphic operations is normally the best way to reduce control coupling. In the example above, there could be two separate classes `Circle` and `Rectangle`; `routineX` could then just call `draw`, with the system choosing the appropriate method to run.

There are cases when control coupling cannot or should not be completely avoided. For example, the SimpleChat server has the method `handleMessageFromClient`. This is tightly coupled to the methods in the SimpleChat client that generate the commands. One way to reduce the control coupling in this case would be to have a look-up table that mapped a command to a method that should be called when that command is issued. There is still some coupling, since the look-up table must be modified when commands are changed; however, look-up tables are simpler in structure than nested if-then-else statements.

Stamp coupling This occurs whenever one of your application classes is declared as the type of a method argument. Some stamp coupling is necessary; however, the following situation illustrates why it is best to try to reduce it.

Imagine a class `Employee` that has many instance variables such as `name`, `address`, `email`, `salary`, `manager`, etc., and many methods to manipulate these variables. Any method that is passed an instance of `Employee` is given the ability to call any of its public methods. The method `sendEmail` in the following `Emailer` class, for example, has this ability.

```
public class Emailer
{
  public void sendEmail(Employee e, String text) {...}
  ...
}
```

The problem here is that the sendEmail method *does not need* to be given access to the full Employee object; it really only needs access to email and name. Giving it full access represents unnecessary stamp coupling. Any time a maintainer changes the Employee class he or she will have to check the sendEmail method to see if it needs to be changed. The Emailer class is also not reusable – it can only be used in applications that use the Employee class.

There are two ways to reduce stamp coupling, a) using an interface as the argument type, and b) passing simple variables. The following illustrates the first way:

```
public interface Addressee
{
  public abstract String getName();
  public abstract String getEmail();
}

public class Employee implements Addressee {...}

public class Emailer
{
  public void sendEmail(Addressee e, String text) {...}
  ...
}
```

The stamp coupling is reduced since the sendEmail method now has access only to the name and email data that it truly needs. Changes to the Employee class will be far less likely to impact it. The sendEmail method will still be impacted if the Addressee interface is changed, although that is probably unlikely to occur. Given that the Addressee interface is easy to reuse, the Emailer class now becomes reusable.

Instead of creating a new Addressee interface, you might have considered using a superclass of Employee (e.g. Person) as the type of the sendEmail method. This can sometimes effectively reduce the stamp coupling; but using an interface is usually a more flexible solution.

The second way to reduce stamp coupling is illustrated as follows:

```
public class Emailer
{
  public void sendEmail(String name, String email, String text)
  {...}
  ...
}
```

In this case the stamp coupling has been replaced with data coupling, discussed below.

Data coupling This occurs whenever the types of method arguments are either primitive or else simple classes such as String. Methods must obviously have arguments, therefore some data coupling or stamp coupling is unavoidable. However, you should reduce coupling by not giving methods unnecessary arguments.

The more arguments a method has, the higher the coupling. This is because each caller to the method must have code to prepare the data for each argument; and any changes to how the method declares or interprets each argument may require changes to each caller's code.

There is a trade-off between data coupling and stamp coupling. In the case of a single argument, data coupling is considered looser, and therefore better, than stamp coupling. However, if you replace a single complex argument (stamp coupling) with many simple arguments (data coupling), the total resulting coupling will be higher. In the above code, it was acceptable to eliminate stamp coupling at the expense of adding one extra argument to the `sendEmail` method. It would not have been acceptable to add three or four extra arguments; in such a case, sticking with the stamp coupling (using the `Addressee` interface) would have been better.

Routine call coupling This occurs when one routine (or method in an object-oriented system) calls another. The routines are coupled because they depend on each other's behavior, and the caller depends on the interface of the called routine.

Routine call coupling is always present in any system. However, if you use a sequence of two or more methods to compute something, and this sequence is used in more than one place, then you can reduce routine call coupling by writing a single routine that encapsulates the sequence.

For example, imagine that to use a graphics package, you had to write the following sequence of code over and over again:

```
aShape.drawBackground();
aShape.drawForeground();
aShape.drawBorder();
```

You would be better off creating a new method that encapsulated this sequence. Should the arguments of the above three methods ever change, the maintainer would now only have to change your encapsulated method.

Type use coupling This occurs when a module uses a data type defined in another module. Type use coupling naturally occurs in typed languages such as Java. It occurs any time a class declares an instance variable or a local variable as having another class for its type.

Type use coupling is similar to common coupling, but instead of data being shared, only data types are shared. The impact of sharing data types is normally less than the impact of sharing data, hence type use coupling is considered less problematic than common coupling.

The consequence of type use coupling is that if the type definition changes, then the users of the type may well have to change.

Stamp coupling is closely related to type use coupling, therefore the techniques for reducing stamp coupling can also be applied to type use coupling. In particular, you should declare the type of a variable to be the most general possible class or interface that contains the required operations. For example, when creating a variable that is to contain a collection, you should normally declare its type to be List, that is, any class that implements the java.util.List interface. The actual instance stored in the variable could be an ArrayList, LinkedList or Vector, or perhaps some other class to be defined later. However, declaring the type to be List is sufficient since all the important operations are defined in that interface. The benefit is that your code would be less likely to need to change were you to later decide to use a different type of collection.

Inclusion or import coupling Import coupling occurs when one component imports a package (as in Java); inclusion coupling occurs when one component includes another (as in C++). Doing this means that the including or importing component is now exposed to everything in the included or imported component – even if it is not actually using the facilities of that component. If the included or imported component changes something on which the includer relies, or adds something that raises a conflict with something in the includer, then the includer must change.

The bigger the imported or included component, the worse the coupling. However, importing a standard package (e.g. one delivered with the programming language) is better than importing a homemade package.

Some inclusion or import coupling is necessary – since it enables you to use the facilities of libraries or other subsystems. However, it is important not to import packages or classes that you do not need: in addition to having to worry about changes to the things you are using, you then also have to worry about changes to things you don't use. For example, your system might suddenly fail if a new item is added to an imported file, and this new item has the same name as something you have already defined in your subsystem.

External coupling This occurs when a module has a dependency on such things as the operating system, shared libraries or the hardware. It is best to reduce the number of places in the code where such dependencies exist.

The Façade design pattern can reduce external coupling by providing a very small interface to external facilities.

Exercises

E175 Another way to resolve control coupling in handleMessageFromClient would be to use Java's reflection mechanism. This permits Java to directly treat a string as a method name, and then to call the method. Investigate reflection, and determine what changes would be required to handleMessageFromClient. Then discuss whether the use of reflection would actually be a good design decision, as opposed to keeping the control coupling.

E176 Categorize the following aspects of a design by the types of *coupling* they exhibit.

(a) Class `CourseSection` has public class variables called `minClassSize` and `maxClassSize`. These are changed from time to time by the university administration. Many methods in classes `Student` and `Registration` access these variables.

(b) A user interface class imports a large number of Java classes, including those that draw graphics, those that create UI controls and a number of other utility classes.

(c) A system has a class called `Address`. This class has four public variables constituting different parts of an address. Several different classes, such as `Person` and `Airport` manipulate instances of this class, directly modifying the fields of addresses. Also, many methods declare one of their arguments to be an `Address`.

E177 Describe ways to reduce the cases of coupling described in the last exercise.

E178 What forms of coupling are present in the SimpleChat system? Describe any ways in which coupling can be reduced.

Design Principle 4: Keep the level of abstraction as high as possible

You should ensure that your designs allow you to hide or defer consideration of details, thus reducing complexity. The general term given to this property of designs is *abstraction*. Abstractions are needed because the human brain can process only a limited amount of information at any one time.

We have discussed many types of abstractions in earlier chapters. In Chapter 2 we introduced procedural abstraction and data abstraction – hiding the details of procedures and data, respectively. In Section 2.7 we discussed several types of abstraction present in object-oriented programs.

Some abstractions, like classes and methods, are supported directly by the programming language. Others, like associations, are present purely in models used by the designer.

Abstractions work by allowing you to understand the essence of something and make important decisions without knowing unnecessary details. The details can be provided in several ways:

■ At a later stage of design. For example, when creating class diagrams, you often initially leave out the data types of attributes, and you do not show the implementation details of associations.

■ By the compiler or run-time system. For example, dynamic binding takes care of which methods will run.

■ By the use of default values. For example, a draw operation that always makes the background white unless some explicit action is taken to change the default.

Design Principle 5: Increase reusability where possible

There are two complementary principles that relate to reuse; the first is to design *for* reuse, and the second is to design *with* reuse. We introduced both of these principles in Chapter 3.

Designing for reusability means designing various aspects of your system so that they can be used again in other contexts, both in your system and in other systems. As discussed in Chapter 3, you can build reusability into algorithms, classes, procedures, frameworks and complete applications. Mechanisms whereby components can be reused include calling procedures and inheriting a superclass.

Important strategies for increasing reusability are as follows:

- Generalize your design as much as possible. As you design a potentially reusable component, imagine several other systems that could use this component. Then design your component so that it could work with the other systems too. For example, if you are creating a facility to draw a particular kind of diagram, why not design it so that it could be used to draw other kinds of diagrams for other applications? Better yet, forget the specific application and focus on the reusable component alone. For example, if you need to create a method to save instances of `Employee` to a binary file, instead consider the problem of saving instances of *any* class to a binary file.

- Follow the preceding three design principles. Increasing cohesion increases reusability since the component has a well-defined purpose. Reducing coupling increases reusability because the component can stand alone. Increasing abstraction increases reusability since abstractions are naturally more general.

- Design your system to contain hooks. As discussed in Chapter 2, a hook is an aspect of the design deliberately added to allow other designers to add additional functionality. One of the barriers to reuse occurs when a component does most of what someone else needs, but not quite everything. If a component has effective hooks, then other people can easily extend it to do what they want. For example, the OCSF system has hooks such as `connectionClosed` that allow application designers to choose to do something interesting when a connection is closed.

- Simplify your design as much as possible. The more complex the component, the less it is likely to be reusable in novel contexts. The most reusable components are those that do one simple thing but do it very well. Basic Unix commands such as `grep`, `cat`, `head`, `tail`, `sort`, `uniq`, `awk`, and `sed` are considered classic examples of reusable components because they are very powerful yet relatively simple. Their simplicity comes from the fact that they all input and output the same data type: streams of characters. Their power comes from the fact that they can be strung together in a large variety of combinations.

There are a number of barriers that tend to thwart attempts to build reusable software. These are discussed in the 'Difficulties and risks' section at the end of Chapter 3.

Design Principle 6: Reuse existing designs and code where possible

Designing with reuse is complementary to designing for reusability. Actively reusing designs or code allows you to take advantage of the investment you or others have made in reusable components.

Cloning should normally *not* be seen as an effective form of reuse. Cloning involves copying code from one place to another; it should be avoided since, when there are two or more occurrences of the same or similar code in the system, any changes made (e.g. to fix defects) will have to be made in all clones. Unfortunately, maintainers are often not aware of all the clones that exist, and hence only make the change in one place. The bug thus remains, even though the maintainer thinks it is fixed.

In general, it can be acceptable to clone a single line of code; perhaps a line that contains a complicated call to a method with many arguments. However, any time you are tempted to clone more than a couple of lines of code, it is normally best to encapsulate the code in a separate method and call it from all the places it is needed. See the sidebar 'Tolerating Clones?' for a discussion of exceptions to this rule.

Tolerating clones?

Developers are often advised, as we have done here, not to clone code, but rather to create a new routine or method and call it from several places. This remains good general advice, but there are exceptions:

Imagine you have a software system, we will call it 'A', that is thoroughly tested and has a high reliability requirement. Imagine then that you need to create a new system 'B' that is similar to A, but has important differences. The standard advice is to build a framework out of A's code and then create both a new A and a new B built on this framework. But then A would have to be tested all over again since its code would not be identical to the original. The cost of doing this might be higher, in some cases, than the expected cost of having to maintain clones caused by the alternative approach: duplicating A and modifying it to create B. However, if we repeated this cloning process over and over, the cost of maintaining clones would eventually exceed the cost of developing a framework and re-doing the various systems.

In the above situation, of course, if the original designers of A had had the foresight to create a framework in the first place, then the above issue would not arise.

Removing clones that already exist in a reliable, tested system might also often cost more than leaving them there.

Design Principle 7: Design for flexibility

Designing for *flexibility* (also known as *adaptability*) means actively anticipating changes that a design may have to undergo in the future and preparing for them. Such changes might include changes in implementation (e.g. to improve efficiency or to handle larger volumes of data) or changes in functional requirements.

Ways to build flexibility into a design include:

> **Cloning objects versus cloning code**
>
> In Java there is an interface `Cloneable`: many classes implement this, meaning that you can call the method `clone` to duplicate instances – that is, to create new, identical, objects.
>
> This is quite different from the 'copying code' sense of cloning discussed here.

■ Reducing coupling and increasing cohesion. This allows you to more readily replace part of a system. For example, if your current application saves data to a file, you might anticipate that in future you will want to use a commercial database package. Placing the data-saving parts of your system in a subsystem that has layer cohesion will greatly facilitate such a change.

■ Creating abstractions. In particular, try to create interfaces or superclasses with polymorphic operations. Doing this allows new extensions to be easily added.

■ Not hard-coding anything. Constants should be banished from code. For example, if you want to limit the number of clients that can connect to a server to 25, do not have a line of code that says: `if(numConnections <= 25)`…. Instead, read the maximum value from a configuration file when the server starts. Better yet, make such values preferences that users can change through a preferences dialog.

■ Leaving all options open. For example, when a method encounters an exception, it is best that the method throws the exception rather than taking a definite action to handle it. The caller of the method then has the flexibility to decide what to do with the exception.

■ Using reusable code and making code reusable. The techniques discussed in the previous two design principles, such as adding hooks, tend also to make designs more flexible.

Design Principle 8: Anticipate obsolescence

Anticipation of obsolescence is a special case of design for flexibility. Changes will inevitably occur in the technology a software system uses and in the environment in which it runs. Anticipating obsolescence means planning for evolution of the technology or environment so that the software will continue to run or can be easily changed.

The following are some rules that designers can use to better anticipate obsolescence:

■ Avoid using early releases of technology. The immediate problem is that early releases are likely to have more defects than later releases. However, even if it is possible to work around a defect, a secondary problem may then arise: if the provider of the technology fixes the defect in a subsequent release of the technology, the original work-around may no longer work. Even where no defect exists, improvements to the technology, which are especially likely in the first few releases, can render designs that use the technology in need of change. For example, early adopters of Java, in the 1995–1997 time frame, were later required to make many changes to their code because some of the classes and methods they used became *deprecated*. The Java designers declared components to be deprecated when they developed improved designs – they do not intend to support the older components indefinitely, therefore users are forced to update their software.

- Avoid using software libraries that are specific to particular environments. For example, software that makes use of specific features found only in one operating system, or one particular type of hardware, is less likely to be supported in the distant future.

- Avoid using undocumented features or little-used features of software libraries. The little-used features are not only more likely to have defects but, more importantly, the manufacturers may feel that little harm will be done if they are removed or changed. On the other hand, if the technology provider makes changes to heavily used features there will be loud protests from many users, therefore such changes are less likely to be made.

- Avoid using reusable software or special hardware from smaller companies, or from those that are less likely to provide long-term support. A smaller company is more likely to go out of business or not to have the resources to support older versions. It may seem harsh to suggest that we should only trust larger companies – they can go out of business too. However, the probability is higher that a small company will have to abandon a product.

- Use standard languages and technologies that are supported by multiple vendors. Doing this gives you some confidence that important technology will not be orphaned. Many software systems still in existence today are based on obscure proprietary languages. However, standards are not a panacea: they can change, and there may be subtle differences in implementations of a standard that make it difficult to switch to a competing vendor, even if the new vendor ostensibly supports the same standard.

Design Principle 9: Design for portability

Designing for portability shares many things in common with anticipating obsolescence, although the objective is different. Anticipating obsolescence has, as its primary objective, the survival of the software. Design for portability has, as its prime objective, the ability to have the software run on as many platforms as possible, although sometimes this might also be a necessity for survival.

An important guideline for achieving portability is to avoid the use of facilities that are specific to one particular environment. Some programming languages, such as Java, make this easy because the language itself is designed to allow software to run on different platforms unchanged. Nevertheless, even with Java, there can be subtle differences regarding how some features work on different platforms – knowing about these and avoiding them is important. One such difference is class libraries; some companies have produced special Java libraries that work only with that company's compiler, which in turn runs on only one platform. Attempting to port software that uses that library to another platform can be difficult.

Other languages such as C++ have many features that are very much dependent on the particular hardware architecture. You have to be aware, for example, of the order of characters within a word (so-called big-endian versus little-endian), and the number of bits in an integer.

Another important portability issue has to do with text files: the characters used to terminate lines differ from platform to platform.

Design Principle 10: Design for testability

During design you can take steps to make testing easier. Testing, which is the subject of the next chapter, can be performed both manually and automatically. Automatic testing involves writing a program that will provide various inputs to the system in order to test it thoroughly. Therefore it pays to design a system so that automatic testing is made easy.

The most important way to design for testability is to ensure that all the functionality of the code can be executed without going through the graphical user interface. You can achieve this by carefully separating the UI from the functional layer of the system. A test harness can then be written that calls the API of the functional layer. Another good strategy is to provide a command-line version of your system, such as the command-line version of SimpleChat that we presented at the beginning of this book. This will allow you to write a test program that automatically issues commands to your application.

In order to design a Java class for testability you can create a `main` method in each class. Such `main` methods simply exercise the other methods of a class and report any problems.

Design Principle 11: Design defensively

You should never trust how others will try to use a component you are designing. Just like automobile drivers are taught not to trust other drivers, and therefore to *drive* defensively, a software designer should not trust other designers or programmers, and so should *design* defensively. In other words, in order to increase the reliability of your system, you not only need to make sure you don't add any defects yourself, but you must also properly handle all cases where other code attempts to use your component inappropriately.

The most important way to design defensively is to check that all of the inputs to your component are valid. Or, more accurately, check the *preconditions* of each component.

For example, imagine you have a method that determines whether a certain date is a working day. The first thing this method would do is check that the date is valid.

Unfortunately, over-zealous defensive design can result in unnecessarily performing the same validity checks over and over again. For example, imagine the following method:

```
public boolean isWorkingDay(String aDate)
  throws InvalidDateException
{
  if(!isValidDate(aDate)) throw new InvalidDateException();
  return !(isWeekEnd(aDate) || isHoliday(aDate));
}
```

The first line of the method body validates the date. However, due to defensive design, isWeekEnd and isHoliday may also validate the date. It is a waste of computing power to check the date up to three times like this.

Design by contract is a technique that allows you to design defensively in an efficient and systematic way. The key idea behind design by contract is that each method has an explicit contract with its callers. The contract has a set of assertions that state:

■ What *preconditions* the called method requires to be true when it starts executing. The caller has the responsibility to make these preconditions true before making the call.

■ What *postconditions* the called method agrees to ensure are true when it finishes executing. The called method has the responsibility to make these postconditions true, before returning.

■ What *invariants* the called method agrees will not change as it executes.

Preconditions, postconditions and invariants are all Boolean expressions. If they ever evaluate to false, this indicates that there is a failure. They are similar to the OCL expressions we discussed in Chapter 5; in fact, OCL can be used to write assertions.

Performing assertion checking inside a program is one of the most effective ways to detect and correct errors. Many languages incorporate different mechanisms to write assertions. The ANSI macro assert(expression) can be used to this end in C++. In Java, the keyword assert has been introduced in version 1.4. For example, in the code below, an explicit precondition assertion has been added, meaning that the method must always be called with a valid date. Not fulfilling this condition would be an error.

```
public boolean isWeekEnd(String aDate)
{
  assert isValidDate(aDate); // precondition.

  return (dayOfTheWeek(aDate)==SUNDAY ||
          dayOfTheWeek(aDate)==SATURDAY);
}
```

Under normal operation, the assertions should not be explicitly evaluated in each method since they have always to be true. However, in the testing phase it is useful to have the assertions explicitly executed, so that you can quickly identify any methods that do not fulfill their contract. In Java, assertions are enabled at compile time by using the -ea switch of javac. In this mode, `assert` will throw an `AssertionError` if the expression evaluates to `false`. When assertion checking is disabled (default mode), the `assert` statements are simply ignored. You should therefore always switch on assertion checking during development and testing, and turn it off when the system is finally released.

Note that design by contract implies a level of trust. It is like having a driving instructor with you, clarifying the rules of the road, and stopping you from having an accident while you are learning. However, if you make mistakes after getting your license (the assertion checking is off) you can still have an accident. Therefore at the boundaries between major components, such as layers, you should always rigorously check inputs. At these boundaries, you would therefore not use an assertion mechanism that can be turned off.

9.3 Techniques for making good design decisions

The principles discussed in the previous section suggest qualities you should strive to build into software as you design it. In this section we describe two approaches that will help you to make decisions.

Using priorities and objectives to decide among alternatives

Before you start design, you should have established priorities and objectives for various aspects of quality. An objective is a measurable value you wish to attain. A priority states which qualities override others in those cases where you must make compromises.

The qualities to consider when setting priorities and objectives include memory efficiency, CPU efficiency, maintainability, portability and usability. In general, the priorities and objectives should be obtained from the non-functional requirements.

In order to make a design decision, you can perform the following steps:

Step 1 List and describe the alternatives for the design decision.

Step 2 List the advantages and disadvantages of each alternative with respect to your objectives and priorities.

Step 3 Determine whether any of the alternatives prevents you from meeting one or more of the objectives. If it does, you may have to rule it out. However, if none of the alternatives permit you to meet your objectives, you may have to adjust your objectives or else go back to earlier design decisions.

Step 4 Choose the alternative that helps you to best meet your objectives. If several alternatives seem equally good in terms of the objectives, then use the priorities to decide among them.

Step 5 Adjust your priorities for subsequent decision making. If you know you have already met your objectives for some aspects of quality, then you can increase the priority of the other qualities, for which you have not yet met your objectives.

Example 9.1   *You are asked to choose between five different algorithms that can be used to perform a particular distributed financial analysis operation. You are given the following objectives. When everything is otherwise equal, highest priority should be given to the qualities at the top of the list.*

- **Security**. Encryption must not be breakable within 100 hours of computing time on a 2GHz Intel processor, using known cryptanalysis techniques.

- **Maintainability**. No specific objective.

- **CPU efficiency**. Must respond to the user within one second when running on an 800MHz Intel processor (the slowest machine the users are likely to use).

- **Network bandwidth** efficiency. Must not require transmission of more than 8 KB of data per transaction.

- **Memory efficiency**. Must not consume over 30 MB of RAM.

- **Portability**. Must be able to run on Windows 2000 and later versions of Windows, as well as Mac OS and Linux.

You evaluate the algorithms and determine the information in Table 9.3. 'DNMO' means that the algorithm *Does Not Meet the Objective*; the objective is met in the other cases. A dash means that you did not evaluate the factor since you found out that the algorithm did not meet two separate objectives.

We first look at whether the objectives are met. It turns out that none of the algorithms meet the CPU efficiency objective. We are, however, unable to find any algorithms that are better in this respect, therefore we have to lower our standards and choose the algorithms that come closest (A, B and D). Algorithm D, however, does not meet the bandwidth efficiency objective and we therefore rule it out.

Next, we use the remaining priorities to decide between algorithms A and B. Both algorithms are equal in terms of our top priority, security. However, algorithm B is better in terms of the second priority, maintainability; it therefore becomes our final choice.

Table 9.3   Algorithm evaluations

	Security	Maintainability	Memory efficiency	CPU efficiency	Bandwidth efficiency	Portability
Algorithm A	High	Medium	High	Medium; DNMO	Low	Low
Algorithm B	High	High	Low	Medium; DNMO	Medium	Low
Algorithm C	High	High	High	Low; DNMO	High	Low
Algorithm D	—	—	—	Medium; DNMO	DNMO	—
Algorithm E	DNMO	—	—	Low; DNMO	—	—

Exercise

E179 You are given Table 9.4 showing the quality levels achieved by various software architectures.

Table 9.4   Quality levels achieved by various software architectures

Software architecture	Maintain- ability	Memory required	CPU speed required	Bandwidth required	Portable to which platforms?
A	High	20 MB	1 GHz needed	35 Kbps	Unix, Windows
B	High	14 MB	500 MHz needed	1 Mbps	Windows only
C	High	8 MB	2 GHz needed	2 Kbps	Windows, Macintosh
D	Medium	20 MB	1 GHz needed	30 Kbps	Unix only

Determine which architecture you might choose if you had the following objectives and priorities. Justify your answer.

(a) Objectives: runs on Windows; works on a 30 Kbps connection or faster; works on a 1 GHz machine or faster; requires no more than 25 MB memory. General priorities, starting with first: bandwidth efficiency, CPU efficiency, portability, memory efficiency, maintainability.

(b) Same as (a) except bandwidth drops to fourth priority.

(c) Objectives: runs on Unix; works on 1 Mbps connection or faster; works on 500 MHz machine or faster; requires no more than 40 MB memory. General priorities, starting with first: maintainability, portability, bandwidth, CPU speed, memory.

Using cost–benefit analysis to choose among alternatives

An important consideration when you do design is finding ways to reduce costs and increase benefits. Whenever you make a design decision in which the alternatives have different benefits or costs, you can therefore perform cost–benefit analysis to ensure you are making the best decision. You would certainly do this if you are adding an optional aspect of the design, or if the priorities and objectives do not lead to a clear decision.

Cost–benefit analysis is widely taught in management courses, but it is not just for project managers. Individual software engineers should be able to use this technique, since they must make day-to-day design decisions.

You cannot expect to be completely accurate when performing cost–benefit analysis. However, even 'back-of-the-envelope' computations based on rough estimates can help you to make better decisions. Often, it becomes very clear that a certain option will cost far more than an alternative.

To estimate the costs of a new feature or design alternative, you should add up estimates of the following:

■ The incremental cost of doing the *software engineering* work, including ongoing maintenance for the life of the system. This includes the work involved in requirements, design, implementation, quality assurance, etc. By 'incremental', we mean the extra cost that would be required if you chose this alternative. The software engineering cost is proportional to the amount of time spent by software engineers, commonly measured in person-days or person-months. Most organizations convert this into monetary terms by multiplying by a factor that accounts for the average salary plus other costs associated with employing a person, such as their office space.

■ The incremental costs of any *development technology* that you will have to buy, such as programming languages, reusable components, databases etc.

■ The incremental costs that *end-users and product support personnel* will experience. These costs include the extra installation time, training time, help-desk time, learning time and data entry time, as well as extra licenses for reused components, and any extra hardware needed.

In Chapter 11, we will look at other aspects of cost estimation, such as techniques for doing it as accurately as possible.

To estimate the *benefits* of a new feature or design alternative, you should add up the following:

■ The incremental software engineering time saved. For example, an improvement in flexibility might considerably reduce maintenance cost.

■ The incremental benefits measured in terms of either increased sales or else financial benefit to users. You can base your estimate on increased sales if your product is generic. On the other hand, if the product is custom in nature, then you can estimate how much money users could make or save if you implemented the alternative under consideration. Both figures will depend heavily on making an accurate estimate of the number of users who will eventually use your system.

Example 9.2　*You are the software architect for the GANA system and you are trying to decide whether it would be cost-effective to develop a generic framework for navigation systems. Outline the costs and benefits that should be considered.*

Costs:

■ Extra software engineering work: you estimate this will take 3 person-months of extra time to work out the generic requirements, 2 person-months of extra time to do the design, 1 extra person-month for the implementation, and 2 extra person-months for the testing.

■ There will be no costs for extra development technology.

■ There will be no extra end-user costs.

Benefits:

■ Software engineering work saved: you estimate that over the next three years, your company will be developing more advanced navigation systems for the trucking industry and the search and rescue industry. These will, together, save 6 person-months of labor if they can build on your framework. You also estimate that the framework will save you 4 person-months of maintenance time for the GANA system itself.

■ You also estimate that the framework will allow you to get new products to market faster. The potential benefit of this is hard to quantify, but it could increase sales by over £200,000.

Even though the above estimates are very approximate, they support your decision to develop a framework. This is true even if you do not consider the uncertain benefits of getting products to market faster.

9.4　Model Driven Development

In Chapters 5, 6 and 8 you learned how to develop models of software using UML. As we mentioned, a model is an abstraction or view of a system that helps you to design it and analyze it. When you study a diagram in a model, what you see should faithfully represent the final system, but only a *simplified* view of an aspect of the system.

Since the earliest days of software engineering, people have used models; and since the mid 1990s these have been typically developed in UML. However, often in the past the models were little more than diagrams – very useful diagrams, but just diagrams. Developers used the diagrams as a guide to their programming. Gradually, various modeling tools were given the capability to *generate* some of the code; programmers could then fill in the missing details.

Now, tools are available which can take models and generate *all* of the code for certain types of applications. The model effectively becomes a form of high-level program and all development work can take place exclusively in the model. This process, known as *model-driven development*, is expected to become more and more widespread over the next 10–20 years as tools become more sophisticated.

Increasing abstraction in programming

In the beginning (the early 1950s) people programmed in *machine language*: directly manipulating the binary op-codes that the CPU uses as its instructions. Then computer scientists had the bright idea of creating *assembly language*: abstracting some of the detail away, making the machine code more human readable using mnemonics for each instruction, and adding higher-level macro capabilities to deal with repetitive tasks. Assemblers translated this into machine language.

The next stage in the evolution of programming was *high-level languages*: this started with Fortran and Cobol, and eventually led to modern languages such as Java, C#, etc. Compilers are programs that initially generated assembler code, and now directly generate machine code or else bytecode for virtual machines. High-level languages added numerous abstractions to make programming simpler: types systems, higher level statements, classes, etc.

Model-driven development simply takes this process further: by modeling in UML the developer can take advantage of abstractions such as states and associations without having to worry about the details of coding them. Tools can generate high-level language code, machine code or bytecode.

Model-driven development does not, however, eliminate the need to code certain types of detailed algorithms. That is why tools that generate entire systems from UML models must also provide a language for implementing the actions and activities that we discussed in Chapter 8. UML provides a lot of detail about the semantics of the actions and activities that must be supported by such a tool; however, it leaves the syntax of an appropriate *action language* to the tool. We will not discuss the details of UML actions any further, except to say that tools can allow the developer to code the actions in a language such as Java.

There are various different approaches to model-driven development. An approach developed by the OMG (who also develop UML) is called *Model Driven Architecture* (MDA).

One of the important features of model-driven development is that the models themselves can be created at several different levels of abstraction. In MDA, one first develops a Platform Independent Model (PIM). This describes the system's data and activities in a very general way. One then adds detail to create one or more Platform Specific Models (PSMs). For example, you could develop a PIM for a Police Information System; this would contain class diagrams representing all the data to be manipulated, various state diagrams, various activity diagrams, as well as other types of diagrams we will discuss in the next section. This model could, however, be implemented as a web-based system, a client–server system using a technology such as OCSF, something else entirely, or even several of these.

To develop the details for each type of implementation of the Police Information System, you would need a PSM. The PSM for a web-based system would describe the various html pages that would be needed, and the various programs that would interpret http form data generated when the user selects 'submit' on a web page.

9.5   Software architecture

Architecture plays a central role in building construction. A building's architecture is described using a set of plans that, taken together, represent all aspects of the building. It describes the building from such viewpoints as electricity, plumbing, structure, etc.

The architect is the person in charge of the whole project. He or she has the responsibility to make sure that the building will be solid, cost-effective and satisfactory to the client.

Software architecture is similar. It plays a central role in software engineering, and involves the development of a variety of high-level views of the system. Furthermore, individuals called software architects often lead a team of other software engineers.

Definition: *software architecture* is the process of designing the global organization of a software system, including dividing software into subsystems, deciding how these will interact, and determining their interfaces.

The term 'software architecture' is also applied to the documentation produced as a result of the process. For clarity, this documentation is often also called the *architectural model*.

The importance of developing an architectural model

Software engineers discuss all aspects of a system's design in terms of the architectural model. Decisions made while this model is being developed therefore have a profound impact on the rest of the design process. The architectural model is the core of the design; therefore all software engineers need to understand it.

The architectural model will often constrain the overall efficiency, reusability and maintainability of the system. Poor decisions made while creating this model will constrain subsequent design.

There are four main reasons why you need to develop an architectural model:

■ **To enable everyone to better understand the system**. As a system becomes more and more complex, making it understandable is an increasing challenge. This is especially true for large, distributed systems that use sophisticated technology. A good architectural model allows people to understand how the system as a whole works; it also defines the terms that people use when they communicate with each other about lower-level details.

■ **To allow people to work on individual pieces of the system in isolation**. The work of developing a complex software system must be distributed among a large number of people. The architecture allows the planning and co-ordination of this distributed work. The architecture should provide sufficient information so that the work of the individual people or teams can later on be integrated to form the final system. It is for that reason that the interfaces and dynamic interactions among the subsystems are an important part of the architecture.

■ **To prepare for extension of the system**. With a complete architectural model, it becomes easier to plan the evolution of the system. Subsystems that are envisioned to be part of a future release can be included in the architecture, even though they are not to be developed immediately. It is then possible to see how the new elements will be integrated, and where they will be connected to the system. Architects designing buildings often use this technique – their drawings show not only the proposed building but also its future extensions (Phase I, Phase II, etc.). Specialists like electrical engineers can then plan the cabling to take into account the future needs of the foreseen extension.

■ **To facilitate reuse and reusability**. The architectural model makes each system component visible. This is an important benefit since it encourages reuse. By analyzing the architecture, you can discover those components that can be obtained from past projects or from third parties. You can also identify components that have high potential reusability. Making the architecture as generic as possible is a key to ensuring reusability.

Contents of a good architectural model

A system's architecture will often be expressed in terms of several different *views*. These can include:

■ The logical breakdown into subsystems. This is often shown using package diagrams, which we will describe later. The interfaces among the subsystems must also be carefully described.

■ The dynamics of the interaction among components at run time, perhaps expressed using interaction or activity diagrams.

■ The data that will be shared among the subsystems, typically expressed using class diagrams.

■ The components that will exist at run time, and the machines or devices on which they will be located. This information can be expressed using component and deployment diagrams, which are discussed later.

An important challenge in architectural modeling is to produce a relevant and synthetic picture of a large and complex system. In other words, the reader should be able to understand the system very quickly by looking at the different views. To enable this, it should be clear how the views relate to each other.

To ensure the maintainability and reliability of a system, an architectural model must be designed to be *stable*. Being stable means that the new features can be easily added with only small changes to the architecture.

When developing custom software, the architecture should be expressed clearly enough that it can be used to communicate effectively with clients. The clients may not need to know other details of the design. However, they often want to understand the architecture so that they can be confident the software is being designed well, and can monitor development progress. The architectural diagrams used for the construction of buildings are also used to communicate with clients.

How to develop an architectural model

The system's architecture must take its overall shape very early in the design process, although it will continue to mature as iterative development proceeds.

The basis for the architectural model will be the system domain model and the use cases. The first draft of the architectural model should be created at the same time as these. These give the architect an idea about which components will be needed and how they will interact. At the same time, the early architecture will give use case modelers guidance about the steps the user will need to perform. For example, if the use cases describe a process of accessing information that is stored centrally in some repository, this guides the architect to think in terms of a client–server architecture. Similarly, the fact that there is a client–server architecture guides the use case modeler to add use cases for logging in, account creation, etc.

The following are some steps that you can use iteratively as you refine the architecture.

1. Start by sketching an outline of the architecture, based on the principal requirements, including the domain model and use cases. At this stage, you can determine the main components that will be needed, such as databases, particular hardware devices and the main software subsystems. You can also choose among the various architectural patterns we will discuss later, such as using a client–server architecture or a pipe-and-filter architecture. It can be worthwhile having several different teams independently develop a first draft of the architecture; the teams can then meet to pick the best architecture, or to merge together the best ideas.

2. Refine the architecture by identifying the main ways in which the components will interact, and by identifying the interfaces among them. Also, decide how each piece of data and functionality will be distributed among the various components. Now is the time to determine if you can reuse an existing framework. If possible, you might decide to transform your architecture into a generic framework that can be reused by others.

3. Consider each use case, adjusting the architecture to make it realizable. At this stage you try to finalize the interface of each component.

4. Mature the architecture as you define the final class diagrams and interaction diagrams.

Describing an architecture using UML

All UML diagrams can be useful to describe aspects of the architectural model. Remember that the goal of architecture is to describe the system at a very high level, with emphasis on software components and their interfaces. Use case diagrams can provide a good summary of the system from the user's perspective. Class diagrams can be used to indicate the services offered by components and the main data to be stored. Interaction diagrams can be used to define the protocol used when two components communicate with each other.

In addition to the UML diagrams we have already studied in this book, three other types of UML diagram are particularly important for architecture modeling: package diagrams, component diagrams and deployment diagrams. These are used to describe different aspects of the organization of the system. In the next three subsections we will survey the essentials of these types of diagram.

Packages

Breaking a large system into subsystems is a fundamental principle of software development. A good decomposition helps make the system more understandable and therefore facilitates its maintainability.

In UML, a *package* is a collection of modeling elements that are grouped together because they are logically related. Note that a UML package is not quite the same thing as a Java package, which is a collection containing only classes. However, a very common use of UML packages is to represent Java packages.

A package in UML is shown as a box, with a smaller box attached above its top left corner. The packages of the SimpleChat system are illustrated in Figure 9.6. Inside the box you can put practically anything, including classes, instances, text or other packages.

When you define a package, you should apply the principles of cohesion and coupling discussed earlier. Increasing cohesion means ensuring that a package only has related classes; decreasing coupling means decreasing the number of dependencies as much as possible.

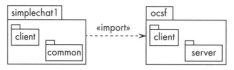

Figure 9.6   An example package diagram

You show dependencies between packages using a dashed arrow. A dependency exists if there is a dependency between an *element* in one of the packages and an *element* in another. To use a package, it is required to have access to packages that it depends on. Also, changes made to the interface of a package will require modification to packages that depend on it.

A package that depends on many others will be difficult to reuse, since using it will also necessitate importing its dependent packages. Circular dependencies among packages are particularly important to avoid. Finally, making the interface of a package as simple as possible greatly simplifies its use and testing. The Façade pattern can help to simplify a package interface.

Component diagrams

A component diagram shows how a system's components – that is, the physical elements such as files, executables, etc. – relate to each other. The UML symbol for a component is a box with a little 'plug' symbol in the top-right corner. An example is shown in Figure 9.7; many more examples can be found in the next section.

Figure 9.7   An example component diagram

A component provides one or more interfaces for other components to use. The same 'lollipop' symbol is used for an interface as was introduced in Chapter 5. To show a component using an interface provided by another, you use a semi-circle at the end of a line. Figure 9.7 show how these two symbols plug together.

Various relationships can exist among components, for example:

■ A component may *execute* another component, or a method in the other component.

■ A component may *generate* another component.

■ Two components may *communicate* with each other using a network.

It is easy initially to confuse component diagrams with package diagrams. The difference is that package diagrams show *logical groupings* of design elements, whereas component diagrams show relationships among types of *physical* components.

Deployment diagrams

A deployment diagram describes the hardware where various instances of components reside at run time. An example is shown in Figure 9.8. A node in a deployment diagram represents a computational unit such as a computer, a processing card, a sensor or a device. It appears as a three-dimensional box.

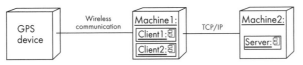

Figure 9.8   An example deployment diagram

The links between nodes show how communication takes place. Each node of a deployment diagram can include one or several run-time software components. Various artifacts such as files can also be shown inside nodes.

9.6   Architectural patterns

The notion of patterns, introduced in Chapter 5, can be applied to software architecture. In this chapter we present several of the most important *architectural patterns*, which are also often called *architectural styles*. Each allows you to design flexible systems using components that are as independent of each other as possible.

The Multi-Layer architectural pattern

Building software in layers is a classical architectural pattern that is used in many systems. It is so important that layer cohesion was one of the types of cohesion we presented earlier when discussing Design Principle 2.

As we discussed, in layered systems each layer communicates only with the layers below it – in many cases, only the layer immediately below it. Each layer has a well-defined API, defining the services it provides.

A complex system can be built by superimposing layers at increasing levels of abstraction. The Multi-Layer architectural pattern makes it possible to replace a layer by an improved version, or one with a different set of capabilities.

It is particularly important to have a separate layer at the very top to handle the user interface. Independence of the UI layer allows the application to have several different UIs. These could be UIs running on different platforms, UIs for 'professional' versus 'standard' versions of the application, or UIs designed for different locales (discussed in Chapter 7). We will look at the UI layer in more detail below when we discuss the Model–View–Controller architectural pattern.

Layers immediately below the UI layer provide the application functions determined by the use cases. Layers at the bottom provide services such as data storage and transmission. This is illustrated in Figure 9.3(a).

Patterns at different levels of abstraction
Patterns can be created for any activity involving human expertise. In software engineering, they occur at many levels of abstraction.

At the lowest level are programming *idioms*; these describe preferred ways to solve detailed programming problems, and are out of the scope of this book. Moving up the abstraction scale are the *design patterns* such as Delegation and Observer, and the *modeling patterns* such as Abstraction–Occurrence presented in Chapter 6. At the top of the abstraction scale are the *architectural patterns* discussed here.

Most operating systems are built according to the Multi-Layer architectural pattern, as shown in Figure 9.3(b). A low-level *kernel* layer deals with such functions as process creation, swapping, and scheduling. Higher-level layers deal with such functions as user account management, screen display, etc. The layers are often further subdivided into smaller subsystems.

Most communications systems exhibit a layered architecture. A simplified illustration of this is shown in Figure 9.3(c). At the bottom level, there are facilities for transmitting and receiving signals. Above this is a layer that deals with splitting messages into packets and reconstructing messages that are received. Still higher is a layer that deals with handling ongoing connections with a remote host (e.g. using sockets). At the top is a layer that handles various protocols, such as http, used by application programs.

The SimpleChat system uses a layered architecture to separate the user interface from the core of the system. For example, the class `ChatClient` is separated from the class `ClientConsole`. The Observable layer of the OCSF allows the core of a client or server to be further separated into a layer that has the application logic, and one that deals with client–server communication.

Although the normal assumption is that the communication between layers will be by procedure calls, it can also be performed in some systems using inter-process communication. In other words, the lower layers can become servers and the higher layers can become clients. This illustrates how the Multi-Layer and Client–Server architectural patterns (discussed next) can be used together. If we did use inter-process communication to implement a layered architecture, we would typically redraw Figure 9.3 using a component diagram.

The Multi-Layer architectural pattern helps you adhere to many of the design principles discussed earlier, in particular:

❶ *Divide and conquer.* The separate layers can be independently designed.

❷ *Increase cohesion.* Well-designed layers have layer cohesion; in other words, they contain all the facilities to provide a set of related services, and nothing else.

❸ *Reduce coupling.* Well-designed lower layers do not know about the higher layers. The higher layers can therefore be replaced without impacting the lower layers. Also, the only connection between layers is through the API.

❹ *Increase abstraction.* When you design the higher layers, you do not need to know the details of how the lower layers are implemented. This makes designing high-level facilities much easier.

⑤ *Increase reusability.* The lower layers can often be designed generically so that they can be used to provide the same services for different systems.

⑥ *Increase reuse.* You can often reuse layers built by others that provide the services you need – a layer for loading and storing from a database, for example.

⑦ *Design for flexibility.* Designing in layers gives you the flexibility to add new facilities that build on lower-level services, or to replace higher-level layers.

⑧ *Anticipate obsolescence.* Databases and UI systems tend to change; by isolating these in separate layers, the system becomes more resistant to obsolescence.

⑨ *Design for portability.* All the facilities that are dependent on a particular platform can be isolated in one of the lower layers.

⑩ *Design for testability.* Individual layers, particularly the UI layer, database layer and communications layer, can be tested independently.

⑪ *Design defensively.* The APIs of layers are natural places to build in rigorous checks of the validity of inputs. You can design a system so that if a higher layer fails, the lower layers continue to run. The opposite can also be made true; for example, if a database layer crashes, it could be made to restart automatically.

Exercise

E180 Describe how you might divide a video-game system into layers. Consider that the system has components which do some of the following activities: display graphics, manage the objects that are displayed on the screen, compute object position and speed, keep track of scores, keep track of various stages of the game.

The Client–Server and other distributed architectural patterns

We discussed the Client–Server architectural pattern in detail in Chapter 3. Its basic principles are: a) there is at least one component that has the role of server, waiting for and then handling connections, and b) there is at least one component that has the role of client, initiating connections in order to obtain some service.

An important variant of the client–server architecture is the three-tier model under which a server communicates with both a client (usually through the Internet) and a database server (usually within an intranet, for security reasons). The server acts as a client when accessing the database server.

A further extension to the Client–Server architectural pattern is the Peer-to-Peer architectural pattern. A peer-to-peer system is composed of various software components that are distributed over several hosts. Each of these components can be both a server and a client. Any two components can set up a communication channel to exchange information as required. Figure 9.9

shows a peer-to-peer architecture for instant messaging. Messages no longer have to be sent through a central server. However, before two peers can communicate, they have to discover each other's existence. A central server may still be used for this.

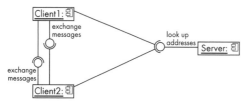

Figure 9.9   A peer-to-peer architecture for instant messaging, retaining a central server only to look up the addresses of clients

Distributed architectures help you adhere to design principles such as the following:

❶ *Divide and conquer.* Dividing the system into client and server processes is a very strong way to divide the system. Each can be separately developed.

❷ *Increase cohesion.* The server can provide a cohesive service to clients. For example, it can provide a single service with no side effects and therefore be functionally cohesive. A server also acts as a lower-level layer that the client accesses.

❸ *Reduce coupling.* There is usually only one communication channel between distributed components, and the data being passed is usually simple messages. This helps reduce coupling, although there is normally control coupling (commands sent by the client control what the server does).

❹ *Increase abstraction.* Separate distributed components are often good abstractions. For example, you do not need to understand the details of how a server operates.

❻ *Increase reuse.* It is often possible to find suitable frameworks on which to build good distributed systems (e.g. OCSF). However, reusability may not be high since client–server systems are often very application specific.

❼ *Design for flexibility.* Distributed systems can often be easily reconfigured by adding extra servers or clients. Furthermore, as discussed in Chapter 3, clients and servers can be developed by competing organizations, giving the customer a choice. However, changing the protocol of the system can be difficult.

❾ *Design for portability.* You can write clients for new platforms without having to port the server.

❿ *Design for testability.* You can test clients and servers independently.

⑪ *Design defensively.* You can put rigorous checks in the message handling code to ensure that no matter what messages you receive, your component will not crash.

Exercise

E181 The original Napster was the most famous and controversial of many peer-to-peer systems for sharing files; in its architecture, it retained a central registry of users. Other peer-to-peer file sharing systems, such as Gnutella and KAZAA, do not require a central registry. Do some research to determine how the various current file-sharing systems work, and how some are able to dispense with a central server. What are the advantages and disadvantages of the two approaches?

The Broker architectural pattern

The idea of the Broker architectural pattern is to distribute aspects of the software system *transparently* to different nodes. This is illustrated in Figure 9.10.

Figure 9.10 The Broker architectural pattern

Using the Broker architecture, an object can call methods of another object without knowing that this object is remotely located. The use of the Proxy design pattern (discussed in Chapter 6) can help achieve this goal. A Proxy object calls the broker, which determines where the remote object can be found.

CORBA is a well-known open standard that allows you to build this kind of architecture – it stands for Common Object Request Broker Architecture. Java has many classes that allow you to use CORBA facilities. There are also several other commercial architectures that also provide broker capabilities.

The Broker pattern is particularly useful in helping you follow these design principles:

❶ *Divide and conquer.* The remote objects can be independently designed.

❺ *Increase reusability.* It is often possible to design the remote objects so that other systems can use them too.

❻ *Increase reuse.* You may be able to reuse remote objects that others have created.

❼ *Design for flexibility.* The broker objects can be updated as required, or you can redirect the proxy to communicate with a different remote object.

❾ *Design for portability.* You can write clients for new platforms while still accessing brokers and remote objects on other platforms.

⑪ *Design defensively.* You can provide careful assertion checking in the remote objects.

Note that the separation of data between a proxy and a remote object tends to reduce communicational cohesion.

Exercise

E182 Do some research to determine the main broker platforms and their differences.

The Transaction Processing architectural pattern

In the Transaction Processing architectural pattern, a process reads a series of inputs one by one. Each input describes a *transaction* – a command that typically makes some change to the data stored by the system. There is a transaction dispatcher component that decides what to do with each transaction; this dispatches a procedure call or message to a component that will handle the transaction.

For example, in the airline system, transactions might be used to add a new flight, add a booking, change a booking or delete a booking. This is illustrated in Figure 9.11.

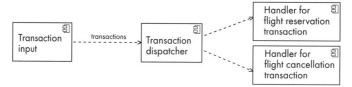

Figure 9.11 The transaction processing architecture used in an airline system

The dynamic binding and dispatching of polymorphic methods is a further example. In fact, it is best to design a system to use this implicit transaction-processing mechanism where possible, rather than designing an explicit version.

Transaction processing systems are often embedded in servers. A typical example is a database engine, where the transactions are various types of queries and updates. The command handler mechanisms in SimpleChat's server and client classes are, in fact, transaction dispatchers, although the pattern would be more strongly followed if they dispatched each command to a separate method.

Transactions themselves vary in their level of complexity. In many cases an update transaction requires that several separate changes be made to a database. For example, as we saw in Chapter 5, booking a passenger on a flight requires creating a `Booking` object, as well as creating bi-directional links from it to a `SpecificFlight` and a `PassengerRole`. It is essential that this whole transaction be fully completed, or else not done at all. Transaction dispatchers and handlers therefore work together to assure the *atomicity* of transactions.

Many transaction processing systems work in environments where several different threads or processes can attempt to perform transactions at once. In these environments the data to be modified by the transaction must be locked first, and the lock must be released afterwards. The situation is further complicated by the fact that an application may need to do a query transaction, then process the data, and finally do an update transaction on the data, while being assured that another thread has not changed the data in the meantime. If a lock is used, then other transactions are delayed until the whole process is complete. There are several strategies for handling this situation – you should read a database design book to learn about them. However, in the next chapter we will raise some relevant issues when we talk about testing systems that have multiple threads.

The Transaction Processing pattern is particularly useful in helping you follow these design principles:

❶ *Divide and conquer.* The transaction handlers are suitable system divisions that you can give to separate software engineers.

❷ *Increase cohesion.* Transaction handlers are naturally cohesive units. They may exhibit functional, sequential or procedural cohesion. However, they tend not to exhibit communicational cohesion.

❸ *Reduce coupling.* Separating the dispatcher from the handlers tends to reduce coupling. However, you have to be careful that the coupling among the transaction handlers is kept under control.

❼ *Design for flexibility.* You can readily add new transaction handlers.

⓫ *Design defensively.* You can add assertion checking in each transaction handler and/or in the dispatcher.

The Pipe-and-Filter architectural pattern

The Pipe-and-Filter architectural pattern is also often called the *transformational* architectural pattern. It works as follows. A stream of data, in a relatively simple format, is passed through a series of processes, each of which transforms it in some way. The series of processes is called a *pipeline*. Data is constantly fed into the pipeline; the processes work concurrently (conceptually at least) so that data is also constantly emerging from the pipeline.

The strength of this pattern is that the system can be modified easily by adding or changing the transformational processes. This is easiest if, at most stages of the pipeline, the data has the same general form. For example, the data might be simply a stream of characters. The processes might do such things as converting the characters to upper case; removing unneeded characters; or encrypting the text.

Another example of a pipe-and-filter architecture is a speech transmission system. This would continuously read sound coming from microphones, process it in various ways, compress it, transmit it over a network and then regenerate sound at a remote location. It would use several different transformational components to do this. The architecture is illustrated in Figure 9.12.

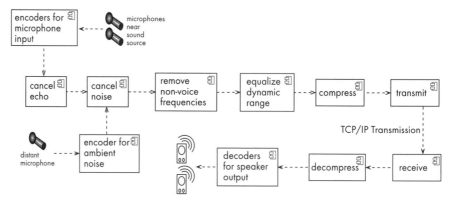

Figure 9.12   A pipe-and-filter architecture for sound processing

Some of the transformational processes are true filters: 'cancel echo', 'cancel noise', 'remove non-voice frequencies' and 'equalize dynamic range' simply remove some of the information, but leave it in the same format. The other processes convert the information into distinctly different formats.

The 'cancel noise' process illustrates how two pipelines can join together. It is also possible for a pipeline to split into two.

In Chapter 3, we saw the use of the classes `ObjectOutputStream`, `DataOutputStream`, `OutputStream`, and the corresponding input streams. These act like filters passing data to each other: for example `ObjectOutputStream` will convert an arbitrary object into bytes which it then passes to `OutputStream` for transmission; after transmission, an `InputStream` will receive the data and pass it to an `ObjectInputStream` for reconstruction of the original objects.

A pipe-and-filter system provides fulfils the following principles:

❶ *Divide and conquer.* The separate processes can be independently designed.

❷ *Increase cohesion.* The processes generally have functional cohesion.

❸ *Reduce coupling.* The processes have only one input and one output, normally using a standard format, therefore coupling is very low. Type use coupling can become an issue if the format of the data needs to change.

❹ *Increase abstraction.* The pipeline components are often good abstractions, hiding their internal details.

❺ *Increase reusability.* The processes can often be used in many different contexts.

❻ *Increase reuse.* It is often possible to find reusable components to insert into a pipeline.

⑦ *Design for flexibility.* There are several ways in which the system illustrated in Figure 9.12 is flexible:

❏ Almost all the components could be removed. For example, 'cancel echo' or 'cancel noise' could be removed. In fact the encoder for microphone input could be directly connected to the decoder for speaker output, drastically shortening the pipeline.

❏ Components could be replaced with different implementations. For example the 'transmit' and 'receive' components could be replaced in order to allow communication over a different type of network. The 'compress' and 'decompress' components could also be replaced in order to use different algorithms.

❏ New components could be inserted, for example to perform encryption.

❏ Certain components could be reordered. For example, removing non-voice frequencies could be done before canceling noise.

❏ The encoders for microphone input and for ambient noise could be instances of the same component type.

⑩ *Design for testability.* It is normally easy to test the individual processes.

⑪ *Design defensively.* You can rigorously check the inputs of each component, or else you can use design by contract, writing careful preconditions and postconditions for each component.

Exercise

E183 Outline the design of a pipe-and-filter system to analyze a continuous stream of quotations from the stock market. One filter might extract only those stocks in which you are interested. Another process might add information to each stock quote, such as the total number of stocks you own, and the amount of profit or loss you have made on the stock. Some components might analyze quotes traveling through the pipe, and might alert you about whether you should buy or sell the stock.

The Model–View–Controller (MVC) architectural pattern

Model–View–Controller, or MVC, is an architectural pattern used to help separate the user interface layer from other parts of the system. Not only does MVC help enforce layer cohesion of the user interface layer, but it also helps reduce the coupling between that layer and the rest of the system, as well as between different aspects of the UI itself.

The MVC pattern separates the functional layer of the system (the *model*) from two aspects of the user interface, the *view* and the *controller*. This is illustrated in Figure 9.13. Although the three components are normally

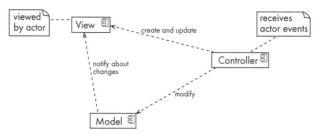

Figure 9.13   The Model–View–Controller (MVC) architectural pattern for user interfaces

instances of classes, we use a component diagram to emphasize the fact that the components could also be separate threads or processes.

The *model* contains the underlying classes whose instances are to be viewed and manipulated.

The *view* contains objects used to render the appearance of the data from the model in the user interface. The view also displays the various controls with which the user can interact.

The *controller* contains the objects that control and handle the user's interaction with the view and the model. It has the logic that responds when the user types into a field or clicks the mouse on a control.

The model does not know what views and controllers are attached to it. In particular, the Observer design pattern is normally used to separate the model from the view. The MVC architectural pattern therefore exhibits layer cohesion and is a special case of the Multi-Layer architectural pattern.

MVC in web architectures

Web architectures generally use MVC as follows:

1. The View component generates html for display by the browser.

2. There is a component that interprets http 'post' transmissions coming back from the browser – this is the Controller.

3. There is an underlying system for managing the information – this is the Model.

Examples of View generation technology are JSP and ASP – you will often see web pages that have these suffixes. These technologies start with an outline of an html document and use programs to fill in missing pieces. Each time the page is displayed, it can therefore have different content (at the very least, advertisements are often inserted). The original Controller technology was called 'CGI' (Common Gateway Interface); there are now, however, many others available.

The View and Controller technologies can be combined: a program that interprets a 'post' transmission will often then generate a new page. The model, however, should always be kept separate.

Sometimes no specific controller component is created – the most important aspect of the MVC pattern is separation of the model and the view. The term model-view separation is used to describe this situation.

The MVC architectural pattern allows us to adhere to the following design principles:

❶ *Divide and conquer*. The three components can be somewhat independently designed.

❷ *Increase cohesion*. The components have stronger layer cohesion than if the view and controller were together in a single UI layer.

❸ *Reduce coupling*. The communication channels between the three components are minimal and easy to find.

❻ *Increase reuse*. The view and controller normally make extensive use of reusable components for various kinds of UI controls. The UI, however will become application specific, therefore it will not be easily reusable.

❼ *Design for flexibility*. It is usually quite easy to change the UI by changing the view, the controller, or both.

❿ *Design for testability*. You can test the application separately from the UI.

MVC in Java

Several of the Swing GUI components of the Java API are based on the MVC architectural pattern.

For example, JList (the view) is a graphical component used to visualize a list of items. This list is the visual representation of data handled by an AbstractListModel (the model). It contains the data and notifies the JList whenever a change is made to the data by the application. These two classes follow the Observer pattern (see Chapter 6); the JList registers itself as an observer of the AbstractListModel instance as follows (note that in the Java API, observers are usually called *listeners*):

```
listModel.addListDataListener(jList)
```

Finally, each time a modification is made to the list, the method fireIntervalAdded or fireIntervalRemoved is called by the controller.

Exercise

E184 Imagine you are designing a system where a user can select a given company and obtain the price of its stock; the stock price is refreshed at regular intervals. Identify the model, the view and the controller in this application. Draw a high-level sequence diagram of a typical interaction.

The Service-Oriented architectural pattern

Now that the Internet has become so pervasive, a new architectural pattern has become prominent: *Service-oriented architecture*. This architecture organizes an application as a collection of services that communicate with each other through well-defined interfaces. In the context of the Internet, the services in question are called *Web services*.

A Web service is an application accessible through the Internet that can be integrated with other web services to form a *Web-based application*. To use a web service, you send a correctly formatted http request to an http server. Unlike normal http requests this is done 'behind the scenes' by the Web application program, not a browser being used by an end user. The server will run the service application and return the response as a document, typically structured using a language called *XML*. This is illustrated in Figure 9.14.

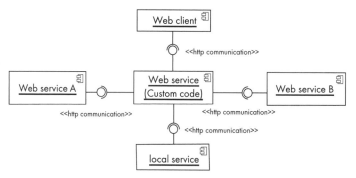

Figure 9.14   The Service-oriented architectural pattern

In Figure 9.14, a client program we are developing obtains information from a Web service provided by some company on the Internet. This in turn calls upon two other Web services, A and B, also available on the Internet. In addition, it uses Web-services protocols to access a local server operated by the same company.

A key aspect of the Web service architecture is that its different components communicate with each other using open Web standards. You build applications whose components are bound together over the Internet. The result is that a Web service can be accessed by many applications in many locations.

Web services can perform a wide range of tasks. Some may handle simple requests for information while others can perform more complex business processing. Enterprises can use Web services to automate and improve their operations. For example, an electronic commerce application can make use of web services to:

■ access the product databases of several suppliers;

■ process credit cards using a Web service offered by a bank;

■ arrange for delivery using a Web service offered by a shipping company.

The toughest challenge facing the developer of a Web service is *security*. The service opens the enterprise's business operations and data to remotely distributed clients. Special care must therefore be taken to protect both customer and business information. Other important considerations are reliability, availability and scalability of the Web service.

Two examples of well-known platforms you can use to build web-services-based applications are Sun's J2EE platform and Microsoft's .NET Framework. These can be seen as large horizontal frameworks providing, among many other things, the required functionality to build interoperable services. They both provide flexible security models and offer other mechanisms to assist with scalability and reliability.

The Web services pattern helps you to adhere to the following design principles:

❶ *Divide and conquer.* The application is made of independently designed Web services, which are distributed and accessible through the Internet.

❷ *Increase cohesion.* Normally, the Web services are structured as layers, where high-level services are built on top of lower-level services. Some Web services can also exhibit functional cohesion.

❸ *Reduce coupling.* Web-based applications are loosely-coupled applications built by binding together distributed components.

❹ *Increase abstraction.* Since the clients communicate with each Web service through well-defined interface, no details about the particular implementation of a given Web service need to be known. However, communication with a Web service can sometimes be quite complex if the protocol is not defined at the right level of abstraction.

❺ *Increase reusability.* A Web service is a highly reusable component.

❻ *Increase reuse.* Web-based applications are built by reusing existing Web services.

❽ *Anticipate obsolescence.* If the technology used inside a given Web service becomes obsolete, then a new implementation of this service can be offered without impacting the applications that use it. The web-service architecture can be seen as a client–server architecture where the obsolescence risk is reduced by relying on open communication standards.

❾ *Design for portability.* A service can be implemented on any platform that supports the required standard protocols.

❿ *Design for testability.* Each service can be tested independently.

⓫ *Design defensively.* Web services enforce defensive design, since many different applications, written by various developers (including malicious ones), can access the service. Each Web service has therefore no choice but to detect and reject any inappropriate or improperly formatted request for service.

Exercise

E185 Search the web for a company offering a public Web service. Describe the service offered and give an example of an application that could use it.

The Message-Oriented architectural pattern

Also known as Message-Oriented Middleware (MOM), this architecture is based on the idea that since humans can communicate and collaborate to accomplish some task by exchanging emails or instant messages, then software applications should also be able to operate in a similar manner. The core of the architecture is an application-to-application messaging system. Senders and receivers need only to know what are the message formats; that is, a receiving (or sending) application does not have to know anything about the software component that sent (or received) the message. Moreover, the two communicating applications do not even have to be available at the same time. This is illustrated in Figure 9.15.

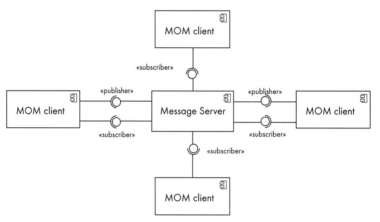

Figure 9.15   The Message-Oriented architectural pattern

The message, which is central to MOM architectures, is a self-contained package containing application data plus some network routing headers used by the messaging system to transmit the message across the network. The messages are sent through virtual channels, also called *topics*. Software components that send messages to topics are called *publishers*. To receive messages, an application must *subscribe* to a topic. In general, any message sent to a given topic is delivered to all the topic's subscribers, each of them receiving a copy of the message. This has similarities to the Observer design pattern discussed in Chapter 6.

The application can choose to ignore a received message or react to it by, for instance, sending a reply containing requested information. The exchange of these messages is governed by two important principles. First, message delivery is completely asynchronous; that means the exact moment at which a given message is delivered to a given subscribing application is unknown. Secondly, reliability mechanisms are in place such that the messaging system can offer the guarantee that a given message is delivered once and only once.

Text messaging using cellular phones can be seen as a simple message-oriented application, but more complex systems can also adopt this architecture. Consider, for example, a sales company where various vendors sell products to consumers. When an item is sold, the vendor's software system can automatically send a message to the appropriate topic. The inventory component, one of the subscribers of this topic, would then be informed and initiate the product delivery process. At the same time, the sales office will receive the same message and use it to, let's say, accumulate statistics about sales trends. The accounting department would calculate the vendor's commission from the information received. And finally, another subscriber could be the factory that would adjust the production rate based on the number of products sold.

Clearly, the effectiveness of such system depends on the messaging system that is used to deliver the messages. Two approaches can be taken when designing such a system. The first is to use a centralized architecture where all messages transit through a message server that is responsible for delivering messages to the subscribers. This is the simpler model, but all functionality then relies on the server. The alternative is to use a decentralized architecture where message routing is delegated to the network layer and where some of the server functionality is distributed among all message clients. The *Java Message Service* (JMS) is an API providing all the required features to develop and deploy message-oriented applications. JMS-based components are portable and can be used by different applications that communicate using different messaging system service providers.

This pattern allows us to adhere to the following design principles:

❶ *Divide and conquer.* The application is made of isolated software components, independently designed and distributed across a network.

❸ *Reduce coupling.* The components are loosely coupled since they share only data format (a form of data coupling).

❹ *Increase abstraction.* The quality of the abstraction mainly resides in the prescribed format for the messages. These are generally fairly simple to manipulate, all the application details being hidden behind the messaging system.

❺ *Increase reusability.* A component will be reusable if its underlying prescribed message formats are flexible enough to adapt to different contexts.

❻ *Increase reuse.* The different components can be reused as long as the new system can adhere to the formats proposed by each reused component.

⑦ *Design for flexibility.* It is always easy to update or enhance the functionality of a message-oriented system just by adding, removing or replacing components in the system.

⑩ *Design for testability.* Each component can be tested independently.

⑪ *Design defensively.* Defensive design in the context of message-oriented systems consists of validating all received messages before processing them and ignore the ones that cannot be properly interpreted.

Exercise

E186 Draw a diagram showing the components of an online auction application designed using a message-oriented architecture. Describe the messages to be exchanged.

E187 Sketch a possible architecture for the following systems. It will be helpful first to sketch the most important use cases. Describe which architectural patterns you are using.

(a) A corporate payroll system. All the information about employees, including their monthly salary and bank account, is kept in a database. Every two weeks, the system pays employees by depositing their salary in their bank account.

(b) A system to buy stocks on the Internet. Clients perform their transactions using a web browser. They are to access their accounts by providing a user ID and password. When an order is made, the system must process it by communicating with the appropriate stock market. The system also has to interact with the bank account of the client once the amount of the transaction is determined.

(c) The GANA system whose requirements were described in Chapter 4.

(d) A system for analyzing signals from a radio-telescope to see if there are signs of extra-terrestrial intelligence. This system takes tapes containing radio signal data, and divides them up into small 'work units' that are distributed to hundreds of thousands of computers running screen savers. These screen savers filter and transform the data in various ways, and then analyze it to detect different kinds of signals. Results are returned to the central site for further analysis. See setiathome.ssl.berkeley.edu for a real implementation of such a system.

9.7 Writing a good design document

Design documents serve two main purposes. Firstly, they help you, as a designer or a design team, to *make good design decisions*. The process of writing down your design helps you to think more clearly about it and to find flaws in it. Secondly, they help you *communicate the design* to others.

We will now examine both of these purposes.

Design documents as an aid to making better designs

Design documents help you, as a designer, because they force you to be explicit and to consider the important issues before starting implementation. They also allow a group of people to review the design and therefore to improve it.

There has been a tendency among software developers to omit design documentation or to document the design only *after* it is complete. In other branches of engineering, doing this has always been considered completely unacceptable: engineers know that it would lead to serious mistakes and in most cases would make planning for construction impossible. For example, without creating plans in advance of building construction it would be impossible to know what building supplies to order, and nobody would be able to review the design to ensure it adheres to standards, such as having adequate fire exits.

Unfortunately, because software is intangible, it is sometimes *possible* to jump directly into programming without any design documents. This does not, however, make doing so a good idea. Plunging directly into programming without writing a design document tends to result in an inflexible and overly complex system.

Design documents as a means of communication

When writing anything, it is important to know the *audience* for your work. Design documents are used to communicate with three groups of individuals. In general, you can expect most documents to be read by all three groups:

- Those who will be *implementing* the design, that is, the programmers.

- Those who will need, in the future, to *modify* the design.

- Those who need to create systems or subsystems that *interface* with the system being designed.

Knowing that these are the audiences for the design document can help the designer decide what information to include. For example, to communicate with designers of other systems, you can make explicit the services that your system provides and how to use them. To communicate with future maintainers, you can give a high-level overview of your design to help them understand it, and explain areas where your design was made flexible to allow for enhancement.

It is crucial to not only include the design as it exists, but also to include the *rationale* for the design: that is, the reasoning you used when making your design decisions. Providing the rationale allows the reader to better understand the design. It also allows reviewers to determine whether good decisions were made, and helps the maintainers determine how to change the design. A maintainer may be tempted to change the design so that it reflects one of the alternatives you rejected. Knowing your reasoning means that the maintainer will not do this capriciously, but with the benefit of your prior insight.

Contents of a design document

We suggest that a design document should contain the following information. As with all the documentation types described in this book, you should use this as a general guide only. Each company should have specific formats you need to follow so as to be consistent with other design documents. You will also need to vary the kinds of information in each section depending on the kind of design (e.g. architectural or detailed) that you are producing.

A. **Purpose**. Specify what system or part of the system this design document describes. Make reference to the requirements that are being implemented by this design – doing so ensures that there is *traceability* from the requirements to the design.

B. **General priorities**. Describe the priorities used to guide the design process. For example, how important was maintainability or efficiency as the design was being prepared?

C. **Outline of the design**. Give a high-level description of the design that allows the reader to get a general feeling for it quickly. A diagram can often serve this purpose.

D. **Major design issues**. Discuss the important issues that had to be resolved. Give the possible alternatives that were considered, the final decision and the rationale for the decision.

E. **Details of the design**. Give any other details the reader will need to know that have not yet been mentioned. These might include detailed descriptions of the protocol used to communicate between client and server, the overviews of data structures and algorithms, as well as how to use various APIs.

In general, when writing a design document, ensure that it is neither too short nor too long. In keeping the document at the right length, be guided by the intended audience; ensure that the information the readers will need to learn is readily available. At the same time, remember that there is no point writing information that would never be read because the reader already knows it or can easily find it from some other source. In particular:

■ Avoid documenting information that would be readily obvious to a skilled programmer or designer.

■ Avoid writing details in a design document that would be better placed as comments in the code.

■ Avoid writing details that can be extracted automatically from the code, such as the list of public methods.

The latter two points deserve some elaboration. When you are doing design, you can actually create skeletons for the files that will contain the code. You write in these skeletons some of the high-level code comments as well as the templates for public methods. If instead you were to write this material in design documents, then when you transfer it to the code, you would have to maintain the information in both places, since it will inevitably change.

9.8 Design of a feature for the SimpleChat instant messaging application

This section presents a short design document that extends the detailed requirements example that was presented in Section 4.12.

A. **Purpose.** This document describes important aspects of the implementation of the `#block`, `#unblock`, `#whoiblock` and `#whoblocksme` commands of the SimpleChat system.

For the requirements, see Section 4.12.

B. **General priorities.** Decisions in this document are made based on the following priorities (most important first): Maintainability, Usability, Portability, Efficiency.

C. **Outline of the design.** Blocking information will be maintained in the `ConnectionToClient` objects. The various commands will update and query the data using `setValue` and `getValue`.

D. **Major design issues.**

Issue 1: Where should we store information regarding the establishment of blocking?

Option 1.1: Store the information in the `ConnectionToClient` object associated with the client requesting the block.

Option 1.2: Store the information in the `ConnectionToClient` object associated with the client that is being blocked.

Decision: *Point 2.2 of the specification requires that we be able to block a client even if that client is not logged on. This means that we must choose option 1.1 since no `ConnectionToClient` will exist for clients that are logged off.*

E. **Details of the design:**

Client side:

❏ The four new commands will be accepted by `handleMessageFromClientUI` and passed unchanged to the server.

❏ Responses from the server will be displayed on the UI. There will be no need for `handleMessageFromServer` to understand that the responses are replies to the commands.

Server side:

❏ Method `handleMessageFromClient` will interpret `#block` commands by adding a record of the block in the data associated with the originating client. This method will modify the data in response to `#unblock`.

❏ The information will be stored by calling `setValue("blockedUsers", arg)` where `arg` is a `Vector` containing the names of the blocked users.

❏ Method `handleMessageFromServerUI` will also have to have an implementation of `#block` and `#unblock`. These will have to save the blocked users as elements of a new instance variable declared thus: `Vector blockedUsers;`

❏ The implementations of `#whoiblock` in `handleMessageFromClient` and `handleMessageFromServerUI` will straightforwardly process the contents of the vectors.

❏ For `#whoblocksme`, a new method will be created in the server class that will be called by both `handleMessageFromClient` and `handleMessageFromServerUI`. This will take a single argument (the name of the initiating client, or else 'server'). It will check all the `blockedUsers` vectors of the connected clients and also the `blockedUsers` instance variable for matching clients.

❏ The `#forward`, `#private` and simple message commands will be modified as needed to reflect the specifications. Each of these will each examine the relevant `blockedUsers` vectors and take appropriate action.

9.9 Difficulties and risks in design

■ **Like modeling, design is a skill that requires considerable experience**. Design requires weighing many alternatives; however, to do so requires knowing about the alternatives and also being able to evaluate their consequences.
Resolution. Do not attempt to design large systems until you have experienced a wide variety of software development projects. Actively study designs of other systems, including designs that have been found to be both good and bad.

■ **Poor designs can lead to expensive maintenance**. A system with high coupling and low cohesion will be very difficult to change, will have many more defects and will deteriorate more rapidly than a well-designed system.
Resolution. Follow the principles discussed in this chapter. Also, use the modeling techniques and patterns discussed in this book. Hold design reviews so that others can find flaws in your designs.

■ **Ensuring that a software system's design remains good throughout its life requires constant effort.** Design tends to deteriorate as a result of adding new features that were not anticipated in the original design. The design also deteriorates as a result of people not understanding it when they make modifications.

Resolution. Make the original design as flexible as possible so as to anticipate changes and extensions. Ensure that the design documentation is usable and at the correct level of detail so that maintainers will be able to make effective use of it. Ensure that change is carefully managed, with all changes to the requirements and design undergoing review. If it appears that implementing a new requirement would necessitate undermining the integrity of the architecture, then perform re-engineering to change and improve the architecture first.

9.10 Summary

In this chapter we have discussed principles, techniques and patterns that, if applied carefully, should lead to software that is flexible and maintainable.

Four of the most important principles are: divide up the system so that you can better handle its complexity, increase cohesion so that each component has a clearly identifiable purpose, reduce coupling so that there is minimal dependency between components, and increase abstraction so that you can work with the design without having to understand its details.

It is important to try to build components that have functional cohesion (the component computes just one output with no side effects), layer cohesion (the component provides a unified set of services at a certain level of abstraction) or communicational cohesion (the component manages all the interaction with a particular class of data). It is also important to reduce content coupling (surreptitious modification of data that is internal to a component), common coupling (use of global data) and control coupling (one component completely controls what another component does).

Other important principles are: strive for high flexibility, reusability, reuse, portability and testability. You should also anticipate obsolescence and design defensively.

Techniques for making good design decisions include carefully analyzing each option against the objectives and priorities, as well as performing cost–benefit analysis to determine whether a particular option is worthwhile.

Software architecture is a cornerstone of any software engineering project. The architectural model forms the basis on which the rest of the system is built. It allows you to divide the system into subsystems, and to distribute the work to team members. It also allows those team members to communicate effectively, and to plan for eventual extension of the system.

The architecture describes the subsystems, the interfaces between those subsystems, as well as their dynamic behavior, interactions and shared data. The architectural model can use all the various kinds of UML diagrams, including the package diagrams, deployment diagrams and component diagrams which we introduced in this chapter.

When building an architecture, you should try to compose the system from various well-known architectural patterns. These include the Multi-Layer pattern, the Client–Server and other distributed patterns, the Pipe-and-Filter pattern, and the Broker pattern.

All aspects of design should be communicated to readers using carefully written documentation. The readers will include those who are implementing the design, those who will modify it and those who will develop other systems that interface with it. Remember to include rationale in your documentation.

9.11 For more information

- J. Bosch, *Design and Use of Software Architectures*, Addison-Wesley, 2000

- M. Jazayeri, A. Ran, F. Van Der Linden and Philip Van Der Linden, *Software Architecture for Product Families: Principles and Practice*, 2nd edition, Addison-Wesley, 2003

- L. Bass, P. Clements, R. Kazman and K. Bass, *Software Architecture in Practice*, Addison-Wesley, 1998

- C. Hofmeister, Robert Nord and Dilip Soni, *Applied Software Architecture*, Addison-Wesley, 1999

- D. Smith, *Designing Maintainable Software*, Springer Verlag, 1999

- A. Rollings and Dave Morris, *Game Architecture and Design: A New Edition*, Coriolis Group, 2003

- M. Fowler, *UML Distilled*, 3rd edition, Addison-Wesley, 2003

- R. Monson-Haefel, D. Chappell, *Java Message Service*, O'Reilly, 2000

- Software architecture resources on the web: http://www.serc.nl/people/florijn/interests/arch.html

- Bredemeyer's resources for software architects: http://www.bredemeyer.com

- CORBA: http://www.corba.org

- The Microsoft web services developer center: http://msdn.microsoft.com/webservices/

- The Sun web site on the J2EE technology: http://java.sun.com/j2ee/

Project exercises

E188 Create requirements documents for the following advanced features of the SimpleChat system.

(a) A capability to allow several servers to be linked together. A user could connect his or her client to any of the servers. The functions of the system would appear to the end-users to work in the same way as if there was just one server.

(b) A capability to allow users to send files to each other. The receiving user would have to acknowledge that he or she is willing to accept the file.

(c) A 'buddy-list' capability. A client can ask to be notified when any of a particular subset of other clients is logged on (currently the system tells you the complete set of people who are logged on).

(d) The ability to conduct votes among all the people on a channel. One user, who proposes a vote, specifies the question and several alternative answers that people can vote for. Voting can be done in a way that is visible to everybody, or else secretly (at the discretion of the proposer). Whenever the proposer desires, the results can be tabulated and transmitted to everybody.

E189 Create a design for each of the features you specified in the last exercise. If you discover defects in the requirements, then update them.

E190 Implement the features you designed in the last exercise. If you discover flaws in the requirements or design, then update those documents as needed.

E191 This exercise requires you to do some research into basic cryptographic techniques. Specify and design an extension to SimpleChat that would allow you to encrypt all the communication that occurs in a particular channel.

E192 Create a complete design document, including an architectural model, for the Small Hotel Reservation System.

Testing and inspecting to ensure high quality

Disciplined attention to requirements analysis, modeling and design helps produce good quality software that solves the customers' problems. However, any human activity, no matter how carefully performed, will involve mistakes. It is therefore necessary to verify meticulously that the system performs as required. In this chapter we discuss two important verification techniques, testing and inspection. We will also put these in the context of quality assurance as a whole.

In this chapter you will learn about the following

- The distinction between such terms as 'failure' and 'defect'.

- Strategies for efficiently and effectively finding defects in software, by testing and inspecting it.

- Particular types of defects and how to detect them.

- How to write test cases.

- Other ways to help ensure quality such as root cause analysis, and implementing a process standard.

10.1 Basic definitions

People often talk rather interchangeably about such things as 'errors', 'mistakes', 'bugs', 'failures' and 'defects'. It is important, however, carefully to define and distinguish among these terms so that the discussion in the remainder of the chapter is clearer.

An extreme and easily understood kind of failure is an outright crash. However, any violation of requirements should be considered a failure,

> **Definition:** a *failure* is an unacceptable behavior exhibited by a system.

including such things as the production of incorrect outputs, the system running too slowly, or the user having trouble finding online help.

The frequency of failures, as encountered by testers and end-users, allows you to measure the *reliability* of a system. An important design objective is to achieve a very low failure rate, and hence high reliability.

Most failures are violations of requirements that are stated *explicitly* in a requirements document. However, it is possible to have a failure resulting from a violation of an *implicit* requirement – something not written in the requirements document, but which the user or tester discovers when running the system. Such a failure indicates that the requirements need improving. Remember that failures may arise from violations of either functional or quality requirements.

> **Definition:** a *defect* is a flaw in any aspect of the system including the requirements, the design and the code, that contributes, or may potentially contribute, to the occurrence of one or more failures. A defect is also known as a *fault*.

The techniques presented in this chapter are intended to enable software engineers to discover and remove defects.

Often it takes several defects, working together, to cause a particular failure. For example, imagine in the SimpleChat program that a user tries to forward messages to himself or herself. It would be a design defect if it were possible to set up such a forwarding situation to start with. Imagine, nevertheless, that this first defect existed. In the worst case, such a defect would result in an infinite loop, and a resulting 'hang' or crash, as the system tries to forward the same message over and over again. However, this worst case could only occur if there were a second defect, where the system does not detect, during the actual sending of a message, that it is forwarding a message around a loop. A tester would only be able to uncover the second defect if the first were present. On the other hand, an inspector, studying the code in detail, might notice both. In this chapter we will study both testing and inspecting.

> **Definition:** an *error* is a slip-up or inappropriate decision by a software developer that leads to the introduction of a defect into the system.

An error can be made at any stage of the software development process, from requirements to implementation and maintenance. Improved education and disciplined approaches to software engineering should lead to fewer errors, and hence fewer defects and fewer failures.

Pejorative words for bad things

There are a wide variety of words for 'bad' things that happen in software engineering, and the words are often used with subtly different meanings.

In colloquial speech, 'failures' and 'defects' are often not distinguished from each other – they are both simply called 'bugs' or 'problems'. However, software developers should make an effort to distinguish consciously between failures and defects. Doing so helps them to think more clearly about the quality, or the lack of quality, in a system. It also allows them to monitor and measure that quality, and thus improve both the product and the development process.

In addition to meaning a 'mistake' made by a person, the word 'error' also has a second meaning: the amount of deviation from the correct value in a numerical calculation, due to rounding off or truncation. We will discuss such errors later in this chapter. When a software engineer makes an error, it is a 'bad thing'; however, when a round-off error occurs, it is only bad (i.e. a defect) if it is not anticipated and correctly handled.

Exercise

E193 Categorize the following according to whether each describes a *failure*, a *defect* or an *error*:

(a) A software engineer, working in a hurry, unintentionally deletes an important line of source code.

(b) On 1 January 2040 the system reports the date as 1 January 1940.

(c) No design documentation or source code comments are provided for a complex algorithm.

(d) A fixed size array of length 10 is used to maintain the list of courses taken by a student during one semester. The requirements are silent about the maximum number of courses a student may take at any one time.

10.2   Effective and efficient testing

Testing is the process of deliberately trying to cause failures in a system in order to detect any defects that might be present. As with all engineering activities, efficiency and effectiveness are both important. To test *effectively*, you must use a strategy that uncovers as many defects as possible. To test *efficiently*, you must find the largest possible number of defects using the fewest possible tests. An effective and efficient testing strategy is often called a *high-yield* strategy.

Black-box and glass-box testing

Most of the time, testers treat a system as a *black box*. This means they provide the system with inputs and observe the outputs, but they cannot see what is

Properly handled exceptions are not failures

Object-oriented programs throw 'exceptions'; these should not be confused with failures. In most cases, exceptions are thrown in situations that are anticipated by programmers, such as reaching the end of a file.

It is a failure, however, when an unexpected exception is thrown. The corresponding defect is the absence of code to handle the exception. Even in these cases, though, it is better that an exception is thrown, and debugging information captured, rather than the program crashing with no clue as to what happened.

It is particularly bad practice to blindly catch all exceptions without justification; defects can then remain hidden. In particular, code like the following should be avoided if possible:

```
try {...} catch(Exception e) {/* do nothing */}
```

going on inside. In particular, they can see neither the source code, the internal data, nor any of the design documentation describing the system's internals.

An alternative approach to testing is to treat the system as a *glass box*. In glass-box testing, the tester can examine the design documents and the code, as well as observe at run time the steps taken by algorithms and their internal data. He or she can therefore design tests that will exercise all aspects of each algorithm and data structure. Glass-box testing is widely referred to as *white-box* testing or structural testing; however, we prefer the term glass-box testing since the notion of looking inside a glass box clearly provides a better metaphor.

Glass-box testing is more time-consuming than black-box testing, but removes much of the guesswork, and allows the tester to be more thorough. When performing glass-box testing, a tester can analyze the code to ensure that his or her testing strategy has reached a targeted *coverage* of statements and branches: the tester can ensure that, for example, 90 per cent of all statements are executed and 80 per cent of all branches are taken.

Individual programmers often informally employ glass-box testing when they are verifying their own code. It is only used as part of a formal testing process when testing critical or complex components. Therefore, most of the techniques we will discuss in this chapter are oriented towards black-box testing.

Example 10.1   *Discuss how you would employ glass-box testing to test the run method of the OCSF* AbstractServer *class found on the book's web site (www.lloseng.com).*

Using glass-box testing means that you will base your testing strategy on the actual implementation, rather than the requirements.

To help do this systematically, you can first draw a flow graph of the code as shown in Figure 10.1. This graph has a node for all the possible places where the code can make a branch (such as if statements, while statements and statements that can throw an exception), the places where those branches can lead (the bodies of loops, if or else clauses, and catch statements), and the places where two separate paths come together (the statements after a loop or if-then-else body, as well as finally clauses or the statements after catch clauses).

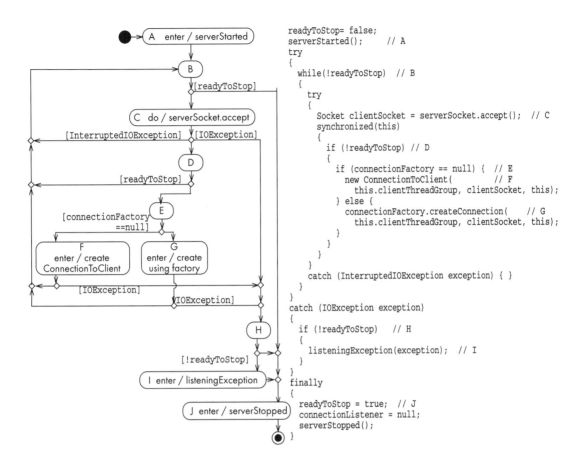

The code shown in the figure:

```
                                    readyToStop= false;
                                    serverStarted();      // A
                                    try
                                    {
                                      while(!readyToStop)  // B
                                      {
                                        try
                                        {
                                          Socket clientSocket = serverSocket.accept(); // C
                                          synchronized(this)
                                          {
                                            if (!readyToStop) // D
                                            {
                                              if (connectionFactory == null) { // E
                                                new ConnectionToClient(         // F
                                                  this.clientThreadGroup, clientSocket, this);
                                              } else {
                                                connectionFactory.createConnection( // G
                                                  this.clientThreadGroup, clientSocket, this);
                                              }
                                            }
                                          }
                                        }
                                        catch (InterruptedIOException exception) { }
                                      }
                                    }
                                    catch (IOException exception)
                                    {
                                      if (!readyToStop)    // H
                                      {
                                        listeningException(exception);  // I
                                      }
                                    }
                                    finally
                                    {
                                      readyToStop = true;  // J
                                      connectionListener = null;
                                      serverStopped();
                                    }
```

Figure 10.1   Flow graph of the OCSF AbstractServer run method. The code is extracted from
that found on the book's web site (http://www.lloseng.com)

In Figure 10.1, we have labeled each node with a letter. This letter is also
shown as a comment in the code. We show calls to callback methods in
appropriate nodes.

Once you have a flow graph you must then choose from the following
strategies for glass-box testing:

■ **Covering all possible paths**. This is infeasible in graphs with loops since there
would be an infinite number of paths (i.e. repeatedly looping).

■ **Covering all possible edges**. This is probably the most efficient strategy. You
devise a sufficient set of tests to make sure that each of the outgoing edges of all
nodes is taken. The following tests would ensure edge coverage of Figure 10.1; a
black-box tester would most likely not be able to devise a similar set of tests.
The most difficult aspect of executing these tests is to force I/O exceptions to be
thrown at the correct time, as in tests 3 through 6. Bold text is used below to
show the first time a given edge is covered.

1. **A-B-C-B**-C-...-B-**C-D-E-F-B**-C-...-B-C-**B-J**: run the server, connect a client, and send the stop command.

2. A-B-C-B-C-...-B-C-D-E-**G-B**-C-...-B-C-B-J: repeat the same sequence, but this time use a connection factory.

3. A-B-C-B-C-...-B-**C-H-I-J**: same as 2, but force an I/O exception to occur while accepting the connection.

4. A-B-C-B-C-...-B-C-D-**E-G-H-J**: same as 2, but force an exception to occur during creation of the connection class (e.g. during stream creation); also send the stop command at the same time so that path H-J is taken.

5. A-B-C-B-C-...-B-C-D-E-**F-H**-J: same as 4, but with a regular `ConnectionToClient`.

6. A-B-C-B-C-...-B-C-**D-B**-J: same as 1, except send the stop command just after the connection is accepted.

■ **Covering all nodes**. This is a less exhaustive, and therefore less effective strategy. For example, in the above, tests 1, 3 and 4 together cover all nodes, but the remainder are needed to cover all the edges.

Testing is like detective work

The job of the tester has certain similarities with that of the detective:

■ A detective must try to understand the criminal mind. Similarly, the tester must try to understand how programmers, designers and users think, so as to better find defects. For example, detectives know that criminals tend to repeat certain patterns of behavior (their *modus operandi*); if detectives know these patterns, they can more easily track down the criminals. Similarly, testers know that software developers implement algorithms in certain ways and tend to have habits that can lead to errors, and hence to defects. Testers can uncover defects by anticipating typical errors made by developers. Testers can also uncover defects by anticipating unusual things that users might try to do.

■ Detective work is painstaking. The detective must not leave anything uncovered, and must be suspicious of everything. Similar suspicion and attention to detail are the hallmark of an effective tester. However, like detective work, it does not pay to take an excessive amount of testing time – as we mentioned earlier, both tester and detective have to be *efficient*.

Equivalence classes: a strategy for choosing what to test

Imagine you are asked to test a Java method `validMonth` that takes an `int` argument that is supposed to correspond to a valid month. The method returns true if the input is in the range 1 to 12 inclusive, and false otherwise. We will look at how you should test such a month-validation method to make sure it behaves correctly.

To confirm correct behavior, it is equally as important to check that the method returns false in the case of an invalid month, as it is to check that it returns true in the case of a valid month.

One possible testing strategy would be to use *brute force*, i.e. to test the method using *every possible* value of Java's int datatype – all integers from -2^{31} to $2^{31}-1$. Common sense, however, tells us that such testing of all possibilities would not only take such a huge amount of time as to be impractical, but would also be pointless. It would be pointless because any given defect is likely to cause failures with many different input values. For example, if a failure always occurs with input 243, then it is almost certain that a failure will also occur with input 245. Hence you do not need to test both values. Our knowledge of software design and programming tells us that there is no reason to believe 243 and 245 would be treated any differently by any reasonable algorithm that might be used to validate a month number.

Therefore, in order to test efficiently, you should divide the possible inputs into groups that you believe will be treated similarly by reasonable algorithms. Such groups are called *equivalence classes*. A tester needs only to run one test per equivalence class, using a *representative* member of that equivalence class as input (plus boundary tests that we will discuss later). For the month-validation problem, there are three equivalence classes, as shown in Table 10.1.

Table 10.1   Equivalence classes for month validation, where the input value is a Java int

Equivalence class	Range of values
Invalid – larger	13 to $2^{31}-1$ (can be loosely expressed as 13 to ∝)
Valid	1 to 12
Invalid – smaller	-2^{31} to 0 (can be loosely expressed as −∝ to 0)

As mentioned, determining equivalence classes helps the tester to do efficient yet thorough black-box testing. However, determining the equivalence classes is often not easy. The tester has to understand the required input and the domain-specific rules that govern what input is acceptable. Also, the tester has to have knowledge of computer science and software design. For example, he or she would have to know about the ranges of integer data types in order to determine the upper and lower bounds of the two invalid equivalence classes in the month-validation problem.

Exercise

E194 Create a table of equivalence classes for each of the following single-input problems. Some of these might require some careful thought and/or some research. Remember: put an input in a separate equivalence class if there is even a slight possibility that some reasonable algorithm might treat the input in a special way.

(a) A telephone number to be used by an automatic dialer.

(b) A person's name (written in a Latin character set).

(c) A time zone, which can be specified either numerically as a difference from UTC (i.e. GMT), or alphabetically from a set of standard codes (e.g. EST, BST, PDT).

(d) The speed of a vehicle, which is a 3-digit integer. This may be followed by the units 'km/h', 'm/s' or 'mph'. 'km/h' is the default.

(e) A credit card number.

(f) An FM broadcast radio frequency.

(g) A URL.

Combinations of equivalence classes

Imagine you are designing a system that is to contain information about all kinds of land vehicles, including passenger vehicles and racing vehicles. Such a system might require the user to enter specifications of a new type of vehicle.

Your job is to decide how to divide this system into equivalence classes for testing. You are told that the user can enter the following data:

1. Whether the manufacturers give data about the vehicle in metric or traditional (Imperial or US) units. The user selects this using pair of 'radio buttons'. This impacts how the rest of the data will be interpreted (two equivalence classes; there is no possibility of invalid input).

2. Maximum speed, an integer ranging from 1 to 750 km/h or 1 to 500 mph (four equivalence classes: $[-\infty..0]$, $[1..500]$, $[501..750]$, $[751..\infty]$).

3. Type of fuel, one of a set of 10 possible strings that the user explicitly types (11 equivalence classes – the eleventh class is any string other than the 10 valid ones).

4. Average fuel efficiency, a fixed-point value with one decimal place, ranging from 1 to 240 L/100 km or 1 to 240 mpg (three equivalence classes).

5. Time to accelerate to 100 km/h or 60 mph. This is a fixed-point value with one decimal place, ranging from 1 to 100s (three equivalence classes).

6. Range, an integer from 1 to 5000 km or 1 to 3000 miles (four equivalence classes: $[-\infty..0]$, $[1..3000]$, $[3001..5000]$, $[5001..\infty]$).

The first thing to notice is that each of the six inputs has its own set of equivalence classes. A second thing to notice is that some of the inputs *depend* on the values of others. In particular, the valid values for inputs 2 and 6 depend on whether metric or traditional units has been specified as input 1. This adds an extra equivalence class for inputs 2 and 6, giving them four each instead of three.

A string-valued input, such as input 3, would have just one equivalence class if any arbitrary string were valid and no algorithm would actually try to process the string. However, in the case of input 3, every legal value should be considered a separate equivalence class because the tester must verify that the designer has explicitly written code to recognize every valid type of fuel. Since the user types strings, the program must do string comparisons to determine which fuel type is entered; a common bug in the code would be to misspell one of the fuel types in the code that makes the comparison.

The set of equivalence classes for the system as a whole is the set of all possible *combinations* of inputs. The total number of equivalence classes for the system is therefore the product of the number of classes of the individual inputs; in this case $2 \times 4 \times 11 \times 3 \times 3 \times 4 = 3168$. Since, like this system, most systems have many distinct inputs, the total number of system equivalence classes can become very large. This is called a *combinatorial explosion* of the space of required tests.

The combinatorial explosion implies that you cannot realistically test every possible system-wide equivalence class. A reasonable approach to testing is therefore as follows. You should first make sure that at least one test is run with every equivalence class of every individual input. Then you should also, where possible, test all combinations where one input is likely to *affect the interpretation of* another. Therefore, for example, you should use both metric and traditional units (specified by input 1) when running tests for inputs 2 and 6.

Using the above strategy, the number of tests for the vehicles example can be reduced to 11. You run one test for each equivalence class of input 3; while doing this you also vary the eight possible combinations of inputs 1 and 2, the eight combinations of inputs 1 and 6, and the three possible equivalence classes of the other two inputs. You should test a few other random combinations of equivalence classes.

In addition to testing representative values from each equivalence class, you should also test values at the boundaries of equivalence classes. This is discussed in the next subsection.

Exercise

E195 Describe a good set of equivalence class tests for the following situations:

(a) A personal information form that asks for family name, first name, date of birth, street address, city, country, postal code and home telephone number.

(b) The set of commands available in the client side of SimpleChat Phase 2.

(c) The GANA system. Hint: inputs come from other places than just the user interface.

Testing at boundaries of equivalence classes

More errors in software occur at the boundaries of equivalence classes than in the 'middle'. For example, when testing a method that inputs an integer and checks whether a valid day number has been entered for the month of November, the valid equivalence classes are integers less than 1, integers from 1 to 30 and integers greater than 30. However, the most likely error is that the number 31 is accepted as valid (i.e. the system treats it the same way as integers from 1 to 30). Another common error might be the acceptance of zero as a valid day number.

Therefore we should expand the idea of equivalence class testing to specifically test values at the extremes of each equivalence class.

Exercise

E196 Expand each of your answers to include equivalence class boundary values that should be tested.

Detecting specific categories of defects

As mentioned earlier, a tester must act like a detective, trying to uncover any defects that other software engineers might have introduced. This means not only testing at equivalence classes and their boundaries, but also designing tests that explicitly try to catch a range of specific types of defects that commonly occur.

The next few sections give a non-exhaustive list of some of these most common categories of defects. This list will help you to design appropriate test cases. It will also be useful when designing software, since it will help you to create designs that avoid these defects.

10.3 Defects in ordinary algorithms

The following subsections list some of the most common kinds of defects found in all types of algorithms. In some cases, these algorithmic defects can be found in the specification, but they are more often introduced by the designer or the programmer.

Incorrect logical conditions

Defects The logical conditions that govern looping and if-then-else statements are wrongly formulated. Sometimes a condition needs completely restructuring, but often the defect is more subtle, such as nesting parentheses incorrectly, reversing comparison operators (e.g. > becomes <), or mishandling the equality case (e.g. >= becomes > or vice versa).

Testing Use equivalence class and boundary testing. To compute the equivalence classes,
strategy consider each variable used in the logical condition as an input.

Example Imagine that an aircraft's alarm is supposed to sound if the landing gear is not deployed when the aircraft is close to the ground. The specifications might state this as follows: 'The landing gear must be deployed whenever the plane is within 2 minutes from landing or take-off, or within 2000 feet from the ground. If visibility is less than 1000 feet, then the landing gear must be deployed whenever the plane is within 3 minutes from the landing or lower than 2500 feet.' Note that in this case a false alarm is just as bad as a failure of the alarm to sound when it should.

Java code for the alarm might be written as follows (in deliberately bad style):

```
if(!landingGearDeployed &&
  (min(now-takeoffTime,estLandTime-now))<
    (visibility < 1000 ? 180 :120) ||
  relativeAltitude <
    (visibility < 1000 ? 2500 :2000)
  )
{
  throw new LandingGearException();
}
```

Unfortunately, this type of bad style that gives rise to defects is rather a common practice. There is at least one critical defect in this code – see if you can understand the code and find the defect. It is likely that a programmer might not notice it due to the nested parentheses and the overall complexity of the condition.

As shown in Table 10.2, the inputs are the variables used in the condition. The total number of system equivalence classes in the aircraft example would be $3\times3\times3\times2\times2 = 108$. Since this number is manageably small, and since this is a safety-critical system, all the classes should be tested.

Figure 10.2 shows how the equivalence classes relate to each other. The gray area indicates the classes where the alarm should sound if the landing gear is not deployed. The most critical classes are those next to the boundary of the gray area, each of which is marked with a letter. In these classes, a change in a single variable can affect the outcome. Table 10.3 describes the equivalence classes we need to test areas *a* and *d*.

We also need to perform boundary tests for each of the equivalence classes. For example, testing what happens if the visibility is zero, very close to 1000 feet, and unlimited. Particularly important boundary cases occur while the plane is on the ground, since it is likely that special processing might take place while there.

Table 10.2 Equivalence classes of conditions that can lead to a decision about whether the landing-gear alarm should sound

Variable affecting condition	Equivalence classes
Time since take-off	3: Within 2 minutes after take-off, 2–3 minutes after take-off, more than 3 minutes after takeoff
Time to landing	3: Within 2 minutes prior to landing, 2–3 minutes prior to landing, more than 3 minutes prior to landing
Relative altitude	3: < 2000 feet, 2000 feet to 2500 feet, 2500 feet
Visibility	2: < 1000 feet, 1000 feet
Landing gear deployed	2: true, false

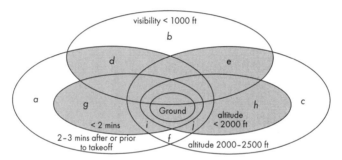

Figure 10.2 Venn diagram, with shading showing situations where the landing gear must be down, and hence the alarm must sound if it is not down. Conversely, the alarm should never sound in the unshaded areas

Table 10.3 The eight system equivalence classes corresponding to the boundary between regions *a* and *d* of Figure 10.2

Flight stage	Visibility	Landing gear	Required result
2–3 minutes after take-off	≤ 1000 ft	Deployed	No alarm
2–3 minutes prior to landing	≤ 1000 ft	Deployed	No alarm
2–3 minutes after take-off	≤ 1000 ft	Not deployed	No alarm
2–3 minutes prior to landing	≤ 1000 ft	Not deployed	No alarm
2–3 minutes after take-off	< 1000 ft	Deployed	No alarm
2–3 minutes prior to landing	< 1000 ft	Deployed	No alarm
2–3 minutes after take-off	< 1000 ft	Not deployed	Alarm sounds
2–3 minutes prior to landing	< 1000 ft	Not deployed	Alarm sounds

You might ask the question, how can I test a landing-gear system like this since it is to be embedded in a real aircraft? The answer is that the alarm module needs to be thoroughly tested in a *simulated* environment before being tested in a real aircraft.

Exercises

E197 Write Java code for the aircraft landing-gear example and test it according to the equivalence classes and boundary cases suggested. Record and fix any defects. Note that to save time, you should write a program to test it automatically (this is called a *test harness*).

E198 Create tables that will help you test the conditions corresponding to the following requirements.

(a) User C sends a message to A. The message must be forwarded from A to B if the following are all true: 1) A has requested that his or her messages be forwarded to B; 2) B is logged on; and 3) B has neither requested that messages from A be blocked nor that messages from C be blocked. Furthermore, if the message is declared to be an emergency message then no blocking occurs.

(b) Applicants under the age of 18 should use form A, while those 18 or above should use form B. However, disabled people of any age, except those on social assistance, should use form C. People on social assistance should complete form D in addition to either A or B. Senior citizens should complete form E in addition to the other forms, unless they are on social assistance or are living in a subsidized nursing home. Anybody who is not disabled and not a senior citizen, and who earns over £15,000 per year, should complete form F in addition to other forms.

(c) The navigation system must announce to drivers that they have to turn onto a new road two minutes in advance of the required turn. Exceptions arise in the following circumstances. Firstly, if a driver is still completing a previous turn, then the warning of the new turn should be delayed until the first turn is complete – although 15 seconds warning must still be given. Secondly, in a city environment (where a driver driving at the speed limit would encounter at least one possible turn every 30 seconds), the system should warn the driver only 30 seconds before the turn is required.

(d) The burglar alarm system should sound the alarm immediately if a movement of magnitude greater than 4 is detected while the alarm is activated. An alarm should also sound if a movement of magnitude 3 persists for more than 5 seconds, or a movement of magnitude 2 persists for more than 15 seconds. Additionally, an alarm should sound if the total amount of magnitude 2 or 3 movement exceeds 30 seconds in any 2-minute period. If two or more sensors detect movement simultaneously, as might be the case in an earthquake, then the above time-periods are doubled. The alarm is never sounded within 1 minute of activation.

Performing a calculation in the wrong part of a control construct

Defect The program performs an action when it should not, or does not perform an action when it should. These are typically caused by inappropriately excluding the action from, or including the action in, a loop or if-then-else construct.

Testing strategies Design tests that execute each loop *zero* times, exactly *once*, and *more than once*. Also, ensure that anything 'bad' or 'unusual' that could happen while looping is made to occur on the first iteration and the last iteration.

This kind of defect is not always reliably caught using black-box testing; in such cases glass-box testing or inspections may be more effective.

Examples The following Java code illustrates a typical case:

```
while(j<maximum)
{
  k=someOperation(j);
  j++;
}
if(k==-1) signalAnError();
```

In this case, `signalAnError` was supposed to be called if any of the calls to `someOperation` resulted in a value of −1. Unfortunately, here it can only be called following the last call to `someOperation`. The final line should therefore have been placed inside a loop. This kind of defect may be missed if the loop normally executes only once.

Another common type of control-construct defect occurs in the following situation (using deliberately bad style):

```
if(j<maximum)
  doSomething();
if(debug) printDebugMessage();
else doSomethingElse();
```

Here, the lack of curly brackets and proper indenting has obscured the logic. A programmer added the third line while debugging, but that means that while not debugging, `doSomethingElse()` is always called, which was not intended. Diligent testing should be able to detect this.

Not terminating a loop or recursion

Defect A loop or a recursion does not always terminate, that is, it is 'infinite'.

Testing strategies Although the programmer should have analyzed all loops or recursions to ensure they reach a terminating case, a tester should nevertheless assume that the programmer has made an error. The tester should analyze what causes a repetitive action to be stopped, and should run test cases that the tester anticipates might not be handled correctly.

Example Imagine that a program is supposed to count the total number of atoms in a complex organic molecule. It might do this by starting at an arbitrary molecule and traversing it from bond to bond, walking down each branch.

A tester might wonder, however, whether the algorithm would work correctly if there were one or more *circular* structures in the molecule; he or she might be suspicious that a circular structure could cause the algorithm to try to loop forever, counting ever higher as it went round and round the molecule. Of course, any reasonable programmer should also have thought of this situation, but the tester must not trust this.

Not setting up the correct preconditions for an algorithm

Defect When specifying an algorithm, one specifies *preconditions* that state what must be true before the algorithm should be executed. A defect would exist if a program proceeds to do its work, even when the preconditions are not satisfied.

Testing strategy Run test cases in which each precondition is not satisfied. Preferably its input values are just beyond what the algorithm can accept.

Example In the organic chemistry program, a precondition might be that the input is a single molecule. The tester should therefore try to test by giving as input two disjoint molecules.

Not handling null conditions

Defect A null condition is a situation where there normally exists one or more data items to process, but sometimes there are none. It is a defect when a program behaves abnormally when a null condition is encountered. In these situations, the program should 'do nothing, gracefully'.

Testing strategy Determine all possible null conditions and run test cases that would highlight any inappropriate behavior.

Examples Imagine you want to calculate the average sales of members of each division in an organization. But what if some division has no members? Perhaps they all quit, or the division has just been formed and nobody has been hired. A typical defect would be that this relatively unusual situation results in an attempt to divide by zero (zero sales, divided by zero members).

As a related example, imagine you are asked to find the salesperson who has sold the most in the above division. In attempting to perform this calculation, an algorithm might loop zero times and hence never actually set the maximum value, or leave it set to some arbitrary, but incorrect value.

Not handling singleton or non-singleton conditions

Defect A singleton condition is like a null condition. It occurs when there is normally *more than one* of something, but sometimes there is only one. A non-singleton condition is the inverse – there is almost always *one* of something, but occasionally there can be more than one. Defects occur when the unusual case is not properly handled.

Testing strategy Brainstorm to determine unusual conditions and run appropriate tests.

Examples The following are two examples of these conditions:

❏ Imagine that in a web browser you can set up a series of 'personal profiles'. Each user of the computer has their own personal profile that includes their name, bookmarks list, and 'cookies'. Imagine you created a personal profile under your name, 'John Smith'. Later on you accidentally created another profile, using the same name. Then you decided to get rid of one of the two profiles; you therefore selected a profile and issued the 'delete' command. Unfortunately, the deletion operation might assume that there can be only one profile using a given name, so that it simply traverses the list of profiles, deleting *all* the profiles by that name. The result? Both of the profiles are deleted. Anticipating this kind of defect, a tester can enter several identically-named profiles and make sure that only one is deleted.

❏ Imagine that a program is designed to randomly assign members of a sports club into pairs who will play against each other. Does the program do something intelligent with the left-over person when there is an odd number of members? And what happens if there is only one member? (Maybe the club should be disbanded, but it would still be best if the program did not crash.)

Off-by-one errors

Defect A program inappropriately adds or subtracts 1, or inappropriately loops one too many times or one too few times. This is a particularly common type of defect.

Testing strategy Develop boundary tests in which you verify that the program computes the correct numerical answer, or performs the correct number of iterations.
Since graphical applications are common places where off-by-one errors are found, study the display to see if objects slightly overlap or have slight gaps.

Examples Assuming 0-based indexing, as is the case in Java, then the following loop would always skip the first element, and loop one too few times.

```
for (i=1; i<arrayname.length; i++) { /* do something */ }
```

If 1-based indexing had been used, as in some other programming languages, then the code would inappropriately skip the *last* element. Note that the use of the Iterator class in Java helps prevent such coding defects, but the job of the tester is to assume the worst and guess that designers have made errors like this.

Similar errors can occur when using a prefix operator instead of the postfix operator in certain calculations. In the following example, the variable val is probably being incremented too early, so that its initial value is not actually passed to anOperation.

```
while (iterator.hasNext())
{
  anOperation(++val);
}
```

Operator precedence errors

Defect An operator precedence error occurs when a programmer omits needed parentheses, or puts parentheses in the wrong place. Operator precedence errors are often extremely obvious, but can occasionally lie hidden until special conditions arise.

Testing strategy In software that computes formulae, run tests that anticipate defects such as those described in the example below. However, code inspections, discussed later, are likely to be better at catching this kind of defect.

Example A program may compute z+(x*y), when it was supposed to compute (z+x)*y. In this case, the programmer probably wrote z+x*y and forgot that multiplication takes precedence over addition. If z is normally zero, or all three variables are normally 1, then this defect could remain hidden. Testing for errors like this therefore means thinking carefully about which values of x, y and z to use.

Use of inappropriate standard algorithms

Defect An inappropriate standard algorithm is one that is unnecessarily inefficient or has some other property that is widely recognized as being bad.

Testing strategies The tester has to know the properties of algorithms and design tests, such as those in the following examples, that will determine whether any undesirable algorithms have been implemented.

Examples There is not enough space in this book to discuss choice of algorithms and algorithm analysis – that is the subject of separate books. Nevertheless, the following are some bad choices of algorithms that testers should try to detect:

❑ **An inefficient sort algorithm**. The most classical 'bad' choice of algorithm is sorting using a so-called 'bubble sort' instead of a more efficient approach to sorting. A tester can test for such a defect by increasing the number of items being sorted and observing how execution time is affected. A bad sorting algorithm will increase with the square of the number of items – if you *double* the number of items a bad sorting algorithm will take about *four* times as long. A better algorithm will normally increase much more slowly. Imagine, for example, that you sort 10,000 items and notice that the system takes 5 seconds. Then you double the number of items to 20,000. If a bad algorithm were being used, you would expect the time to increase to about 20 seconds. On the other hand, if a better quality algorithm were being used, you would expect sorting time to be instead about 11 seconds on average, which is slightly more than double the time.

❑ **An inefficient search algorithm**. You would expect that searching through a very large list of sorted items should be done quite rapidly. You can test for this in a similar manner to testing for an inefficient sort algorithm. Ensure that the search time does not increase unacceptably as the list gets longer. Also check that the position in the list of the item you are looking for does not have a noticeable impact on search time.

❑ **A non-stable sort**. A non-stable sort will take equal elements and sometimes switch their order after the sorting process. For example, imagine that you start with a list of people ordered alphabetically by their name. If you now sort the people alphabetically by city, you would normally want to see the people in each city still sorted by name. A tester should therefore deliberately run an experiment like this to see if the results are as expected. A non-stable sort would make the names of people in each city appear randomly, or at best imperfectly ordered.

❑ **A search or sort that is case sensitive when it should not be, or vice versa**. The tester should test algorithms with mixed-case data to see if the algorithm behaves as expected.

Note that the first two types of inappropriate algorithm will only be noticed by users when the amount of data to be handled is very large. In either of these cases, if only a few dozen items are ever likely to be in a list, then the tester need not worry about the algorithm.

Exercise

E199 Java has a built-in sorting capability, found in classes `Array` and `Collection`. Test experimentally whether these classes contain efficient and stable algorithms.

10.4 Defects in numerical algorithms

Numerical computation defects are a special class of algorithmic defect. They can occur in any software that performs mathematical calculations, especially calculations involving floating point values. Whole books are devoted to numerical algorithms; the following are some of the typical classes of defects that testers should try to find.

Not using enough bits or digits to store maximum values

Defect   A system does not use variables that are capable of representing the largest possible values that could be stored. When the capacity of a data type is exceeded, an unexpected exception might be thrown, or else the data may be stored incorrectly.

Testing strategies   Test using very large numbers to ensure that the system has a wide enough margin of error.

Example   Imagine that you were going to be storing the monthly salary of an employee in a short integer (whose value ranges up to 32765). Although this limit would work for most employees, failures would occur in the case of a) highly-paid executives, b) a period of high inflation, or c) a foreign currency that has previously experienced high inflation and now uses very large numbers for ordinary transactions.

Using insufficient places after the decimal point or too few significant figures

Defects   This problem occurs with floating point or fixed-point values. A floating-point value might not be 'wide' enough to store enough significant figures. A fixed-point value might not store enough places after the decimal point. These defects force the system to round excessively, which can mean that data is stored inaccurately and can also lead to a build-up of errors as discussed in the next defect category.

Testing strategies   Perform calculations that involve many significant figures, and large differences in magnitude. Verify that the calculated results are correct in such cases.

Example   Imagine an investment application that tracks a portfolio of shares. Typical shares are quoted using three or four significant digits, hence, prices might be $135.5 or $33.16. However, if a share 'crashes' in value for some reason, it might drop to only a few cents. In such a case, your system might have to record its value as $0.0344. If your system were only able to record values to two decimal places after the point, then it could not correctly manipulate such stocks.

Ordering operations poorly so that errors build up

Defects   This defect occurs when you do small operations on large floating-point numbers, and excessive rounding or truncation errors build up. In particular, if you take a very large floating-point number, for example 3.54×10^{28}, and add or subtract a very small number from it, for example 1, then the answer will be exactly equal to the large number. This is because the large floating-point number does not store enough significant figures for the operation to have any effect on it. It is not, per se, a defect that this occurs. However, it is a defect if the programmer intended the large number to be modified. Although the above example was an extreme case, this kind of defect can also occur in less obvious situations, as illustrated in the examples below.

Testing strategies If a numerical application is designed to work with floating-point numbers, then make sure it works with inputs that vary widely in magnitude, including both large positive and large negative exponents. Pay particular attention to the accuracy of the result when a floating-point value is being repeatedly decremented or incremented by small amounts.

Examples Imagine a fictitious processor that stored only four significant figures. Now imagine you stored the value 9876 in a variable and wanted to subtract the following values from it: 0.42, 0.35, 0.27 and 0.47. If you subtracted these values from 9876 one after the other, the result would remain 9876. This is a defect because you know that subtracting any very small value from 9876 will always result in 9876, to four decimal places. On the other hand, if you perform the calculation by first adding the small values to each other (result = 1.51) and then subtracting this from 9876, the result will be 9874, which is correct.

A similar example: imagine you are adding a large number of small credits to an account. If the account's total were in the thousands of dollars, you might always round it to the nearest dollar. However, in this situation, small transactions of a few cents would never affect the account balance.

Assuming a floating-point value will be exactly equal to some other value

Defect If you perform an arithmetic calculation on a floating-point value, then the result will very rarely be computed exactly. It is therefore a defect to test if a floating-point value is exactly equal to some other value. You should instead test if it is within a small range around that value.

Testing strategies Standard boundary testing should detect this type of defect.

Example The following is at risk of resulting in an infinite loop, since d may never equal precisely 10.0, but may instead equal 9.99999999999 after 10 iterations.

```
for (double d = 0.0; d != 10.0; d+=2.0) {...}
```

The correct expression should have been:

```
for (double d = 0.0; d < 10.0; d+=2.0) {...}
```

Exercise

E200 Describe the type of numerical defects present when the following are implemented in a program. Assuming you did not actually know the implementation, describe how you would attempt to detect such defects.

(a) `double x, y;... if(x/3.0 == y) {...}`

(b) `int totalCorporateAssets; // In Euros`

(c) `short priceOfOil; // In US 10ths of a cent per gallon`

(d) You run a web site that implements micro-payments; it charges users a third of a cent for every page click. You accumulate each client's bill in an integer where each unit represents a 10th of a cent. However, you record the money earned by each page in a float value.

10.5 Defects in timing and co-ordination: deadlocks, livelocks and critical races

Timing and co-ordination defects arise in situations involving some form of concurrency. They occur when several threads or processes interact in inappropriate ways. In this section we will use the word 'thread' to mean both 'thread' and 'process'.

The three most important kinds of timing and co-ordination defects are *deadlocks*, *livelocks* and *critical races*. Ways to design software so as to avoid these situations are discussed in books on real-time and concurrent software. Here we present the concepts of these defects and some thoughts about how to test for them.

Deadlock and livelock

Defects A deadlock is a situation where two or more threads or processes are stopped, waiting for each other to do something before either can proceed. Since neither can do anything, they permanently stop each other from proceeding. A classic example of real-life deadlock is the 'gridlock' sometimes encountered in busy cities. This is illustrated in Figure 10.3. Vehicles waiting to move in one direction hold up vehicles waiting to travel in other directions; however, each set of vehicles is ultimately delaying itself. Everybody therefore waits indefinitely.

As a software example of deadlock, imagine that thread A is waiting to access object O. Object O is locked by thread B, perhaps using Java's synchronization mechanism. Thread B, however, might be waiting to access object P, which is in turn locked by thread A. Neither thread can ever continue its work unless some outside thread forces a break in the deadlock. This situation is illustrated in Figure 10.4.

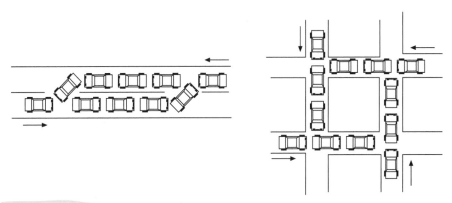

Figure 10.3 Two examples of gridlock: a form of deadlock

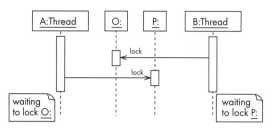

Figure 10.4   A deadlock situation in software

Livelock is similar to deadlock, in the sense that the system is stuck in a particular behavior that it cannot get out of. The difference is as follows: whereas in deadlock the system is normally hung, with nothing going on, in livelock, the system can do some computations, but it can never get out of a limited set of states.

The left part of Figure 10.5 shows livelock in traffic. Several cars are trapped in a grid of one-way streets, in which some directions are blocked, perhaps by accidents or road construction. The cars can keep moving round and round in circles, but they cannot go anywhere outside of the loop.

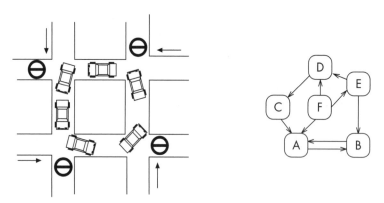

Figure 10.5   Livelock in traffic (left) and software (right)

The right part of Figure 10.5 shows a livelock situation in a state diagram. There are several transitions leading into states A and B; but once there, the system can only alternate backwards and forwards between the two states.

Both deadlocks and livelocks can appear as 'hung' systems. The difference is that in livelock the system can continue to consume CPU time. When you encounter a hung system it is certainly a failure, but it is not necessarily caused by a deadlock or livelock: the hang could result from a single thread waiting for an unavailable resource, an infinite loop, or a crash. Also, not all deadlocks and livelocks will completely hang a system, since other threads may still be running.

Testing strategies Deadlocks and livelocks tend to occur as a result of unusual combinations of conditions that are hard to anticipate or reproduce. It is often most effective to use *inspection* to detect such defects, rather than testing alone. There are some tools that can be used to detect deadlock potential, but these are beyond the scope of this book.

Whether testing or inspecting, a person with a background in real-time systems should be employed – such a person can apply his or her knowledge and experience to best anticipate timing and co-ordination defects.

If its cost is justifiable, glass-box testing is one of the best ways to uncover these defects, since you can actually study the progress of the various threads.

If black-box testing is the only possibility, then you can try some of the following tactics:

❑ Vary the time consumption of different threads by giving them differing amounts of input, or running them on hardware that varies in speed.

❑ Run a large number of threads concurrently.

❑ Deliberately deny resources to one or more threads (e.g. temporarily cut a network connection, or make a file unreadable).

Critical races

Defects A critical race is a defect in which one thread or process can sometimes experience a failure because another thread or process interferes with the 'normal' sequence of events. The defect is not that the other thread tries to do something, but that the system allows interference to occur. Critical races are often simply called 'race conditions', although the word 'critical' should be used to distinguish a defect from a race that has no bad consequences.

One type of critical race occurs when two processes or threads normally work together to achieve some outcome; however, if one is sped up or slowed down then the outcome is incorrect. This is illustrated in Figure 10.6, where in the abnormal case the data is read by thread B before it is created by thread A.

(a)   (b)

Figure 10.6   A critical race situation caused by a change in speed of execution

A second type of critical race occurs when one thread unexpectedly changes data that is being operated on by another thread, resulting in incorrect results. This is illustrated in Figure 10.7.

Designers can prevent critical races by using various mechanisms that allow data items to be locked so that they cannot be accessed by other threads when they are not ready. One widely used locking mechanism is called a *semaphore*.

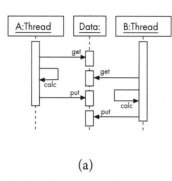
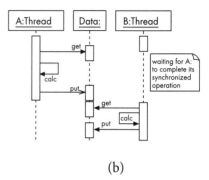

(a)   (b)

Figure 10.7   A critical race situation caused by a second thread unexpectedly accessing non-synchronized data

In Java, the **synchronized** keyword can be used to ensure that no other thread can access an object until the synchronized method terminates.

Unfortunately, overuse of locking can result in deadlocks or livelocks. Locking can also dramatically slow performance since it takes a lot of extra work to manipulate and check the locks.

Testing strategies   Testing for critical races is done using the same strategies as testing for deadlocks and livelocks. Once again, inspection is often a better solution.

It is particularly hard to test for critical races using black-box testing alone, since you often do not know the extent of the concurrency going on inside the system, and you cannot always manipulate the various threads to cause race conditions. The timing differences that can give rise to problems can be on the order of milliseconds. Therefore, even if you detect a critical race during testing, you may not be able to reproduce the problem reliably. One possible, although invasive, strategy is to deliberately slow down one of the threads by adding a call to the **sleep** method.

Exercise

E201   Write a short program to generate a critical race situation. Your program will start two threads that sleep for a random amount of time and then do a calculation based on a stored value. They also update the stored value. The result of the calculations should be different depending on which thread sleeps for the longest period of time. This exercise is designed to heighten your awareness of critical races, not to teach you good practice!

10.6 Defects in handling stress and unusual situations

The defects discussed in this section are encountered only when a system is being heavily used, or forced to its limits in some other way. These defects represent a lack of robustness. To test for such defects you must run the system intensively, supply it with a very large amount of input, run many copies of it, run it on a computer or network that is busy running other systems, and run it in atypical environments.

The following subsections give some of the most important categories of stress defects. Many of the kinds of defects discussed here are not explicitly discussed in typical requirements documents. However, they *should* be in the requirements since designers need to arrange explicitly for them to be handled, and testers need to write test cases for them.

Insufficient throughput or response time on minimal configurations

Defect A minimally configured platform is one that barely conforms to the environment specified in the requirements. It has exactly the minimum amount of memory and disk space specified, the slowest CPU, the oldest permitted release of the operating system and other support software, as well as the slowest allowed network connection.

It is a defect if, when the system is tested on a minimal configuration, its throughput or response time fails to meet requirements.

Testing strategy Perform testing using minimally configured platforms. For extra reliability, you could test the system in an environment that has a configuration that is worse than the minimum. In such conditions, it should report that it could not run properly.

Incompatibility with specific configurations of hardware or software

Defect It is extremely common for a system to work properly with certain configurations of hardware, operating systems and external libraries, but fail if it is run using other configurations.

Testing strategy Extensively execute the system with a wide variety of configurations that might be encountered by users. By a 'configuration' we mean a particular combination of hardware, operating system and other software.

Examples A system might fail if a different graphics card is installed, if certain fonts are missing, or a newer or older version of a web browser is installed.

Defects in handling peak loads or missing resources

Defects If a computer becomes short of resources such as memory, disk space or network bandwidth, then programs cannot be expected to continue running normally. However, it is a defect if the system does not gracefully handle such situations.

Other types of shortage of resources include missing files or data, lack of permission to perform certain operations, inability to start new threads, or running out of space in a fixed size data structure. Such problems might be temporary, resulting from a peak in the workload of the software system, of the computer or of the network. On the other hand, the problem might be more permanent, resulting from a failure of some other system.

No matter what the cause, the program being tested should report the problem in such a way that the user will understand. It should then either wait for the problem to be resolved, terminate gracefully or deal with the situation in some other sensible way.

Testing strategies In any of these cases, the tester has to deny the program under test the resources it normally uses, by employing such methods as deleting files, concurrently running other resource-hungry programs, making less memory available, or disconnecting the system from the network. The tester can also run a very large number of copies of the program being tested, all at the same time. To do this effectively, you have to write a special program called a *load generator* that constantly provides input to the system. Load generators are available commercially.

Inappropriate management of resources

Defect A program does not manage resources effectively if it uses certain resources but does not make them available to other programs when it no longer needs them.

Testing strategy Run the program intensively over a long period of time in such a way that it uses many resources, relinquishes them and then uses them again repeatedly.

Examples A program might open many files, but not close them so as to enable other programs to open them. Or a program might abusively consume a very large amount of bandwidth on a network.

A memory leak is a special case of in-appropriate management of resources. Programs written in C, C++ and certain other languages can request memory but not release it when it is no longer needed. If this occurs repeatedly and a program runs for an extended period of time, the computer can eventually begin to perform poorly or even run out of memory. To detect a memory leak, a tester has to run a program for an extended period, and use a utility (see the sidebar) that indicates the amount of memory being used. If the amount of memory steadily increases, this suggests that a memory leak is present.

Although memory leaks are a widespread problem in languages such as C++, you can also get a similar effect in Java if you add objects to an instance of some collection class, and then do not remove them when no longer needed – the garbage collector only removes objects that are not referenced by any other object.

Defects in the process of recovering from a crash

Defects Any system will undergo a sudden failure if its hardware fails, or if its power is turned off. When this occurs, it is a defect if the system is left in an unstable state and hence is unable to recover fully once the power is restored or the hardware

How to determine if a program has a memory leak

The most definitive way to determine whether a program has a memory leak is to run it for a period of time and watch how much memory it uses. If the amount of memory steadily increases, yet the application is not dealing with larger volumes of data, then there is probably a leak.

Most computers allow you to study the memory usage of a computer in detail. On Unix, Linux, and Mac OS X you can type `ps -aux` or `top` in a terminal window to get memory usage data. You can also find out the complete memory map of a process using `pmap` on Solaris systems. Several programs are available to do similar things in the Windows environment.

Besides the above, there are also software libraries that you can link with C or C++ code that replace the normal memory management utilities. These will allow you to obtain a listing of all blocks of allocated memory and make leaks easier to find. An example of such a package is Purify from IBM Rational Software http://www.ibm.com/software/awdtools/purify/.

repaired. It is also a defect if a system does not correctly deal with the crashes of related systems.

Testing strategies An approach for testing for defects in the recovery process is to kill either your program or the programs with which it communicates, at various times during execution. You could also try turning the power off; however, operating systems themselves are often intolerant of doing that.

Examples Unstable states occur when data is half-written, or if a client program does not detect that a server has been restarted.

It is often permissible for a system that recovers from a catastrophic failure to lose the data that was in the process of being entered. However, any earlier transactions should be fully recoverable.

Exercises

E202 Run the SimpleChat server (Phase 3 or higher) and connect a few clients to it. Then make the `passwords.txt` file write-protected so that the server cannot register new clients. Try to connect a new guest client. Does the server react in a sensible way?

E203 If you were designing the following types of software, what stress tests and unusual situations should you subject the system to?

(a) A new web browser.

(b) A flight simulator.

(c) The SimpleChat system.

(d) The GANA navigation system.

10.7 Documentation defects

In the previous sections we have discussed how to detect classes of defects that arise from errors on the part of designers. However, we pointed out at the beginning of the chapter that a failure occurs any time a user has difficulty – and one source of difficulty is using the documentation. You therefore need to 'test' the documentation carefully.

Defect The software has a defect if the user manual, reference manual or online help gives incorrect information or fails to give information relevant to a problem.

Testing strategy Examine all the end-user documentation (in both paper and online forms), making sure it is correct. In particular, make sure it has correct solutions to problems that users might encounter, and correct instructions to help beginners learn how to use the software. Work through the use cases, making sure that each of them is adequately explained to the user. You should use the strategies we discussed in Chapter 7 for evaluating usability: ask users to read the documentation and tell you what they do not understand or do not like.

10.8 Writing formal test cases and test plans

A *test case* is an explicit set of instructions designed to detect a particular class of defect in a software system, by bringing about a failure.

A test case can give rise to many *tests*. Each test is a particular run of the test case on a particular version of the system.

A *test plan* is a document that contains a complete set of test cases for a system, along with other information about the testing process. The test plan is one of the standard types of documentation that should be produced in most software engineering projects. If a project does not have a test plan, then testing will inevitably be done in an ad-hoc manner, leading to poor quality software.

The test plan should be written long before the testing starts. You can start to develop the test plan once you have developed the requirements. A set of use cases can help you design test cases, as discussed in Chapter 4.

Information to include in a formal test case

Each test case should have the following information:

A. **Identification and classification**. Each test case should have a number, and may also be given a descriptive title that indicates its purpose. The system, subsystem or module being tested should also be clearly indicated, with a reference to the related requirements and design documents. Finally, the importance of the test case should be indicated, as discussed in the next subsection.

B. **Instructions**. These tell the tester exactly what to do. The instructions must tell the tester how to put the system into the required initial state and what inputs to provide. The tester should not normally have to refer to the specifications or to any other documentation in order to execute the instructions.

C. **Expected result**. This tells the tester how the system should behave in response to the instructions – i.e. what it should output and what state it should then be in. The tester reports a failure if he or she does not encounter the expected result.

D. **Cleanup (when needed).** This tells the tester how to make the system go 'back to normal' or shut down after the test. For example, if a test case requires that some erroneous data be added to a database, then the cleanup section of the test case would require that the data be deleted (or that the database be reloaded from a backup) so as not to disrupt future tests.

Test cases can be organized into groups or tables, and some of the classification information and instructions can be associated with an entire group, rather than repeated for each test case.

It is becoming increasingly common to completely automate the testing process. Each test case then may become a method that throws an exception if the test fails. The same information described above would still be needed; for example, the test case method would need to report an identification of what failed.

Levels of importance of test cases

It is a good idea to classify test cases according to their importance, or severity level. The most important test cases are executed first, and are designed to detect the most severe classes of defect. A typical scheme for levels of importance is as follows, although each organization may develop its own scheme:

Level 1 First pass critical test cases. These are designed to verify that the system runs and is safe. Any level 1 failure normally means that no further testing is possible.

Level 2 General test cases. These verify that the system performs its day-to-day functions correctly and is therefore a 'success'. A level 2 failure, while important to fix, may still permit testing of other aspects of the system to continue in the meantime.

Level 3 Test cases of lesser importance. For example, these may test 'cosmetic' aspects of the user interface such as the whether a button or menu item is 'grayed out' when it cannot be used. If desired, level 3 test cases can also be used to provide some redundancy – for example, extra testing of additional combinations of input. If there are many failures of level 3 test cases then the system can probably be used, but is lacking in overall quality.

> **JUnit**
> JUnit is a Java framework for automated testing. It is becoming widely used among Java developers. See http://junit.org.

Determining test cases by enumerating attributes

It is important that the test cases test every aspect of the requirements. Each detail in the requirements is called an *attribute* – an attribute can be thought of as something that is testable. A good first step when creating a set of test cases is to *enumerate* the attributes.

A simple approach to enumerating attributes is to circle all the important points in the requirements document. However, there are often many attributes that are *implicit*. For example, the requirements may simply state that the look and feel of a program will conform to Microsoft Windows look and feel guidelines. That means that the guidelines contain hundreds of implicit attributes to be tested. The requirements may be silent about all the various versions of software and hardware on which the system should run, and will probably not mention that the program should have no memory leaks. Nevertheless, these should be considered attributes, since a good test plan will include test cases to detect these situations.

Structuring the requirements as a set of use cases (using the format discussed in Chapter 4) can often make the explicit attributes easy to determine. For example, the system's responses to each step performed by the user become attributes, as do the postconditions. Since exceptional situations are listed as separate use cases, these give rise to their own sets of attributes.

Once you have determined the attributes, the next thing to do is to think of all the various tests you need to create to actually test the attributes. You will need to consider equivalence class and boundary tests, as well as tests that try to discover the sets of defects discussed in the last few sections.

Example 10.2 *Create a list of attributes for the following example: a dialog box is to be displayed when the user quits an email program before sending a message he or she is composing. The dialog is to say, 'You have not yet sent your mail, do you want to send it before quitting?' The user has the option of selecting, 'Cancel', 'Send then quit', or 'Quit without sending'. The last is the default.*

Here are some of the testable attributes of this example. Most of these are implicit. These would expand into a much longer list of test cases.

- Are the three buttons lined up at the bottom of the screen?

- Does the dialog box follow the standard appearance of the platform?

- Is the 'Quit without sending' button darkened, indicating that it is the default, and is its action taken when the user hits the return key?

- Can the user (in Windows) press the ALT key plus a letter to invoke any of the options without the mouse?

- Does the dialog box fail to appear when the user quits while not in the middle of composing mail?

- Does the dialog box appear when the user has just started composing mail, but has not yet typed anything? (The requirements need clarifying about this – note that it is not sensible to actually send such a message.)

- Are 'tool tips' displayed when the user passes the mouse over each button?

- When each button is clicked, does it do what it says it will do?

- Does the system behave reasonably when the user selects 'Send then quit', but the system encounters an error when trying to send (the requirements are unclear whether the quitting is abandoned or not)?

- Does the system behave reasonably if the user tries to switch to another program while this dialog is displayed?

- Does the system behave reasonably when the dialog box is brought up and dismissed many times (this helps detect memory leaks)?

Example 10.3   *Discuss the attributes that will need to be tested to test a method with the following specification: method* `mutPrime(x,y)` *takes two* `int` *values and returns* `true` *if* `x` *and* `y` *are mutually prime (have no common divisors except 1) and returns* `false` *otherwise.*

It will be necessary to test situations in which either or both of `x` and `y` are a) equal to one, b) equal to zero, c) negative, d) prime, e) non-prime, but mutually prime with respect to the other, and f) non-mutually-prime.

Exercises

E204   Write four complete test cases for each of the testing situations listed in Exercise E198.

E205   Expand Table 10.3 into a complete test plan.

Test-first development

It has always been recommended to develop test cases well before testing starts. However, there is a trend now towards developing test cases even earlier, and using the process to *drive* design and programming. This is particularly popular when following an agile process.

In *test-first development* you first write an automated set of tests for the next iteration of development. Then you design and write the code such that the tests will pass. The tests are therefore basically a re-stating of the requirements in an automated, testable form. In agile test-first development, the tests may actually be the only way that the requirements are stated in detail.

Testing programs versus proving programs correct

When engineering artifacts are built, engineers try to use analysis techniques to *prove* that they will behave as expected. As engineering has advanced, engineers have learned increasingly sophisticated analysis techniques. In the early days of aviation, for example, it was essential to experiment with and extensively test new aircraft to make sure they flew properly. Today, we understand how to analyze and simulate aerodynamics so well that engineers can be confident that a new aircraft will fly properly when it first takes off. Some testing is still performed in case the analytical and simulation techniques (or control software) have defects, but the time and cost to test a new aircraft is greatly reduced.

Many people yearn for the day when we will be able to use similarly powerful analytic techniques to prove that software adheres to its specifications, and that we will thus be able to reduce the need for software testing. In fact, there are tools that allow you to prove certain assertions about programs, although there are some things that cannot be completely proved, such as whether an arbitrary program will terminate.

However, economics dictate that the extra effort to prove most programs correct is currently not worth the benefits. This is because the analytic techniques for software are labor-intensive, and testing is relatively cheap. This contrasts with testing aircraft, where a failure results in an expensive crash. Formal proof techniques should, however, be used for safety-critical software – such as an aircraft's control software.

A recommended practice in test-first development is to run the test cases prior to developing the code. This helps test the test cases themselves – they should all, of course, fail at this point.

A key advantage of test-first development is that writing the automated tests helps ensure the requirements are properly understood.

10.9 Strategies for testing large systems

In the earlier sections we have discussed the kinds of defects to find, as well as how to write clear and effective test cases. But what strategy should you use to test an entire system that has many subsystems and thousands of test cases? In this section we discuss several approaches to testing such a system.

Integration testing: big bang versus incremental approaches

Testing how the parts of a system or subsystem work together is commonly called *integration testing*. It can be contrasted with *unit testing*, which is testing an individual module or component in isolation.

The simplest approach to integration testing is *big bang* testing. In this approach, you take the entire integrated system and test it all at once. This strategy can be satisfactory when testing a small system; however, when a failure occurs while testing a larger system, it may be hard to tell in which subsystem a defect lies.

A better integration testing strategy in most cases is *incremental testing*. In this approach, you first test each individual subsystem in isolation, and then continue testing as you integrate more and more subsystems.

The big advantage of incremental testing is that when you encounter a failure, you can find the defect more easily. You know it is most likely to be in the subsystem you most recently added.

Incremental testing can be performed *horizontally* or *vertically*, depending on the architecture of the system. Horizontal testing can be used when the system is divided into separate sub-applications, such as 'adding new products' and 'selling products'; you simply test each sub-application in isolation. However, for any sub-application that is complex, it is necessary to divide it up vertically into layers.

There are several strategies for vertical incremental testing: top-down, bottom-up and sandwich. The various strategies are illustrated in Figure 10.8.

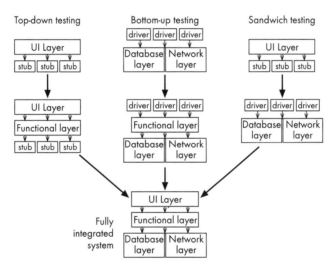

Figure 10.8   Vertical strategies for incremental integration testing

Top-down testing

In top-down testing, you start by testing only the user interface, with the underlying functionality simulated by *stubs*. Then you work downwards, integrating lower and lower layers, each time creating stubs for the layers that remain un-integrated. As you integrate each lower layer, you test the system again.

Stubs are pieces of code that have the same interface (i.e. API) as the lower-level layers, but which do not perform any real computations or manipulate any real data. Any call to a stub will typically immediately return with a fixed default value.

If a defect is detected while performing top-down testing, the tester can be reasonably confident that the defect is in the layer that calls the stubs. It could also be in the stubs, but that is less likely since stubs are so simple.

The big drawback to top-down testing is the cost of writing the stubs. However, there are a few automated testing tools that can help generate skeleton code for stubs, relieving the software engineer of some of the tedium of writing them.

Bottom-up testing

To perform bottom-up testing, you start by testing the very lowest levels of the software. This might include a database layer, a network layer, a layer that performs some algorithmic computation, or a set of utilities of some kind.

You need *drivers* to test the lower layers of software. Drivers are simple programs designed specifically for testing; they make calls to the lower layers. Drivers in bottom-up testing have a similar role to stubs in top-down testing, and are time-consuming to write. A driver that fully automates the testing of lower layers is called a *test harness*.

Example 10.4   *Drivers to test OCSF.*

Because of the infinite number of possibilities in the chaining of events, writing a complete set of independent test cases that would exhaustively test the OCSF framework is not possible. The glass-box testing described in Example 10.1 tests several crucial aspects of the framework that might not be thought of in black-box testing. But, as mentioned in that example, it is impossible to cover all paths using glass-box testing. Also, timing and co-ordination failures are more likely to occur under stress situations where several clients are connected; therefore the robustness of the server in these cases has to be assessed.

We have therefore written a test harness consisting of two drivers. This simulates a SimpleChat session where several clients connect to the server and exchange messages. These drivers bypass the user interfaces normally used by end users. They automate the execution of several timing, co-ordination and stress test cases.

On the server side, the `EchoServer` class written using OCSF is put under the control of the first driver. This driver simply calls the service methods, causing the server to transition from one state to another (see Figure 3.3 on page 82). It uses the following sequence of actions in order to take all possible transitions: Listen–Close–Listen–Stop–Close–Listen–Stop. This sequence is infinitely repeated, the server staying in each state for a random period of time. A complete log of all server actions, including any exceptions thrown, is displayed for the tester.

The role of the second driver is to randomly generate and control a set of clients. A `Frame` containing information about each created client is displayed on a grid (Figure 10.9). At random intervals, the client driver takes one of the following actions:

■ It creates a new client and connects it to the server. Information about this client is put in a panel of the grid that is not already running a client.

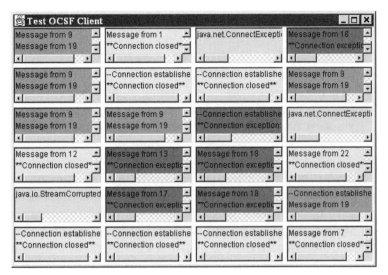

Figure 10.9   Test driver for the OCSF client

- It randomly selects a client and makes it send a message (the simple string 'Message from X', where X is the grid number).

- It disconnects a random client.

Figure 10.9 is a snapshot of the client driver window. A color convention has been used to help identify each client's state (although the colors are shown here using shades of gray).

At the time the snapshot was taken, six clients were simultaneously connected – these are shown in medium-gray. The panels in dark gray correspond to clients that have been killed by the server. The panels in light gray show other situations such as when the client closed itself, or unsuccessfully attempted to connect. Any exceptions thrown by the OCSF `AbstractClient` class while trying to connect, disconnect or send messages are also displayed in the corresponding panel.

To perform a more severe stress test, the client side of this testing system should be run simultaneously on several machines. The two drivers can be found on the book's web site (www.lloseng.com). You should experiment with these to learn about how to write and use test drivers.

Sandwich testing

Sandwich testing is a hybrid between bottom-up and top-down testing – it is sometimes therefore called *mixed testing*. A typical approach to sandwich testing is to test the user interface in isolation, using stubs, and also to test the very lowest-level functions, using drivers. Then, when the complete system is integrated, only the middle layer remains on which to perform the final set of tests.

For many systems, sandwich testing will be the most effective form of integration testing.

The test–fix–test cycle and regression testing

When a failure occurs during testing or after deployment, most organizations follow a carefully planned process. Each failure report is entered into a failure tracking system. It is then is screened and assigned a priority. It is often too expensive to fix every defect, therefore low-priority failures might be put on a *known bugs list* that is included with the software's *release notes*. Some failure reports might be merged if they appear to result from the same defects.

When a decision is made to resolve a failure, somebody is assigned to investigate it, track down the defect or defects that caused it, and fix those defects. Finally a new version of the system is created, ready to be tested again.

Unfortunately, there is a high probability that efforts to remove defects will actually add new ones – either because the maintainer tries to fix problems without fully understanding the ramifications of the changes, or because he or she makes ordinary human errors. This phenomenon is known as the *ripple effect*, because new defects caused by erroneous fixes of other defects tend to spread through a system like a ripple. The system regresses into a more and more failure-prone state.

You can minimize the ripple effect by applying a very disciplined approach to the process of fixing defects. For example, you can perform *impact analysis* to carefully explore and document all possible effects of a change. You can then have others inspect each change before it is made. However, experience shows that the ripple effect will still persist if you do not have an appropriate testing strategy.

After making any change, you must therefore not only re-run the test case that led to the detection of the defect, but you must also re-test the rest of the system's functionality. This latter process is called *regression testing*. It is normally far too expensive to re-run every single test case whenever a change is made to software, so regression testing involves running a subset of the original test cases. The regression tests are carefully selected to cover as much of the system as possible.

Deciding when to stop testing

You might imagine that you should go on re-testing software until all the test cases have passed. Unfortunately, this is not a practical approach. For the reasons discussed in the last subsection, it is too expensive, and perhaps futile, to try to remove every last bug from most systems. Perfection will normally remain forever elusive.

However, it is also a poor strategy to stop testing merely because you have run out of time or money. This will result in a poor-quality system.

You should, instead, establish a set of criteria like the following to decide when testing should be considered complete:

- All of the level 1 test cases must have been successfully executed.

- Certain predefined percentages of level 2 and level 3 test cases must have been executed successfully. Suitable levels will vary from system to system. In a non-critical system used by a small number of people, test case pass targets of 95% for level 2 and 75% for level 3 might be appropriate. In a more critical system, or one used by a large number of people, then test case pass targets of 99% for level 2 and 90% for

> **The law of conservation of bugs**
> The 'law of conservation of bugs' states that the number of bugs remaining in a large system is proportional to the number of bugs already fixed. In other words, a defect-ridden system will always tend to remain a defect-ridden system. This is because a poorly designed system will not only have more defects to start with, but will also be harder to fix correctly and hence will suffer more strongly from the ripple effect.

level 3 might be set. Ultimately the targets will depend on the cost of failures versus the cost of continued testing and fixing of defects.

- The targets must have been achieved and then maintained for at least two cycles of 'builds'. A *build* involves compiling and integrating all the components of the software, incorporating any changes since the last build. Many organizations do this on a daily or weekly basis; they then perform regression testing on the build. Failure rates can fluctuate from build to build as different sets of regression tests are run or new defects are introduced. It might be by chance that the targets are reached one day but are not met the next day.

The roles of people involved in testing

Testing is an intellectual exercise that is just as challenging and creative as design. All software engineers should develop their testing skills, although some have a particular talent for testing and may specialize in it.

In a software development organization, the first pass of unit and integration testing is often called *developer testing*. This is preliminary testing performed by the software developers who do the design and programming. Organizations should then employ an *independent testing group* that runs the complete set of test cases, seeking defects left by the developers.

An advantage of having a separate group perform testing is that they do not have a vested interest in seeing as many test cases pass as possible. Although it would be unprofessional for developers to claim that a test case has passed when it has not, they may nevertheless be less hard on themselves than an independent group. Also, an independent group that specializes in testing will develop specific expertise in how to do good testing, and how to use testing tools.

Testing performed by users and clients: alpha, beta and acceptance

So far, our discussion of testing has assumed that it is performed by software engineers in the development organization. However, the testing process also normally involves users. We have already seen in Chapter 7 that users should be heavily involved in testing and evaluating prototypes. In this section we will discuss the involvement of users in testing versions of the system that are almost ready to be put into production. Such testing should occur once the developers believe that the software has reached a sufficient level of quality (it is approaching the quality targets specified in the non-functional requirements).

Alpha testing is testing performed by users and clients, under the supervision of the software development team. The development team normally invites some users to work with the software and to watch for problems that they encounter.

Beta testing is testing performed by the user or client in their normal work environment. It can be initiated either at the request of the software developers, or at the request of users who want to try the system out. Beta testers are selected from the potential user population and given a pre-release version of the software. They know that the software will contain more defects than the final version, but they have the benefit of using the features of the software before others have access to them. Beta testers are responsible for reporting problems when they discover them.

The advantages of alpha and beta testing are the following. You typically are able to have a much larger volume of testing performed, and the users use the software in the same manner that they will use it when it is formally released. Very often, the users do things that the developers of the test plan never anticipated; hence users encounter failures that no test case was written to detect. In the worst case, discovery of these defects during alpha and beta testing may require major changes to the software – but it is better that the defects be found at this stage, rather than following the software's general release.

Some organizations rely very heavily on beta testing, and will release low-quality software to the general population in what is called an *open beta release*. If the software is in heavy demand, this can result in the effective discovery of problems. It may make economic sense to do this from the perspective of the developers, but it is not good engineering practice. It results in wasted time on the part of the users, since many people will discover the same problems. It can also damage the reputation of the developers if many failures occur.

Acceptance testing, like alpha and beta testing, is performed by users and customers. However, the customers do it on their own initiative – to decide whether software is of sufficient quality to purchase. Many large organizations also perform acceptance testing before they will pay a developer they have contracted to develop custom software for them. Other organizations use acceptance testing in order to choose between several competing generic products.

Exercise

E206 Discuss how integration testing could be performed in the SimpleChat system. What stubs or drivers could be written to permit separate testing of individual layers?

Object-oriented testing

All of the testing strategies we have discussed work just as well for object-oriented software as for non-OO software. Nevertheless, there is a special set of techniques called object-oriented testing. These techniques focus on the properties of object-oriented programs. Examples include:

■ Writing methods within each class to act as drivers that will test the methods of that class. We mentioned this in the discussion of Design Principle 10 in the last chapter.

■ Testing to ensure that the behavior of a subclass is consistent with the behavior of its superclass. This can be done by running, in each subclass, the driver methods of the superclass.

10.10 Inspections

An inspection is an activity in which one or more people systematically examine source code or documentation, looking for defects. Normally, inspection involves a meeting, although participants can also inspect alone at their desks.

Roles on inspection teams

Typically an inspection team will consist of software engineers, who fill the following roles:

■ The *author*.

■ A *moderator*. This person calls and runs the meeting and makes sure that the general principles of inspection are adhered to. These principles are discussed in the next subsection.

■ A *secretary*. He or she is responsible for recording the defects when they are found. This is not an office administrative assistant, but rather a software engineer just like the other inspectors. It takes a thorough knowledge of software engineering to understand and record defects.

■ *Paraphrasers*. These people will step through the document explaining it in their own words. We will explain the paraphrasing process in more detail below.

In a small inspection team, an individual can perform more than one of the latter three roles.

Principles of inspecting

Some general principles of inspecting are as follows:

■ **Inspect the most important documents of each type**. Inspection should be performed on code, design documents, test plans and requirements. It is not always necessary or economical to inspect every single piece of code or every document, but the most important ones should certainly be inspected. Quality will be higher if more are inspected, but costs will also be higher. When inspecting code, all aspects of code should be considered, including the comments.

- **Choose an effective and efficient inspection team**. Two or more people should participate in an inspection, since more pairs of eyes are better than one. However it is uneconomical to have a very large number of people involved; between two and five people (including the author) is probably a good range; the exact number can depend on the importance of the item being inspected. The inspection team should include experienced software engineers, who are more likely to uncover defects.

- **Require that participants prepare for inspections**. The inspection team should study the code or other documents prior to the meeting and come prepared with a list of defects. If a participant has not prepared, then he or she will spend most of his or her mental energy at the inspection meeting trying to understand the document, rather than helping to find defects.

- **Only inspect documents that are ready**. Inspections should be held once specifications, design documents or code are believed by their authors to be final. However, when preparing for an inspection meeting, the inspectors might immediately realize that the document represents very poor design, that its layout is messy and hard to read, or that it needs some other major change; in these circumstances it is probably best to call off the meeting. The author should be asked to make changes before a new attempt is made at inspection. Attempting to inspect a very poor document will result in defects being missed – and the document will have to be re-inspected anyway.

- **Have 'finding defects' as the only goal**. It is best not to mix inspection meetings with meetings in which other activities are involved. For example, if you are inspecting code, you should not at the same time be teaching newcomers how the system works. Having the secondary goal would detract from the primary goal, which is to find defects. You should also not mix inspections with meetings whose primary role is to make decisions. For example, requirements and design reviews are often arranged so that the teams can debate alternatives – doing this should not be confused with inspecting.

- **Avoid discussing how to fix defects**. Fixing defects is a design issue that can be left to the author. There is no need to consume the time of the entire team during the meeting. If the author needs help with a particular defect, he or she can always ask for it later.

- **Avoid discussing style issues**. It is important that inspections do not become bogged down debating such issues as the naming convention used for variables, or whether the '{' and '}' should always line up with each other vertically or not. Issues such as these may be important, but should be discussed separately, in the context of the project as a whole. A good rule of thumb is the following: an issue should be raised in an inspection meeting only if it may represent a defect. Note, however, that bad style is often a maintainability defect.

- **Do not rush the inspection process**. The schedule should be arranged so that there is time both to complete the necessary inspections and to fix the defects found. A common problem is to be rushing to meet deadlines and hence to skip inspection or to fail to properly fix the defects found. A good speed to inspect is about 200 lines of code per hour (including comments), or ten pages of text per hour.

- **Avoid making participants tired**. Since inspection is very mentally taxing, it is best not to inspect for more than two hours at a time, or for more than four hours a day.

- **Keep and use logs of inspections**. Logs of inspections should be kept. These will list what was inspected and the defects found. Follow-up should be done after every inspection session to ensure that all the defects have, in fact, been resolved. You can also use the logs to track the quality of the design process – ideally as a team gets better at design, the number of defects found per line of code will decrease.

- **Re-inspect when changes are made**. You should re-inspect any document or code that is changed more than 20% for any reason; for example, as a result of adding new features, or fixing problems arising from testing or inspection.

A peer-review process: managers are normally not involved

It is common practice to exclude managers from inspection activities, that is, to have inspections performed only by the peers of the author. The rationale for this is that it may allow the participants to express their criticisms more openly, not fearing repercussions from the manager.

In small organizations, however, there may not be enough people to perform inspections if the manager is not involved. Also, if the team members are professional in their work practices, then management involvement may have no negative consequences. It may also be beneficial for managers to participate since it can help them stay involved in the team's work and hence make better management decisions.

Whether or not a manager participates in inspections, the members of an inspection team should feel they are all working together to create a better document. The author should be made to feel comfortable, and not 'blamed' when defects are found.

Conducting an inspection meeting

The following is a suggested approach to running an inspection meeting:

1. The moderator calls the meeting and distributes the documents to be inspected.

2. As mentioned above, the participants prepare for the meeting in advance.

3. At the start of the meeting, the moderator explains the procedures and verifies that everybody has prepared.

4. At the meeting, paraphrasers take turns explaining the contents of the document or code, without reading it verbatim. Paraphrasing forces everybody to *think* about what they are reading; merely reading verbatim can become a mindless exercise that can be done while almost asleep. Requiring that the paraphraser not be the author ensures that the paraphraser says what he or she *sees*, rather than what the author *intended* to say. Differences between these two views will therefore become clear and thus highlight defects. The author, in particular, may notice the paraphraser say something different from what he or she thought was written.

5. Everybody speaks up when they notice a defect or when the paraphrasing reaches a defect that they had found while preparing. There may be a very brief discussion to ensure that it really is a defect, and then the secretary makes a record of it. After this, paraphrasing continues.

As an alternative to paraphrasing, the inspectors can simply walk through the lists of defects found while each member was preparing. Some organizations even dispense with meetings entirely, and have the moderator gather lists of defects produced by individual inspectors working alone.

Inspecting compared to testing

Inspection is a quality assurance activity that is complementary to testing:

■ Both testing and inspection rely on different aspects of human intelligence. To test effectively, testers have to develop a good set of test cases. They need an aptitude for thinking of what could go wrong without actually studying the software. In an inspection meeting, on the other hand, the participants have to uncover defects by understanding what would happen if the system were run – they have to mentally *execute* the software. Both activities require attention to detail, and people can make mistakes in both activities. However, the chances of mistakes are reduced if both activities are performed, since chances of the same defect slipping by both activities are greatly reduced.

■ Testing can find defects whose consequences are obvious but which are buried in complex code, and thus will be hard to detect when inspecting. Inspecting, on the other hand, can more easily find defects whose consequences might be subtle; hence the tester might not have thought to test for them. They become clear when reading the source code or design documents.

■ Inspecting can find defects that relate to maintainability or efficiency that are not readily detectable when testing. For example, a tester may observe that the results of a computation take one second. He or she may not be able to tell, without inspecting the code, that an inefficient algorithm is being used, and that the computation time could be dramatically reduced by changing the code. Similarly, very messy code might work adequately when tested; but the maintainability problems would only be noted during an inspection.

Testing or inspecting, which comes first?

It is important to inspect software *before* extensively testing it. This considerably speeds up the overall verification process. The reason for this is that inspecting allows you to get rid of many defects quickly. Not only would testing take a lot longer to find the same number of defects, but then every one of them must be individually investigated and fixed. Also, if you test before inspecting, and the inspectors then recommend that redesign is needed, the testing work has been wasted.

There is a growing consensus that it is most efficient to inspect software before any testing is done – even before developer testing.

Exercise

E207 Working in groups of four or five, conduct inspections of some code and documents you have produced while working on the exercises in this book. Each member of the group should have their turn as author, presenting the group with one item of about 100 lines of code or five pages of text. The members of the group should exchange material several days before the inspection meeting. Group members should prepare for the meeting by making sure they understand what is to be inspected. The meetings themselves, which should last for about half an hour for each author, should be conducted as discussed above. The role of moderator can be rotated among the various group members. The deliverables from this exercise are the inspection logs.

10.11 Quality assurance in general

In this chapter, so far, we have looked at two important and inter-related approaches to ensuring the quality of software: testing and inspecting. Both of these are disciplined processes that software engineers and their organizations should implement.

Quality assurance should, however, be an activity that pervades all aspects of software development. In Chapter 4, for example, we discussed how you can review requirements to ensure that they are valid.

In the following subsections we will look at some other things that can be done to help increase software quality.

Root cause analysis

The objective of root cause analysis is to determine why a software engineer made the error that resulted in a defect occurring. It might have been simple human error – it will never be possible to completely prevent all such errors. However, often there are one or more root causes that you can correct in order to reduce the number of errors made.

The following are examples of root causes.

■ Lack of training and experience.

■ Schedules that are too tight.

■ Building on poor designs or reusable technology.

There are other possible root causes, including unanticipated design complexity, failure to adhere to design or management principles, lack of discipline in the process, failure to properly review requirements and designs, and failure to keep track of the details of the project. These, however, are often not root causes, but rather are due to lack of training and experience. Even too-tight schedules and building on poor designs are signs of project management failure, and hence have lack of training or experience as the ultimate root cause.

Measuring quality as a means to strive for continuous improvement

It is essential to measure quality of both the product and the process. This allows you to plot the quality over a period of time and to determine whether it is improving or not. Measuring quality allows you to set objectives for quality improvement and to motivate yourself and others to meet those objectives.

Two historic software failures that could have been prevented

Better quality assurance could have prevented a number of high-profile disasters, such as the following. To learn more, see the 'For more information' section.

■ **Therac-25**. The Therac-25 was a machine designed for radiation therapy in cancer patients. Unfortunately, a software defect resulted in it delivering far more radiation than intended under certain circumstances, with several resulting deaths.

■ **Ariane-5**. In 1996 the first flight of the $500 million French Ariane-5 Launcher failed due to a software defect. The failure occurred due to an attempt to fit an integer greater than 2^{15} into a 16-bit integer. That, in turn, was caused by reusing an older piece of code without verifying that the code would work properly in the new release

Entire books have been written about metrics; the following are some of the things you can measure regarding the quality of a software product, and indirectly of the quality of the process.

■ The number of failures encountered by users.

■ The number of failures found when testing a product.

■ The number of defects found when inspecting a product.

■ The percentage of code that is reused (more is better, but don't count clones).

■ The number of questions posed by users to the help-desk (as a measure of usability and the quality of documentation).

You can compare how these change over time. You can also compare the quality of two systems, after normalizing by dividing by the size of the system.

Post-mortem analysis

Post-mortem analysis involves looking back at a project after it is complete, or after a release. You look at the design and the development process and identify those aspects, which, with benefit of hindsight, you could have done better. You then make plans to do better next time.

Process standards

Organizations can collectively improve software quality by following the guidelines found in several different standards. The following is a list of standardized approaches; the first three of these were developed at the Software Engineering Institute of Carnegie Mellon University.

Spectacular software successes

In several places in this book we have pointed to software projects or systems that have failed and resulted in disasters. However, the quality and reliability of many systems is remarkable. The software that runs the space shuttle is a key example: although shuttles have suffered tragic accidents, the software that controls all aspects of space flight has worked with flying colors, despite its incredible complexity. The shuttle software team was one of the first to achieve a CMM level 5 rating. Highly reliable and complex software also controls airplanes, railway systems, telecommunications systems and banking systems. Failures of hardware tend to be at least as common as software failures in these types of systems.

- **The Personal Software Process** (PSP™). This defines a disciplined approach that an individual software developer can use to improve the quality and efficiency of his or her personal work. Two of the key tenets of the psp are personally inspecting your own work, and measuring the progress you make towards improving the quality of your work.

- **The Team Software Process** (TSP™). This describes how teams of software engineers can work together effectively.

- **The Software Capability Maturity Model** (CMM™). This contains five levels. Organizations start at level 1, and as their processes become better they can move up towards level 5.

- **ISO 9000-3**. This is an international standard that lists a large number of things an organization should do to improve its overall software process.

These standards include testing and inspecting among the things to do; however, they include a great many other best practices as well. In this book we do not have the space to discuss these standards in detail, but references to these and other standards are found in the 'For more information' section at the end of the chapter.

Any practicing software engineer should have a good understanding of these standards and their suitability for his or her organization.

10.12 Test cases for phase 2 of the SimpleChat instant messaging system

On the book's web site (http://www.lloseng.com) you will find a complete set of test cases to test Phases 1 and 2 of SimpleChat. The following is a selection of those test cases.

General setup for test cases in the 2000 series

System: SimpleChat/ocsf   Phase: 2
Instructions:

1. Install Java, minimum release 1.2.0, on Windows 95, 98 or ME.

2. Install Java, minimum release 1.2.0, on Windows NT or 2000.

3. Install Java, minimum release 1.2.0, on a Solaris system.

4. Install the SimpleChat – Phase 2 on each of the above platforms.

Test Case 2001
System: SimpleChat   Phase: 2
Server startup check with default arguments
Severity: 1
Instructions:

1. At the console, enter: `java EchoServer`.

Expected result:

1. The server reports that it is listening for clients by displaying the following message:
   `Server listening for clients on port 5555`

2. The server console waits for user input.

Cleanup:

1. Hit ctrl+c to kill the server.

Test Case 2002
System: SimpleChat   Phase: 2
Client startup check without a login
Severity: 1
Instructions:

1. At the console, enter: `java ClientConsole`.

Expected result:

1. The client reports it cannot connect without a login by displaying:
   `ERROR - No login ID specified. Connection aborted.`

2. The client terminates.

Cleanup: (if client is still active)

1. Hit ctrl+c to kill the client.

Test Case 2003
System: SimpleChat   Phase: 2
Client startup check with a login and without a server
Severity: 1
Instructions:

1. At the console, enter: `java ClientConsole <loginID>` where `<loginID>` is the name you wish to be identified by.

Expected result:

1. The client reports it cannot connect to a server by displaying:
   `Cannot open connection. Awaiting command.`

2. The client waits for user input

Cleanup: (if client is still active)

1. Hit ctrl+c to kill the client.

Test Case 2007
System: SimpleChat   Phase: 2
Server termination command check
Severity: 2
Instructions:

1. Start a server (Test Case 2001 instruction 1) using default arguments.

2. Type #quit into the server's console.

Expected result:

1. The server quits.

Cleanup: (If the server is still active):

1. Hit ctrl+c to kill the server.

Test Case 2013
System: SimpleChat   Phase: 2
Client host and port setup commands check

Severity: 2
Instructions:

1. Start a client without a server (Test Case 2003).

2. At the client's console, type #sethost <newhost> where <newhost> is the name of a computer on the network.

3. At the client's console, type #setport 1234.

Expected result:

1. The client displays
   Host set to: <newhost>
   Port set to: 1234.

Cleanup:

1. Type #quit to kill the client.

Test Case 2016
System: SimpleChat   Phase: 2
Multiple remote client disconnections and re-connections
Severity: 2
Instructions:

1. Start a server (Test Case 2001, instruction 1).

2. On different computers, start clients (1 or 2 per computer) and connect them to the server.

3. Exchange data among all the clients and the server.

4. Close the server using the #close command.

5. Change the server's listening port by using the #setport <newport> command.

6. Restart the server using the #start command.

7. Change the ports of the clients, using #setport, to correspond to the new port of the server.

8. Reconnect the clients to the server by using the #login <loginID> command.

Expected results:

1. The first set of connections occur normally.

2. When the server is closed, all clients are disconnected.

3. The server displays the following message when the #setport command is used:
   port set to: <newport>.

4. The server restarts and displays:
   `Server listening for connections on port <newport>.`

5. The clients change port as in Test Case 2013.

6. The clients reconnect normally.

Cleanup:

1. Type #quit to kill the clients.

2. Type #quit to kill the server.

Test Case 2017
System: SimpleChat   Phase: 2
Client changing hosts
Severity: 2
Instructions:

1. On two different computers, start servers on the default port.

2. On a third computer, start a client and connect it to one of the two servers.

3. Logoff from that server using the #logoff command.

4. Change the host name by using the #sethost <otherhost> where <otherhost> is the name of the computer running the other server.

5. Log the client on again using the #login <loginID> command.

Expected results:

1. The two servers start up normally.

2. The client connects to the first server normally.

3. When the client disconnects it displays
   `Connection closed.`

4. When the client disconnects, the server displays:
   `<loginID> has disconnected.`

5. The client changes host as in Test Case 2013.

6. The client reconnects normally as in Test Case 2016.

Cleanup (Unless proceeding to Test Case 2018):

1. Type #quit to kill the servers.

2. Type #quit to kill the client.

> **Test Case 2019**
> System: SimpleChat   Phase: 2
> **Different platform tests**
> Severity: 3
> Instructions:
>
> 1. Repeat test cases 2001 to 2018 on Windows 95, 98, NT or 2000, and Solaris.
>
> **Expected results:**
>
> 1. The same as before.

10.13 Difficulties and risks in quality assurance

- **It is very easy to forget to test some aspects of a software system**. In some projects, the team members feel that 'running the code a few times' is sufficient. Even when a formal test plan is in place, testers often forget to do such things as stress tests and documentation tests. Forgetting certain types of tests diminishes the system's quality.

  Resolution. Use all the testing strategies described in this chapter.

- **There is a conflict between achieving adequate quality levels, and 'getting the product out of the door'**. Although almost everybody recognizes the importance of quality, those activities that can ensure quality are often sacrificed in order to meet deadlines. In particular, companies often judge developers or project managers purely on when they deliver product, not on its quality level. Quality assurance activities are often seen as an overhead expense to be reduced. The result is poor-quality software.

  Resolution. Create a separate department to oversee quality assurance. Publish statistics about quality (within the organization) so that people will be motivated to increase their quality. Build adequate time for all quality assurance activities into the schedule. Consider quality assurance to be an integral and ongoing part of development. Publish cost–benefit analyses to demonstrate to everyone that deadlines should not override a need for quality.

- **People have different abilities and knowledge when it comes to quality**. Some people have a natural tendency to pay attention to detail, whereas other people are better at seeing the 'big picture'. When it comes to testing, the former people might help uncover more problems. Many people are not trained adequately in various aspects of quality, particularly usability and maintainability.

  Resolution. Give people tasks that fit their natural personalities. Train people in testing and inspecting techniques. Give people feedback about their performance in terms of producing quality software so that they have something measurable to improve. Have developers and maintainers work for several months on a testing team; this will heighten their awareness of quality problems they should avoid when they return to designing software.

10.14 Summary

In this chapter we have given you an overview of several important strategies for efficiently verifying that a system is of sufficient quality, as well as for supporting quality development more generally.

We discussed key terminology, in particular that human errors cause defects, and defects cause failures.

We then looked at strategies for testing. Black-box testing allows you only to control a system's inputs and observe its outputs, whereas glass-box (or white-box) testing allows you to examine the system's internals. Big bang testing involves testing an integrated system all at once, whereas incremental approaches to integration testing involve first testing individual subsystems, and then testing repeatedly as subsystems are put together to create the complete system.

Testing a selected member of each equivalence class, as well as equivalence class boundaries, allows you to detect different defects without exhaustively trying all possible inputs. However, determining suitable equivalence classes is hard. In particular, it is necessary to apply knowledge of the most common types of defects and program design strategies. Typical types of defects to seek include algorithmic defects (such as incorrect logical conditions, or not handling null conditions), defects in which the system cannot handle stress, and defects resulting from failure to adhere to standards.

We discussed how to systematically write both test cases and complete test plans, and to consider test-first development where an automated test plan is used to drive development. We also pointed out that it is important to plan in advance when to stop testing. In addition, we looked at regression testing, which is testing with a subset of tests when the system is changed, alpha testing, which is testing by users under the supervision of developers, and beta testing, which is testing by users in their own environment.

Inspections are another way of verifying software that should be used in conjunction with, and prior to, testing. We suggested a strategy for inspection that involves a team. Team members include the author, a paraphraser and a moderator. The paraphraser proceeds through the code or other documents, explaining the material in his or her own words. The Personal Software Process is a disciplined approach to individual software development that, among other things, emphasizes careful inspection of your own work.

Finally, we looked at quality assurance as a whole, including the notion of continuous improvement.

10.15 For more information

Software quality assurance in general

- Hotlist about software quality assurance and process improvement: http://www.tantara.ab.ca/info.htm

- G. Gordon Schulmeyer (Ed), *Handbook of Software Quality Assurance*, Prentice Hall, 1999

Important software failures

- Peter G. Neumann's Risks Digest. http://catless.ncl.ac.uk/Risks/. Contains numerous reports of software failures. Software engineers should study these failures to ensure they do not re-create them

- N. G. Leveson and C. S. Turner, 'An Investigation of the Therac-25 Accidents', *IEEE Computer*, Vol. 26, No. 7, July 1993, pp. 18–41

- J-M. Jézéquel and B. Meyer, 'Design by Contract: The Lessons of Ariane', *IEEE Computer*, Vol. 30, No. 2, January 1997, pp. 129–130

Software testing

- T. Koomen, M. Pol, H. W. Broeders and H. Voorthuyzen, *Test Process Improvement: A Practical Step-by-Step Guide to Structured Testing*, Addison-Wesley, 1999

- W. E. Lewis, *Software Testing and Continuous Quality Improvement*, CRC Press, 2000

- C. Kaner, H. Q. Nguyen and J. Falk, *Testing Computer Software*, 2nd edition, Wiley, 1999

- Software testing online resources by Roland Untch at Middle Tennessee State University: http://www.mtsu.edu/~storm

- Newsgroup comp.software.testing and its FAQ: http://www.faqs.org/faqs/software-eng/testing-faq

- The DMOZ Open Directory on software testing: http://dmoz.org/Computers/Programming/Software_Testing

- Aptest's software testing links; a particularly strong list of testing tools: http://www.aptest.com/resources.html

Software inspection

- D. A. Wheeler, B. Brykczynski, and R. N. Meeson, Jr. (Eds.), *Software Inspection An Industry Best Practice*, IEEE CS Press, 1996

- T. Gilb, D. Graham and S. Finzi, *Software Inspection*, Addison-Wesley, 1993

Books about process standards

- P. Jalote, *CMM in Practice: Processes for Executing Software Projects at Infosys*, (SEI Series in Software Engineering), Addison-Wesley, 1999

- W. Humphrey, *Introduction to the Personal Software Process*, (SEI Series in Software Engineering), Addison-Wesley, 1996

- W. Humphrey, M. Lovelace and R. Hoppes, *Introduction to the Team Software Process*, (SEI Series in Software Engineering), Addison-Wesley, 1999

- D. Hoyle, *ISO 9000 Quality Systems Handbook*, 4th edition, Butterworth-Heinemann, 2000

Standards

The following are some of the IEEE and British standards covering quality assurance and testing. As mentioned in Chapter 4, access to these requires a subscription. See: http://www.standards.ieee.org/software/index.html for the IEEE standards, and bsonline.techindex.co.uk for the British standards.

- ISO 9126, *Software Product Quality Characteristics*

- IEEE Standard 730, *Software Quality Assurance Plans*

- IEEE Standard 829, *Software Test Documentation*

- IEEE Standard 1012, *Software Verification and Validation*

- IEEE Standard 1028, *Software Reviews*

- British Standard 7925, *Software Testing*

Project exercises

E208 Perform a test case inspection of the test cases for Phase 2 of the SimpleChat system. The purpose of this inspection will be to detect defects in the test cases, not in SimpleChat itself. A legitimate part of an inspection is to uncover important test cases that are missing from the set, therefore make sure the test plan has tests that detect all the types of defects discussed in this chapter.

E209 Create a set of test cases for Phase 3 of the SimpleChat system. This is the version of SimpleChat you created at the end of Chapter 4. Once you have created your test plan, use it to test your work, recording any failures when they occur. (Suggestion: test the work of another group while they test your work.)

E210 Perform a root cause analysis of the failures you encountered in the last exercise.

E211 Stress test the SimpleChat program by having a very large number of people connect clients to the same server and issue many different commands. Try to determine the capacity of the server (or the network) before it slows down to an unacceptable level of performance. Write a summary of your experiences.

E212 Create a complete set of test cases for the Small Hotel Reservation System.

Managing the software process

11

Earlier in this book, we made the point that software engineering is a labor-intensive activity. Performing software engineering successfully therefore means carefully managing the people who perform it and organizing the tasks they perform. Project management is an activity that all software engineers will perform to some extent, even though they might not be officially given the title of manager or leader. In this chapter we introduce some of the basic principles of project management that all software engineers should know.

In this chapter you will learn about the following

- The different process models and methodologies that can be used to plan and conduct a software project.

- Techniques for estimating the amount of work it will take to develop a system.

- The basics of organizing software engineering teams.

- Techniques for planning, scheduling and tracking the work.

11.1 What is project management?

Project management encompasses all the activities needed to plan and execute a project. The following are specific activities often done by a project manager:

1. **Deciding what needs to be done**. Finding customers; working with customers to determine their problem and the scope of the project; prioritizing the work; selecting the overall processes that will be followed, and negotiating contracts.

2. **Estimating costs**. The most important aspect of this is estimating the amount of elapsed time and effort that will be required to complete the project. We will discuss this in Section 11.3.

3. **Ensuring there are suitable people to undertake the project**. This includes finding people, and ensuring that people have appropriate training. It can also include firing people who are not performing adequately.

4. **Defining responsibilities**. Determining how people will work together in teams and who will be responsible for what. Teams are the subject of Section 11.4.

5. **Scheduling**. Determining the sequence of tasks, plus setting deadlines for when tasks must be complete. Major deadlines are called *milestones*. Scheduling is discussed in Section 11.5.

6. **Making arrangements for the work**. Initiating the paperwork involved in hiring or subcontracting; setting up training courses; finding office space; ensuring that hardware and software is available; ensuring that people have the requisite security clearance, etc.

7. **Directing**. Telling subordinates and contractors what to do. Many of the other activities in this list involve making decisions; but acting on those decisions by ordering people to do things is a distinct activity. Directing is not as simple as issuing orders – you have to get people to commit to deliver what they promise.

8. **Being a technical leader**. Giving advice about engineering problems; helping people solve problems by leading discussions; pointing people to appropriate sources of information; acting as a mentor, and making high-level decisions about requirements and design.

9. **Reviewing and approving decisions made by others**. In certain types of projects, the project manager will have to take the ultimate legal responsibility for declaring that proper engineering practice has been followed, and that the manager believes the resulting system will be safe. However, a certain amount of reviewing and approving is a part of every project.

10. **Building morale and supporting staff**. Helping resolve interpersonal conflicts; ensuring that people feel rewarded, respected and motivated; giving people feedback to help them improve their work; and ensuring that people always have somebody to talk to about problems.

11. **Monitoring and controlling**. Finding out what is going on, determining how the plans need to change, and taking action to keep the project on track. The risk management process, which we have talked about throughout this book, is a central aspect of this.

12. **Co-ordinating the work with managers of other projects**.

13. **Reporting**. Telling customers and higher-level managers what they need and want to know.

14. **Continually striving to improve the process**.

Project management disasters

Periodically in the news, there are reports of major failures of software projects: projects that are canceled, in whole or in part, after spending large amounts of money and running far over budget and behind schedule. There are always many contributing factors to these failures, such as changing requirements or unexpected technological problems. However, with improved project management, the problems could have been detected and resolved without wasting so much money.

■ The United States Internal Revenue Service struggled for years to update its software. The cost overruns and opportunity costs (failure to collect revenue) were estimated to exceed $50 billion per year.

■ Attempts from the early 1980s to the mid-1990s to update the air traffic control systems in the United States met with many failures. One after another, components of the system were abandoned after billions of dollars had been spent and many years of elapsed time had passed.

■ Early in 1993, the London Stock Exchange abandoned the development of its Taurus paperless share settlement system after 10 years and £400m were wasted.

■ In 1995, the Canadian Auditor General's annual report found that large amounts of money had been wasted due to poorly managed projects in the Canadian Federal Government (see http://www.oag-bvg.gc.ca/domino/reports.nsf/html/9512ce.html).

Other references that discuss project management failures such as these can be found under the 'Important software failures' heading of the 'For more information' section in the previous chapter.

In some organizations, the role of 'project manager' is separated from the role of 'departmental manager'. Activities such as hiring, building morale, and issuing the final directions may then be performed by the latter individual instead.

We are introducing project management in this book since all software engineers need to have a basic understanding of how their managers run projects. Furthermore, all software engineers from time to time perform project management tasks. For example, software engineers have to estimate the amount of time their personal work will take; schedule their personal work; help to define the project by working on requirements analysis; act as a leader in their area of technical expertise; review the work of others; participate in risk management; co-ordinate with others; report to managers and work with others to improve the process.

In the next four sections, we will look at key project management skills: choosing an overall process model, estimating costs, building a team and scheduling. We will conclude the chapter by describing the project plan – an essential document maintained by the project manager.

Exercise

E213 Review the work you performed while you were doing group-oriented exercises in this book. For each of the project management activities, listed above, write down a) what you did (if anything), and b) how you believe you could do better.

11.2 Software process models

Software process models are general approaches for organizing a project into activities. They help the project manager and his or her team to decide what work should be done and in what sequence to perform the work. The models should be seen as *aids to thinking*, not rigid prescriptions of the way to do things – each project will end up with its own unique plan.

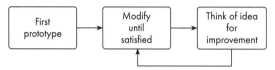

Figure 11.1   The opportunistic approach, a poor model for software development

Organizations that don't follow good software engineering practices often end up following what is often called an *opportunistic approach*, illustrated in Figure 11.1. In the opportunistic approach, developers keep on modifying the software until they or their users are satisfied. This approach has several important problems:

- It does not acknowledge the great importance of working out the requirements and the design before starting implementation. The system might satisfy certain user needs, but reaching a high level of user satisfaction will require many changes.

- The design of software deteriorates faster if it is not well designed. In the opportunistic model, design is an ad-hoc activity, therefore rapid deterioration is to be expected.

- Since there are no plans, there is nothing to aim towards. Since there is nothing to aim towards, you can never know if you are doing well or poorly. Therefore there is no *control* of costs or schedule in an opportunistic project.

- There is no explicit recognition of the need for systematic testing and other forms of quality assurance. Many undetected defects therefore remain, giving rise to never-ending changes that make the system worse and worse. As a result, the system most often collapses at some point and becomes unusable and irreparable. The only solution is then to rebuild the system from scratch (until it collapses again).

- The above problems make the cost of developing and maintaining software very high.

The waterfall model

The *waterfall* model is a significant improvement over the opportunistic approach. It is a classic way of looking at software engineering that accounts for the importance of requirements, design and quality assurance. The model is so named because diagrams of it, such as Figure 11.2, tend to look like cascading waterfalls.

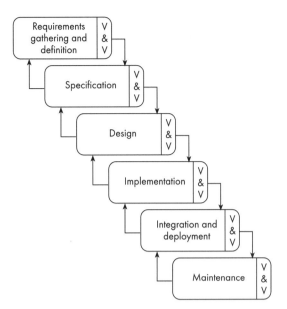

Figure 11.2   The waterfall model

Rather than jumping in and immediately developing a product, the waterfall model suggests that software engineers should work in a series of stages. Before completing each stage, they should perform quality assurance (verification and validation) so that the next stage can be built on a good foundation. The waterfall model also recognizes, to a limited extent, that you sometimes have to step back to earlier stages when you discover a problem in a subsequent stage.

The waterfall model forms the foundation of many software development methodologies in use today. However, it has some limitations and, if followed too strictly, can lead to the following types of problems:

■ The model implies that you should attempt to complete the entire specification before moving on to the design, and the entire design before moving on to implementation. This is an overly rigid viewpoint since it does not account for the fact that requirements constantly change. It also means that customers cannot use anything until the entire system is complete.

■ The waterfall model makes no allowances for prototyping and implies that you can get the requirements right by simply writing them down and reviewing them. In practice, this only works for simple, well-understood types of software development.

■ The model implies that once the product is finished, everything else is maintenance. Relegating maintenance to be the 'last step' makes it appear that all you have to do at that point is to make minor adjustments, perhaps without requirements and design. Unfortunately, most of the costs occur after the initial system is developed as the system is repeatedly changed.

The phased-release model

The *phased-release model* of software development, shown in Figure 11.3, rectifies some, but not all, of the problems of the waterfall model. The most important change is that it introduces the notion of *incremental* development. It suggests that, after requirements gathering and planning, the project should be broken into separate subprojects, or phases. Each phase can then be released to customers when ready. Parts of the system will be available earlier than would have been possible when using a strict waterfall approach.

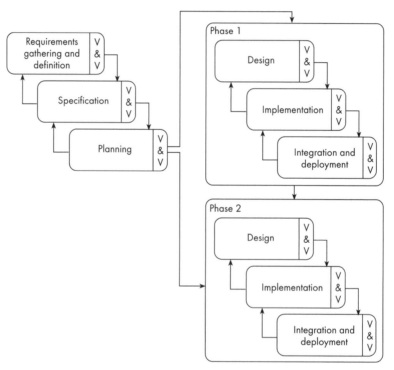

Figure 11.3   The phased-release model

The phased-release model still retains some of the important weaknesses of the waterfall model. It continues to suggest that all requirements be finalized at the start of development, and it continues to downplay the possibility of prototyping. When the time comes to develop Phase 2, and subsequent phases, the design is based on the original specifications – in other words, the model does not facilitate learning lessons from Phase 1, which could result in improvements to subsequent phases.

The spiral model

The *spiral model*, as shown in Figure 11.4, is another view of incremental development that explicitly embraces prototyping and an *iterative* approach to software development. This model takes the position that you should start to

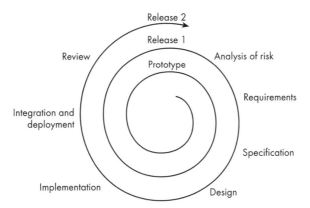

Figure 11.4   The spiral model

develop software by developing a small prototype (innermost loop of the spiral). This first prototype follows a mini-waterfall process, but is very quickly developed and serves primarily to gather requirements. The last stage of this inner loop is review, or evaluation, of the first prototype.

Project managers embrace the spiral model because it acknowledges one of the most famous quotations in software engineering. It was Fred Brooks who said, 'The question is not whether to build a pilot system and throw it away. You will do that. The question is whether to plan in advance to build a throwaway.'

In subsequent loops of the spiral, the project team performs further requirements, design, implementation and review. There may be several cycles of prototyping; however, subsequent cycles become official releases.

Before each cycle of the spiral ends, a review is held. At this review, the stakeholders discuss their experiences with the previous release and decide whether to proceed to another cycle.

The spiral model also adds the notion of *risk analysis* to process modeling. The first thing to do before embarking on each new loop of the spiral is to decide what are the major difficulties to be handled. After determining these, you then make adjustments to the architecture, the requirements or the project plan as necessary.

When following the spiral model, a project undergoes a large number of cycles. The cycling only ends when the system is finally retired. This model therefore incorporates the idea that maintenance is simply a type of ongoing development.

The evolutionary model

The *evolutionary model* (Figure 11.5) shows software development as a series of hills, each representing a separate loop of the spiral. This is a third way of thinking about incremental development.

This model shows two things that are not always clear from the spiral model. First, it shows that loops, or releases, tend to overlap each other. As testing and

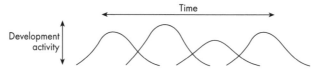

Figure 11.5   The evolutionary model

preparations for deployment of one release are under way, planning for the next release has already started.

Secondly, the evolutionary model makes it clear that development work tends to reach a peak, at around the time of the deadline for completion of implementation. Finally, the model shows that each prototype or release can take different amounts of time to deliver, and can take differing amounts of effort.

The concurrent engineering model

The *concurrent engineering model* (Figure 11.6) explicitly accounts for the divide and conquer principle. Each team works on its own component, typically following a spiral or evolutionary approach.

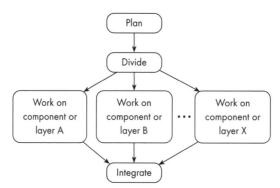

Figure 11.6   The concurrent engineering model

In the concurrent engineering model, there has to be some initial planning, and periodic integration. The diagram therefore only shows a picture of a single iteration.

The Rational Unified Process

Many of the features of the above models are embodied in what is known as the *Rational Unified Process (RUP)*. This is the most widely known published methodology that embraces UML and most of the other techniques discussed in this book.

RUP is designed to be adaptable: it suggests a framework and a set of disciplined practices to follow, but encourages you to vary the level of rigor depending on your organization's needs.

See the 'For more information' section at the end of Chapter 5 for the definitive book about RUP.

Agile approaches

We have discussed agile approaches periodically throughout this book. These approaches embrace the iterative model, encouraging the development of particularly small iterations, and the reassessment of the direction of the project as each new iteration is being considered. The techniques also explicitly disavow 'big' processes: by which we mean processes that require the development of lots of documentation and have delivery dates far in the future.

Agile approaches are gaining popularity for small projects that involve uncertain, changing requirements and other sources of high risk. Risk is reduced because nothing big is produced – if a small iteration fails to meet the needs of the users and has to be re-done, only a small amount of money is wasted.

Some people, upon initially hearing of agile techniques, think that they are perhaps throwing away all the discipline inherent in some of the other techniques we have talked about. This misconception is far from the truth: all the agile approaches promote using disciplined techniques; the key is that each of these techniques is lightweight – that is, it is not something that will bog down the project or cost a lot of money. In fact many of the techniques are explicitly designed to save money.

The most famous of the agile techniques is eXtreme Programming (XP). Some of the tenets of eXtreme Programming are:

- The development team includes all the stakeholders, who work very closely together. In particular, it is considered important to have a customer or user on site.

- You do not develop large requirements documents. Instead, you write a series of up to about 80 *user stories* that describe things the users want the system to do for them (see the sidebar in Section 4.8). Each user story must take a couple of weeks to develop and test; if developers estimate it would take longer, then it must be broken down into smaller stories.

- Project planning is based on the user stories. There must be a series of small and frequent releases. A release is divided into iterations of between 1 and 3 weeks. The stakeholders work together to determine which stories will be released in each iteration. Planning takes place just before the start of each iteration, and *project velocity* is measured and used to gauge how much time a set of user stories will actually take to develop. During each iteration, programmers sign up to do tasks that must take between 1 and 3 days – programmers do their own estimates of how much time each task should take.

- There are three project variables that can be changed: *scope*, *resources* and *time*. Management is only allowed to dictate any two of these; the developers determine the third. Quality, a fourth variable, should not be sacrificed.

■ In order to ensure high quality, design for testability and test-first development (see Chapter 10) are emphasized: automated test cases are written before the software is developed. As failures occur, new automated test cases are written. Acceptance testing is based on the user stories.

■ A large amount of *refactoring* is encouraged. Refactoring means transforming the design to ensure internal qualities such as maintainability are promoted. Simple examples of refactoring include adding a superclass that contains common features of existing classes, and adding a Façade design pattern around a package to reduce coupling. Frequent refactoring ensures the design retains high internal quality despite the fact that design only considers one small iteration at a time. We will have more to say about refactoring in the context of re-engineering below.

■ *Pair programming* is recommended. The idea behind this is that defects are much less likely to creep into code if two people are involved in its creation. Both people also keep each other engaged and focused on the task.

Extreme programming also promotes many other ideas, such as the use of CRC cards, a focus on simplicity, creation of 'spike' throwaway prototypes when difficult technical issues are encountered, frequent integration, and continual improvement. Another part of the philosophy is that software developers should not need to be overworked; overtime is therefore frowned on.

There are some drawbacks to agile methods. It is harder to write a contract for development of a system when neither party knows the direction the project will take. Also, some of the techniques become less and less appropriate as the system becomes larger and larger. Nevertheless, many developers and managers now enthusiastically support the use of agile techniques for a wide variety of types of project.

The open source model

A model that is widely used for software development is the open source model. In this model software is distributed for free along with the source code, and interested people contribute improvements, without being paid by users.

Many open source projects were founded by enthusiasts who initially developed a system largely as a hobby, or perhaps as a student research project. People who contribute to the projects often benefit because they are users of the software and want it to become better and better. The idea is that community members will make the software ever better for themselves and others in the community.

The open source movement has resulted in a wide variety of important systems, including the Linux operating system and the GNU tools. Some companies allow their developers to participate in open source projects; IBM, for example, has heavily promoted the Eclipse software development tool.

In the open source model, a small group of leaders must retain control of which contributions make it into the final release. Quality assurance is performed by the community: those interested in the project scrutinize and criticize any suggested contributions.

Choosing a process model

When planning a particular project, the important thing to recognize is that you can combine the features of the models that apply best to your current project.

From the waterfall model, you will always incorporate the notion of stages, but you will most likely want to avoid having a single cascade ending in maintenance.

From the phased-release model, you can incorporate the notion of doing some initial high-level analysis, and then dividing the project into releases. You can also incorporate the notions of prototyping and risk analysis from the spiral model.

Next, from the evolutionary model you can incorporate the notion of varying amounts of time and work, with overlapping releases. And from the concurrent engineering model, you can break the system down into components and develop them in parallel.

Finally, even if you are developing a large system, you can adopt many of the features of the agile model: smaller releases, on-site users, test-first development and frequent refactoring can all be adopted in projects both large and small.

Re-engineering

No matter what process model you use, in any large or long-lived project, the design will deteriorate. Periodically, therefore, project managers should set aside some time to re-engineer part or all of the system. The extent of this work can vary considerably: it could include cleaning up the code to make it more readable, completely replacing a layer, or refactoring part of the design.

In general, the objective of a re-engineering activity is to increase maintainability. It should not normally involve adding any new features for users, but should make the system more flexible so that adding such features in the future becomes easier.

Although periodic re-engineering will reduce long-term costs, it is often hard to convince managers and customers of this. You need to present them with a detailed analysis of how much the re-engineering will cost, and what cost savings will result. As with many aspects of software engineering, you should follow the 80–20 rule: you can get 80 per cent of the benefits of re-engineering with only 20 per cent of the work, therefore focus re-engineering efforts on the parts of the system most in need of it.

11.3 Cost estimation

One of the biggest challenges in software engineering is accurately forecasting how much time and effort it will take either to develop a system, or to make a specific set of changes. All software developers have to participate in cost

Chaos in project management

The Standish Group's reports on project management chaos contain some of the most respected statistics about software project failures. According to the Standish Group, the average project exceeds its budget by 90%, and its schedule by 120%. Furthermore, over 30% of projects are canceled before completion. In the United States alone, this represents about $100 *billion* in wasted money per year. See http://www.standishgroup.com.

estimation, no matter whether they are the managers or architects of a large system, or whether they are the engineers responsible for the design and programming of a single component.

There is an old cliché that 'time is money'. In software project management, this is literally true. When you estimate the cost of doing some work, you focus on estimating how much software-engineering time will be required. However, there are two distinct aspects of time. The first is *elapsed time*; this is the difference in time from the start date to the end date of a task or project. The second aspect of time is probably better called *development effort* (or simply *effort*); this measures the amount of labor used and is expressed in *person-months* or *person-days*.

When planning a project, you budget a certain amount of effort for each task, and you schedule the start and end times for that task. If you schedule a task to take two weeks of elapsed time, but take six person-weeks of effort, that means that you must also ensure that an average of three people are working on the task at any given point in time.

The elapsed time of a project is important – you might have a contractual obligation to deliver software by a certain day, or you might want to ensure that your product reaches the market before the competition. However, the actual cost of a project is primarily a function of development effort.

To convert an estimate of development effort to an amount of money, you multiply it by the *weighted average cost* (also called the *burdened* cost) of employing a software engineer for a month (or a day). The weighted average cost not only includes the average salary of a software engineer, but also the cost of providing that person with benefits, an office, a desk, a computer as well as technical and managerial support. The weighted average cost is therefore often two to three times average salary.

Example 11.1 *In your organization, although the average salary is $4,000 /month, the weighted average salary for cost estimation purposes is $11,000/month. You have determined that a particular project will take 7 person-months to complete. How much would you estimate this project will cost financially?*

You estimate that the project will cost 7×$11,000 = $77,000.

Principles of effective cost estimation

Cost estimation is notoriously difficult, as witnessed by the large number of projects that are completed behind schedule and over budget, or are not completed at all. There are several key principles that can help you to make better estimates. These can be applied whether you are estimating the time for your personal work, or for an entire project.

Cost Estimation Principle 1: Divide and conquer

In Chapter 9, we said that divide and conquer was one of the essential principles of design. In Chapter 10, we said it also applies to testing. It turns out to be just as important to cost estimation.

If you try to estimate the entire cost of a project as a single number, you are likely to be very inaccurate. To make a better estimate, you should divide the project up into individual subsystems, and then divide each subsystem further into the activities that will be required to develop it. Next, you make a series of detailed estimates for each individual activity, and sum the results to arrive at the grand total estimate for the project.

Although your detailed estimates may be inaccurate, your final estimate will be more accurate, for two reasons. Firstly, you will be more likely to account for all the subsystems and activities. Secondly, if you underestimate the time required for some subsystems or activities, this should be at least partly compensated for by overestimates in other places.

Although it will help you improve estimates, the divide and conquer principle is not a panacea. You might miss activities or systematically underestimate each activity, leading to a total estimate that is too low. The other principles listed below will help to combat this.

Cost Estimation Principle 2: Include all activities when making estimates

If you do not appreciate the amount of effort required for certain activities, or omit them entirely, then your estimate of total effort will be too low.

For example, when asked to estimate the cost of a new feature for SimpleChat, a beginner might focus primarily in the amount of time required to write the requirements document and the code. However, the time required for *all* development activities must be taken into account, including prototyping, design, inspecting, testing, debugging, writing user documentation and deployment.

Cost Estimation Principle 3: Base your estimates on past experience combined with what you can observe of the current project

The only way to predict the future is to reason by analogy with the past. If you are developing a project that has many similarities with a past project, then you can expect it to take a similar amount of work.

In practice, no two projects are the same. However, the more you follow Principle 1 and divide the estimation task into fine-grained detailed estimates, the more likely you are to be able to find similarities with aspects of past projects.

There are two general strategies for using past experience. The first is to base your estimates purely on the personal judgment of experts within your team. Such people will have worked on other projects and can extrapolate their experience to the current project. The second strategy is to use algorithmic models that have been developed in the software industry as a whole by analyzing a wide range of development projects. They take into account various aspects of a project's size and complexity, and provide formulas to compute anticipated cost.

The algorithmic models allow you to systematically base your estimate of development effort on an estimate of some other factor that you can measure, or that is easier to estimate. Project managers base their estimates on factors such as the following:

- The number of use cases.

- The number of distinct requirements.

- The number of classes in the domain model.

- The number of widgets in the prototype user interface.

- An estimate of the number of lines of code.

Which of the above factors you use as a basis for your estimate depends on how far you have progressed in development. For example, you may have completed an initial use case model, but have not yet finalized the detailed requirements or developed a prototype user interface.

Example 11.2   *You have been asked to estimate the cost of a project for which you developed a system domain model composed of 24 classes. In a recent similar project, the average development effort (including all testing etc.) was 10 person-days per class. What would be your cost estimate for the current project?*

You might first assume from past experience that the system domain model classes represent half of the total number of classes in the final system. The other classes would be user interface and architectural classes. The development effort estimate would therefore be $24 \times 2 \times 10 = 480$ person-days = 16 person-months. Using the burdened cost from Example 11.1, this results in a cost estimate of 16x$11000 = \$176,000$.

Project managers often use lines of code to give an intermediate estimate of system size that people can easily understand. For example, you might convert an estimate of use cases to an estimate of lines of code, and then convert the lines of code to an effort estimate using one of the formulas discussed below. However, you can only effectively base cost estimates on lines of code when you have almost completed design.

Example 11.3   *Your records of previous projects show that an average class has 6 attributes, and 14 methods, averaging 6 lines of code each. The average lines of code per class is 90. How many lines of code would you expect to have to develop in the system of Example 11.2?*

You would expect to develop $90 \times 48 = 4.3$KLOC.

A typical algorithmic model uses a formula such as the following:

$$E = a + bN^c$$

In this formula, E is the effort estimate and N is the estimate or measure being used as the basis for the effort estimate (e.g. number of use cases or lines of code). The values a, b and c are obtained by extensive analysis of past projects, and determinations of the differences that will effect the current project (these will be discussed in Cost Estimation Principle 4).

The exponent c is particularly interesting. If it is not equal to one, it means that the effort increases *non-linearly*. If $c < 1$, there would be *economies of scale* as a project gets larger, which turns out *not* to be the case in software. In real projects $c > 1$, which means that the effort grows increasingly rapidly relative to project size; this is due to the increasingly large amount of co-ordination and complexity involved.

Figure 11.7 shows the effect of typical values of the c parameter used by one of the best-known algorithmic cost estimation models, COCOMO II (COnstructive COst Model, version II). COCOMO II computes effort, in person-months, from an estimate of size, measured in lines of code.

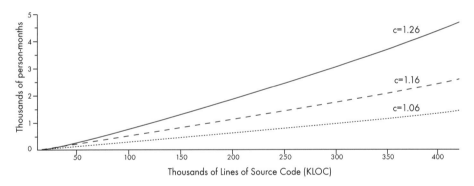

Figure 11.7   Effect of non-linearity in cost estimation

Another important algorithmic method is *Function Point Analysis*. In this approach, and several related approaches, you count features of the requirements and use these to compute an estimate of the system's size. You can then apply COCOMO to the size estimates.

The basic equation used by approaches like Function Point Analysis is:

$$S = W_1F_1 + W_2F_2 + W_3F_3 + \dots$$

The F_i represent counts of features of the requirements such as number of inputs, number of tables in the database, number of use cases etc. These counts are multiplied by weights (the W_i values) calculated using industry-wide experience. The results are summed to produce a system size, S.

To find out more about Function Points and COCOMO, see the references in the 'For more information' section at the end of the chapter.

Estimating the cost of construction – false analogies

Some people yearn for the day when it will be as easy to estimate software development time as it is for a civil engineer to estimate the cost to construct a small building. Civil engineers and builders have tables that allow them, for example, to calculate how much time it will take to lay a certain amount of concrete, or to perform each of the other construction tasks.

Why can't we do this in software engineering? The answer, as we hinted in Chapter 1, is that it is false to draw analogies between 'construction' of buildings and the latter stages of software development that are sometimes (unadvisedly we believe) also called 'construction'.

Software development is an intensely mental activity. Like the *design* of buildings, it is full of decision-making and other intellectual challenges, all the way to the end of programming and testing. Constructing a building should actually be seen as analogous to the printing of disks or making the executables available for downloading. Because software is largely intangible, this real construction process is very inexpensive.

The dominant costs in software engineering are therefore design costs, which are hard to estimate. The dominant costs in many other branches of engineering are true construction costs, which are much easier to estimate.

This does not mean we are doomed to failure; it just means that we should expect a realistic level of uncertainty in our estimates, and that we should practice iterative development and risk management so as to mitigate the effects of those uncertainties.

Cost Estimation Principle 4: Be sure to account for differences when extrapolating from other projects

Although experience from other projects can be a good guide, there are often many subtle differences between projects. You have to consider carefully the effect of differences such as the following when making an estimate for a new project:

- **Different software developers**. People differ dramatically in their skill and experience levels; a skilled programmer can be up to ten times as productive as a less skilled programmer. In projects with only a few people, this can therefore significantly influence the accuracy of estimates.

- **Different development processes and maturity levels**. Teams that have skilled management and a mature development methodology that includes such things as quality assurance, risk management and iterative development will be able to work more efficiently than organizations that follow an ad-hoc approach.

- **Different types of customers and users**. Project teams that have good access to and rapport with both their customers and users can often proceed faster than organizations lacking these advantages. In the latter case, delays are caused by slow or poor decision making. Projects that have a single user or customer will often also proceed faster than projects with many users and customers. Not only does it take time to negotiate decisions when many people are involved, but the resulting compromises may be difficult to develop efficiently.

- **Different schedule demands**. Ironically, if a project team is under intense pressure to deliver software by a certain date they may cut corners and make mistakes that actually end up delaying them. On the other hand, a certain amount of deadline pressure can have a positive effect.

- **Different technology**. The effort required can be affected by changes in hardware, other software systems with which your system must interact, database management systems, operating systems and programming languages. For example, if you change to a new programming language, that language can take considerable time to learn. Also, some languages are known to be less productive than others. For example, programming in assembler is unproductive because it takes many statements to express a given computation, and furthermore the complexity of assembler gives rise to more bugs. Programming in C or C++ is likely to result in faster development. Using Java or C# is likely to decrease development time still further.

- **Different technical complexity of the requirements**. Some systems are intrinsically more complex than others, because they require greater reliability, are distributed, or for many other reasons.

- **Different domains**. A team embarking on a project in a domain in which it has not worked before will undoubtedly take more time than a team that has been working in the same domain for years.

- **Different levels of requirement stability**. Some projects are easier to define in advance. On the other hand, some projects must proceed in an exploratory fashion since the requirements will not be clearly known until prototyping is complete. The total effort will thus vary substantially. Also, some domains are more prone to changes in requirements than others.

The algorithmic cost-estimation techniques explicitly take into account factors such as the above, by multiplying the estimate by a small factor, or increasing the value of an exponent.

In COCOMO II, the basic value of the exponent c in the formula presented earlier is 1.01. You add to this exponent amounts ranging from 0.00 to 0.05 depending on the impact you expect from: a) the level of experience with this kind of project; b) the amount of flexibility you have in the development process; c) the amount of risk management performed; d) the quality of the development team, and e) the process maturity of the organization.

COCOMO II also has a series of multiplicative factors that modify the value of b in the formula. These factors are divided into four categories: Personnel, Product, Project and Platform attributes. Typical initial values of b might be 2.4 for a small project and 3.0 for a medium-sized project.

Example 11.4   *This example continues examples 11.2 and 11.3. Assume that you are working on a small project and will use 2.4 as your multiplicative value, b. To compute the exponent, suppose we have, for this project, good experience with similar project*

(0.01), no involvement of the client in the process (0.00), little risk analysis carried out (0.04), a relatively good team of developers (0.02) and an average process maturity (0.03). Use this data to compute a cost estimate in person-months.

The exponent value will be $1.01+0.10 = 1.11$. The effort would then be $2.4\times4.3^{1.11} = 12.1$ person months.

Example 11.5   Looking up in COCOMO II tables, you find that the following multiplicative factors need to be applied to adjust the value of the b (multiplicative) parameter:

(a) Personnel factor: your team has good experience with the programming language to be used: 0.95

(b) Product factor: the system will be running under very tight memory constraints: 1.21

(c) Project factor: you have to put up with a schedule that is a bit tight: 1.04

(d) Platform factor: particularly high reliability is required: 1.4

Revise your effort estimate from Example 11.4, given this new data, and convert the result to dollars.

The effort estimate is $0.95 \times 1.21 \times 1.04 \times 1.4 \times 12.1 = 20$ person-months, for a cost of $20 \times \$11,000 = \$220,000$.

Exercise

E214   Using your judgment, what would be reasonable multiplicative parameters for the following (you could do this with reference to the COCOMO II documents).

(a) Personnel factor: your team has in the past developed many similar applications.

(b) Product factor: the system includes a particularly large database.

(c) Project factor: some of your development team will be located in the US, some in Canada, some in India and some in South Africa.

(d) Platform factor: the application will run under the Linux operating system.

Cost Estimation Principle 5: Anticipate the worst case and plan for contingencies

In accordance with Murphy's Law, if something can go wrong in a project, it probably will. For example, you might have difficulty deciding on the requirements; there might be unexpected technical challenges in the design process; or somebody might quit or not perform up to expectations.

One way to plan for contingencies is to prioritize all the use cases according to their benefit to the customer. If, as the project progresses, your revised cost estimates show that you will exceed your budget or deliver the software too late, you can drop the lowest priority use cases, and update your estimates accordingly.

Another important thing to do is to build enough 'cushion' into your cost estimate so as to account for typical delays. One way to do this is as follows. For every detailed estimate, make an 'optimistic' (O) estimate, a 'likely' (L) estimate and a 'pessimistic' (P) estimate. Your O estimate suggests the minimum time you reasonably think the activity might take. Your L estimate accounts for what you think would be a typical number of things going wrong. Your P estimate suggests what you think the activity would consume if many difficulties were experienced. You then add up the O estimates, the L estimates and the P estimates separately to arrive a global estimates of the best-case, typical-case and worst-case cost for the project.

Having these three separate estimates ensures that you are not making the mistake of providing only a best-case estimate. Your pessimistic estimate also helps you to become conscious of all the things that could go wrong, so that you can take active steps to avoid them.

Example 11.6   *You are asked to estimate the cost of developing the Release 2 of the GANA system introduced in Chapter 4. The new release would:*

■ *Constantly update the estimated time of arrival at the destination, based on typical travel speeds on the roads to be taken, the time of day, and day of the week (accounting for rush hours).*

■ *Dynamically adjust the scale of the map based on the local population density, the distance of the driver to his or her origin or destination, and the driver's speed. The map would not jump from one scale to another but would smoothly increase or decrease its scale.*

The following table shows Optimistic, Likely and Pessimistic estimates for the work required, expressed in person-months. Note that more detailed estimates could be created if some of the tasks were divided into subtasks.

	Optimistic	*Likely*	*Pessimistic*
Requirements gathering	2.5	3	4
Prototyping	2	3	5
Specification	1	1.5	3
Design	4	6	8
Implementation	5	8	16
Software inspection and testing	6	10	13
Hardware integration and system test	1.5	2.5	4
Total Time	22	34	53

Exercise

E215 Evaluate the cost estimates presented in Example 11.6; discuss potential sources of error in these estimates.

E216 Search the Internet for the source code of an open-source Java project (you can also select a package from the Java API). Then do the following:

(a) Compute some basic metrics: the average number of attributes and methods per class; and the average number of lines per method.

(b) Imagine you are planning to add a new subsystem of 40 classes very similar to the system you have studied. Use the numbers computed in part a) to derive likely, optimistic and pessimistic estimates for the number of lines of code you would expect to find in this system.

(c) Use the COCOMO approach discussed earlier to arrive at optimistic, likely and pessimistic estimates for the effort required to develop the subsystem.

Cost Estimation Principle 6: Combine multiple independent estimates

No matter how good your estimation process, you are likely to have overlooked some factors that will affect the accuracy of your estimate.

You should therefore use several different techniques and compare the results. If there are discrepancies, you can analyze your calculations to discover what factors are causing the differences. For example, you can make one estimate based on your experience with a similar project; you can then use COCOMO or Function Points to make a second estimate.

A well-respected approach to making multiple estimates is the Delphi technique. To use this technique, several individuals initially make cost estimates in private. They then share their estimates to discover the discrepancies. Each individual repeatedly adjusts his or her estimates until a consensus is reached.

Example 11.7 *Discuss the discrepancies between the cost estimates presented in Examples 11.2 and 11.5, and suggest a course of action.*

The estimate of $176,000 from example 11.2 was based purely on extrapolating from this organization's typical costs per class developed. The $220,000 estimate of example 11.5 was based on a much more sophisticated sequence of computations, with a lines-of-code estimate as an intermediate value. In particular, the specific attributes of the *current project* that differentiate it from previous projects were taken into account. You should probably therefore put more weight on the second estimate, although it has one weakness: some factors used in the calculations were based on industry-wide data, not your own company's data.

You should probably attempt to use other cost-estimation techniques to see if they provide any more evidence that would help make the estimate more accurate. You should also closely monitor progress and revise your estimate regularly.

Cost Estimation Principle 7: Revise and refine estimates as work progresses

When you set out to solve a customer's problem you will have very little idea what software is needed (if any), therefore your estimate of the amount of work required can only be very rough. You will refine your estimates for three reasons:

- **As you add detail**. As you gather requirements and begin specifying details, you will be able to increase the accuracy of your estimate. As you move into the design phase, you can again increase the accuracy of your estimates.

- **As the requirements change**. You will adjust your estimates as requirements change, or features are dropped in order to meet a budget or deadline.

- **As the risk management process uncovers problems**. Similarly, as you encounter problems during design and implementation, you will be able to adjust your estimates to take these into account.

Cost estimation should therefore be a continuous activity. Updated estimates should be reported regularly to other members of the team, to management and to customers. A classic project management failure is to keep reporting that the project is 'on time and on budget' until the expected delivery date, and then to announce that the project is six months behind schedule.

Exercise

E217 Working in groups of four, estimate the cost of developing Release 1 of the GANA software, whose requirements were described in Chapter 4. Use as many of the techniques described in this section as possible. Among other things, this means you will use the 'divide and conquer' strategy to divide the software into parts, and divide the development process into detailed activities. You should also make optimistic, likely and pessimistic estimates. Each group should initially split into pairs, with each pair doing the estimation independently. Then the two pairs can come together to compare and reconcile their estimates.

11.4 Building software engineering teams

Software engineering is a human process. Choosing appropriate people for a team, and assigning roles and responsibilities to the team members, is therefore an important project management skill.

Software development contracts based on uncertain cost estimates

Customers often want a contract for custom software development to have a 'fixed price' so that they are not exposed to the risk of inaccurate estimates. On the other hand, software developers want a contract to allow them to charge for whatever 'time and materials' they use; this protects the developers from inaccurate cost estimates but exposes the customers to all the risk.

A solution to this conflict is to make an estimate for the entire project, but only initially sign a fixed-price contract for the first step. After each step, the developers and the customer revise the estimates. Either party can walk away if they believe their risk is growing too high; otherwise they repeat the process, signing a new fixed price contract for each successive step.

This approach reduces risk for both parties. It also encourages the developers to control costs, and discourages the customers from trying to add requirements.

Strict hierarchy versus more flexible arrangements

Software engineering teams can be organized in many different ways. One approach is to use a hierarchical manager–subordinate structure. In this approach, each individual reports to a manager and is responsible for performing the tasks delegated by that manager. At the opposite extreme is the egoless team: in such a team everybody is equal, and the team works together to achieve a common goal. In most organizations today, software engineering is performed using teams that fall in the middle of the spectrum.

In the *egoless approach*, decisions are made by consensus; this can lead to more creative solutions, since group members spontaneously get together to solve problems when they arise. In general, the egoless approach is most suited to difficult projects with many technical challenges. However, it is dependent on the personalities of the individuals, and hence is more likely to run into trouble if personal conflicts arise. Also, the assumption that everybody is equal is often wrong when a team is composed of people whose levels of skill and knowledge vary widely.

The *hierarchical approach* is reminiscent of the military, or large bureaucratic organizations. It is suitable for large projects with a strict schedule and where everybody is well trained and has a well-defined role. However, since everybody is responsible only for their own work, problems may go unnoticed.

The '*chief programmer team*' is a model that is midway between egoless and hierarchical. It works very much like the surgical team in an operating room. The chief programmer leads and guides the project; however, he or she consults with, and relies on, individual specialists. As with the egoless approach, everybody's goal is the success of the project.

Figure 11.8 shows how the main channels of communication differ among the team structures. In each case the same eight people are involved. In the idealized egoless approach shown on the left, everybody communicates with everybody else: this can result in a lot of communication, which may be reasonable when difficult technical problems are to be solved. The total number of potential communication channels is $(n^2-n)/2$. The rightmost diagram shows the

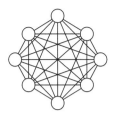 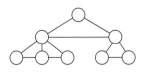 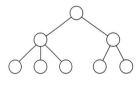

(a) Egoless   (b) Chief programmer   (c) Strict hierachy

Figure 11.8   Idealized communication patterns in different team structures

idealized hierarchical approach, where communication links are dramatically reduced (to $n-1$), but the risk is run that important information will not be communicated.

In reality, whatever team structure is formally adopted, people will tend to consult people with whom they do not have a formal relationship, and may fail to communicate details to people who need to know them. A project manager should therefore monitor and encourage all necessary communication.

Choosing an effective size for a team

We have already discussed the fact that you should divide a system into subsystems. Each subsystem is then assigned to a team; the various teams have to co-ordinate their work.

For a given estimated development effort in person-months there is an optimal team size. Doubling the size of a team will not halve the development time.

Making subsystems, and hence teams, too large or too small tends to make the development more complex and lead to designs that have higher coupling. Subsystems and teams should be sized such that the total amount of required knowledge and exchange of information is reduced – each team needs to understand only the overall software architecture, the details of its own subsystem, plus the interfaces to related subsystems.

For a given project or project iteration, the number of people on a team will not be constant. Initially, just a few people will be involved in defining the scope; later on, additional people will become involved as requirements, design, implementation and testing get under way. As the project or iteration nears completion, people will start moving on to the next iteration or to other work, leaving only a few people to undertake deployment. This change in team size is illustrated in Figure 11.5.

It is important to remember the following rule, however: if your team has an appropriate number of people to start with, then you cannot generally add people if you get behind schedule, in the hope of catching up. In fact, in his book *The Mythical Man Month*, Fred Brooks made one of the most well-known statements in software project management: 'Adding more people to a late project makes it even later.' This occurs because the new people will take time to learn what has been done, and will require support from the other people in the meantime, slowing them down. Furthermore, as mentioned above, if the team was the 'right' size to start with, adding more people may well be making it too big and inefficient.

Skills needed on a team

No matter how the team is organized, individual people are often assigned specific roles based on their particular skills. The following are some of the more common roles found on a development team:

- **Architect**. This person is responsible for leading the decision making about the architecture, and maintaining the architectural model.

- **Project manager**. Responsible for doing the project management tasks described in this chapter. Even in an egoless team, somebody has to be the custodian of the cost estimates and the schedule.

- **Configuration management and build specialist**. This person ensures that, as changes are made, no new problems are introduced. Everyone relies on builds as the baselines for quality assurance and subsequent development. This person also makes sure that documentation for each change is properly updated.

- **User interface specialist**. Although everybody should interact with users, this person has the particular responsibility to make sure that usability is kept at the forefront of the design process.

- **Technology specialist**. Such a person has specialized knowledge and expertise in a technology such as databases, networking, operating systems etc.

- **Hardware and third-party software specialist**. This person makes sure that the development team has appropriate types of hardware and third-party software on which to develop and test the software. This person will install and perform acceptance testing on any reusable components the team plans to use.

- **User documentation specialist**. This person, who should have a technical writing background, ensures that online help and user manuals are well written.

- **Tester**. Even though there should be an independent test group, the development group may have a person who is responsible for the first stage of testing.

Within any development team, the same individual may have more than one of these roles. The important point, from a project management perspective, is that the needed roles be filled. If not, then some of these tasks may not be properly done. It is also important that there be at least two people capable of performing each role, so that if somebody leaves or is sick, the project is not paralyzed.

The roles listed above require specific skills and knowledge. The project manager can either select people with appropriate background, or ensure that people obtain appropriate training. The project manager should also ensure that all team members continue to augment their education in software engineering, as well as in general skills such as leadership, technical writing, and running meetings.

Exercises

E218 Discuss what you think the best team structure would be for each of the following projects:

(a) The replacement of the income tax system of a country.

(b) The GANA software, whose requirements we introduced in Chapter 4.

(c) The control software for a new interplanetary probe.

(d) Software to provide a more useful front-end to a university registration system, so that students can make better choices of courses.

E219 Design a team for implementing Release 1 of the GANA software whose cost you estimated in Exercise E217. Specify an appropriate team structure, the number of people you believe should be on the team, how the team structure would evolve as the project progresses, and the skills you believe team members should have.

11.5 Project scheduling and tracking

Scheduling is the process of deciding in what sequence a set of activities will be performed, as well as when they should start and be completed. Tracking is the process of determining how well you are sticking to the cost estimate and schedule.

Two types of diagram are particularly important in scheduling: *PERT charts* and *Gantt charts*. *Earned value charts* are useful for tracking. In this section, we will show you how to use all three diagram types. A variety of commercial tools are available to help draw these diagrams.

PERT charts

A PERT chart shows the sequence in which tasks must be completed. Each task has zero or more predecessors on which it depends, and zero or more successors, which depend on it. The whole diagram therefore forms a graph, whose nodes are tasks, and whose arcs are dependencies.

In each node of a PERT chart, you typically show the elapsed time and effort estimates. You can also show optimistic, likely and pessimistic estimates.

PERT

PERT stands for 'Program Evaluation Review Technique' and is very similar to techniques called the 'Critical Path Method' and 'Precedence Networks'.

One of the most important uses of a PERT chart is to determine the *critical path*. The critical path indicates the minimum time in which it is possible to complete the project. It is computed by searching for the path through the chart that has the greatest cumulative elapsed time and no idle time. If any task on the critical path is delayed, then the completion date of the project will be delayed.

Figure 11.9 shows a PERT chart for Release 2 of the GANA system, corresponding to the cost estimates in Example 11.6. Note that some of the tasks have been broken down into subtasks. Each task box shows both the expected elapsed time, in weeks, as well as the expected effort in person-months. The critical path is shown in bold. You can calculate the minimum elapsed time (35 weeks) by summing the elapsed times on this path.

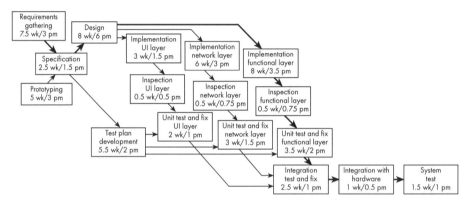

Figure 11.9   A PERT chart for Release 2 of the GANA system

Gantt charts

A Gantt chart is used to graphically present the start and end dates of each software engineering task. A Gantt chart is like a UML sequence chart: one axis shows time and the other axis shows the activities that will be performed.

Figure 11.10 shows a Gantt chart for Release 2 of the GANA system. The black bars are the top-level tasks; the white bars are subtasks, and the diamonds are milestones – important deadline dates, at which specific events may occur.

Note how requirements gathering and prototyping overlap each other. Also note that inspection can be started as soon as the first parts of the implementation are complete, and testing can start as soon as some inspection is complete.

This chart does not yet show the allocation of people to the tasks. Nor have we chosen to show the breakdown of implementation and testing by layer; this latter detail can be added once requirements are clearer.

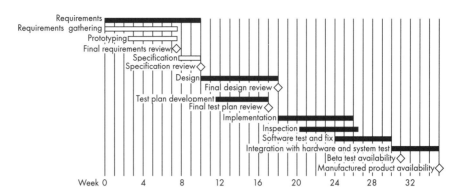

Figure 11.10   A Gantt chart for Release 2 of the GANA system

Earned value charts

Earned value is the amount of work completed, measured according to the *budgeted* effort that the work was supposed to consume. It is also called the *budgeted cost of work performed*. As each task is completed, the number of person-months originally planned for that task is added to the earned value of the project.

For example, in the GANA Release 2 project, the total planned effort for all the tasks is 32.5 person-months. Therefore, when the project is complete, its earned value will be 32.5 person-months.

However, tasks may be completed late, and may take more effort than planned. An *earned value chart* such as Figure 11.11 can be used to measure the extent to which the project is behind schedule and over budget.

An earned value chart has three curves:

■ **The budgeted cost of work scheduled**. This is the planned amount of effort that was supposed to have been expended by any point in time. It is computed by examining at the cost estimates and the Gantt chart. It is shown here as the solid black curve.

■ **The earned value** – that is, the budgeted cost of the work performed. This is shown here as the dotted curve.

■ **The actual cost of the work performed so far**. This is shown as a dashed curve.

At any point in the project, you can tell how far behind schedule you are by measuring the horizontal distance between the earned value curve and the budgeted cost of work scheduled. You can also tell the extent to which you are over budget by measuring the vertical distance between the earned value curve and the actual cost curve. Armed with this information, you can take steps to get the project back on track, for example by postponing less important requirements.

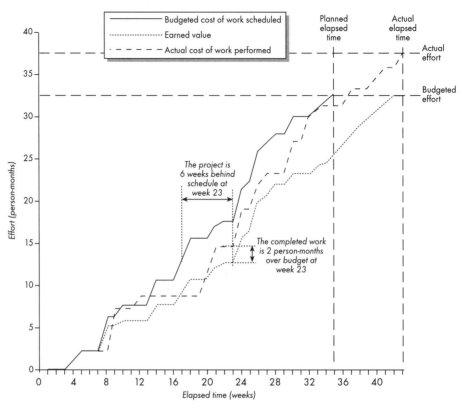

Figure 11.11 Earned value chart showing how development of Release 2 of the GANA system was 8 weeks behind schedule and cost 10 person-months more than expected

Exercises

E220 Draw a PERT and a Gantt chart for the project to develop Release 1 of the GANA software, whose cost you estimated in Exercise E217. Make sure you show the critical path on your PERT chart.

E221 In light of the last exercise, review your proposed cost estimate and team structure for the GANA system. Explain any changes you would make.

11.6 Contents of a project plan

You should write a project plan document that has the following types of information. This document should be regularly updated as the project progresses. As with other documents, when writing a project plan, be concise and understand the audience. The audience will be all the team members, the customers, the project managers of related projects, anybody else who has to implement aspects of the plan, and anybody who has to take over as project manager for any reason.

A. **Purpose**. Describe the problem to be solved, as in the requirements document. State the business objectives for the project, including anticipated benefits. Quantify the benefits as much as possible.

B. **Background information**. Give a brief history of the project to date – you can update this as the project proceeds. Describe the stakeholders. Give references to related projects and any documents produced so far, such as requirements definitions.

C. **Processes to be used**. Describe the overall process model (e.g. spiral model, eXtreme Programming, etc.). Outline the techniques to be employed for requirements gathering, design, implementation, quality assurance, change management, risk management, and ongoing project management. Also describe the documents to be produced, including the contents of these documents, and how you will measure and track the project. Some of this information can be given as pointers to standards.

D. **Subsystems and planned releases**. Show the division of the system into subsystems and releases that can be allocated to people or teams. This can be provided as a reference to the architectural model.

E. **Risks and challenges**. Describe the risks and difficulties that are expected to be most critical to this project, or to specific subsystems. Indicate how they are to be monitored and resolved. This will be updated as the project progresses.

F. **Tasks**. List the tasks to be completed for each subsystem and release.

G. **Cost estimates**. Give the present cost estimates for the tasks and subsystems. Show all calculations, and include pessimistic and optimistic values.

H. **Team**. Describe the team structure, the skills needed on that team, the plan for ongoing training and the allocation of general responsibilities to team members.

I. **Schedule and milestones**. Give reasonable deadlines for completion of tasks. Use Gantt and PERT charts showing the allocations of tasks to people, the periods of time they will work on each task, as well as the critical path(s).

11.7 Difficulties and risks in project management

The problems faced by software engineers in general, as discussed in earlier chapters, are also faced by project managers. The following are some of the particular difficulties faced by those given management tasks.

■ **Accurately estimating costs is a constant challenge**. As discussed in this chapter, there are many sources of uncertainty that result in inaccurate estimates.
Resolution. Follow the cost estimation guidelines presented in this chapter.

■ **It is very difficult to measure progress and meet deadlines**. Despite your best planning efforts, last-minute problems and inaccurate progress reports can confound attempts to meet deadlines with a high-quality result. Quite often, members of a team have a false sense of optimism, blindly ignore some of the tasks that lie ahead, or are fearful to report potential delays.

Resolution. Improve your cost estimation skills so as to account for the kinds of problems that may occur. Develop a closer relationship with other members of the team so that you are more keenly aware at all times about the progress achieved, and the potential risks. Be realistic in initial requirements gathering, and follow an iterative approach, since smaller projects are easier to deliver on time. Use earned value charts to monitor progress.

■ **It is difficult to deal with lack of human resources or technology that is needed to successfully run a project**. People differ widely in skills, and there may be a shortage of software developers with the skills you need. Much of the technology that we use also has deficiencies.

Resolution. When determining the requirements and the project plan, take into realistic consideration the resources available. If you cannot find skilled people or suitable technology then you must limit the scope of your project.

■ **Communicating effectively in a large project is hard**. Many people lack training in the listening and communications skills needed to exchange information effectively with other stakeholders. This results in errors and delays. Both lack of information and information overload are equally problematic.

Resolution. Take courses in communication, both written and oral. Learn how to run effective meetings. Review what information everybody should have, and make sure they have it. Make sure that project information is readily available for browsing, e.g. using an intranet web site. Use 'groupware' technology to help specific groups of people exchange the information they need to know.

■ **It is hard to obtain agreement and commitment from others**. People have different ideas about the requirements, the design and the project plan. Progress can be paralyzed by indecision. People can be reluctant to commit to plans if they feel they have too much work to do, or if they feel there are not enough benefits accruing from the plan as compared to the costs.

Resolution. Take courses in negotiating skills and leadership. Ensure that everybody understands the position of everybody else, the costs and benefits of each alternative, and the rationale behind any compromises. Ensure that everybody's proposed responsibility is clearly expressed. Listen to everybody's opinion, but take assertive action, when needed, to ensure progress occurs.

Exercise

E222 Now you have completed this chapter, go back and review your answer to Exercise E213. What have you learned in the chapter that would have enabled

Software patents: a big source of risk

A patent is a license, given by a government, to hold a monopoly on a new invention for a limited time, typically 20 years. Although laws differ from country to country, you can generally obtain a patent if you can show that your invention is new, useful and non-obvious.

In the past, patents have been very important, ensuring that those who invest effort in developing an innovation will not be immediately undercut in price by people who merely copy their idea. Within the last 20 years, however, patents on *software* have become available in many jurisdictions. The majority of software engineers see this as a bad thing, although many patent holders will obviously hold the opposite opinion.

Software patents certainly are a big source of risk for developers. In the early days of technology, if you marketed an innovation it tended to represent a *single* invention, or perhaps a few. You could therefore reasonably easily tell whether you were infringing on someone's patent. Developing software, however, involves building a system by composing vast numbers of ideas; therefore you are quite likely to accidentally infringe on patents and hence risk being sued by patent holders.

Many people feel software patents should be disallowed since research has shown they probably have the opposite effect from what was intended. They most likely stifle invention – they consume time and money as people defend themselves against claims, or file their own patents so that they can counter-claim against others. They also result in people having to be very cautious in their development and therefore avoid innovation.

To make matters worse, it seems that many patents that have been issued have in fact been neither new nor non-obvious. However, patent examiners have often lacked the time or the sources of information to determine this. Although a bad patent can be overturned in court, doing so is very expensive. This means that if you are sued for infringement of a patent that you know should be invalid, it may still put you out of business.

you to do a better job, if you could go back in time and repeat the group work you did in this book?

11.8 Summary

In this chapter we have briefly introduced some important techniques required to manage a software project.

We started by discussing process models. Although the waterfall model is the classic model, it is recognized today that a more iterative approach is generally superior, and an agile approach may be ideal for a smaller project.

Next we discussed cost estimation, an activity that all software engineers need to perform to some extent, but which is particularly difficult. We outlined a series of principles you can apply, including: dividing and conquering, making sure you account for all activities, basing your estimates on past experience, combining estimates from different people, making pessimistic and optimistic estimates, and regularly revising estimates.

Then we discussed structuring teams. Members of a rigid, hierarchical team will consume less time communicating with each other, but may not exchange essential information. More flexible team structures such as chief programmer or egoless teams work best, especially for smaller and high-risk projects.

We discussed using Gantt, PERT and Earned Value charts for scheduling and tracking projects. Gantt charts show a series of timelines for each task, whereas PERT charts show the interrelationships among tasks, including the critical path. Earned value charts help you determine the extent to which the project is behind schedule and over budget.

All of the information discussed above should be summarized in a project plan that team members can read.

11.9 For more information

The following are some important resources related to project management:

- B. Hughes and M. Cotterell, *Software Project Management*, 3rd edition, McGraw-Hill, 2002. http://www.mcgraw-hill.co.uk/hughes

- S. McConnell, *Software Project Survival Guide*, Microsoft Press, 1997, http://www.stevemcconnell.com/sg.htm

- R. L. Glass, *Software Runaways*, Prentice Hall, 1998

- F. Brooks, *The Mythical Man-Month*, 20th Anniversary Edition, Addison-Wesley, 1995

- R. M. Belbin, *Beyond the Team*, Butterworth-Heinemann, 2000, http://www.belbin.com/book-btt.html

- A good website for COCOMO: http://sunset.usc.edu/research/COCOMOII/

- Dave Farthing's software project management page at the University of Glamorgan: http://www.comp.glam.ac.uk/pages/staff/dwfarthi/projman.htm

- The Extreme Programming web site: http://www.extremeprogramming.org. This web site is a particularly good project management resource, whether or not you are currently thinking of doing eXtreme Programming

- M. Stephens and D. Rosenberg, *Extreme Programming Refactored: The Case Against XP*, Apress, 2003. http://www.softwarereality.com/lifecycle/xp/case_against_xp.jsp

- All project management: http://www.allpm.com

- The project management institute http://www.pmi.org. They have also published their Project Management Body of Knowledge in book form as *A Guide to the Project Management Body of Knowledge*

Standards

The following are some of the IEEE, British and ISO standards covering project management. As mentioned in Chapter 4, standards require a subscription. For ISO standards, see http://www.iso.ch. For IEEE standards, see: http://www.standards.ieee.org/software/index.html. For British standards, see: http://bsonline.techindex.co.uk.

- IEEE Standard 828, *Software Configuration Management Plans*
- IEEE Standard 1219, *Software Maintenance*
- IEEE Standard 1490, *Adoption of the Project Management Institute's Project Management Body of Knowledge*
- ISO Standard/British Standard/ IEEE Standard 12207, *Software Lifecycle Processes*
- ISO Standard/British Standard 15504, *Software Process Assessment*

Project exercises

E223 Look back over all the work you and your group have performed on project work from this book, and write a report about the results. Include the following information:

(a) How much effort you spent in total, for all aspects of the work.

(b) How much you produced, measured in use cases implemented, test cases written, and lines of code.

(c) Your productivity: how much you produced, per person-hour.

(d) Sources of inaccuracy in your estimation of the above.

(e) The technological problems you encountered.

(f) The project management problems you encountered.

E224 Compare your results of the previous exercise with the results of other groups. Explain any differences.

E225 Develop an outline of requirements and a project plan for the following problem. Imagine you were asked to extend SimpleChat Phase 5 so that it can be used to transmit low-resolution, low frame-rate video images of the people participating in a channel. The objective is to make SimpleChat work like video-conferencing software. Include in your project plan the information suggested in Section 11.6. Use data from the last exercise to help calibrate your cost estimates, and use OLP and Delphi estimating techniques.

Review 12

We have incorporated nine themes into many of the chapters in this book. These themes will serve in this chapter as a way to gather together and relate many of the concepts we have discussed.

12.1 Theme 1: Understanding the customer and user

We have emphasized in this book that software engineers must continually focus on the customers and users. Customers are those who pay, while users are those who use. In some cases they are the same people, but often not.

The definition we gave of software engineering from Chapter 1 places customers at the center – we must ensure that everything we do is directed towards solving their problems.

Solving customers' problems is difficult: software engineers must spend considerable effort trying to understand their problems and then develop requirements that address the problems. Techniques for doing this were discussed in detail in Chapter 4; these include domain analysis, interviewing, brainstorming, use case analysis and prototyping.

In Chapter 7, we focused on the users. Unless the users can learn the software effectively, and work efficiently with it, the customer's problem will not be adequately solved. We emphasized that involving users in all activities, and designing the user interface effectively, will ensure that both utility and usability are maximized.

12.2 Theme 2: Basing development on solid principles and reusable technology

We have emphasized throughout the book that software engineering is an *engineering* activity. Like other engineers, a software engineer solves problems by applying well-understood knowledge and technology in a disciplined way. However, the types of knowledge and technology required for the different engineering disciplines differ: other engineers design artifacts made of atoms and are subject to the laws of physics, whereas software engineers design artifacts made of bits, and are subject to the principles of logic, computability and human psychology.

The following are some of the types of knowledge and technology applied – i.e. *reused* – by software engineers:

- **Software engineering principles:** reuse of experience. Table 12.1 reiterates the general principles that we have encountered throughout the book. This book has discussed only a sample of the principles you can apply while developing software, but if you focus on the principles listed here you will be well on your way to being a good software engineer.

Table 12.1   **Summary of software engineering principles presented in this book**

Principles for gathering good requirements (Chapter 4)

1. Perform domain analysis so that you know enough to communicate effectively and avoid misunderstandings
2. Keep the scope of the system narrow enough by understanding and focusing on the customers' real problem
3. Keep the system general enough by finding out the higher-level goals of the customers and users
4. Gather all kinds of requirements: functional, quality, platform and process requirements
5. Combine techniques such as interviewing, brainstorming, use case analysis and prototyping to gather requirements most effectively

Principles for writing good requirements documents (Chapter 4)

1. Ensure that the benefit of each requirement outweighs its cost
2. Ensure that each requirement contributes to the solution of the problem
3. Ensure that each requirement is expressed clearly and consistently
4. Ensure that each requirement is unambiguous
5. Ensure that each requirement is consistent with each of the others
6. Ensure that each requirement contributes to a system that has a sufficient level of quality
7. Ensure that it is possible to develop each requirement with the resources available
8. Ensure that each requirement is written in a verifiable way
9. Ensure that each requirement is uniquely identifiable
10. Ensure that no requirement over-constrains the design of the system
11. Ensure that the requirements document as a whole is sufficiently complete
12. Organize the requirements document effectively
13. Give clear rationale for requirements that needed careful analysis or may be controversial
14. Obtain agreement from all stakeholders for the requirements document

Principles of user-centered design (Chapter 7)

1. Design software based on an understanding of users' tasks

Table 12.1   Summary of software engineering principles presented in this book (cont.)

2. Ensure users are involved in decision-making processes

3. Have users work with, and give feedback about, prototypes of the system and documentation

4. Design the user interface following guidelines for good usability (such as those below)

Principles that lead to good usability (Chapter 7)

1. Do not rely only on usability guidelines – always test with users

2. Base UI designs on users' tasks, as expressed in use cases

3. Ensure that the sequences of actions to achieve a task are as simple as possible

4. Ensure that the user always knows what he or she can and should do next, and what will happen when he or she does it

5. Provide good feedback including effective error messages

6. Ensure that the user can always get out, go back or undo an action

7. Ensure that response time is adequate

8. Use understandable labels and other encoding techniques

9. Ensure that the UI's appearance is neat and uncluttered

10. Consider the needs of different groups of users

11. Provide all necessary help

12. Be consistent

Principles for making good design decisions (Chapter 9)

1. Use priorities and objectives to decide among alternatives

2. Use cost–benefit analysis to choose among alternatives

Principles of effective design (Chapter 9)

1. Divide and conquer

2. Increase cohesion where possible

3. Reduce coupling where possible

4. Keep the level of abstraction as high as possible

5. Increase reusability where possible

6. Reuse existing designs and code where possible

7. Design for flexibility

8. Anticipate obsolescence

9. Design for portability

10. Design for testability

11. Design defensively

Principles of testing (Chapter 10)

1. Treat testing like detective work: be suspicious of everything

2. Be both effective and efficient while testing

Table 12.1   Summary of software engineering principles presented in this book (cont.)

3. Divide the inputs into equivalence classes, based on whether the inputs may cause different code to execute, and run tests in each equivalence class and their boundaries

4. Test for all categories of defects, including algorithmic defects, timing and co-ordination defects, defects in handling unusual situations, and defects in documentation

Principles of inspecting (Chapter 10)

1. Inspect the most difficult documents of each type

2. Choose an effective and efficient inspection team

3. Require that participants prepare for inspections

4. Only inspect documents that are ready

5. Have 'finding defects' as the only goal

6. Avoid discussing how to fix defects

7. Avoid discussing style issues

8. Do not rush the inspection process

9. Avoid making participants tired

10. Keep and use logs of inspections

11. Re-inspect when changes are made

Principles of cost estimation (Chapter 11)

1. Divide and conquer

2. Include all activities when making estimates

3. Base your estimates on past experience combined with what you can observe of the current project

4. Be sure to account for differences when extrapolating from other projects

5. Anticipate the worst case and plan for contingencies

6. Combine multiple independent estimates

7. Revise and refine estimates as work progresses

■ **Patterns: reuse of problem-solving experience.** Patterns express well-understood solutions to problems. In this book we introduced some useful modeling and design patterns in Chapter 6; we also presented some architectural patterns in Chapter 9. Table 12.2 summarizes the main features of the patterns we discussed. There are many hundreds of other patterns – as you develop your software engineering knowledge, you will become familiar with more of them.

■ **Frameworks: reuse of implemented technology.** In Chapter 3, we discussed the benefits of basing design on frameworks. To reinforce this, we based the project work on the Object Client–Server Framework (OCSF).

Table 12.2   The patterns discussed in this book

Type of pattern	Description
Design patterns (Chapter 6)	
Abstraction–Occurrence	Represents abstract sets and their occurrences, while avoiding duplication of information
General Hierarchy	Represents hierarchies of objects (as opposed to hierarchies of classes)
Player–Role	Allows an object to change roles or play multiple roles, avoiding multiple inheritance
Singleton	Guarantees that a certain class can have only one instance
Observer	Reduces coupling by ensuring that an object can communicate with others without knowing their class
Delegation	Reduces coupling and increases reusability by providing methods that do nothing but call methods in neighboring classes
Adapter	Improves reuse and flexibility by translating the interface of a class so that its facilities can be used polymorphically
Façade	Provides a simplified interface for a subsystem, reducing coupling
Immutable	Allows you to create instances that cannot be changed
Read-only Interface	Allows you to select which classes can modify instances of a given class
Proxy	Provides a lightweight stand-in for a heavyweight object
Factory	Allows a framework to create instances of an application-specific class
Architectural patterns (Chapter 9)	
Multi-Layer	Adds flexibility by separation of concerns: in particular, ensuring that the user interface is kept separate from the functional layer
Client–Server	The simplest pattern for distributed computing (discussed in detail in Chapter 3)
Broker	Transparently distributes aspects of a software system to different nodes
Transaction Processing	Provides a uniform interface for handling transactions, permitting easy addition of new types of transaction
Pipe-and-Filter	Divides the system into units where input data is in a relatively simple form, and output data in a similar form, so that sets of the units can be chained together in different ways
Model–View–Controller	Builds on the multi-layer pattern, allowing for separation of concerns within the user interface
Service-Oriented	Enables creation of applications that call on distributed services available on the Internet using standard protocols, and which return their results as XML documents
Message Oriented	Allows applications to be built that communicate transparently through 'topics' to which other applications or subsystems may subscribe

Frameworks are skeletal applications or subsystems on which many different applications can be built. They contain the essential services needed by a class of systems. Software engineers adapt them to the needs of a particular system by writing code that fills slots (required functionality missing from the framework) or hooks (places where the system explicitly anticipates you may want to add extensions). The code written to fill slots and hooks will call the services of the framework.

Since the designers of frameworks have already done much of the hard work, developing applications based on them should be much easier than designing from scratch.

12.3 Theme 3: Object orientation

We introduced the basic principles of object orientation in Chapter 2. We pointed out that an object-oriented system benefits from the synergy arising out of abstraction, inheritance and polymorphism. Under the object-oriented paradigm, both data and procedural abstractions are grouped together into the cohesive units, the classes.

In Chapter 3, we presented the OCSF as an illustration of an object-oriented framework. In Chapters 5 and 6 we discussed class diagrams and patterns, which provide abstract views of the static relationships among classes in a system. Chapter 8 presented several other diagrams that can be used to describe the dynamic aspects of an object-oriented system. In Chapter 9 we showed how object-oriented principles help to achieve better design.

12.4 Theme 4: Visual modeling using UML

All engineers model their products visually. Mechanical engineers and civil engineers have an advantage: since their products are very tangible, most of their diagrams are direct projections of their finished products. Software engineers, in a similar manner, draw pictures of their user interfaces.

However, like electrical engineers with their circuit diagrams, software engineers have to do most of their diagramming using notations that represent abstractions of their product. Over the 50-year history of computing, many different types of diagram have been used to represent software, but the UML notations are now becoming standardized for most purposes.

In this book we gave you a taste of UML in Chapters 2 and 3. We then formally introduced use case diagrams in Chapter 4, class diagrams in Chapter 5, interaction, state and activity diagrams in Chapter 8, and the remaining diagrams in Chapter 9. As a software engineer, you should feel fluent at using these diagrams to represent any design that comes to your mind.

We have also pointed out that the diagrams are more than just pretty pictures: they should be used to help you create better designs and implementations. In Chapters 5 and 6, for example, we showed many examples of good object-oriented design that would have been hard to communicate without UML class diagrams. In Chapter 8, we showed an example piece of code that implements a state and a sequence diagram: without the diagrams, we would have been much more likely to make a mistake in the code.

In Appendix A, we provide a summary of the parts of UML syntax we have introduced in this book.

12.5   Theme 5: Evaluation of alternatives in requirements and design

In Chapter 9, we pointed out that design is a systematic problem-solving process. Many engineering problems involve evaluating the advantages and disadvantages of several alternatives, and then deciding which alternative leads to the best solution to the problem.

As early as Chapter 2, we started to train you to think in this way. There were several exercises where we asked you to evaluate the pros and cons of different design alternatives for a Point class. In Chapter 3 we presented the client–server architecture and discussed the pros and cons of thin-client versus fat-client alternatives.

In Chapter 4, we pointed out that you should evaluate competing software when doing domain analysis. We also showed you examples of carefully documenting the rationale for decisions you make when establishing requirements.

In Chapters 5and 6, we emphasized the process of evaluation while modeling. For example, we asked you to justify your multiplicity decisions. We also pointed out that the process of choosing a pattern requires evaluating whether that pattern correctly balances the 'forces'.

Evaluation of alternatives is central in user interface design. In Chapter 7 we suggested that you follow a process of parallel design so as to explicitly capture different alternatives. You can then evaluate these alternatives by observing users, and by determining the extent to which the designs adhere to usability principles.

In Chapter 9, we presented several principles of design that can serve as a guide in making design decisions, and we discussed cost–benefit analysis as a systematic evaluation process.

12.6   Theme 6: Incorporating quantitative and logical thinking

We taught you to think in a quantitative way in several places in this book. We introduced metrics in Section 2.10, describing them as well-defined methods and formulae for computing values of interest to a software engineer. We pointed out that computing metrics for its own sake is not very useful: it is important to have a goal, and compute metrics that will help you achieve that goal.

In Chapter 2 we introduced a variety of metrics you can use to judge the internal quality of your programs.

In Chapter 4 we introduced quality requirements, pointing out that it is essential to specify them in a quantitative way. We suggested ways to measure such things as response time, throughput, reliability, and availability.

In Chapter 7 we discussed usability metrics, such as the time taken to learn a particular set of features, or the number of instances of a specific task that the user can do per hour (to measure efficiency of use).

In Chapter 9 we talked about cost–benefit analysis, and considered the various things you should measure when doing this.

In Chapter 10 we discussed metrics that can be used to evaluate various aspects of external quality: examples include the number of failures encountered by users, or the number of questions to the help desk.

Finally, in Chapter 11, we discussed metrics in the context of cost estimation. We gave several examples of the use of COCOMO II.

The other aspect of mathematics we applied in this book was logic. In Chapter 5, we showed how you can specify details of UML models using OCL, which is based on logic and set theory.

12.7 Theme 7: Iterative and agile development

Although we discussed the waterfall process model in Chapter 11, we made it clear that modern software engineering should almost always be based on an iterative approach, such as the spiral or agile models. In the iterative approach, you develop a small version of the final system with fewer features; then you continue creating versions, each one with small improvements over the last. In most iterative approaches, the first versions are prototypes, designed purely for requirements analysis. The prototypes are then deliberately thrown away once their lessons are learned.

There are several major advantages to the iterative approach:

■ Risks are reduced, for several reasons. Each piece of development is smaller and simpler; the requirements are less likely to change in the period of time it takes to deliver a small iteration; and you will rapidly detect problems with earlier exposure of the system to customers.

■ Customers are happier since they get something in their hands sooner.

■ If the project fails in a later iteration, at least you have delivered earlier ones.

In Chapter 4, we discussed the 80–20 rule, also called the Pareto Principle, which says, among other things, that 80 per cent of the value to the customer is delivered with 20 per cent of the work. Therefore, you can solve most of the customer's problem in the first iteration.

In the project work in this book, we asked you to practice iterative development: you were given the first iteration of the SimpleChat system in Chapter 3. In several subsequent chapters you then added particular features to it.

12.8 Theme 8: Communicating effectively using documentation

Communication is central to software engineering. You must communicate with customers and users in order to develop requirements and refine the user interface. You must communicate with managers and subordinates as part of project management. And you must communicate your designs to other software engineers who will be implementing them, interfacing to them or modifying them in future.

All of these communication activities require writing some form of documentation. Throughout the book, we suggested the kinds of information that should be put in each type of document. In Chapter 2 we trained you to become used to using documentation by looking up information about Java. Looking up specifications in reference manuals is a hallmark of engineering. In Chapter 4 we described domain analysis documents and requirements documents, and gave detailed examples of the latter. In Chapter 9 we presented design documents, and again gave an example. In Chapter 10 we discussed how to write a test plan and test cases. Finally, in Chapter 11, we indicated the kind of information that should be present in a project plan.

Although we suggested what should be contained in each type of document, we pointed out that organizations tend to have their own standards. The content, and the accessibility of that content to your audience, should be given priority over rigidly following a format.

We also stressed the importance of carefully reviewing documents. In Chapter 4 we gave a long list of things to look for in a requirements document. In Chapter 10 we discussed inspecting documents.

12.9 Theme 9: Risk management in all software engineering activities

We have presented a selection of software engineering risks at the end of each chapter. According to Barry Boehm (in 'Software risk management: principles and practices', *IEEE Software* 8 (1), pp. 32–41, January 1991), the following are the top ten risks that software engineers have to face. Note that this is an extension of the list of root causes of software defects, given in Section 10.11.

1. **Personnel shortfalls**. Software developers and project managers often lack sufficient training or experience to develop a system successfully. This in turn leads to many of the risks listed below. Improving personnel training and education is probably, therefore, the easiest way to reduce long-term risk. If people with sufficient skill are simply not available, however, then the only solution is to reduce the scope of the project. Planning and development effort estimation as presented in Chapter 11 are therefore the key to reduce this important risk.

2. **Unrealistic schedules and budgets**. There is a tendency, probably intrinsic to human nature, to believe you can get more done than is really possible. This is

partly due to not fully appreciating the details and complexity of the proposed system, and partly due to the fact that the early prototyping stages can appear to produce results extremely fast, leading to over-optimism. Sometimes, belief in an unrealistic schedule can persist up to the planned delivery date, giving rise to a well-known 'joke' that would be funny if it were in fact false: many software developers estimate their percent done in stages – they report that they are 20% done, 40% done, 80% done, 99% done, 99% done, 99% done… The solution to this problem is to better understand the requirements, as discussed in Chapter 4, and to better manage the project using the techniques from Chapter 11.

3. **Developing the wrong software functions**. This arises from inadequate requirements analysis. The consequences are software that does not solve the customer's problem, software that is not used, and endless requests for change, leading to deterioration of the design. The solution is better requirements analysis, following the principles discussed in Chapter 4, as well as developing in smaller iterations. It is particularly important to develop prototypes and to interact closely with users, as discussed in Chapter 7.

4. **Developing the wrong user interface**. This means developing a user interface that is not usable for the task at hand and for the intended users. It might be the case, for example, that the interface is efficient for use by experts, yet most users are not experts and find it hard to learn. The solution to this problem is to follow the user-centered design techniques and usability principles discussed in Chapter 7.

5. **Gold-plating**. We mentioned this in Chapter 4: gold-plating occurs when you have requirements that are not necessary to solve the problem. The solution is to be disciplined about cutting such requirements and to focus on developing software that is 'good enough'.

6. **Permitting a continuing stream of requirements changes**. This was another problem we discussed in Chapter 4. It takes considerable discipline to specify a good set of requirements initially so as to minimize the need for changes. It also takes discipline to say no to requests for non-critical changes (or to defer them). Often the requester of the change has a good argument about why the change would be good idea, and it is hard to comprehend the fact that, one by one, a series of changes can seriously impact your ability to deliver the system on time. There is a well-known saying: 'How does a project get to be one year late? One day at a time.' In Chapter 4 we emphasize the importance of clearly defining the scope of the problem; sticking to this definition helps to keep the project focused and to resist the temptation of adding extra features.

7. **Shortfalls in externally performed tasks**. 'Contracting out' is an accepted management approach to reduce costs and take advantage of external expertise. However, if you contract out the development of part of your system, you must ensure that your contractor follows the software engineering

principles discussed in this book. One way to do that is to require that they be certified under ISO-9000 or the CMM, as discussed in Chapter 10. You should also carefully and regularly evaluate the work done by contractors, and take corrective action if shortfalls are detected. Performing integration tests and acceptance tests, as discussed in Chapter 10, is a good way to assess the quality of the work done.

8. **Shortfalls in externally furnished components**. As mentioned in Chapter 3, reusing components developed by others is essential to reduce development costs and simplify design. However, you need to perform acceptance testing and other quality assurance activities, as discussed in Chapter 10, to ensure the reused components do not become an Achilles' heel for you.

9. **Real-time performance shortfalls**. In Chapter 4, we pointed out that it is essential to define real-time performance in the requirements. Designing real-time systems so as to ensure that their timing constraints are always met, however, is a very difficult technical problem. There are advanced techniques to help prevent such failures, but when failures occur they can be catastrophic. We briefly discussed testing for such problems as deadlocks and critical races in Chapter 10, but you should read a real-time design book if you intend to design or test such systems.

10. **Straining computer science capabilities**. This means trying to compute things that intrinsically take an increasingly large amount of CPU time or memory, or would naturally require a very complex design. Some kinds of problems are known to be 'difficult' using today's technology. Technology being developed at the forefront of computer science may in the future help resolve some of these problems; examples of such technology include DNA computing, quantum computing and artificial intelligence techniques. Meanwhile, learning about algorithm analysis and advanced design techniques will help you avoid this risk. Also, as we mentioned in Chapter 4, producing prototypes is a good way to determine the feasibility of very challenging requirements.

12.10 Where next?

This brings us to the end of the book. However, we hope you will continue your studies in software engineering. As we mentioned at the beginning of the book, our intent has been to give you a broad overview of software engineering, with enough depth in areas such as UML and object orientation, so that you can immediately apply what you have learned in the work environment.

After reading this book, you should now be primed to learn about many areas of software engineering in much more depth. For example, there is much more to be learned about software design and architecture, user interface design, quality assurance and project management. You will also want to learn about advanced techniques in which discrete mathematics or statistics can be applied to software engineering, such as formal specification methods and reliability engineering. Many of you will want to study specialized techniques that can be applied to develop real-time or data-processing systems. Finally, you will want to learn more about how to conduct your work in a professional manner – with concern for customers, users, your employer, your peers and society as a whole.

We therefore hope you will continue your studies, both as your formal education continues, and as you embark on a lifelong professional development process.

Summary of the UML notation used in this book

Since this is an introductory textbook, we have discussed only a subset of UML features. The following provides a simple overview of what has been covered. The reader is invited to examine a more complete guide to UML in order to learn about features we have omitted.

Classes (Section 5.2)

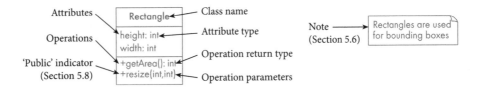

Associations and multiplicity (Section 5.3)

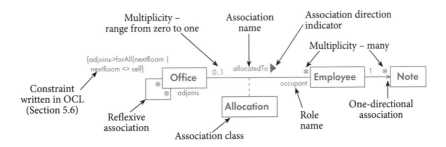

Aggregations (Section 5.6)

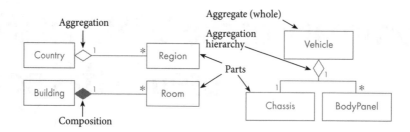

Generalizations (Section 5.4) and interfaces (Section 5.6)

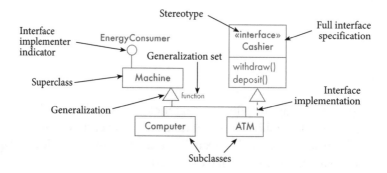

Object diagram (Section 5.5)

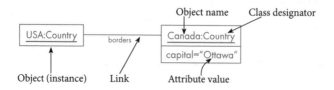

Sequence and communication diagrams (Section 8.1)

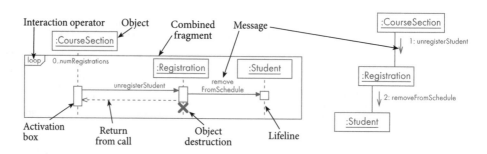

State diagrams (Section 8.2)

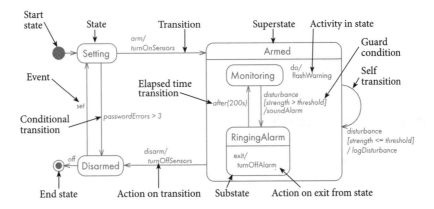

Activity diagrams (Section 8.3)

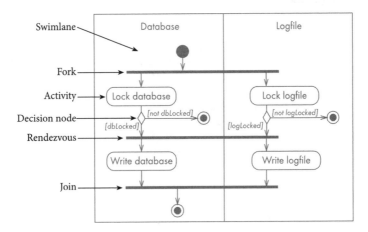

Use case diagrams (Section 4.6)

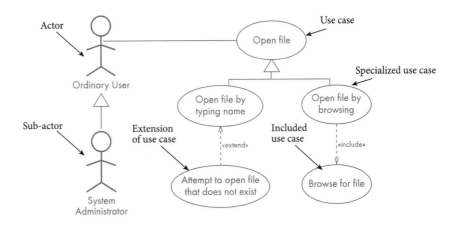

Package diagrams (Section 9.4)

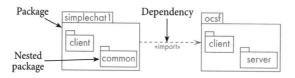

Component diagrams (Section 9.5)

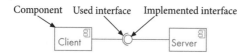

Deployment diagrams (Section 9.5)

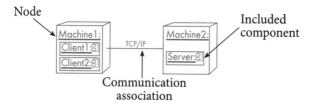

Summary of the documentation types recommended in this book

Throughout this book we have suggested what various types of documentation should contain. The following is a quick reference guide that will help software engineers remember the kinds of information they should include. Each organization should adopt more comprehensive format standards so as to ensure uniformity, although overly rigid formats should be avoided.

When writing documents, remember that their objective is effective communication, therefore keep the intended audience in mind, be as concise as possible, and pay attention to organization and clarity of the writing. Each document should also include, at the beginning, the name of the authors, a version number and a history of changes. This will ensure that change management is done properly.

Domain analysis document (Chapter 4)

A. Introduction. Name of the domain; reasons for the analysis.

B. Glossary. Meanings of terms used in the domain.

C. General knowledge about the domain. Important facts or rules: scientific principles; business processes; analysis techniques; how any technology works.

D. Customers and users. Those who will or might buy the software, and in what industrial sectors they operate. Others who work in the domain.

E. The environment. Equipment and systems used.

F. Tasks and procedures currently performed. What people do as they go about their work, including shortcuts they take.

G. Competing software. Software already in use, and on the market.

H. Similarities across domains and organizations. What is generic versus what is specific to this organization.

Requirements document (Chapter 4)

A. Problem. A succinct description of the problem the system is solving.

B. Background information. Whatever will help readers understand the requirements – references to domain analysis documents, standards and the requirements of related subsystems; important issues you considered, and the rationale for your decisions.

C. Environment and system models. Context and global overview; hardware on which the system will run; other subsystems or software with which it will interact.

D. Functional requirements. The services provided to the user and to other systems – inputs, outputs, computations and timing.

E. Non-functional requirements. Constraints that must be imposed on the design of the system – response time; resource usage; reliability; availability; recovery from failure; allowances for maintainability; enhancement and reusability; platform; technology and development process to be used.

Use case (Chapter 4)

A. Name. Short and descriptive.

B. Actors. Users or other systems that can perform this use case.

C. Goals. What the actor or actors are trying to achieve.

D. Preconditions. The state of the system before the use case – any conditions that must be true before an actor can initiate this use case.

E. Summary. What occurs as the actor or actors perform the use case.

F. Related use cases. Use cases that may be generalizations, specializations, extensions or inclusions.

G. Steps. Use a two-column format, with the left column showing the actions taken by the actor, and the right column showing the system's responses.

H. Postconditions. The state the system is in following completion of the use case.

Design document (Chapter 9)

A. Purpose. The system or part of the system this design document describes; references to the requirements.

B. General priorities. Priorities used to guide the design process.

C. Outline of the design. High-level description of the design.

D. Major design issues. For each issue, the alternatives that were considered, the final decision and the rationale for the decision.

E. Details of the design. Whatever else should be understood by implementers, maintainers and those who will interface to the system.

Test case (Chapter 10)

A. Identification and classification. Test case number; descriptive title; the system, subsystem or module being tested; reference to related requirements and design documents; importance of the test case.

B. Instructions. Tell the tester exactly what to do – how to put the system into the required initial state and what inputs to provide.

C. Expected result. What the system should do in response to the instructions.

D. Cleanup (when needed). How to make the system go 'back to normal'.

E. Purpose. Problem to be solved; business objectives.

Project plan (Chapter 11)

A. Background information. Brief history of the project to date; stakeholders; references to related projects and any documents produced so far, such as requirements definitions.

B. Processes to be used. Overall process model; techniques for requirements gathering, design, implementation, quality assurance, change management, risk management, and project management; documents to be produced; ways to measure and track the project. (These can all be pointers to standards.)

C. Subsystems and releases. Division of the system into subsystems and releases that can be allocated to people or teams. (This can employ references to the requirements or architectural model.)

D. Risks and challenges. Risks and difficulties that are expected to be most critical to this project; how they are to be monitored and resolved.

E. Tasks. List of tasks to be completed.

F. Cost estimates. Cost estimates for the tasks and subsystems.

G. Team. Team structure; skills needed; training plan; allocation of responsibilities.

H. Schedule and milestones. Deadlines for completion of tasks; Gantt and PERT charts allocating tasks to people, showing the times they will work on each task, and showing the critical path(s).

System descriptions

In several places in this book there are examples and exercises demonstrating analysis and design. Below are short outlines of the requirements for these systems. Additional similar requirements descriptions are available on the book's web site (http://www.lloseng.com). This will enable instructors to vary the details of the assignments they give students.

Additional system descriptions can be found in the body of the book:

- Small Hotel Reservations: Exercises at the end of Chapter 4.

- SimpleChat: Introduction in Section 3.9; requirements for a feature in section 4.12.

Police Information System

This system helps the Java Valley police officers keep track of the work they are assigned to do. Officers may be assigned to investigate particular cases, to patrol particular areas or to attend particular events such as court cases. Some work assignments are regular ongoing assignments, while others are for a particular period of time. The system information is updated by the logistics administrator, but individual officers have an interface to display their assigned work.

Household Alarm System

This software will be embedded in an alarm system controller built by Use Case Industries. In conjunction with various hardware devices, it will be able to detect and report such problems as intruders and fires.

GPS-Based Automobile Navigation System (GANA)

This system, manufactured by Use Case Industries, will be used by drivers to navigate around the state of Ootumlia. It uses GPS (Global Positioning System) technology and Internet access to a map database to provide a driver with route maps of various levels of detail, as well as spoken directions to guide the driver to his or her destination.

Airline Reservation System

Ootumlia Airlines runs sightseeing flights from Java Valley, the capital of Ootumlia. The reservation system keeps track of passengers who will be flying in specific seats on various flights, as well as people who will form the crew. For the crew, the system needs to track what everyone does, and who supervises whom. Ootumlia Airlines runs several daily numbered flights on a regular schedule. Ootumlia Airlines expects to expand in the future, therefore the system needs to be flexible; in particular, it will be adding a frequent-flier plan.

Bank Accounts Management System

This system provides the basic services to manage bank accounts at a bank called OOBank. OOBank has many branches, each of which has an address and branch number. A client opens accounts at a branch. Each account is uniquely identified by an account number; it has a balance and a credit or overdraft limit. There are many types of accounts, including: a mortgage account (which has a property as collateral), a checking account, and a credit card account (which has an expiry date and can have secondary cards attached to it). It is possible to have a joint account (e.g. for a husband and wife). Each type of account has a particular interest rate, a monthly fee and a specific set of privileges (e.g. ability to write checks, insurance for purchases etc.). OOBank is divided into divisions and subdivisions (such as Planning, Investments and Consumer); the branches are considered subdivisions of the Consumer Division. Each division has a manager and a set of other employees. Each customer is assigned a particular employee as his or her 'personal banker'.

Elections Management System

The Ootumlia Elections Commission is designing a system to manage elections. The system will manage elections for a variety of different elected bodies (e.g. school boards, city councils, etc.). Each elected body can have various positions (also called seats, e.g. mayor, councilor, etc.). Elections are scheduled for a specific date, and usually several (or all) positions are voted on together; however, sometimes there may be the need for a by-election (e.g. to elect a particular councilor because the incumbent – the previous person who held the position – has resigned).

The system will keep track of candidates for each seat. The system will also record who is the incumbent for a seat, since newspaper reporters are interested in reporting whether incumbents have won again or lost. The system records the name and address of each candidate and incumbent.

The system will also keep track of the list of eligible voters. Each voter can only vote for certain positions (e.g. a particular council seat that represents their area). Each voter is also assigned to vote at a specific poll – each poll has a number and is located in a polling station. The system records the name and address of each voter.

Finally, the system will keep track of the number of votes for each candidate at each poll. However, under no circumstance will it record which voter voted for which candidate, nor whether a voter voted at all.

Geographical Information System

A system used by map makers at the Government of Ootumlia contains information about various maps. Each map has a scale, a name and a set of features. Each map also has information that defines the latitude and longitude of the top left corner of the map, and the height and width of the map in meters.

Features can be of three types: point features, curve features and region features. In general, all features have a name that is displayed on the map next to the feature.

A point feature has a single coordinate, the location at which it is to appear on the map. Examples of point features include transmission towers, mountain peaks, etc. Each type of point feature has a special symbol associated with it; this symbol is a simple bitmap.

A curve feature contains a list of points that define its path. Examples of curve features are roads, railways and rivers. Each type of curve feature has a line pattern associated with it. The line pattern specifies the color, the line thickness, the length of dashes in the line, and the length of gaps in the line.

A region feature is very similar to a curve feature, except that when drawn on the map, it encloses a complete region (the last point connects to the first point). Additionally, it has an optional fill pattern which is a simple bitmap or a color.

Investments System for OOBank

OOBank has a separate investment division. This division manages various mutual funds in which investors may invest and also looks after the investment portfolios of investors.

An investor may at any point in time have several investment advisors. These help the investor decide in what to invest. Different investment advisors specialize in different types of investments.

Investors make a series of transactions and may have to pay a commission on each transaction. The commission is paid to the investment advisor that arranged the transaction.

For each investment the system must keep track of the number of shares (also called units) in addition to the amount the investment is worth today and the amount originally invested.

Each mutual fund invests its money in various securities. The securities can be stocks, bonds or other mutual funds. We must be able to calculate the original amount invested in each security as well as how much that investment is worth today. Each mutual fund may have several investment advisors that help the fund decide what securities in which to invest.

The mutual funds in which investors invest may be managed by OOBank or by some other company. Each mutual fund company may manage several mutual funds.

Manufacturing Plant Controller

This system will be used to manage and control the production processes at Use Case Industries' manufacturing plant. The plant makes several types of mechanical devices. It has 10 assembly lines, each of which can be used in the manufacturing of any of its products. An assembly line is allocated to a product for a fixed period of time (anywhere from a few hours to a few days) – this is called a product run. During a product run, the assembly line makes a specified number of units of the product.

Each product is assembled in several steps. As the product-under-construction moves down the assembly line, it will be worked on in turn by a series of robots. Each robot completes one step before the product moves on to the next step (and a different robot). Each robot is dedicated to just one manufacturing step.

Each product is composed of parts. Parts may be bought from suppliers, or they may in fact be smaller products that are built by this company (in earlier product runs). In each manufacturing step, a given subset of these parts is put together. Parts waiting for assembly are kept in numbered bins; the robots know which bins to go to in order to get the required parts.

Each completed assembly is given a serial number. When orders for products are filled, the serial numbers of the products sold are recorded with the order.

Corporate Event Information System

This program will allow the employees of Ootumlia airlines to keep themselves informed of the various events that are organized by and for company management and employees. Events can be meetings as well as social events.

Woodworking design system

This program is designed to let carpenters, cabinet makers and other wood craftspeople perform computer aided design. The system allows you to make and store any number of designs. Designs can also have design variants (most of the design is the same) but some parts have substitutions.

A design comprises a series of atomic components (pieces of wood, metal hardware attached to the wood, and a few other types of things). Designs are also broken down into a hierarchy of assemblies. Assemblies and components can also be reused in different assemblies.

Each piece of wood is described in terms of its 3-D geometry, the recommended type of wood, and the sequence of cuts and other operations required in order to make it. The 3-D geometry is described in terms of arcs and line-segments that connect to each other at vertices. A group of arcs or line-segments outline a face. Junctions between pieces of wood are described in terms of the faces that touch each together.

The system allows its users to do a wide variety of operations to create and edit designs. Also, the system can visually display a design (or assembly, or component) in three dimensions (allowing the user to rotate it in space), and as various two-dimensional projections.

Glossary

The numbers in square brackets are the sections where each item is discussed. Words in italics are cross-references to other glossary items. You will find an extended cross-linked 'knowledge base' containing this information and much more on the book's web site (www.lloseng.com).

80–20 rule [4.9] A rule that states that 80% of the benefit can often be obtained with 20% of the work; the remaining 20% of the benefit then takes 80% of the work. Also called the *Pareto principle*, it is used to justify cutting less important *requirements* to significantly reduce costs. It also applies in many other situations; for example 80% of the CPU time is spent executing 20% of the statements.

Abstract class [2.6] A class that cannot have any *instances*, and defines a set of methods that must be implemented. Contrast with *concrete class*, and *interface*.

Abstract operation [2.6] An *operation* in a class that makes logical sense for all *subclasses*, but that is not implemented (i.e. has no method) in the class.

Abstraction [2.1 and 9.2] A representation that captures only essential aspects of something, reducing the complexity apparent to the abstraction's user.

Abstraction–Occurrence [6.2] A *pattern* in which two classes are related by a 1–many *association*, and the first class represents an abstraction of the second.

Acceptability [7.3] The extent to which *customers* and *users* like a system.

Acceptance testing [10.9] Testing performed by *customers*, on their own initiative, to decide whether software is sufficiently acceptable to pay for.

Action [8.2] In a *state diagram*, something that takes place effectively instantaneously when a *transition* occurs, or upon entry or exit from a *state*.

Activation box [8.1] A box on a *lifeline* in a *sequence diagram* indicating the period of time during which an object is performing work. See *live activation*.

Activity [8.2] Something that occurs over a period of time and takes place while the system is in a *state*.

Activity diagram [8.3] A UML diagram showing sequences of *activities*; it typically shows multiple *threads*.

Actor [4.6] A role that a *user* or some other system plays when interacting with your system; a class of user of a system.

Adapter [6.8] A *pattern* found in class diagrams in which you are able to reuse an 'adaptee' class by providing a class (the adapter) that *delegates* to the adaptee. It is useful when the adaptee could not have been used directly because its interface does not match what users of the adapter expected.

Adaptive maintenance [1.6] A type of *maintenance* performed to change software so that it will work in an altered environment, such as when an operating system, hardware platform, compiler, software library or database structure changes. Maintenance that is purely adaptive does not result in new capabilities for the user, except the ability to operate the software in the changed environment.

Affordance [7.3] The set of operations that the user can do in a user interface at any given point in time.

Aggregate [5.6] The class on the 'whole' side of an *aggregation*.

Aggregation [5.6] An *association* which specifies that instances of one class contain instances of the other class as parts. In a UML *class diagram*, an aggregation is shown as a diamond next to the 'whole' end of the association.

Agile approach [1.8, 11.2] A *development process* that is disciplined but lightweight. Such approaches are characterized by many short iterations, *test-first development*, and similar techniques. *eXtreme Programming* (XP) is the most well-known such approach.

Algorithmic cost estimation [11.3] An approach to cost estimation such as *COCOMO* or *Function Points*, which uses mathematical formulas whose parameters are based on industrial experience.

Alpha testing [10.9] Testing performed by *users* and *clients*, under the supervision of the software development team.

API [9.2] See *application programming interface*.

Application framework [3.3] A *framework* that provides many of the functions needed by a particular class of *applications*, and which is designed to be reused in the development of such applications. A near-synonym for *vertical framework*.

Application programming interface [9.2] The set of public procedures or methods through which a *layer* provides its services. Also called *API*.

Architect [9.5 and 11.4] The person responsible for leading the decision-making about the *architecture*, and maintaining the *architectural model*.

Architectural model [9.5] The document produced as a result of performing *software architecture*.

Architectural pattern [9.6] A pattern used in *software architecture*. Also called *architectural style*.

Architectural style [9.6] See *architectural pattern*.

Architecture [9.5] See *software architecture*.

Architecture design [9.5] See *software architecture*.

Assertion [9.2] A statement that must be true; if it becomes false then the software has encountered a *failure*.

Association [2.2 and 5.3] A relationship between two *classes*. It represents the existence of a set of *links* between *objects* of the two classes. In a UML *class diagram*, an association is drawn as a line between two classes.

Association class [5.3] A *class* whose instances are associated with links of a (usually many-to-many) *association*. In a UML *class diagram*, it is drawn as an ordinary class with a dotted line connecting it to the association in question.

Asymmetric reflexive association [5.3] A *reflexive association* in which the *roles* at either end are different.

Atomicity [9.6] A property of a transaction that ensures it is completed entirely, or not at all.

Attribute (1) [2.2] A simple piece of information representing a property that is present in the all instances of a class. The term attribute is used in the analysis and design stage before it is known how the attribute will be implemented (in contrast to *instance* *variable*). (2) [10.8] In testing, something that is testable; a detail of the requirements.

Availability [4.5] A *quality* that measures the amount of time that a *system* is running and able to provide services to its users. See also *reliability*.

Beta testing [10.9] Testing performed by the *user* or *client* in their normal work environment.

Big bang testing [10.9] An inappropriate approach to *integration testing* in which you take the entire integrated system and test it as a unit.

Black-box testing [10.3] A form of *testing* in which you manipulate inputs and observe outputs, but cannot observe the internals of the entity being tested. In contrast to *glass-box testing*.

Bottom-up design [9.1] An approach to *design* in which you start by designing the low-level details such as the utilities, and then decide how these will be put together to create successively higher-level components, and ultimately the entire system. In contrast to *top-down design*.

Bottom-up testing [10.9] A *incremental testing strategy* in which you start by testing the very lowest levels of the software using drivers, and then work upwards, as you integrate successive *layers*.

Boundary testing [10.3] A testing strategy based on testing at the boundaries of *equivalence classes*, where most *defects* occur.

Brainstorming [4.7] The process of obtaining ideas, opinions, and answers to a question in a group environment in which all members of the group are given the opportunity to contribute.

Broker [9.6] An *architectural pattern* in which parts of the system are transparently distributed to different nodes of a network.

Budgeted cost of work performed [11.5] See *earned value*.

Bug [10.1] A colloquial term for *defect* or *failure*.

Build [10.9] The process of compiling and integrating all the components of the software, incorporating any changes since the last build.

Burdened cost [11.3] See *weighted average cost*.

Business process [4.10] A process performed by people in an organization. Software systems often automate business processes.

Capability Maturity Model [10.11] A *process standard* containing five levels of maturity; developed at Carnegie Mellon University.

Chartered Engineer [1.3] A term used in the United Kingdom, and certain other jurisdictions, that is equivalent to *professional engineer*.

Chief programmer team [11.4] A team structure midway between a *hierarchical team* and an *egoless team*, in which a chief programmer leads and guides the project, in consultation with experts in various specialties.

Class [2.1 and 2.2] A software *module* that provides both procedural and data *abstraction*. It describes a set of similar *objects*, called its *instances*.

Class design [9.1] The design of the various features of classes such as *associations*, *attributes*, *interactions* and *states*.

Class diagram [5.1] A *UML* diagram that primarily indicates *classes* and the *associations* between those classes.

Class method [2.8] A *method* that, unlike an *instance method*, does not execute in the context of a particular *instance* of a class. It is normally used for such functions as initializing a class, or operating on the complete set of instances of a class.

Class variable [2.3] A data item present in a class that is shared by all instances of that class; also called a *static variable*. (In contrast with *instance variable*).

Classifier A *UML* entity that can have *instances*. Examples are *classes*, *associations* and *use cases*.

Client (1) [1.4] A synonym of *customer*. (2) [3.4] A program or process that connects to another program or process, using a communication channel, in order to request a service. See also *server* and *client–server*.

Client–server [3.4 and 9.6] An *architectural pattern* in which the system is divided into *clients* and *servers*.

Cloning [9.2] (1) The practice of duplicating chunks of code; considered something to avoid unless the benefits can clearly be shown to outweigh the costs. (2) Duplicating an object using the Cloneable interface in Java.

COCOMO [11.3] An *algorithmic cost estimation* method that computes *effort*, in *person-months*, from an estimate of size, measured in lines of code.

Cohesion [9.2] A measure of the extent to which related aspects of a system are kept together in the same module, and unrelated aspects are kept out. An important design principle is to increase cohesion. See also *coupling* and *modularity*, as well as the various types of cohesion: *functional, layer, communicational, sequential, procedural, temporal* and *utility.*

Communication diagram [8.1] A UML *interaction diagram* showing a set of objects connected by *communication links.* Formerly called a collaboration diagram.

Combinatorial explosion [10.3] In the context of *testing,* the observation that the number of required tests for exhaustive testing will increase exponentially as the number of inputs increases.

Combined Fragment [8.1] A group of messages in a *sequence diagram* that are treated specially; for example they may be optional or repeated. Represented by a box with a code in the top-left corner indicating the kind of fragment.

Commercial off-the-shelf software [1.1] A term for *generic software,* often abbreviated as *COTS.*

Common coupling [9.2] A form of *coupling* in which components share data using a global variable and thus become dependent on each other.

Communication link [8.1] In a *communication diagram,* a line drawn between each pair of *objects* involved in the sending of a *message.*

Communicational cohesion [9.2] A form of *cohesion* in which procedures that access the same data are kept together.

Component [9.1] Any piece of software or hardware that has a clear role and can be isolated, allowing you to replace it with a different component with equivalent functionality.

Component diagram [9.5] A *UML* diagram showing *components* and their relationships.

Composite [6.3] A specialization of the *general hierarchy* pattern that uses an *aggregation* instead of an ordinary association.

Composition [5.6] A strong kind of *aggregation* in which if the *aggregate* is destroyed, then the parts are destroyed as well.

Concrete class [2.6] A class that can have *instances.* In contrast to *abstract class.*

Concurrent engineering model [11.2] A *process model* in which each team works on its own *component,* typically following a *spiral* or *evolutionary* approach.

Configuration management [1.7] The process of identifying all the *components* that constitute a system or subsystem, and ensuring that changes to these components and to the configuration are made systematically.

Constraint [5.6] A small block of text in curly brackets embedded in a *UML* diagram. It is normally written in a formal language which can be interpreted by a computer. See also *Object Constraint Language*.

Construction [11.3] A term often applied to the latter stages of *design* and to programming, even though the analogy with construction in other areas of engineering is weak.

Content coupling [9.2] An undesirable form of *coupling* in which a *component* surreptitiously modifies internal data of another component.

Contracting-out [1.1] Paying to have software (typically custom software) developed by some other organization. Also known as *outsourcing*.

Control [7.3] In a user interface, a near-synonym for *user interface component* and *widget*.

Control coupling [9.2] A form of *coupling* in which one *component* affects the sequence of execution in another.

Controller [9.6] In the *MVC* architectural pattern, the *class* or classes used to control and handle the user's interaction with the *view* and the *model*.

CORBA [9.6] A well-known standard *broker* architecture.

Corrective maintenance [1.6] A type of *maintenance* performed to correct a *defect* in software.

Cost–benefit analysis [9.3] The process of deciding whether to do something by evaluating the costs of doing it and the benefits of doing it, and then choosing to do it if the benefits sufficiently exceed the costs.

Cost estimation [11.3] The process of estimating the *effort* and *elapsed time* of an activity or project.

COTS [1.1] Commercial off-the-shelf software. A term for *generic software*.

Coupling [9.2] A measure of the extent to which interdependencies exist between software modules. An important design principle is to reduce coupling. See also *cohesion* and *modularity*, as well as the various types of coupling: *content, common, control, stamp, routine call, type use, data, inclusion, import,* and *external*.

Coverage [10.3] A measure of the percentage of either paths, statements or branches taken by a set of *tests*.

Critical path [11.5] A path through a *PERT* chart indicating the minimum time in which it is possible to complete a project, and the tasks that, if delayed, will delay the whole project.

Critical race [10.5] A defect in which one *thread* or *process* can sometimes experience a *failure* because another thread or process interferes with the 'normal' sequence of events.

Custom software [1.1] Software that is developed to meet the specific needs of a particular *customer* (in contrast to *generic software*).

Customer [1.4] A person who makes decisions about ordering and paying for software (in contrast to a *user*); the customer is the one who has the problem that is being solved by the development of software. Also called a *client*.

Data coupling [9.2] A form of *coupling* in which one *component* passes simple data to another as an argument.

Data processing software [1.1] Software used for running businesses, managing data such as payroll, purchases, sales, product inventory etc.

Decision Node [8.3] A diamond-shape node in an *activity diagram* that represents a decision. It has one incoming arrow, and multiple outgoing arrows, each with a guard. Flow must follow one of the outgoing paths. Compare to *fork* and *merge node*.

Deadlock [10.5] A failure in which two or more processes or *threads* are stopped, waiting for each other to do something before either can proceed.

Defect [10.1] A flaw in any aspect of the system, including the *requirements*, the *design* or the code, that contributes, or may potentially contribute, to the occurrence of one or more *failures*. A defect is also known as a *fault*. See also *error*.

Defensive design [9.2] *Design* with awareness that other *components* cannot be trusted.

Delegation [6.7] A *pattern* in which one procedure does nothing more than call another in a neighboring *class*.

Delphi technique [11.3] An approach to *cost estimation* in which several individuals initially make cost estimates in private, and then share their estimates to discover the discrepancies.

Deployment [1.7] The process of distributing and installing software as well as any other *components* of a system; deployment also includes managing the transition from any previous system.

Deployment diagram [9.5] A *UML* diagram showing hardware nodes, how they are interconnected, and what *components* will exist on them at run time.

Design [9.1] The problem-solving process whose objective is to find and describe a way to implement the system's *functional requirements*, while respecting the constraints imposed by the *quality requirements*, *platform requirements* and *process requirements*, and while adhering to general principles of good quality. Often the term is used to refer to a *design document*.

Design by contract [9.2] An approach to design in which each *method* has a contract with its callers regarding *preconditions*, *postconditions* and *invariants*.

Design decision [9.1] A decision made in the process of *design* which involves listing *design options*, evaluating them according to pre-determined criteria, and choosing the alternative that has the best cost–benefit trade-off.

Design document [9.1] Documentation produced as a result of *design*.

Design issue [9.1] A sub-problem of the overall design problem.

Design option [9.1] An alternative solution to a design issue.

Design pattern [6.1] A *pattern* useful for the design of software.

Design space [9.1] The space of possible design options.

Detailed design [1.7] The *design* of the internals of individual subsystems.

Deterioration [1.1] The tendency of software to accumulate defects as time passes due to errors being made during *maintenance*.

Development effort [11.3] See *effort*.

Development process [4.5 and 11.2] The process used by a particular project, normally following some *process model*.

Dialog [7.4] (1) A specific window with which a user can interact, but which is not the main UI window; also called a dialog box. (2) The back-and-forth interaction between user and computer.

Distributed system [3.4] A *system* in which computations are performed by separate programs that co-operate to perform the task of the system as a whole.

Divide and conquer [9.2 and 11.3] The principle of dividing something large into smaller units, so that it can be dealt with more easily. Applies to *cost estimation*, *design* and *testing*.

Domain (1) [3.5] A named computer network. Individual *hosts* on the network are identified by prepending characters to the domain's name. (2) [4.1] A general field of business or technology in which users work, and which is learned by the software engineer during *domain analysis*.

Domain analysis [4.1] The process by which a software engineer learns enough background information so that he or she can understand the problem and make good decisions during *requirements analysis* and other stages of the software engineering process. See also *domain*.

Domain expert [4.1] Somebody with expertise in a given *domain*, but who may or may not have expertise in software.

Driver [10.9] In the context of *testing*, a simple program that tests services of lower-level *layers* when performing *bottom-up* or *sandwich testing*.

Dynamic binding [2.6] The process of binding a call to a particular *method*. This is performed dynamically at run time due to the presence of *polymorphism*. Also called *late binding* or *virtual binding*.

Earned value [11.5] The amount of work completed, measured according to the budgeted effort that the work was supposed to consume (also called *budgeted cost of work performed*).

Earned value chart [11.5] A diagram used in project tracking, that allows you to compute the amount by which you are behind schedule and over budget; it shows *elapsed time* on one axis, and *effort* expended on the other axis. See also *earned value*.

Economies of scale [11.3] Sub-linear growth in effort as size increases. Not the case in software engineering.

Efficiency [1.5] The extent to which a product or process can operate using the fewest possible *resources*. Efficiency is an important *quality* attribute.

Effort [11.3] The amount of labor used in a task or project, expressed in *person-months* or *person-days*.

Egoless team [11.4] A team structure in which everybody is equal, decisions are made by consensus, and the team works together to achieve a common goal.

Elapsed time [11.3] The difference in time from the start date to the end date of a task or project.

Elapsed-time transition [8.2] A transition that occurs in a *state diagram* due to the passage of a period of time.

Elicitation See *requirements elicitation*.

Embedded software [1.1] Software that is designed to run specific hardware devices, and thus is embedded in the devices, usually in a form of read-only memory (ROM). Much embedded software is also *real-time software*.

Encapsulation [2.7] Creating a module to contain some algorithm or data structure, thus hiding its details behind the module's interface. See also *information hiding*.

Encoding technique [7.3] In a user interface, a way of representing information so as to communicate it to the user; e.g. using text, color, icons, grouping, sound etc. Also known as 'coding technique'.

Engineer [1.3] A person who performs *engineering*. The term engineer is legally reserved, in many jurisdictions, for those who have obtained engineering education and experience, and perform engineering within a company or else have been granted a license, or some other form of certification, to offer engineering services to the public. See also *professional engineer*.

Engineering [1.3] The process of solving *problems* by applying, in a disciplined, systematic and ethical way, scientific and economic knowledge and principles to the *design* and *maintenance* of products or processes. See also *software engineering*.

Enhancement [1.6] A type of *maintenance* performed to add a new capability to software.

Equivalence class [10.3] A set of inputs that a tester believes will be treated similarly by reasonable algorithms.

Equivalence class testing [10.3] A testing strategy based on determining the possible equivalence classes and creating a *test case* for each.

Error [10.1] (1) A slip or inappropriate decision made by a software engineer that leads to the introduction of a *defect* into the system. (2) A mistake made by a *user*. (3) An inaccuracy in a numerical computation. See also *failure* and *defect*.

Event [8.2] In a *state diagram*, something that causes a system or object to change state. May be a *message*, the passage of elapsed time, a condition becoming true, or completion of an *activity*.

Evolution [1.6] The process by which software is modified over the course of its lifetime to meet changing requirements and as problems are fixed or *re-engineering* is performed. This term is often preferred in place of *maintenance* when describing the entire set of changes made to a system.

Evolutionary model [11.2] A *process model* that views development as a series of hills, each representing a separate loop of the *spiral model*.

Exception [2.6] A situation that arises in a program requiring special handling, and hence deviation from the normal path of control.

Extension use case [4.6] A *use case* that makes optional interactions explicit or handles exceptional cases.

External coupling [9.2] A form of *coupling* in which a software component has a dependency to software written by a third party, to the operating system, or to a particular type of hardware.

eXtreme programming [11.2] An *agile process model* and methodology that provides a disciplined approach to highly incremental and user-centered development of small projects.

Façade [6.9] A *pattern* in which you create a class that provides a simplified interface to a package. Users of the Façade class will have reduced *coupling* to the package.

Factory [6.13] A *pattern* that enables a framework to create instances of an application specific class.

Failure [10.1] An unacceptable behavior exhibited by a system. See also *defect* and *error*.

Fat-client system [3.4] A *client–server system* in which the *client* does a large amount of computation. In contrast to *thin-client system*.

Feature (1) [1.6] An identifiable set of requirements that can be added to (or removed from) a system as a unit; (2) [2.5] A *method* or a *variable* defined in a class. Also sometimes called a member or property.

Feedback [7.3] Any response in the system's user interface to a user's actions.

Filter [9.6] A *component* that inputs simple data, processes it and outputs data of a similar kind. See the *pipe-and-filter* architectural pattern

Flow graph [10.3] A graph showing all possible paths through an algorithm.

Force [6.1] In a *pattern*, an issue or concern that you need to consider when solving the problem, including criteria for evaluating a good solution.

Fork [8.3] A symbol in an *activity diagram* indicating splitting of control into multiple threads.

Formal method [5.7] An approach to software engineering in which everything is specified in logic, and mathematical techniques are used to verify the logic.

Formal language [4.8 and 5.7] A language that uses mathematics for the purpose of *modeling*.

Framework [3.3] A skeletal software *component* that performs functions needed by a class of systems, and which is intended to be incorporated into the design of such systems. See also *reuse*.

Function Points [11.3] An *algorithmic cost estimation* method in which you count features of the requirements and use these to compute an estimate of the system's size.

Functional cohesion [9.2] A form of *cohesion* in which modules which together perform a function (a computation that returns a result and has no *side effects*) are kept together, and everything else is kept out.

Functional requirement [4.5] A *requirement* that describes a service provided by a system. See also *quality requirement*, *platform requirement*, *process requirement* and *non-functional requirement*.

Gantt chart [11.5] A diagram used to graphically present the start and end dates of each software engineering task; it shows time on one axis, and tasks on the other.

General hierarchy [6.3] A *pattern* in which two classes are related both by a generalization and by a one to many association, such that the *generated* graph of instances forms a hierarchy.

Generalization [2.5 and 5.4] (1) The relationship between a classifier and another classifier that contains a subset of the features of the former. The former is considered a kind of the latter. In a UML *class diagram*, the generalization relationship between a *subclass* and a *superclass* is indicated by a small triangle pointing towards the *superclass*. Generalizations are also found in *use case diagrams*. (2) The process of creating the above.

Generalization set [5.4] A label on a group of *generalizations* that describes the criteria used to specialize a *superclass* into two or more *subclasses*.

Generic software [1.1] Software designed to be sold on the open market and to perform functions on general-purpose computers that many people need (in contrast to *custom software*). Generic software is also often called commercial off-the-shelf software (COTS).

Glass-box testing [10.3] A form of testing in which the tester can examine the design documents and the code, as well as analyze and possibly manipulate the internal state of the entity being tested. Also called *white-box* or *structural testing*. In contrast to *black-box testing*.

Glue code [3.1] Code that is written to connect reused *COTS* (commercial off-the-shelf) applications.

Goal [4.6] What the user hopes to accomplish by using a system.

Gold-plating [4.9] Building a list of *requirements* that does more than needed.

Green-field development [1.6] Development of a completely new system, as opposed to *evolution* of an existing system.

Guard condition [8.2] A condition that determines whether a certain *transition* will occur in a *state diagram* when an *event* happens.

Heuristic evaluation [7.5] The process of systematically looking for *usability* defects in a user interface, based on a set of usability guidelines or principles.

Hierarchy See *general hierarchy, inheritance hierarchy*.

Hierarchical team [11.4] A rigid team structure in which each individual reports to a manager and is responsible for performing the tasks delegated by that manager.

High-yield testing [10.2] A testing strategy that is both efficient and effective.

Hook [3.3 and 9.2] An aspect of the design deliberately added to allow other designers to add additional functionality. It does nothing in the basic version of the system, but is designed to be implemented or overridden when the system is extended or reused. See also *hook method*.

Hook method [3.7] A *method* that does nothing other than returning to its caller, but is designed to be overridden in subclasses. See also *hook*.

Horizontal framework [3.3] A framework that provides facilities that many different types of applications will need. In contrast to *vertical framework*.

Host [3.5] A computer on a network.

Host name [3.5] An alphanumeric name given to a *host*, normally divided into several components separated by dots. The components of the name following the first dot are called the *domain*. The host name can often be used interchangeably with the computer's IP address.

Hung system [10.5] A system that appears to the user to not be doing anything, caused by such things as a crash, a *deadlock*, a *livelock* or an *infinite loop*.

Identity [2.7] The characteristic of having a distinct existence, such that each entity can be uniquely referred to.

Immutable [6.10] A *pattern* in which the *instances* of a class cannot change state after creation.

Impact analysis [10.9] The process of exploring and documenting all possible effects of a change.

Implementation [1.7] The process of converting a design into an executable software system by programming and related activities.

Implicit requirement [10.1] A requirement not stated explicitly in the requirements document.

Import coupling [9.2] A form of *coupling* in which one component declares that it imports (makes use of the definitions in) another. Import coupling, as found in Java, is similar to *inclusion coupling*, as found in C++.

Inclusion [4.6] A *use case* that captures commonality among a set of other use cases.

Inclusion coupling [9.2] A form of *coupling* in which one component includes the source code of another component. All the includers of a component are coupled to each other and to the included file. See also *import coupling*.

Incremental development [11.2] A *process model* in which the software is developed in a series of releases.

Incremental testing [10.9] A *integration testing* strategy in which you test subsystems in isolation, and then continue testing as you integrate more and more subsystems (see also *top-down testing*, *bottom-up testing*, and *sandwich testing*). In contrast to *big bang testing*.

Information hiding [2.7 and 9.2] Hiding details so as to reduce complexity. Achieved by *abstraction*, *modularity* and *encapsulation*.

Inheritance [2.5] The possession by one *class* of features defined in another class, by virtue of the fact that the former class is defined to be a *subclass* of (to extend) the latter.

Inheritance hierarchy [2.5] The hierarchy formed by the *generalization* relationships among a set of classes.

Inspecting [10.10] A *verification* process that involves several people systematically proceeding through a document searching for *defects*. See also *reviewing*.

Instance [2.2] A role term referring to object that is a member of a class; can also be applied to other *classifiers*, i.e. a *scenario* is an instance of a *use case*. This term is used when talking about an object in the context of its class, as in, 'Object X is an instance of class Y'.

Instance diagram [5.5] See *object diagram*.

Instance method [2.4] A *method* that executes in the context of a particular object; it has access to the *instance variables* of the given object, and can refer to the object itself using the 'this' keyword (in Java and C++).

Instance variable [2.3] A data item present in each instance of a class, normally used to implement *associations* and *attributes*. In contrast with *class variable*.

Integration testing [10.9] Testing during or following the process of integrating a system. See also *incremental testing*.

Interaction diagram [8.1] A *sequence diagram* or *communication diagram* used to model the dynamic aspects of a software system.

Interface [2.6] (1) The public operations provided by a module for other modules to use (see also *Application Program Interface*). (2) A software *module* in which these are listed. A class can implement many interfaces.

Internationalization [7.4] The process of ensuring that a system can be easily adapted to different *locales*.

IP [3.5] Abbreviation for 'Internet Protocol', the low-level *protocol* used by all computers on the Internet, in which messages are divided into packets for delivery to a remote host. See also *TCP/IP*.

IP address [3.5] The address of a computer (i.e. a *host*) connected to an *IP* network. It is composed of a series of numbers. Instead of the IP address, a more human-readable *host name* is often used.

Isa hierarchy [2.5] Another term for *inheritance hierarchy*.

ISO 9000-3 [10.11] An international standard describing activities an organization should perform in order to have an effective software *development* process.

Iterative development [1.8 and 11.2] An approach to development by which software is developed in stages, with the first stage being very simple, and subsequent stages adding more features. See also *incremental development*.

JAD [4.7] Abbreviation for 'Joint Applications Development'. An approach to defining *requirements*, in which all the *stakeholders* meet intensively for several days in a secluded location.

Join [8.3] A symbol in an *activity diagram* indicating a point where several *threads* wait for each other. When all threads reach the join, control continues in a single thread.

Layer [9.2] A *subsystem* that provides a set of services and has *layer cohesion*.

Layer cohesion [9.2] A form of *cohesion* in which the facilities for providing or accessing a set of services through an *API* or hardware interface are kept together. There must also be a strict hierarchy in which higher-level layers can access only lower-level layers.

Leaf class [2.6] A class at the very bottom of an *inheritance hierarchy*.

Learnability [7.3] The speed with which a new *user* can become proficient with the system. An aspect of *usability*.

Learning curve [7.3] A curve on a diagram that plots the time spent learning on one axis, and the amount of functionality learned on the other axis.

Legacy system [1.6] A software system which is still undergoing *evolution*, but on which some or all of the original developers are no longer working.

License [1.3] A legal document authorizing the holder to perform some activity. In many jurisdictions an engineer must hold a license to offer *engineering* services to the public. See also *professional engineer*.

Lifeline [8.1] A dashed line in a *sequence diagram* indicating the period of time during which an object exists.

Link [5.3] A reference from one object to another. An instance of an association. In a UML *object diagram*, a link is drawn as a line connecting two objects. In a communication diagram there are also *communication links*.

Listening [3.4] A state in which a *server* is waiting for clients to connect.

Live activation [8.1] The period of time when an object is performing work. See *activation box*.

Livelock [10.5] A *failure* in which a system can never get out of a limited set of *states*, although it is not in *deadlock*.

Locale [7.4] An environment where the language, culture, laws, currency and many other factors may be different.

Localhost [3.5] A special *host name* that always refers to the current computer.

Localization [7.4] The process of adapting a system to a specific *locale*.

Locking [10.5] A mechanism for reserving a *resource* so as to avoid inappropriate concurrent access.

Maintainability [1.5] An important internal *quality* of software that measures the extent to which the software can be modified at the lowest possible cost, that is, *maintenance* can be made easier.

Maintenance [1.6] In the context of software, any process involving modifying software following its general release to users. See also *evolution*. Important types of maintenance include *adaptive maintenance*, *corrective maintenance*, *enhancement* and *re-engineering*.

Memory leak [10.6] A situation in which a program requests memory but does not release it when it is no longer needed.

Merge Node [8.3] A diamond-shape node in an *activity diagram* that represents the coming together of two non-concurrent paths. Contrast with *join* and *decision node*.

Message [8.1] Any information sent as a *component* interacts with another, including using procedure calls, or network communication. Explicitly shown in *interaction diagrams*.

Message-Oriented Architecture [9.6] An *architectural pattern* in which subsystems communicate by sending messages to virtual topics; other subsystems subscribe to these topics.

Method [2.4] A concrete implementation of an *operation*; a procedure in a *class*.

Methodology [5.1] A description of a *process*; it usually prescribes how to do things in a step-by-step manner.

Metric [2.10, 10.11] A well-defined method and formula for computing some value that helps a software engineer answer a question about a software product or process.

Milestone [11.5] An important deadline date, at which a specific event may occur, and when a specific deliverable may be required.

Mixed testing [10.9] See *sandwich testing*.

Modal dialog [7.4] A *dialog (1)* that the user must dismiss before interacting with any other window. While in the modal dialog, the system is in a very restrictive *mode*.

Mode [7.3] In the context of user interfaces, a state in which the UI restricts the *affordance*.

Model (1) [5.1] A representation of a system that conveys one or more aspects of it in an analyzable way. (2) [9.6] The functional layer in the MVC architectural pattern – the underlying classes whose instances are to be viewed and manipulated. See also *view* and *controller*.

Model Driven Development [9.4]. An approach to software development in which the *architecture* and *design* are specified by developing *models*. The implementation of the software is then generated automatically from the models. A special case of this is called Model Driven Architecture.

Model–View–Controller [9.6] A *architectural pattern* used to separate the functional layer of the system (the model) from two aspects of the user interface, the *view* and the *controller*. Normally abbreviated as *MVC*.

Modeling [5.1] The process of creating a model. Modeling is performed both in design and *requirements analysis*. Modeling may use *formal languages* or diagrams.

Modularity [2.7] The extent to which software is divided into *components*, called *modules*, which have high internal *cohesion*, low *coupling* between each other, and simple *interfaces*. A factor contributing to *maintainability*.

Module [9.1] A *component* that is defined at the programming language level, such as file, *method* or *package*.

Multi-Layer [9.6] An *architectural pattern* in which a system is divided into *layers*.

Multiple inheritance [5.4] *Inheritance* from more than one *superclass*. Best avoided if possible, e.g. by using the *player–role* pattern.

Multiplicity [5.3] Information placed at each end of an association indicating how many instances of one class can be related to instances of the other class. In UML *class diagrams* it is shown as a range separated by two dots (e.g. 1..∗). The asterisk represents 'any number'.

MVC [9.6] The abbreviation normally used for *Model–View–Controller*.

Non-functional requirement [4.5] An old term for *quality requirements*, *platform requirements* and *process requirements*; i.e. all requirements except the *functional requirements*.

Object [2.1] A data element in an object-oriented system, which has its own *identity*, belongs to a particular class, and has behavior and properties. In a *UML object diagram*, an object is drawn as a rectangle containing the name of the class, which is underlined. See also *instance*.

Object Constraint Language [5.7] A language used to write Boolean *constraints* and *assertions* in UML. Also called *OCL*.

Object diagram [5.5] A UML diagram that shows objects and the links between them. Common alternative name: *instance diagram*.

Object orientation [2.1] A near-synonym for the *object-oriented paradigm*.

Object-oriented analysis [2.2] The process of deciding which *classes* will be important to the users, and working out the structure, relationships and behavior of these classes.

Object-oriented paradigm [2.1] An approach to software design and programming in which software is primarily thought of as a collection of classes that each have responsibilities for various operations, and which are instantiated at run time to create *objects*. See also *object orientation* (in contrast to the *procedural paradigm*).

Object-oriented testing [10.9] Testing that focuses on the specific properties of object-oriented programs.

Observer [6.6] A *pattern* found in *class diagrams* in which *instances* of one *class* are informed of changes to instances of a second class.

Obsolescence [9.2] The tendency for a technology to reach a state where it is no longer useful, is superseded by better technology or must be upgraded in order to continue to function correctly.

OCL [5.7] An abbreviation for *Object Constraint Language*.

Off-by-one error [10.4] A *defect* in which a program inappropriately adds or subtracts one, or inappropriately loops one too many times or one too few times.

Open beta release [10.9] A version of a system released for *beta testing* by any member of the general public who wishes to participate.

Open source [11.2] A *process model* in which software is developed by a community, and source code is distributed with the software, so that community members can change it.

Operation [2.4] The abstract notion of something that can be done by one or more classes. An operation is implemented as a set of *methods*. The word is also used in the context of what the user can do in the user interface, i.e. part of the *affordance*.

Operator precedence error [10.4] A *defect* in which an expression in a program lacks needed parentheses, or has parentheses in the wrong place.

Opportunistic approach [11.2] An unsatisfactory *process model* in which developers keep on modifying the software until they or their users are satisfied.

Optimistic–likely–pessimistic estimation [11.3] An approach to *cost estimation* in which you make three estimates for each task and for the project as a whole: an optimistic estimate (in which everything goes well), the likely estimate and a pessimistic estimate (where you account for everything that could go wrong).

Over-constrain [4.8] To make a decision that constrains future choices, with insufficient justification. A typical mistake made during *requirements analysis*.

Overriding [2.6] The situation where a *method* local to a *class* is used in place of a method that otherwise would have been *inherited*.

Package (1) [9.5] A collection of modeling elements that are grouped together because they are logically related. (2) [2.8] A Java facility for grouping a set of classes.

Package diagram [9.5] A type of UML *class diagram* showing *packages* and their relationships.

Paper prototype [4.6] A set of pictures of the user interface of a system used to demonstrate how the system would work if implemented.

Parallel design [9.1] See *parallel development*.

Parallel development [9.1] Independent development of a system or subsystem by several developers, with the objective of exploring *design space* and generating a variety of different design ideas; the best ideas are generally chosen for further development.

Paraphraser [10.10] A person in an *inspection* who steps through the document explaining it in their own words.

Pareto principle [4.9] See *80–20 rule*.

Pattern [6.1] A widely understood and well-defined solution to a particular type of problem. See also *design pattern* and *architectural pattern*.

Pattern language [6.1] A group of interrelated *patterns*.

Peer-to-peer [9.6] A variant of the *client–server* architectural pattern in which components can serve as both servers and clients to each other.

Perfective maintenance [1.6] A type of maintenance that includes *re-engineering*, and is sometimes applied more broadly to include *enhancement*.

Person-month [11.3] A measure of *effort*. One person-month is the amount of work done by one person in one month if they are working full time.

Personal Software Process [10.11] A disciplined approach that an individual software developer can use to improve the *quality* and efficiency of his or her personal work.

PERT chart [11.5] A diagram showing the sequence in which tasks must be completed.

Phased-release model [11.2] An approach to *incremental development* in which, after requirements gathering and planning, the project is broken into separate subprojects, or phases.

Pilot system [11.2] A synonym for *prototype*.

Pipe [9.6] A connection between two *filters* in a *pipe-and-filter* architecture. It joins the output of one filter to the input to another.

Pipe-and-Filter [9.6] An *architectural pattern* in which data in a standard format is passed through a series of processes (*filters*) that transform it in some way. Also called a *transformational architectural pattern*.

Pipeline [9.6] A series of processes that transform data in the *pipe-and-filter* architectural pattern.

Platform requirement [4.5] A type of *requirement* that specifies an aspect of the technology that must be used or the deployment platform for the software. See also *quality requirement*.

Player–role [6.4] A *pattern* found in *class diagrams* in which one class (the player) has several associated *role* classes. Instances of the role classes can change over the lifetime of a player. The pattern reduces the need for *multiple inheritance*.

Polymorphism [2.4] A property of object-oriented software by which an abstract operation may be performed by different *methods* in different *classes*. Polymorphism exists when several classes which each implement the operation either have a common *superclass* in which the operation exists, or else implement an *interface* that contains the operation.

Port [3.5] A number associated with a server on a *host*, used by a client that wishes to connect to that server. Each server on a host must have a different port number.

Portability [9.2] The ability for software to be run in a variety of different hardware or software environments with no or minimal changes.

Postcondition [4.6] A statement that is guaranteed to be true following the successful completion of some algorithm, *method* or *use case*. In contrast to *precondition*.

Post-mortem analysis [10.11] The process of looking back at a completed project's *design* and its *development process*, in order to identify those aspects where improvements can be made in future projects.

Precondition [4.6 and 10.4] A statement that must be true before some algorithm, method or *use case* is executed. In contrast to *postcondition*.

Problem [1.2] In the broad context of *software engineering*, a difficulty, challenge, need or desire faced by a *customer* that is to be solved by developing software.

Procedural cohesion [9.2] A form of *cohesion* in which procedures that are called one after another are kept together.

Procedural paradigm [2.1] An approach to software design and programming in which software is primarily thought of as a hierarchy of procedures – the root of the hierarchy is typically a main procedure, which calls other procedures, etc. (in contrast to the *object-oriented paradigm*).

Process Anything that operates for a period of time, normally consuming *resources* during that time and using them to create a useful result. In software engineering, the word is also applied to mean the *development process* of a software project.

Process model [11.2] A general approach for organizing a project into activities; an aid to thinking, not a rigid prescription of the way to do things.

Process requirement [4.5] A type of *requirement* that specifies an aspect of the *process model* that must be followed. Must be measurable. See also *quality requirement*.

Process standard [10.11] A document describing a well-respected way of developing software.

Product line [3.3]. A set of products based on a common framework, designed with different sets of features so as to satisfy different market needs.

Professional engineer [1.3] A person who has been issued a license, by some jurisdiction, to perform *engineering*. See also *chartered engineer*.

Project management [11.1] All the activities needed to plan and execute a project.

Project manager [11.4] The person responsible for performing *project management* tasks.

Project plan [11.6] A document used in *project management* describing all aspects of the project's process, including the process model, tasks, risks, cost estimates, team structure and schedule.

Propagation [5.6] A mechanism whereby an *operation* in an *aggregate* is implemented by having the aggregate perform that operation on its parts – in other words, the operation is propagated to the parts.

Property See *feature* (2).

Protocol [3.4] The languages and rules by which two programs or processes communicate, as in a *client–server* system.

Prototype [1.8 and 4.7] A version of a system created primarily to learn more about the *requirements*, and not intended to be the final product. It normally contains only certain aspects of the system's eventual functionality.

Prototyping [4.7] The process of developing *prototypes*.

Proxy [6.12] A *pattern* found in which a lightweight object stands in place of a heavyweight object that has the same interface. It transparently loads the heavyweight object when needed.

Quality [1.5] An attribute of a product or process that, if improved, would better satisfy one or more of the *stakeholders* of that product or service. Examples of qualities relevant to software engineering include: *usability*, *efficiency*, *reliability* and *maintainability*. When performing engineering, it is desirable to set measurable objectives for quality and perform *quality assurance*.

Quality assurance [1.7 and 10.11] The process of ensuring that the *quality* of a product or process is sufficient to meet the needs of the stakeholders. Quality assurance includes both *validation* and *verification*; important techniques include *reviewing*, *inspecting* and *testing*.

Quality requirement [4.5] A type of *requirement* that specifies an aspect of software *quality*. Must be measurable. See also *functional requirement*, *platform requirement* and *process requirement*.

Race condition [10.5] See *critical race*.

Rationale [4.9 and 9.7] The reasoning underlying *requirements* or *design decisions*. It should be documented.

Read-only interface [6.10] A *pattern* in which an *interface* is used to restrict which classes have privileges to call update *methods* of a class.

Real-time software [1.1 and 10.5] Software that must react immediately to stimuli from the environment.

Re-engineering [1.6 and 11.2] A type of *maintenance* performed to improve or replace some part of a software system so that it has higher *maintainability*. In general, no new features are added for users. See also *perfective maintenance*.

Refactoring [11.2] Changing part of the *design* by following systematic rules that result in an equivalent design with an increase in certain desirable *qualities*; performed as part of *re-engineering* and promoted in *agile approaches*.

Reflexive association [5.3] An association in which both ends connect to the same class. See also *symmetric reflexive associations* and *asymmetric reflexive association*.

Regression testing [10.9] The process of re-testing a system, using a selected subset of *test cases*, after changes are made.

Release notes [10.9] A document describing a particular release of software, including a known bugs list.

Reliability [10.1] An important *quality* of software that measures the frequency of *failures*, as encountered by testers and end-users.

Rendezvous [8.3] In concurrent programming, a situation where several *threads* meet and wait for each other. See also *join* and *fork*.

Requirement [4.4] A statement describing either 1) an aspect of what the proposed system must do, or 2) a constraint on the system's development; it must contribute in some way to adequately solving the *customer's problem*; the set of requirements as a whole represent a negotiated agreement among all *stakeholders*.

Requirement stability [11.3] A measure of the extent to which *requirements* are likely to change.

Requirements analysis [4.7] The process of deciding on the requirements of a software system. See also requirements gathering.

Requirements creep [4.10] The tendency for the set of *requirements* to relentlessly increase in size during the course of development, resulting in a system that is more expensive and complex than originally intended.

Requirements definition [4.8] A high-level *requirements document* that describes requirements using language understandable by customers and end users. See also *requirements specification*.

Requirements document [4.8] Any document describing a set of requirements. *Requirements definitions* and *requirements specifications* are specific kinds of requirements document.

Requirements elicitation [4.7] The process of actively asking stakeholders to describe their view of the requirements; an important aspect of *requirements gathering*.

Requirements gathering [4.7] A step in *requirements analysis* in which information is obtained that will form the basis of the requirements. See also *requirements elicitation*.

Requirements review [4.9] The process of systematically evaluating a *requirements document*.

Requirements specification [4.8] A *specification of requirements*; i.e. a requirements document that is more detailed than a *requirements definition*.

Resource [1.5] Anything consumed in the development, operation or maintenance of a product or process. Important resources used in software engineering include the time and money of the *stakeholders*, and the CPU-time, memory and files of computers. See also *efficiency*.

Response time [7.4] The time that elapses from when a user issues a command to when the system provides enough results so that the user can continue his or her work.

Responsibility [5.8] Something a system is required to do that is allocated to a particular *class*.

Reusability [3.2 and 9.2] A *quality* that measures of the extent to which a product or *process* can be used in different contexts from which it was originally designed.

Reuse [3.2 and 9.2] The practice of using the same code or design in more than one place. In contrast to *cloning*. See also *reusability*.

Reviewing [4.9] The process of systematically proceeding through a software document to perform a function such as *validation*, or *verification*.

Ripple effect [10.9] The situation in which removing *defects* causes new ones to be added.

Risk management [1.8] The process of evaluating risks and taking corrective action, including revising plans, on a regular basis.

Role (1) [5.3] A name given to one end of an *association* that acts as a synonym for the *class* at that end. (2) [6.4] A class in the *player–role* pattern whose instances can be attached to player objects.

Root cause analysis [10.11] The process of determining the ultimate reason why a software engineer made the error that introduced a defect.

Routine call coupling [9.2] A form of *coupling* in which one routine calls another.

Sandwich testing [10.9] An *incremental testing* strategy in which you test the top *layers* and bottom layers, and finally test the integrated system. It is partially *bottom-up* and partially *top-down*, hence is also called *mixed testing*.

Scenario [4.6] An instance of a *use case*, involving a specific actor instance, at a specific time and using specific data.

Schedule [11.3] (1) The allocation of tasks to time periods. (2) The total elapsed time of a project.

Scheduling [11.1, 11.5] Determining the sequence of tasks, plus deciding when the tasks should start, and setting deadlines for when they must be complete.

Scope [4.3] The extent of a software project.

Sequence diagram [8.1] A UML *interaction diagram* showing the sequence of *messages* exchanged by the set of *objects* and optionally an *actor*. Actors and objects are on one axis, and time is on the other.

Sequential cohesion [9.2] A form of *cohesion* in which a series of procedures, where one provides input to the next, are kept together.

Server [3.4] A program or process that, in response to requests from *clients*, provides some kind of service.

Server socket [3.5] Data in a server used to generate connections on a *port*.

Service-Oriented Architecture [9.6] An *architectural pattern* in which subsystems obtain information by calling on standard services available on the Internet, called *Web Services*. The information is typically delivered in *XML* format.

Severity level [10.8] A number given to a *failure*, *defect* or *test case*, indicating the amount of impact it has on the user or customer.

Shelfware [4.7] Software that is not used.

Shrink-wrapped software [1.1] A term for *generic software*, so-called because it is often sold in boxes tightly wrapped in plastic.

Side effect [9.2] A change to the state of the system made by a procedure, other than merely returning a result. See also *functional cohesion*.

Signature [5.2] The format of an *operation* or message, including arguments and return value.

Singleton [6.5] (1) A *pattern* that ensures that a certain class can have only one *instance*. (2) A class for which only one instance should exist.

Slot [3.3] A missing part in a *framework* that is filled in by the application developer who is adapting the framework to suit his or her needs. See also *hook*.

Socket [3.5] Data in a *client* or *server* that represents an end of a *TCP/IP* connection. A complete connection has two sockets, one in the client and one in the server.

Software [1.1] Programs and related data that run on a computer. See also *custom*, *data processing*, *embedded*, *generic* and *real-time software*.

Software architecture [9.5] (1) The process of designing the global organization of a software system, including dividing software into *subsystems*, deciding how these will interact, and determining their *interfaces*. (2) Documentation produced as a result of this process (the *architectural model*). (3) The field of study of how to effectively do the above.

Software construction [11.3] See *construction*.

Software crisis [1.1] The situation that is said to have existed since at least the late 1970s, characterized by an inability of software developers to deliver good quality software on time and on budget.

Software developer [1.4] A person involved in the development of software. These include *software engineers*, but may also include others who have specific technical training, but may not be considered to be software engineers.

Software engineer [1.1] A person who has education in, and experience performing, *software engineering*. An *engineer* who specializes in *software*.

Software engineering [1.2] (1) The process of solving customers' problems by the systematic development and evolution of large, high-quality software systems within cost, time and other constraints. The application of *engineering* to software systems of any kind. (2) The field of study of how to effectively do the above.

Software process model [11.2] See *process model*.

Specialization [5.4] The inverse of *generalization*.

Specification [4.8] A document that gives complete detail about something. Normally implicitly means *requirements specification*, but the term design specification is sometimes also used to mean a detailed and precise *design document*.

Spiral model [11.2] An incremental process *model* that explicitly embraces *prototyping* and an *iterative development approach*.

Stable architecture [9.5] An *architecture* that permits changes to a system to be made without the architecture having to change.

Stable sort [10.4] A sort algorithm that leaves equal items in the same order they were in prior to sorting.

Stakeholder [1.4] A person or organization that may be affected by the success or failure of a project or organization. Stakeholders for software projects include *users*, *customers*, *software developers* and managers of the development team.

Stamp coupling [9.2] A form of *coupling* in which one of the argument types of a method is an application class. In contrast to *data coupling*.

Standard [10.11] A document describing a body of well-respected information that engineers should conform to in order to ensure they are following best practice, and will consistently produce good-quality products. See also *process standard*.

State [8.2] A situation in which a system or object behaves in a specific way in response to any *events* that occur.

State diagram [8.2] A UML diagram showing *states* and *transitions*, used to describe the externally visible behavior of a system or of an individual *object*. Near-synonyms include 'state machine', 'statechart diagram' and 'finite state machine'.

Static method [2.9] A synonym for *class method*, so named because one declares a method to be a class method in Java and C++ using the 'static' keyword.

Static variable [2.3] A *class variable*. The term class variable is normally preferred; in C++ and Java, such variables are labeled with the keyword 'static'.

Stereotype [5.6] A way to use some of the standard *UML* notation to represent something special. Created using a label in «guillemets».

Stress testing [10.6] Testing on minimal configurations and at peak loads or with missing resources.

Structural testing [10.3] See *glass-box testing*.

Stub [10.9] A piece of code that has the same *interface* (i.e. *API*) as the lower-level *layers*, but which does not perform any real computations or manipulate any real data. Used in *top-down testing*.

Subclass [2.5] A class that is an extension of another class, and hence *inherits* from the other class. See *generalization*.

Substate [8.2] A *state* within a state.

Subsystem [9.1] A *system* that is part of a larger system, and which has a well-defined *interface*.

Superclass [2.5] A *class* of which another class is an extension, and hence defines features that are inherited by the other class.

Swimlane [8.3] A division in a UML *activity diagram* showing the activities performed by a particular object.

Symmetric reflexive association [5.3] A *reflexive association* in which the *roles* and multiplicity at either end are identical.

Synchronization [3.8] A mechanism to guarantee that only one *thread* can access an object at a time.

System [9.1] A logical entity, having a set of definable responsibilities or objectives, and consisting of hardware, software or both.

Systems engineering [1.7] A type of *design* that involves deciding which *requirements* should be implemented using hardware, and which using software.

Task analysis [4.6] The process of determining the detailed steps needed to perform a task effectively and efficiently. See also *use case analysis*.

TCP [3.5] Transmission Control Protocol. An important protocol used to establish and manage *connections* between computers. See also *TCP/IP*, *IP* and *Socket*.

TCP/IP [3.5] Transmission Control Protocol/Internet Protocol. An important pair of protocols used to establish connections and send data between computers. See also *TCP* and *IP* separately.

Temporal cohesion [9.2] A form of *cohesion* in which aspects of a system are grouped together which are used during the same phase of execution of a program, i.e. they execute close together in time.

Test [10.8] A particular run of a *test case* on a particular version of a system.

Test case [10.8] An explicit set of instructions designed to detect a particular class of *defect* in a software system, by bringing about a failure.

Test-first development [10.8] An approach, commonly used in *agile approaches*, in which you first define the *test cases*, then design the software to make the test cases pass.

Test harness [10.9] A program that automates testing of a system. See also *driver*.

Test plan [10.8] A document that contains a complete set of test cases for a system, along with other information about the testing process.

Test–fix–test cycle [10.9] The cycle in which software developers repeatedly run tests, discover and fix *defects*, and then re-test. This continues until quality objectives are met.

Testability [9.2] The ability for software to be instrumented so that it can be automatically tested using a *test harness*. An important internal *quality* of software.

Testing [10.2] An approach to *verification* that involves systematically executing software to detect *defects*.

Thin-client system [3.4] A *client–server* system in which the *client* is as small as possible and the server does most of the computation. In contrast to *fat-client system*.

Thread [3.4] In general, a path of execution that can run concurrently with other paths of execution. In Java, a class that implements the general concept of a thread. A lightweight *process*.

Top-down design [9.1] An approach to *design* in which one starts with the high-level architecture of the system, then works downwards until finally designing the low-level details such as the structure of individual classes. In contrast to *bottom-up design*.

Top-down testing [10.9] An *incremental testing* strategy in which you start by testing only the user interface, with the underlying functionality simulated by stubs, then you work downwards, integrating lower and lower layers.

Topic [9.6] The channels by which subsystems communicate in the *Message-Oriented Architecture*.

Traceability [4.9] The ability to determine the information that led to a decision being made. For example, aspects of a design should be traceable to specific *requirements*.

Tracking [11.5] In the context of *project management*, the process of determining how well you are sticking to the *cost estimate* and *schedule*. See *earned value chart*.

Transaction-processing [9.6] An *architectural pattern* in which a transaction dispatcher inputs transactions and dispatches them to handlers.

Transformational architectural pattern [9.6] A near-synonym for *Pipe-and-Filter* architectural pattern.

Transition [8.2] A change of *state* in response to an *event*.

Type use coupling [9.2] A form of *coupling* in which several components make use of the same globally-defined data type.

UML [5.1] Abbreviation for the *Unified Modeling Language*.

Unified Modeling Language [5.1] A standard language for modeling various aspects of software, which includes, among other things, a set of diagrammatic notations. UML was invented by Booch, Rumbaugh and Jacobson.

Unit testing [10.9] Testing an individual module or component in isolation. In contrast to *integration testing*.

Usability [7.3] An important *quality* of software that measures the extent to which a product or process is learnable, enables users to be productive and avoid *errors*, and also subjectively satisfies them (in contrast to *utility*).

Usability testing [7.5] The process of evaluating a user interface by having users perform tasks and observing them, noting any usability *defects*.

Use case [4.6] A way in which a system can be used, described as a step-by-step sequence of actions, along with the system's response and certain other information.

Use case analysis [4.6] The process of dividing up the functionality of the system into use cases, and determining the relationships among those use cases. A useful technique for *requirements analysis*. Very similar to *task analysis*.

Use case diagram [4.6] A UML diagram showing *actors*, *use cases* and their relationships.

Use case instance [4.6] See *scenario*.

Usefulness [7.3] The extent to which a system can be used to perform a task; combines *usability* and *utility*.

User [1.4] A person who uses software (in contrast to *customer*). One of the *stakeholders*.

User-centered design [7.1] An approach to software engineering using techniques that focus on *users* and their needs.

User interface component [7.3] A *component* used to create the user interface such as a menu, list, input field etc. Also called a *control* or *widget*.

User interface design [7.3] The *design* of the user interface of a software system.

Utility (1) [9.2] A method or class that has wide applicability to many different subsystems and is designed to be *reusable*. (2) [7.3] The extent to which, independent of *usability*, a product or process provides capabilities needed to solve a customer's *problem*.

Utility cohesion [9.2] A form of *cohesion* in which *utilities* (1) which cannot be logically placed in other cohesive units are kept together.

Validation [1.7] The *process* of ensuring that *requirements* and *designs* solve the customer's problem (in contrast to *verification*).

Verification [1.7] The *process* of ensuring that the *design* or *implementation* conforms to the *requirements*; the process of ascertaining that the software has no *defects* (in contrast to *validation*). See also *inspecting* and *testing*.

Vertical framework [3.3] A complete framework for a particular class of *applications*. A near-synonym for *application framework*.

View [9.6] In the *MVC* architectural pattern, the class or classes used to render the appearance of the data from the model in the user interface.

Waterfall model [11.2] A *process model* in which the software engineer works in a series of stages. The basis for many process models, but not the recommended model to use in modern software engineering. In contrast to *incremental development* and *iterative development*.

Weighted average cost [11.3] The cost of employing a person, including the cost of benefits, office and management support. Also called *burdened cost*.

Web service [9.6] A service available on the Internet, delivered using the http *protocol*, and designed to be used by applications, as opposed to end users. Data is normally delivered in XML format. See *service-oriented architecture*.

White-box testing [10.3] A synonym for *glass-box testing* or *structural testing*.

Widget [7.4] A synonym for *user interface component* and *control*.

XML [9.6] A textual markup language in which tags are used to provide meanings to various types of information.

Index